# CLINICAL PSYCHOLOGY AND PEOPLE WITH INTELLECTUAL DISABILITIES

## Second Edition

Edited by

Eric Emerson (Lancaster University
and University of Sydney)

Chris Hatton (Lancaster University)

Kate Dickson (Betsi Cadwaladr University Health Board)

Rupa Gone (Enfield Integrated Learning Disabilities
Service)

Amanda Caine (Pennine Care NHS Foundation Trust)

Jo Bromley (Central Manchester University Hospitals
NHS Foundation Trust)

## WILEY-BLACKWELL

A John Wiley & Sons, Ltd., Publication

This edition first published 2012
© 2012 John Wiley & Sons, Ltd

Wiley-Blackwell is an imprint of John Wiley & Sons, formed by the merger of Wiley's global Scientific, Technical and Medical business with Blackwell Publishing.

*Registered Office*
John Wiley & Sons Ltd, The Atrium, Southern Gate, Chichester, West Sussex, PO19 8SQ, UK

*Editorial Offices*
350 Main Street, Malden, MA 02148-5020, USA
9600 Garsington Road, Oxford, OX4 2DQ, UK
The Atrium, Southern Gate, Chichester, West Sussex, PO19 8SQ, UK

For details of our global editorial offices, for customer services, and for information about how to apply for permission to reuse the copyright material in this book please see our website at www.wiley.com/wiley-blackwell.

The right of Eric Emerson, Kate Dickson, Rupa Gone, Chris Hatton, Jo Bromley and Amanda Caine to be identified as the authors of the editorial material in this work has been asserted in accordance with the UK Copyright, Designs and Patents Act 1988.

Wiley also publishes its books in a variety of electronic formats. Some content that appears in print may not be available in electronic books.

Designations used by companies to distinguish their products are often claimed as trademarks. All brand names and product names used in this book are trade names, service marks, trademarks or registered trademarks of their respective owners. The publisher is not associated with any product or vendor mentioned in this book. This publication is designed to provide accurate and authoritative information in regard to the subject matter covered. It is sold on the understanding that the publisher is not engaged in rendering professional services. If professional advice or other expert assistance is required, the services of a competent professional should be sought.

*Library of Congress Cataloging-in-Publication Data*

Clinical psychology and people with intellectual disabilities / edited by Eric Emerson ... [et al.]. – 2nd ed.
    p. ; cm.
  Includes bibliographical references and index.
  ISBN 978-0-470-02971-8 (cloth) – ISBN 978-0-470-02972-5 (pbk.)
I. Emerson, Eric, 1953–
[DNLM: 1. Mental Retardation–complications.   2. Mentally Disabled Persons–psychology.   3. Mental Disorders–therapy.   4. Psychology, Clinical–methods. WM 300]
  616.89–dc23
                                                                        2011043016

A catalogue record for this book is available from the British Library.

Wiley also publishes its books in a variety of electronic formats. Some content that appears in print may not be available in electronic books.

Set in 10/12pt Palatino by SPi Publisher Services, Pondicherry, India
Printed in Singapore by Ho Printing Singapore Pte Ltd

1   2012

*In memory of our colleague
and friend Amanda Caine (1954–2011)*

# CONTENTS

About the Editors ............................................................................ ix
List of Contributors ........................................................................ xi
Preface ............................................................................................ xiii

**Part 1:    Setting the Scene** ........................................................ 1

Chapter 1    Intellectual Disabilities – Classification,
             Epidemiology and Causes ................................... 3
             *Chris Hatton*

Chapter 2    Service Provision ................................................ 23
             *Rupa Gone, Chris Hatton and Amanda Caine*

Chapter 3    Social Context ........................................................ 51
             *Eric Emerson and Rupa Gone*

Chapter 4    Cognitive Assessment ......................................... 63
             *Isobel Lamb*

Chapter 5    Common Legal Issues in Clinical Practice ....... 83
             *A.J. Holland*

**Part 2:    General Clinical Issues** ............................................ 105

Chapter 6    Interviewing People with Intellectual
             Disabilities ........................................................... 107
             *Helen Prosser and Jo Bromley*

Chapter 7    Working with People: Direct Interventions .... 121
             *Nigel Beail and Andrew Jahoda*

Chapter 8    Working with Families ....................................... 141
             *Jo Bromley and Christine Mellor*

Chapter 9    Working with Organisations or:
             Why Won't They Follow My Advice? .............. 161
             *Judith McBrien and Sue Candy*

Chapter 10   Reflections on 25 Years Working
             in the NHS .......................................................... 181
             *Ian Fleming*

**Part 3:   Working with...** ......................................................... **203**

Chapter 11   Working with People Whose Behaviour
Challenges Services ........................................... 205
*Alick Bush*

Chapter 12   Working with Offenders or Alleged
Offenders with Intellectual Disabilities .......... 235
*Glynis H. Murphy and Isabel C.H. Clare*

Chapter 13   Sexual Exploitation of People
with Intellectual Disabilities ............................ 273
*Paul Withers and Jennifer Morris*

Chapter 14   Working with Parents Who Happen
to Have Intellectual Disabilities....................... 293
*Sue McGaw*

Chapter 15   People with Intellectual Disabilities
and Mental Ill-Health......................................... 313
*D. Dagnan and W.R. Lindsay*

Chapter 16   Working with People with Autism ................. 339
*Jo Bromley, Elizabeth Crabtree, Christine
Mellor and Mary Delaney*

Chapter 17   Older Adults with Intellectual Disabilities:
Issues in Ageing and Dementia ....................... 359
*Sunny Kalsy-Lillico, Dawn Adams
and Chris Oliver*

Index ................................................................................................. 393

# ABOUT THE EDITORS

**Eric Emerson** is Professor of Disability and Health Research at the Division for Health Research, Lancaster University (UK) and Professor of Disability and Population Health in the Faculty of Health Sciences at the University of Sydney (Australia). His research addresses the health and social inequalities faced by people with disabilities and, in particular, people with intellectual and developmental disabilities.

**Chris Hatton** is currently Professor of Psychology, Health and Social Care at the Centre for Disability Research at Lancaster University, where he has worked since 2000. His research has principally involved people with intellectual disabilities, focusing on documenting the nature and scale of inequalities experienced by people with intellectual disabilities and their families and evaluating policy and practice innovations to reduce/eliminate these inequalities.

**Kate Dickson** is a Clinical Psychologist working for the Betsi Cadwaladr University Health Board in North Wales. She specialises in work with children with intellectual and developmental disabilities and their families.

**Rupa Gone** qualified as a Chartered Clinical Psychologist in 2002. She is currently working with adults with intellectual disabilities as head of psychology in an Integrated Learning Disabilities Service in Enfield. Previously she has worked as a clinical psychologist with children who have intellectual disabilities and/ or autistic spectrum disorders for Hertfordshire Community NHS Trust; and with people with intellectual disabilities in Bury and in Rochdale, for Pennine Care NHS Foundation Trust.

**Amanda Caine** was Consultant Clinical Psychologist in the Psychological Therapies Service Pennine Care NHS Foundation Trust. She had always worked in the NHS with several different client groups including adults with learning disabilities.

**Jo Bromley** is Service Lead for the Clinical Psychology Service for Children with Disabilities in Manchester (Central Manchester Foundation Hospitals NHS Trust). She has a particular interest in making Child and Adolescent Mental Health Services accessible to children with disabilities and their families.

# LIST OF CONTRIBUTORS

**Dawn Adams**
School of Psychology, University of Birmingham, UK

**Nigel Beail**
Professor and Clinical Lecturer, Department of Psychology, University of Sheffield; Professional Head of Psychology Services, Barnsley NHS, UK

**Alick Bush**
Psychological Services, Sheffield Health and Social Care NHS Foundation Trust

**Sue Candy**
Consultant Clinical Psychologist and Managing Director Psychology Associates, Saltash Cornwall.

**Isabel C.H. Clare**
Consultant Clinical and Forensic Psychologist, Cambridgeshire and Peterborough NHS Foundation Trust and Cambridge Intellectual and Developmental Disabilities Research Group, Department of Psychiatry, University of Cambridge

**Elizabeth Crabtree**
Consultant Clinical Psychologist, Alder Hey Children's NHS Foundation Trust

**D. Dagnan**
Honorary Professor, Lancaster University; Clinical Director, Cumbria Partnership NHS Trust

**Mary Delaney**
Specialist Clinical Psychologist, Oldham Community Stroke Team, Pennine Care NHS Foundation Trust, Integrated Care Centre, New Radcliffe Street, Oldham, OL1 1NL

**Ian Fleming**
Consultant Clinical Psychologist PennineCare NHS Trust, Lancashire, UK

**A.J. Holland**
Health Foundation Chair in Learning Disabilities, CIDDRG, Section of Developmental Psychiatry, University of Cambridge

**Andrew Jahoda**
Professor (Learning Disabilities), Glasgow University Centre for Excellence in Disabilities Development, University of Glasgow; Honorary Consultant Clinical Psychologist, Glasgow Learning Disability Partnership

**Dr Sunny Kalsy-Lillico**
Consultant Clinical Psychologist, Birmingham Learning Disabilities Service, Birmingham Community Healthcare NHS Trust, UK

**Dr Isobel Lamb**
Consultant Clinical Psychologist, Head of Learning Disability Speciality Blackburn with Darwen and Hyndburn Ribble Valley, Lancashire Care NHS Foundation Trust, UK

**W.R. Lindsay**
Consultant Clinical Psychologist, Lead Clinician in Scotland and Head of Research, Castlebeck Care; Chair of Learning Disabilities and Forensic Psychology, University of Abertay, Dundee

**Judith McBrien**
Consultant Clinical Psychologist, Cornwall Foundation NHS Trust.

**Sue McGaw**
Consultant Clinical Psychologist, PAMS Training Ltd, Cornwall

**Christine Mellor**
Clinical Psychologist, Central Manchester Foundation NHS Trust

**Jennifer Morris**
Clinical Psychologist, Mersey Care NHS Trust

**Glynis H. Murphy**
Professor of Clinical Psychology & Learning Disabilities, Tizard Centre, University of Kent

**Chris Oliver**
School of Psychology, University of Birmingham, UK

**Helen Prosser**
School of Health Sciences, University of Salford

**Paul Withers**
Head of Psychological Treatment Services, Calderstones Partnership NHS Foundation Trust

# PREFACE

In compiling the second edition of our book *Clinical Psychology and People with Intellectual Disabilities* we have attempted to provide a resource that will support the training of clinical psychologists and other professionals to work with people with intellectual disabilities. Our aim was to produce a text that covered the middle ground between a 'how to do it' manual and an academic review of the relevant literature.

The book consists of three sections. In the first section (creatively called Part 1: Setting the Scene) we have attempted to cover a range of issues that are likely to (or should) underpin the provision of clinical psychology (and other) services for people with intellectual disabilities. These include summaries of what is known about the number of people who have intellectual disabilities, the needs of people with intellectual disabilities, trends in service provision for people with intellectual disabilities and the legal framework within which services are provided.

In Part 2, we address a range of issues pertinent to clinical practice. These include general issues related to interviewing people with intellectual disabilities, structuring interventions and building rapport, working with families and with (and within) organisations.

In Part 3, we focus more specifically on issues related to clinical practice when working with some particular client groups; people with challenging behaviours or mental health problems, older people, parents who themselves have learning disabilities, people at risk of (or who have experienced) sexual exploitation and people with autism spectrum disorders. This list was not meant to be (and could not be) exhaustive. Instead our aim was to address clinical issues pertinent to supporting some of the more common reasons for intervention.

We hope that this comprehensive revision of *Clinical Psychology and People with Intellectual Disabilities* provides clinical psychologists and other professionals with the context, evidence and expert guidance required for effective clinical practice.

*Eric Emerson*
*Chris Hatton*
*Kate Dickson*
*Rupa Gone*
*Amanda Caine*
*Jo Bromley*

# Part 1
# SETTING THE SCENE

Chapter 1

# INTELLECTUAL DISABILITIES – CLASSIFICATION, EPIDEMIOLOGY AND CAUSES

Chris Hatton

## INTRODUCTION

Epidemiology has been defined as 'the study of the distribution and determinants of health, disease, and disorder in human populations' (Fryers 1993). Although intellectual disability can be argued to be neither a disease nor a disorder, understanding the epidemiology of intellectual disability is of fundamental importance for service planning. Quite simply, to provide a needs-led service you have to know how many people with intellectual disabilities there are, what services they are likely to need, and whether there will be any changes in the need for services in the future.

However, determining the epidemiology and causes of intellectual disabilities is at best an inexact science. As 'intellectual disability' is socially constructed, what it means, how it is measured, and therefore who counts as having an 'intellectual disability' has varied over time (Trent 1995; Wright and Digby 1996) and across cultures and countries (Emerson *et al.* 2007; Jenkins 1998). Current professionally driven conceptualisations of 'intellectual disability' as largely a deficit in intelligence (Wright and Digby 1996) often have little resonance for people labelled with intellectual disability or their families (Finlay and Lyons 2005; Jenkins 1998). Therefore, before looking more closely at the literature concerning epidemiology and causes, we must first look at how people are currently classified as having an 'intellectual disability'.

*Clinical Psychology and People with Intellectual Disabilities*, Second Edition. Edited by
Eric Emerson, Chris Hatton, Kate Dickson, Rupa Gone, Amanda Caine and Jo Bromley.
© 2012 John Wiley & Sons, Ltd. Published 2012 by John Wiley & Sons, Ltd.

## CLASSIFICATION

As mentioned above, 'intellectual disability' is socially constructed. The classification system used will determine who counts as having an 'intellectual disability', with obvious consequences when considering epidemiology and causes. In high-income English speaking countries, over the last 100 years classification systems have largely located intellectual disability as a series of deficits within the individual; typically in terms of deficits in intelligence and 'adaptive behaviour' (the behaviours necessary to function within society) that become apparent before cultural norms of adulthood (Emerson *et al.* 2007) – the so-called 'medical model'. In more recent times, the social model of disability (where it isn't a person's 'impairment' that disables them, but the oppressive organisation of society that acts to create disability) has presented a fundamental challenge to traditional classification systems (Thomas 2007).

Classification systems have changed in different ways to meet the challenge laid down by the social model of disability. For example, the American Association on Mental Retardation (AAMR), now renamed the American Association on Intellectual and Developmental Disabilities (AAIDD), produced the most recent revision of their classification system in 2010 (AAIDD 2010), presented in Box 1.1; similar (although less precise) definitions are used by the Department of Health (Department of Health 2001). This revision still locates intellectual disability as largely a function of individual deficits, although in their guidance they do state that adaptive skills are a result of the 'fit' between a person's capacities and their environment. In a supportive environment a person may be able to function perfectly well (thus not meeting the criteria for intellectual disability) – in a less supportive environment the same person may have problems and meet criteria for intellectual disability.

A more thoroughgoing attempt to incorporate social model ideas into medical model classification systems has come from the World Health Organization's International Classification of Functioning, Disability and Health (ICF) (World Health Organization 2001). This classification system attempts to describe intellectual disability in terms of interactions between the person's impairment (i.e. intellectual ability), their potential capacity and their actual performance across a range of activities, taking into account the person's environmental, cultural and personal context.

Whichever classification system is used, there are a number of issues regarding classification which are likely to arise when working in services for people with intellectual disabilities.

**Box 1.1**    AAIDD 2010 Definition of 'Intellectual Disability'

'Intellectual disability is characterized by significant limitations both in intellectual functioning and in adaptive behaviour as expressed in conceptual, social, and practical adaptive skills. This disability originates before age 18.'

## OPERATIONAL DEFINITIONS:

'*Intellectual functioning*: an IQ score that is approximately two standard deviations below the mean, considering the standard error of measurement for the specific assessment instruments used and the instruments' strengths and limitations.'

'*Adaptive behavior*: performance on a standardized measure of adaptive behavior that is normed on the general population including people with and without ID that is approximately two standard deviations below the mean of either (a) one of the following three types of adaptive behavior; conceptual, social, and practical or (b) an overall score on a standardized measure of conceptual, social, and practical skills.'

## Important elements of the definition:

*...significant limitations ...*

Intellectual disability is defined as a fundamental difficulty in learning and performing certain daily life skills. There must be significant limitations in conceptual, social and practical adaptive skills, which are specifically affected. Other areas (e.g. health, temperament) may not be.

*...in intellectual functioning...*

This is defined as an IQ standard score of approximately 70 to 75 or below (approximately two standard deviations below the mean), based on assessment that includes one or more individually administered general intelligence tests.

*...and in adaptive behavior...*

Intellectual functioning alone is insufficient to classify someone as having an intellectual disability. In addition, there must be significant limitations in adaptive skills (i.e. the skills to cope successfully with the daily tasks of living.

*...originates before age 18...*

The 18th birthday approximates the age when individuals in this society (i.e. USA) typically assume adult roles. In other societies, a different age criterion might be more appropriate.

## Levels of Intellectual Disability

Although some classification systems do not define levels of intellectual disability and regard the labels attached to levels of intellectual disability as misleading (AAIDD 2010), the concept of different degrees of severity of intellectual disability is commonly used in policy and practice in the UK. These classifications are typically based on standardised IQ scores. A typical system is that of the International Classification of Diseases (or ICD), produced by the World Health Organisation:

Mild        50–70
Moderate    35–49
Severe      20–34
Profound    <20

For many purposes (such as epidemiological studies), all people with IQ<50 are classified as people with severe intellectual disabilities. While these labels of levels may assist heuristically in getting a sense of a person's likely capabilities and support needs, they do not map reliably on to capabilities that are potentially important for the clinician, such as capacity to give informed consent or capacity to participate effectively in clinical interventions requiring significant linguistic, memory or other cognitive capabilities. There is no substitute for individual assessment of a person's individual profile of capabilities and support needs.

## Cultural and Linguistic Diversity

'Intellectual disability' is socially constructed, and can be regarded as a product of specific English-speaking cultures at a particular point in history (Emerson *et al.* 2007). This is particularly important when considering the reliance of epidemiological research on IQ tests, which can dramatically over-estimate prevalence rates of intellectual disability amongst minority ethnic communities (Hatton 2002; Leonard and Wen 2002). There are also highly likely to be cultural differences in perceptions of which behaviours are considered to be adaptive (Jenkins 1998).

## Present Functioning

'Intellectual disability' is not necessarily a life-long trait or condition, and depending on people's circumstances and responses to them they may not be regarded as having intellectual disabilities throughout their lives. Indeed, many people with 'mild' intellectual disabilities (but see AAIDD 2010) have only intermittent and time-limited contact with services, usually to assist at times of crisis.

## Classification in Service Settings

Formal classification systems like the ones outlined above, with their associated assessment tools, are rarely used in existing services to make decisions about whether a person has intellectual disabilities. Also, because such assessments are made by professionals within services, decisions about whether a person has intellectual disabilities are frequently influenced by the availability of services and the professional's judgement of what is in the best interests of the individual. Many factors can impact upon this decision; financial, political, ideological, and administrative.

Consequently, there may be people within intellectual disability services who would not meet systematic classification criteria (e.g. people who were institutionalised many years ago). It is also highly likely that there are people not in contact with intellectual disability services who would meet standard classification criteria. Services are increasingly tightening eligibility criteria to decide who is eligible for intellectual disability services and to 'prioritise' (i.e. ration) service provision. These eligibility criteria vary widely between different services, and use widely different methods of assessment.

## EPIDEMIOLOGY

The general epidemiological literature generally has two ways of counting the number of people with a particular disorder in a given population, *prevalence* and *incidence* (see Box 1.2), although as the above discussion will have made clear this is a very inexact science when applied to people with intellectual disabilities.

**Box 1.2**   Definitions of prevalence and incidence

*Prevalence* is the number of cases, old and new, existing in a population at a given point in time or over a specified period.
*Incidence* refers to the number of new cases of a disorder arising in a population in a stated period of time.

(Richardson and Koller 1985)

## Prevalence

Epidemiological studies of the prevalence of intellectual disabilities of children and adults across the world's high income countries are becoming more common (see Leonard and Wen 2002; McLaren and Bryson 1987; Murphy *et al.* 1998; Roeleveld *et al.* 1997 for reviews). Prevalence estimates for the world's middle and low income countries are more sparse and varied for a number of reasons, but rates may be higher than those found in high income countries (Durkin *et al.* 2006; Emerson and Hatton 2007; Maulik *et al.* 2011). Much of the variance in prevalence rates reported across studies can be accounted for by methodological factors, including:

1) *Sampling method*. Studies which use total population samples, and assess all members of a population for intellectual disability, typically report much higher overall prevalence rates than studies using administratively defined populations (i.e. those currently using services for people with intellectual disabilities or those known to services). This discrepancy is much less for studies of the prevalence of severe intellectual disabilities.

2) *Classification criteria*. As discussed earlier, classification systems for deciding whether a person has an intellectual disability vary over time and across different geographical areas, and different researchers have used more or less stringent criteria for classifying people with intellectual disabilities.

3) *Assessment method*. Reliance on IQ alone almost inevitably results in higher prevalence rates than those using IQ and adaptive behaviour assessment methods. Other factors, such as the skills of the professional conducting the assessment and the language and culture of people being tested (and those doing the testing) will all influence the prevalence rate reported.

*People with Mild Intellectual Disabilities (i.e. IQ 50 or 55 to 70)*

Studies of high income countries (see Leonard and Wen 2002; McLaren and Bryson 1987; Murphy *et al*. 1998; Roeleveld *et al*. 1997) report the following findings (see Durkin *et al*. 2006, for information on low and middle income countries):

1) General prevalence rates (i.e. across all ages) of mild intellectual disabilities from *3.7 to 5.9 per 1,000* based on administratively defined populations (i.e. those known to services), with total population studies reporting much higher prevalence rates (based on IQ assessment only) of around 30 per 1,000, although a recent UK study has produced an estimated prevalence rate of 80 per 1,000 (Simonoff *et al*. 2006).
2) More males with mild intellectual disabilities than females (ratio approx. 1.6:1, although gender ratios vary widely across studies).
3) An increase in the apparent prevalence of mild intellectual disabilities throughout the school years, followed by a sharp drop around the school leaving age.
4) A disproportionate number of people with mild intellectual disabilities come from disadvantaged socio-economic backgrounds.

These findings illustrate clearly the complex processes involved in the classification of people as having intellectual disabilities. For example, changes in age-specific prevalence rates (e.g. increasing across school age, then dropping beyond school-leaving age) may simply reflect people's identification by and ongoing contact with services, or they may be a consequence of people on adulthood demonstrating a good adaptive fit to their circumstances, thereby no longer meeting the classification criteria for intellectual disability.

*People With Severe Intellectual Disabilities (i.e. IQ < 50 or 55)*

Studies of high income countries (see Leonard and Wen 2002; McLaren and Bryson 1987; Murphy *et al*. 1998; Roeleveld *et al*. 1997) report the following findings (see Durkin *et al*. 2006, for information on low and middle income countries, where prevalence rates are likely to be at least double):

1) General prevalence rates (i.e. across all ages) of severe intellectual disabilities from *3 to 4 per 1,000*, with total population studies reporting higher prevalence rates (e.g. 6.3 per 1,000) than studies using administratively defined populations.

2) More males with severe intellectual disabilities than females (ratio approx 1.2:1).
3) An increase in the apparent prevalence of severe intellectual disabilities throughout the school years, with little if any reduction at school-leaving age.
4) Less association between prevalence and socio-economic background.

For people with severe intellectual disabilities, the classification of intellectual disability is usually made with more confidence and earlier than for people with mild intellectual disabilities. Also, children with severe intellectual disabilities are likely to continue receiving services after leaving school, and are less likely to move out of a classification of intellectual disability due to changes in circumstances.

## Incidence

Epidemiological studies of the incidence of intellectual disability are scarcer than studies of prevalence, largely due to their methodological difficulty (Fryers 1993). These studies tend to rely on administratively defined populations of people with intellectual disabilities (typically people identified as such by service systems) rather than independently assessing entire populations, resulting in possible under-estimates of incidence for people with mild intellectual disabilities. Studies across the US and Northern Europe have reported similar incidence rates – for example a US study reported a cumulative incidence at age 8 years of 4.9 children with severe intellectual disabilities per 1,000 births and 4.3 children with mild intellectual disabilities per 1,000 births (Katusic *et al.* 1995; see also Rantakallio and von Wendt 1986).

### UK Trends – Prevalence and Service Need

It is not possible to estimate the number of number of people with intellectual disabilities in the UK either from information held by central government departments or from large-scale population based surveys. Robust estimates of current and future numbers of people with intellectual disabilities, based on data from registers and general population data, have been recently derived (Emerson and Hatton 2008, 2011). These estimates conclude that:

- 169,000 people aged 20 or more (0.46% of the adult population) were known users of learning disability services in England. Of these, 26,000 were aged 60 or more.

- 985,000 people in England have an intellectual disability, including people not identified by specialist services (2% of the general population). This included 796,000 people aged 20 or more, of whom 174,000 were people aged 60 or more.
- Overall, there will be sustained growth over the next two decades in both the numbers of people with intellectual disabilities known to learning disability services (11% over the decade 2001–2011, 14% over the two decades 2001–2021) and the estimated 'true' number of people with intellectual disabilities in England (15% over the decade 2001–2011, 20% over the two decades 2001–2021).
- Within the 50+ age range there will be very marked increases in both the numbers of people with learning disabilities known to learning disability services (28% over the decade 2001–2011, 48% over the two decades 2001–2021) and in the estimated 'true' number of people with intellectual disabilities in England (31% over the decade 2001–2011, 53% over the two decades 2001–2021).

When considering the service needs of people with intellectual disabilities in the UK, three issues stand out:

1) In common with other high income countries, the life expectancy of people with intellectual disabilities in the UK is increasing, although still lower than that of the general population (Carter and Jancar 1983; Hollins et al. 1998; McGuigan et al. 1995). Combined with bulges in prevalence rates for the 'baby boom' generation (Fryers 1993) and the increasing survival throughout adulthood of people with more complex and multiple needs, this increased life expectancy suggests a sharp rise in demand for adult services, particularly housing support services.

2) There is some tentative evidence (Emerson and Hatton 2004; Emerson et al. 1997; Kerr 2001; but see McGrother et al. 2002) of higher prevalence rates of severe intellectual disability for children in some South Asian communities in the UK. Combined with the relatively young age structure of minority ethnic communities in the UK, the need for services directed to South Asian people with intellectual disabilities (and possibly other minority ethnic communities, although prevalence data are unavailable) will continue to increase over the next 20 years (Emerson and Hatton 1999).

3) There is a consensus among practitioners that increasing numbers of children with intellectual disabilities and very complex medical needs are surviving into adulthood as a result of improved medical care and nutrition (e.g. tube feeding). At present, however, no data are available with which to evaluate this claim.

## Disorders and Conditions Associated with Intellectual Disabilities

A range of disorders have been found to be more likely amongst people with intellectual disabilities. While the number of additional disorders a person is likely to have increases with the severity of the intellectual disability, the type of additional disorder reported does not seem to vary significantly across the range of intellectual disabilities (McLaren and Bryson 1987). The wide variation in prevalence rates for associated disorders reflect a wide range of methodological, classification, and assessment differences across studies, and therefore should not be treated as definitive. The most common disorders or conditions associated with intellectual disabilities include:

1) *Epilepsy.* Between 15% and 30% of people with intellectual disabilities have been reported to have epilepsy (McLaren and Bryson 1987).
2) *Cerebral palsy/other motor impairments*; reported in 20% to 30% of people with intellectual disabilities (McLaren and Bryson 1987).
3) *Sensory impairments*; reported in 10% to 33% of people with intellectual disabilities, although studies using clinical criteria for sensory impairments report much higher rates than studies using functional criteria (Hatton and Emerson 1995; McLaren and Bryson 1987).
4) *Challenging behaviour*; reported in 6% to 14% of people with intellectual disabilities, although there are widely different criteria for determining and measuring challenging behaviour (Emerson 2001; McLaren and Bryson 1987).
5) *Mental health problems.* Due to difficulties in accurately identifying mental health problems in people with intellectual disabilities and differences in definition, the range of prevalence rates reported are particularly wide (10% to 80%), although studies using more stringent criteria tend to report rates of mental health problems among adults (around 20% to 40%) similar to or slightly higher than the general population (Hatton and Taylor 2005). Among children, there is growing evidence of a four to five fold elevation in rates of mental health problems among children with intellectual disabilities (Einfeld and Emerson 2008; Emerson and Hatton 2007).

## CAUSES OF INTELLECTUAL DISABILITY

Understanding the causes of a person's intellectual disability can have a potentially crucial impact on prevention, treatment and management programmes for that individual (AAIDD 2010). The 'new genetics' (Dykens *et al.* 2000) is driving much of the research attempting to link genetic 'causes' to treatment and management, although much of this work is the subject of intense ethical debate. For clinical psychologists, the most important issue is that understanding the cause of a person's intellectual disability may have implications for management programmes. One well-known example is phenylketonuria, a deficit in metabolising a particular protein which causes severe intellectual disabilities if untreated. However, such intellectual disabilities can be completely avoided by a diet low in the protein phenylalanine.

The 'new genetics' has also introduced the concept of the 'behavioural phenotype' (Dykens *et al*. 2000; Hodapp and Dykens 2004). Proto-typically, 'a behavioral phenotype should consist of a distinct behavior that occurs in almost every case of a genetic or chromosomal disorder, and rarely (if at all) in other conditions' (Flynt and Yule 1994, p. 666). This strict definition would limit the study of behavioural phenotypes to a small number of genetic/chromosomal conditions with clear behavioural consequences (e.g. self-mutilation in Lesch-Nyhan syndrome; hyperphagia in Prader-Willi syndrome). This original concept of behavioral phenotypes has been broadened to a more probabilistic definition, for example 'the heightened probability or likelihood that people with a given syndrome will exhibit certain behavioral and developmental sequelae relative to those without the syndrome' (Dykens 1995; p. 523). Clearly, understanding the behavioural phenotype associated with a specific condition is vital when supporting that individual, for example in terms of the person's physical environment, routines, learning style, challenging behaviours, etc. (Dykens *et al*. 2000). However, some caution needs to be expressed regarding the behavioural phenotype approach. Correspondences between genetic syndrome and particular behaviours are rarely perfect; many people with the genetic syndrome do not show the behaviour and many people without the genetic syndrome do show the behaviour. There is also a danger that self-fulfilling prophecies may occur within services (for example, the belief that if a person has a particular genetic syndrome, then particular behaviours are inevitable and not amenable to intervention).

The incidence, prevalence and consequences of different aetiologies are dynamic over time, due to factors such as changes in the age of parents at the child's birth, changes in parental health behaviours such as smoking and alcohol use prenatally, prenatal screening programmes, the survival and treatment of low birthweight babies, and interventions for specific factors associated with intellectual disabilities (Brosco *et al*. 2006; Leonard and Wen 2002), although overall prevalence rates seem relatively stable (Leonard and Wen 2002).

Generally, studies estimate that for people with severe intellectual disabilities, aetiology is unknown for between 20% and 40% of cases, although figures in recent studies are at the lower end of this range

(Leonard and Wen 2002; McLaren and Bryson 1987; Partington *et al*. 2000). For people with mild intellectual disabilities, aetiology is unknown for a somewhat higher 45% to 62% of cases (McLaren and Bryson 1987). For perhaps the majority of people, the determinants of intellectual disability will involve a complex interaction between biomedical, social, behavioural and educational factors. These factors may influence the individual at the prenatal, perinatal, and postnatal stages of life.

## Prenatal Causes

Overall, studies estimate that more than 20% of cases of severe intellectual disability can be accounted for by chromosomal disorders, and that a further 20% to 40% of cases accounted for by other prenatal factors, such as single gene disorders, multi-factorial/polygenetic causes and environmental effects (McLaren and Bryson 1987; Partington *et al*. 2000). For people with mild intellectual disabilities, only 4% to 10% of cases are generally accounted for by chromosomal disorders (McLaren and Bryson 1987; Matilainen *et al*. 1995), with a further 11% to 23% of cases assumed to be due to other prenatal causes (McLaren and Bryson 1987; Matilainen *et al*. 1995).

### Biomedical Factors

Prenatal biomedical factors potentially determining intellectual disability include chromosomal disorders, single gene disorders and other syndrome disorders (see Connor and Ferguson-Smith 1993; Plomin *et al*. 1997). Advances in medical genetics are being made at a rapid pace, with an increasing number of genetic abnormalities and associated syndromes being identified, although how many cases of currently unknown aetiology will become newly identified is open to debate (McLaren and Bryson 1987).

*Chromosomal disorders*   These account for between 20% and 40% of all live births of people with severe intellectual disabilities. This range of estimates possibly reflects differences across studies in the availability of amniocentesis and genetic screening, and differences in maternal age (McLaren and Bryson 1987). The majority of conceptions with chromosomal disorders spontaneously abort (Connor and Ferguson-Smith 1993).

By far the most common chromosomal disorder associated with intellectual disability is Down syndrome (Trisomy 21, where a person has an extra whole or part chromosome-21). Approximately 1 in 700 live births have Trisomy 21, and almost all people with Down syndrome have an additional intellectual disability to some degree. People with Down syndrome are at risk for congenital heart problems, thyroid problems, epilepsy, immunological deficiencies, vision and hearing loss, and reduced life-span with early-onset dementia (Dykens *et al.* 2000). Other less common chromosomal disorders are listed in Table 1.1.

*Single gene disorders*    In recent years, there has been increasing interest in Fragile-X syndrome, which occurs more commonly in males, and has been claimed to be the most common hereditary cause of intellectual disability. Recent estimates of the frequency of Fragile-X are at around 1 in 4000 males and at least half as many females (Dykens *et al.* 2000). Common (although not conclusive) indicators of Fragile-X include an elongated face with large ears, and enlarged testes in males. Other single-gene disorders associated with intellectual disabilities are listed in Table 1.1.

*Other syndrome disorders*    There are a wide range of other relatively rare biomedical syndromes that may have a prenatal causal effect on later intellectual disabilities. These often have a genetic basis in that they are the result of dominant or recessive genes, but they may also have a poly-genetic basis, and vary widely in the severity of the effect. These include neurofibromatosis, tuberous sclerosis, myotonic dystrophy, craniosynostosis syndromes, and inborn errors of metabolism. Other prenatal biomedical causes of intellectual disabilities may not be associated with genetic disorders, but may be the result of disorders of brain formation at the prenatal stage. Spina bifida is probably the most well known of this group of disorders (Connor and Ferguson-Smith 1993).

*Environmental Factors*

Whilst the importance of prenatal environmental effects has long been recognised, assessing the degree of their causal influence on the later development of intellectual disabilities has still to be conclusively determined. Studies have produced a wide range of estimates for the number of cases attributable to the prenatal environment (0.7% to 11.2% for people with severe intellectual disabilities; 8.2% to 8.8% for people with mild intellectual disabilities; McLaren and Bryson 1987; Matilainen *et al.* 1995). Factors here include maternal malnutrition and ingestion of drugs and toxins during pregnancy (e.g. fetal alcohol syndrome), maternal diseases during pregnancy, and irradiation during pregnancy, although the relative impact of these factors in influencing intellectual disability is unknown (McLaren and Bryson 1987).

## Perinatal Causes

Overall, studies estimate that approximately 10% of cases of severe intellectual disability are due to perinatal causes. Figures for mild intellectual disability are more variable, ranging from 1% to 19% of cases (McLaren and Bryson 1987; Matilainen *et al.* 1995).

**Table 1.1** Genetic disorders associated with intellectual disabilities (from connor and ferguson-smith 1993; Einfeld and Emerson 2008; McLaren and Bryson 1987; Plomin et al. 1997).

*Chromosomal Disorders*

| Name | Syndrome Name | Birth Prevalence | Associated Features |
|---|---|---|---|
| Trisomy 21 | Down's syndrome | 1 in 700 (related to maternal age) | Almost all some intellectual disability. Most survive well into adulthood; some evidence of early onset dementia. |
| Trisomy 18 | Edward's syndrome | 1 in 3,000 | All have severe intellectual disability. 10% survive to age one year. |
| Trisomy 13 | Patau's syndrome | 1 in 5,000 | All severe intellectual disability / seizures. 18% survive to age one year. |
| 15q- (maternal) | Angelman syndrome | 1 in 20,000 | Generally moderate intellectual disability. |
| 15q- (paternal) | Prader-Willi syndrome | 1 in 10,000 | Almost all some intellectual disability. Short stature, over-eating. |
| 7p- | Williams syndrome | 1 in 25,000 | Almost all some intellectual disability by later childhood. |
| 5p- | Cri-du-chat syndrome | Very rare | Half show severe intellectual disability. |
| | Klinefelter syndrome (XXXY) | 1 in 1,000 males | Some reduction in verbal skills, severe intellectual disability uncommon. |

Other very rare chromosomal disorders include Trisomy 8, 9p+ and 4p-

## Single Gene Disorders

| | | |
|---|---|---|
| Fragile-X syndrome (X-linked) | 1 in 4,000 males; at least half in females | Mild-moderate intellectual disability in one third of boys and girls. |
| Lesch-Nyhan syndrome (X-linked) | 1 in 20,000 males | Almost all severe intellectual disability. All show severe self-injury, usually hand and lip biting. |
| Duchenne's muscular dystrophy | 1 in 3,500 males | Variable effect on intellectual ability: verbal skills more impaired. Progressive muscle wastage, almost all die before age 20. |
| Phenylketonuria | 1 in 10,000 | Untreated, some severe intellectual disability. |

*Biomedical Factors*

Intrauterine infections are the most common biomedical perinatal cause of intellectual disabilities, accounting for 2% to 6% of people with severe intellectual disabilities, and 1% of people with mild intellectual disabilities. Such infections include cytomegalovirus, toxoplasmosis, rubella, neonatal herpes and bacterial meningitis (McLaren and Bryson 1987).

*Environmental Factors*

The most common perinatal cause of severe intellectual disability is asphyxia (lack of oxygen), with 4% to 8% of people with severe intellectual disability suffering asphyxia during birth. The figures for asphyxia in people with mild intellectual disabilities vary widely, from 5% to 19%. Another common cause of intellectual disability is premature birth of the child (3% to 5% of people with severe intellectual disabilities; figures for people with mild intellectual disabilities unknown). Other perinatal traumas that may result in intellectual disability include haemorrhaging in the brain due to abnormal labour and/or delivery, premature birth, and umbilical cord accidents (McLaren and Bryson 1987).

## Postnatal Causes

Very little is known about the relative impact of postnatal factors on the development of intellectual disabilities. Studies of people with severe intellectual disabilities report a wide range of estimates (1% to 13%) of people influenced by postnatal factors (McLaren and Bryson 1987; Matilainen *et al.* 1995). For people with mild intellectual disabilities, there is a common assumption that environmental factors, particularly those associated with socio-economic disadvantage, are the predominant causal factor, although these links are usually inferred rather than demonstrated (Emerson *et al.* 2007; McLaren and Bryson 1987).

*Biomedical Factors*

There are a wide range of postnatal biomedical factors that may impact upon the development of intellectual disability, although estimates of their prevalence are as yet unavailable. Such factors include infections (e.g. encephalitis, meningitis), diseases affecting the central nervous system, degenerative disorders (e.g. Rett syndrome, Friedrich's ataxia and basal ganglia disorders), and epilepsy and related disorders (Connor and Ferguson-Smith 1993).

*Environmental Factors*

Again, a wide range of environmental factors, probably in a multifactorial fashion, can influence the development of intellectual disabilities. Traumatic injuries to the brain, various toxic disorders (e.g. high levels of lead or mercury, dehydration, hypoglycemia) and malnutrition can all cause intellectual disabilities. Environmental deprivation, such as psychosocial disadvantage, child abuse and neglect, and chronic social/sensory deprivation, have all been hypothesised to influence the development of intellectual disability, although the relative impact they have compared to other factors is largely unknown (Durkin *et al*. 2006; Einfeld and Emerson 2008; Emerson *et al*. 2007; World Health Organization and World Bank 2011).

## CONCLUSIONS

Understanding the epidemiology and causes of intellectual disabilities is important for developing needs-led services, and developing treatment and management programmes for people with intellectual disabilities. As 'intellectual disability' is socially constructed and subject to variations in definition and identification, studying the epidemiology and causes of intellectual disability is an at best inexact science. Despite these variations, it is clear that there are substantial and increasing numbers of people with intellectual disabilities who require a variety of services. Research is developing more sophisticated methods of identifying potential causes of intellectual disability, tracking their behavioural effects, and therefore suggesting new methods for treatment and management.

## FURTHER READING

American Association on Intellectual and Developmental Disabilities (2010). *Intellectual Disability: Definition, Classification, and Systems of Supports* (11th edn). Washington DC: American Association on Intellectual and Developmental Disabilities.

Dykens, E.M., Hodapp, R.M. and Finucane, B.M. (2000) *Genetics and Mental Retardation Syndromes*. Baltimore: Brookes.

Maulik, P.K., Mascarenhas, M.N., Mathers, C.D., Dua, T. and Saxena, S. (2011) Prevalence of intellectual disability: A meta-analysis of population-based studies. *Research in Developmental Disabilities*, **32**, 419–36.

World Health Organization and World Bank (2011) *World Report on Disability*. World Health Organization: Geneva.

## References

American Association on Intellectual and Developmental Disabilities (2010). *Intellectual Disability: Definition, Classification, and Systems of Supports* (11th edn). Washington DC: American Association on Intellectual and Developmental Disabilities.

Brosco, J.P., Mattingly, M. and Sanders, L.M. (2006) Impact of specific medical interventions on reducing the prevalence of mental retardation. *Archives of Pediatric Adolescent Medicine*, **160**, 302–9.

Carter, G. and Jancar, J. (1983) Mortality in the mentally handicapped: a 50 year survey at the Stoke Park group of hospitals (1930–1980). *Journal of Mental Deficiency Research*, **27**, 143–56.

Connor, J.M. and Ferguson-Smith, M.A. (1993) *Essential Medical Genetics* (4th edn). Blackwell: Oxford.

Department of Health (2001) *Valuing People: A new strategy for learning disability for the 21st century*. London: Department of Health.

Durkin, M.S., Schneider, H., Pathania, V.S., Nelson, K.B., Solarsh, G.C., Bellows, N., Scheffler, R.M. and Hofman, K.J. (2006) Learning and developmental disabilities. In World Health Organization (eds), *Disease Control Priorities related to Mental, Neurological, Developmental and Substance Abuse Disorders* (pp. 39–56). Geneva: World Health Organization.

Dykens, E.M. (1995) Measuring behavioral phenotypes: Provocations from the 'new genetics'. *American Journal on Mental Retardation*, **99**, 522–32.

Dykens, E.M., Hodapp, R.M. and Finucane, B.M. (2000) *Genetics and Mental Retardation Syndromes*. Baltimore: Brookes.

Einfeld, S. and Emerson, E. (2008) Intellectual disabilities. In M. Rutter, D. Bishop, D. Pine, S. Scott, J. Stevenson, E. Taylor and A. Thapar (eds). *Rutter's Child and Adolescent Psychiatry* (5th edn). Blackwell: London.

Emerson, E. (2001) *Challenging Behaviour: Analysis and intervention in people with severe intellectual disabilities* (2nd edn). Cambridge: Cambridge University Press.

Emerson, E. and Hatton, C. (1999) Future trends in the ethnic composition of British society and among British citizens with learning disabilities. *Tizard Learning Disability Review*, **4**, 28–32.

Emerson, E. and Hatton, C. (2004) Letter to the editor: response to McGrother *et al.* (2002). *Journal of Intellectual Disability Research*, **48**, 201–2.

Emerson, E. and Hatton, C. (2007) The mental health of children and adolescents with intellectual disabilities in Britain. *British Journal of Psychiatry*, **191**, 493–99.

Emerson, E. and Hatton, C. (2008). *Estimating Future Need for Adult Social Care Services For People With Learning Disabilities in England*. Centre for Disability Research, Lancaster University: Lancaster.

Emerson, E. and Hatton, C. (2011). *Estimating Future Need for Social Care Among Adults With Learning Disabilities in England: an update*. Improving Health & Lives Learning Disabilities Observatory, Lancaster University: Lancaster.

Emerson, E., Azmi, S., Hatton, C., Caine, A., Parrott, R. and Wolstenholme, J. (1997) Is there an increased prevalence of severe learning disabilities among British Asians? *Ethnicity and Health*, **2**, 317–21.

Emerson, E., Fujiura, G. and Hatton, C. (2007) International perspectives. In S. Odom, R. Horner, M. Snell and J. Blacher (eds), *Handbook on Developmental Disabilities* (pp. 591–613). New York: Guilford.

Finlay, W.M.L. and Lyons, E. (2005) Rejecting the label: a social constructionist analysis. *Mental Retardation*, **43**, 120–34.

Flynt, J. and Yule, W. (1994) Behavioural phenotypes. In M. Rutter, E. Taylor and L. Hersov (eds) *Child and Adolescent Psychiatry: Modern approaches* (3rd edn, pp. 666–87). London: Blackwell Scientific.

Fryers, T. (1993) Epidemiological thinking in mental retardation: Issues in taxonomy and population frequency. In *International Review of Research in Mental Retardation: Volume 19* (ed. N.W. Bray). Academic Press: San Diego.

Hatton, C. (2002) People with intellectual disabilities from ethnic minority communities in the US and the UK. *International Review of Research in Mental Retardation*, **25**, 209–39.

Hatton, C. and Emerson, E. (1995) Services for people with learning disabilities and sensory impairments: Results of a national survey of local authorities. *British Journal of Learning Disabilities*, **23**, 11–17.

Hatton, C. and Taylor, J.L. (2005) Promoting healthy lifestyles: mental health. In G. Grant, P. Goward, M. Richardson and P. Ramcharan (eds), *Learning Disability: A Life-Cycle Approach To Valuing People* (pp. 559–603). Maidenhead: Open University Press/McGraw Hill Educational.

Hodapp, R.M. and Dykens, E.M. (2004) Studying behavioral phenotypes: issues, benefits, challenges. In E. Emerson, C. Hatton, T. Thompson and T. R. Parmenter (eds), *The International Handbook for Applied Research in Intellectual Disabilities* (pp. 203–20). Chichester: John Wiley and Sons, Ltd.

Hollins, S., Attard, M.T., von Fraunhofer, N. and Sedgwick, P. (1998) Mortality in people with learning disability: risks, causes, and death certification findings in London. *Developmental Medicine and Child Neurology*, **40**, 50–6.

Jenkins, R. (1998) (ed.) *Questions of Competence: Culture, classification and intellectual disability*. Cambridge, UK: Cambridge University Press.

Katusic, S.A., Colligan, R.C., Beard, M., O'Fallon, M., Bergstralh, E.J., Jacobsen, S.J. and Kurland, L.T. (1995) Mental retardation in a birth cohort, 1976–1980, Rochester, Minnesota. *American Journal on Mental Retardation*, **100**, 335–44.

Kerr, G. (2001) Assessing the needs of learning disabled young people with additional disabilities. *Journal of Learning Disabilities*, **5**, 157–74.

Leonard, H. and Wen, X. (2002) The epidemiology of mental retardation: challenges and opportunities in the new millennium. *Mental Retardation and Developmental Disabilities Research Reviews*, **8**, 117–34.

McGrother, C.W., Bhaumik, S., Thorpe, C.F., Watson, J.M. and Taub, N.A. (2002) Prevalence, morbidity and service need among South Asian and white adults with intellectual disability in Leicestershire, UK. *Journal of Intellectual Disability Research*, **46**, 299–309.

McGuigan, S.M., Hollins, S. and Attard, M. (1995) Age-specific standardized mortality rates in people with learning disability. *Journal of Intellectual Disability Research*, **39**, 527–31.

McLaren, J. and Bryson, S.E. (1987) Review of recent epidemiological studies of mental retardation: Prevalence, associated disorders, and etiology. *American Journal of Mental Retardation*, **92**, 243–54.

Matilainen, R., Airaksinen, E., Mononen, T., Launiala, K. and Kaariainen, R. (1995) A population-based study on the causes of mild and severe mental retardation. *Acta Paediatrica*, **84**, 261–6.

Maulik, P.K., Mascarenhas, M.N., Mathers, C.D., Dua, T. and Saxena, S. (2011) Prevalence of intellectual disability: A meta-analysis of population-based studies. *Research in Developmental Disabilities*, **32**, 419–36.

Murphy, C.C., Boyle, C., Schendel, D., Decoufle, P. and Yeargin-Allsopp, M. (1998) Epidemiology of mental retardation in children. *Mental Retardation and Developmental Disabilities Research Reviews*, **4**, 6–13.

Partington, D., Mowat, D., Einfeld, S., Tonge, B. and Turner, G. (2000) Genes on the X chromosome are important in undiagnosed mental retardation. *American Journal of Medical Genetics*, **92**, 57–61.

Plomin, R., DeFries, J.C., McClearn, G.E. and Rutter, M. (1997) *Behavioral Genetics* (3rd edn.). W.H. Freeman and Co.: New York.

Rantakallio, P. and von Wendt, L. (1986) Mental retardation and subnormality in a birth cohort of 12,000 children in Northern Finland. *American Journal of Mental Deficiency*, **90**, 380–7.

Richardson, S.A. and Koller, H. (1985) Epidemiology. In *Mental Deficiency: The Changing Outlook* (4th edn) (ed. A.M. Clarke, A.D.B. Clarke and J.M. Berg). Methuen: London.

Roeleveld, N., Zielhuis, G.A. and Gabreels, F. (1997) The prevalence of mental retardation: a critical review of the recent literature. *Developmental Medicine and Child Neurology*, **39**, 125–32.

Simonoff, E., Pickles, A., Chadwick, O., Gringras, P., Wood, N., Higgins, S. *et al.* (2006) The Croydon Assessment of Learning Study: Prevalence and educational identification of mild mental retardation. *Journal of Child Psychology and Psychiatry*, **47**, 828–39.

Thomas, C. (2007) *Sociologies of Disability and Illness: Contested ideas in disability studies and medical sociology*. Palgrave MacMillan: Basingstoke.

Trent, J.W. (1995) *Inventing The Feeble Mind: A history of mental retardation in the United States*. University of California Press: Berkeley CA.

World Health Organization (2001) *International Classification of Functioning, Disability and Health*. World Health Organization: Geneva.

World Health Organization and World Bank (2011) *World Report on Disability*. World Health Organization: Geneva.

Wright, D. and Digby, A. (1996) (eds). *From Idiocy to Mental Deficiency: Historical perspectives on people with learning disabilities*. Routledge: London.

# Chapter 2

# SERVICE PROVISION

## Rupa Gone, Chris Hatton and Amanda Caine

## A BRIEF HISTORY OF SERVICE PROVISION

A historical perspective is useful in a number of ways. It reinforces the notion that 'intellectual disability' is socially constructed and, in a climate where claims are often made about marvellous new ways of providing radically new services (e.g. Bradley and Knoll 1995), it can provide a sobering perspective with which to evaluate such claims (Trent 1995; Wright and Digby 1996).

### Before the Institutions: The Poor Laws and 'Community Care'

The period from medieval times to the nineteenth century is often viewed as radically different from today, either a golden age or an era of neglect. However, the continuities between this period and today's era of 'community care' are as notable as the differences. Despite the legal system distinguishing between 'lunacy' (acquired and punctuated by 'lucid intervals') and 'idiocy' (congenital and irreversible) (Andrews 1996; Neugebauer 1996; Rushton, 1996), in practice, the classification of 'idiocy' was dependent on a number of pragmatic factors. People would only come to the attention of the courts or poor law administrators if they needed financial support, usually triggered by family life-cycle crises or disruptive behaviour on the part of the person with 'idiocy' (Andrews 1996; Rushton 1996).

The responses of poor law administrators to 'idiocy' varied and incarceration in asylums or workhouses was rare. Poor law relief was more often directed towards providing basic necessities. Such relief could

*Clinical Psychology and People with Intellectual Disabilities*, Second Edition. Edited by
Eric Emerson, Chris Hatton, Kate Dickson, Rupa Gone, Amanda Caine and Jo Bromley.
© 2012 John Wiley & Sons, Ltd. Published 2012 by John Wiley & Sons, Ltd.

be directed towards family members, same-sex 'keepers' or 'nurses', who provided lodgings and care for the person (Andrews 1996; Rushton 1996), or to the person themselves to enable them to live independently.

## Institutions as Social Reform: The Victorian Era

The reasons for the rise in institutions for people with intellectual disabilities are complex, unclear and hotly debated (Scheerenberger 1983; Trent 1995; Wright and Digby 1996). However increasingly urban, industrialised societies, with their associated changes in family structures and household economies, changing conceptions of 'idiocy', and the Victorian penchant for social reform all combined to create fertile ground for the rise of the institution in the late nineteenth century.

The first institutions for 'idiots' were founded on the basis of a new optimism about the possibilities of teaching skills to people formerly regarded as incurable (Gladstone 1996). The first specialised institutions, run by voluntary agencies, were designed to take in 'idiot' children for a maximum of five years and train them to become productive members of society. This was not borne out in practice; stories of spectacular success were not repeated, and children tended to remain in institutions much longer than their allotted five years.

Institutions provided by state agencies were different in size, ethos, and character from the earlier voluntary 'idiot asylums' and did not select on the basis of likely trainability. They were much larger, with advocates of large institutions citing advantages such as rapidly increasing demand, economies of scale, and increasing precision of classification for the purposes of education, training and treatment. Indeed, to keep costs low, many 'idiot asylums' encouraged the retention of adult 'idiots' within the institution, to carry out necessary work at minimal cost (Gladstone 1996). This resulted in an ethos of permanent containment and regimented routines necessary to ensure the smooth running of the institution (Gladstone 1996; Jackson 1996).

## Private Problem to Social Threat: The Early Twentieth Century

By the end of the nineteenth century a rise in the number of people classified as 'idiots' was apparent. Debates continue concerning how much of this rise was 'real' (Day and Jancar 1991; Race 1995; Ryan 1987). While improved living conditions and health care throughout the nineteenth century may have contributed to an actual rise in the number of people with intellectual disabilities, social factors appeared to be the major fuel for the increased demand for institutional places, including changing demands on families and expanding concepts of 'idiocy'.

Several strands of thought around this time converged to reconceptualise the 'idiot' as a threat to society. First, the increasingly influential medical profession began to conceptualise 'idiocy' as an organic disease, with a concomitant pessimism about training or 'cure' and a reinforcement of the idea of 'idiots' as qualitatively different from the rest of society. Second, the eugenics movement claimed that social ills, including poverty, crime and 'immoral' sexual behaviour, were caused by people of inferior genetic stock. Third, educationalists and psychologists developed the theory of unified intelligence, which in its IQ test form could be used as an impeccably 'scientific' method for classifying people as being mentally deficient at a young age. Through the use of terms such as 'moral imbecility', many people engaging in behaviour unacceptable to Edwardian sensibilities, such as drunkenness or 'immoral' sexual behaviour, were brought under the umbrella definition of 'mental deficiency' (Cox 1996; Jackson 1996).

The permanent segregation of people with 'mental deficiency' now became an explicit goal for institutions (Jackson 1996), a stark contrast to the early Victorian aims of training and re-integration into society. It was argued that this would result in a great saving of money to the community at large, while protecting society from people with 'mental deficiency' and also protecting people with 'mental deficiency' from themselves and society (Jackson 1996).

The Royal Commission on the Care and Control of the Feeble-Minded (1904–1908) was in part a response to this changed atmosphere, and recommended the setting up of an expanded nation-wide network of permanent, segregated institutions (or 'colonies') for people with 'mental deficiency'. The Mental Deficiency Act of 1913 went part of the way towards trying to achieve this goal. These colonies were to be controlled by Boards of Control of local authorities, who had wide-ranging powers both to admit people to institutions and to detain them once they were institutionalised (Digby 1996; Race 1995; Ryan 1987). However, the Act failed to provide adequate new resources for local authorities, leading to its uneven and incomplete implementation (Digby 1996; Thomson 1996).

In addition to enabling the institutionalisation of people with 'mental deficiency', the 1913 Act also allowed for local authorities to place people with 'mental deficiency' under 'supervision' with their families, or under 'guardianship' with a range of service providers (Thomson 1996) which sometimes included their families. Families were also supported by newly opened 'occupation centres', which provided activities during the day for people with 'mental deficiency' (Thomson 1996).

## The NHS and Community Care

The setting up of the welfare state in the UK after the Second World War provided a framework for services which is still present today. The 1944 *Education Act*, for example, led to the establishment of a number of special schools for children with intellectual disabilities, although the terms of the Act also excluded children with severe disabilities who were deemed to be 'ineducable'. The establishment of the National Health Service (NHS) in 1948 also brought all institutions under the aegis of the health service, an arbitrary decision but one with long-term consequences. As institutions became hospitals, people with intellectual disabilities became patients with health problems.

The number of people with intellectual disabilities in institutions rose to a peak of approximately 60,000–64,000 in the 1950s and 1960s, although another 35,000–40,000 people were living outside institutions under care or guardianship orders at this time (Felce 1996; Race 1995). At around this time doubts were voiced about whether the institution was a desirable place for people with intellectual disabilities to live. First, many of the claims made by eugenicists, for example about the heritability of intelligence, had been discredited by the 1950s, and a gradual shift in social mores meant that people with intellectual disabilities became seen as less of a threat to society. Second, a renewed interest in the rights of individuals after the Second World War led to increasing calls for people with intellectual disabilities to enjoy the same civil rights as other citizens (Emerson 1992).

Research demonstrating the debilitating effect of institutions on child development in general and the development of people with intellectual disabilities in particular proliferated. Some of this research suggested that people with intellectual disabilities previously thought to be 'ineducable' could develop their skills with appropriate education and support; the kind of education and support that was not provided in institutions. Furthermore, these alternatives seemed to provide a much better social and material environment than that provided by large, barren institutions. Finally, and possibly most damagingly, there were a series of scandals concerning hospitals for people with intellectual disabilities, starting with the Committee of Enquiry into Ely Hospital in 1969, which castigated the ill-treatment meted out by staff on their patients (Mittler and Sinason 1996; Race 1995).

Thus, throughout the 1960s alternatives to institutionalisation were firmly on the agenda. At the level of 'high politics', the Seebohm Report of 1968 (enacted in 1970; Seebohm, 1968) recommended the setting up of social services departments in local authorities to provide a more proactive, comprehensive and integrated service for families and individuals requiring help, including people with intellectual disabilities living outside institutions. The White Paper of 1971, *Better Services for the Mentally Handicapped,* advocated a massive increase in community-based services for people with intellectual disabilities and a consequent reduction in hospital places, although the White Paper stopped some way short of proposing total hospital closure. From this point, children became less likely to be admitted to mental handicap hospitals, and some adults began to leave to community-based units or hostels (Felce 1996; Race 1995).

This equivocal stance gradually changed throughout the 1970s and 1980s, with Government-sponsored committees such as the Jay Committee becoming increasingly influenced by the ideas of normalisation as they were promoted in the UK (Emerson 1992; King's Fund 1980; O'Brien and Tyne 1981; Wolfensberger 1972). In the UK the means adopted to achieve these ends focused on moving people with intellectual disabilities out of hospitals into ordinary houses, on the assumption that if institutional environments created institutional behaviour, it followed that 'ordinary' environments would create more valued, 'ordinary' behaviour.

After the demonstrated success of pilot projects providing 'ordinary life' services to people with severe and profound intellectual disabilities (Felce 1989; Lowe and de Paiva 1991), the implementation of 'ordinary living' services became more widespread throughout the UK, although there is evidence that 'ordinary living' services were geographically patchy and by no means the dominant model of residential provision (Emerson and Hatton 1996; 1997). In line with developments in North America, Australasia and Scandinavia, the number of people with intellectual disabilities living in institutions fell sharply throughout the 1980s (Emerson *et al.* 1996; Hatton, Emerson, & Kiernan, 1995), with the number of hospital places approximately halving between 1980 and 1992 (Emerson and Hatton 1994). Day services in the form of day centres (first named 'Adult Training Centres', where industrial work was carried out for little money; later re-named 'Social Education Centres', where the ostensible aims were educative) also expanded during this period, as did family support services such as respite and domiciliary care (Gray 1996; Stalker 1996).

## POLICY AND LEGISLATIVE CONTEXT

Current international and national policies and legislation regarding people with intellectual disabilities are outlined. We then focus on UK policy and legislation pertaining to the health and community care of the general population including shifts in commissioning arrangements, since these inevitably also impact on the lives of people with intellectual disabilities.

## International Legislation

The UK has international commitments specific to the human rights of children and young people and adults with intellectual disabilities. For adults, an international legislative framework in force from May 2008 is provided by the United Nations (UN) Convention on the Rights of Persons with Disabilities. The Convention affirms that all individuals with all types of disabilities must enjoy all human rights and fundamental freedoms. The Convention is explicit in making a paradigm shift from viewing people with disabilities as recipients of charity, medical treatment and social protection towards viewing people with disabilities as equal citizens, who are capable of claiming their rights and making decisions about their lives based on their free and informed consent. As a signatory the UK is obliged to ensure all categories of rights apply to individuals with disabilities and identify areas where adaptations have to be made for people to effectively exercise their rights, areas where their rights have been violated, and where protection of rights must be reinforced.

Children and young people with intellectual disabilities have been identified as extremely vulnerable to having their rights violated. A World Health Organization and UNICEF partnership initiative aims to ensure that all children and young people with intellectual disabilities are fully participating members of society, living with their families, integrated in the community and receiving health care and support proportional to their needs. Launched in November 2010 the resultant *European Declaration on the Health of Children and Young People with Intellectual Disabilities and their Families* sets out four key objectives:

- Promote and support good physical and mental health and well-being.
- Eliminate health and other inequalities and prevent other forms of discrimination, neglect and abuse.
- Provide support that prevents family separation and allow parents to care for and protect children and young people with intellectual disabilities.
- Support children and young people in the development of their potential and the successful transitions through life (WHO, 2010).

## National Policy and Legislation Relating to People with Intellectual Disabilities

In 2001 the UK Government published the White Paper *Valuing People: A New Strategy for Learning Disability for the 21st Century* (DOH 2001) laying out plans for improving the lives of children and adults with intellectual disabilities and their families and carers. Building on the principles of previous legislation and policies, the central tenets of the Government's plans were to:

- tackle social exclusion and achieve better life chances;
- ensure value for money from investment in intellectual disability services;
- promote consistency and equity of services across the country;
- promote effective partnership working at all levels to ensure a person-centred approach to delivering quality services;
- drive up standards by encouraging an evidence-based approach to service provision and practice.

*Valuing People* stated that the Government's objective was to enable people to have access to a health service designed around their individual needs, with fast and convenient care delivered to a consistently high standard and with additional support where necessary (DOH 2001). However, Valuing People has not yet resulted in equitable access to health care. The gap between the aims of *Valuing People* and the actual life experiences of people with intellectual disabilities were apparent as a series of independent inquiries reported that people:

- reported substantial physical health inequities (Disability Rights Commission 2006);
- experienced severe inequities in health care provision (Michael 2008);
- continued to have their human rights breached (Joint Committee of Human Rights 2008).

To increase the progress towards the vision set out in *Valuing People*, the UK government outlined a three year strategy and implementation plan; *Valuing People Now* (DOH 2009b). The strategy incorporated each of the ten recommendations made by the *Healthcare for All* report (itself a response to Mencap's 2007 *'Death by indifference'* campaign).

*Valuing People Now* has also brought the 2001 *Valuing People* white paper up to date with recent government policy. Throughout each strand the strategy reflects the personalization agenda of social care services in the policies it sets out for housing, employment, healthcare, education and family.

## The Disability Discrimination Act and 'Reasonable Adjustments'

Since the *Disability Discrimination Act (1995)*, people with intellectual disabilities (along with other groups of disabled people) have had an entitlement to equal access to public sector services, including NHS Trust-provided health services and local authority-provided social care services. Over time, principally through the *Disability Discrimination Act (2005)* and reinforced in the recent *Equality Act (2010)*, this fundamental entitlement to equal access has been increasingly well-defined as the Disability Equality Duty. In law, all public sector services have a legal duty to provide 'reasonable adjustments' for people with intellectual disabilities, so that a person with intellectual disabilities can expect to receive health and social care that is equally accessible and designed to be equally effective compared to people without disabilities. Reasonable adjustments include removing physical barriers to accessing health and social care services, but importantly also include changing the ways in which services are delivered and ensuring that policies, procedures and staff training all ensure that services work equally well for people with intellectual disabilities (Equality and Human Rights Commission 2010a, b; Government Equalities Office 2010). The legal duty for health and social care services is 'anticipatory'. This means that a health or social care service should be thinking in advance of how to make reasonable adjustments for people with intellectual disabilities, rather than waiting until a person with intellectual disabilities tries to use the service to put reasonable adjustments into place.

Over the past 20 years, the substantial and wide-ranging health inequalities experienced by people with intellectual disabilities have become increasingly well-documented (Emerson and Baines 2010). A major factor contributing to these health inequalities are stark inequalities in the access that people with intellectual disabilities have to health services, and equally stark inequalities in how people with intellectual disabilities are treated (or not treated) when using health services. These inequalities in access and treatment to health services have been thoroughly documented in a series of investigations and inquiries. These include:

- The Disability Rights Commission formal investigation into the physical health inequalities experienced by people with learning disabilities and/or mental health problems (Disability Rights Commission 2006).
- A national audit of specialist inpatient healthcare services for people with learning disabilities carried out by the Healthcare Commission (Healthcare Commission 2007).
- Mencap highlighted the cases of six people with learning disabilities who their families believed had died avoidably whilst in NHS or social services (Mencap 2007; see also the 'Six Lives' report of the investigation into these six cases by the Parliamentary and Health Service Ombudsman and Local Government Ombudsman in 2009).

These and evidence from other inquiries resulted in the Department of Health setting up an independent inquiry into the healthcare experienced by people with learning disabilities, which reported in 2008 (Michael 2008). This report reinforced the findings of previous inquiries, stating that 'There is a clear legal framework for the provision of equal treatment for people with disabilities and yet it seems clear that since services are not yet being provided to an adequate standard (sic)' (Michael 2008 p. 55).

However, the robust legal framework of the *Disability Equality Duty* and strong policy leadership from the Department of Health (Giraud-Saunders 2009) have not resulted in health services routinely providing comprehensive reasonable adjustments for people with learning disabilities. As the current Mencap campaign *'Getting It Right'* emphasises (Mencap 2010), institutional discrimination within health services towards people with learning disabilities still exists, with many barriers relating to the attitudes, knowledge and skills of health service staff, and the routine operation of the health systems within which staff work.

## Reforming the National Health Service

*The NHS Plan* (DOH 2000) set out a ten-year plan to create a modern and dependable NHS.

Throughout this and other national policy there was an explicit expectation that services involve their users in a broad range of issues. There is now a broad knowledge base of experience across the country on effective, non-tokenistic approaches to achieve this, varying from direct involvement in assessment and individual planning through to involvement in wider strategic issues. Organisational structures should enable service users and advocates to have an impact on debates about the future style and direction of services in a way that is beyond the token user in a planning group.

These principles are reiterated in the White Paper *Equity and Excellence: Liberating the NHS* (DOH, 2010a). This is the latest long-term plan for the NHS which purports to give the NHS a coherent, stable, enduring framework for quality and service improvement. It aims to move beyond the debate about structures and processes in health care delivery and focus on improved health outcomes for all citizens. It describes a challenging and far-reaching set of reforms, which will drive cultural change in the NHS with the following aims:

- to improve health outcomes;
- to focus on outcomes and the quality standards to deliver them;
- to increase the autonomy of providers in return for;
- more accountability for the results they achieve;

- to demonstrate democratic legitimacy (accountable to patients through choice and accountable to the public) at local level;
- to cut bureaucracy and improve efficiency.

At the time when *Liberating the NHS* is supposed to be implemented the NHS has to achieve unprecedented efficiency gains, with savings reinvested in front-line services, to meet the financial challenge and the costs of demographic and technological change.

A further change is that the guidance compiled by the National Institute for Health and Clinical Excellence (NICE) will no longer be binding on commissioners (see commissioning section below). NICE is an independent organization responsible for providing national guidance on promoting good health and preventing and treating ill health. NICE guidance has been produced for over 50 conditions all of which may be applicable to someone with intellectual disabilities.

## Funding for Long-Term Care

Uncertainty about how to access and who is responsible for funding long-term care can affect the lives of people with intellectual disabilities and their families. *Continuing NHS Care* (DOH 1995) stated that where it is thought continuing NHS care might be appropriate then multi-professional assessment and consultation with parents and carers are necessary to determine whether the services needed could only be provided by the NHS or whether other alternatives would be more appropriate and cost effective. However, the Health Service Ombudsman for England (2003) report on NHS funding for the long term care of older and disabled people concluded that:

- The Department of Health's guidance and support to date had not provided the secure foundation needed to enable a fair and transparent system of eligibility for funding for long-term care to be operated across the country.
- What guidance there is has been misinterpreted and misapplied by some health authorities when developing and reviewing their own eligibility criteria.
- Further problems have arisen in the application of local criteria to individuals.
- The effect has been to cause injustice and hardship to some people.

Recommendations were that strategic health authorities and primary care trusts should:

- Review the criteria used by their predecessor bodies, and the way those criteria were applied, since 1996. They will need to take into account the *Coughlan* judgment (England and Wales Court of Appeal 1999);

According to this judgment, the boundary between health and social care is not one of policy, but of law. The judgment establishes that where a person's primary need is for health care, and that is why they are placed in nursing home accommodation, the NHS is responsible for the full cost of the package.
- Pay compensation to patients, where the criteria, or their application, were unfair. This could include patients who may wrongly have been made to pay for their care in a home.

It also proposed that the Department of Health should:

- consider how they can support and monitor the performance of authorities and primary care trusts in this work. Consider reviewing whether, from 1996, criteria being used were lawful and in accordance to guidance;
- review the national guidance on eligibility for continuing NHS health-care, making it much clearer in new guidance the situations when the NHS must provide funding and those where it is left to the discretion of NHS bodies locally;
- become proactive in checking that future criteria follow that guidance;
- consider how to link assessment of eligibility into the single assessment process and whether the Department should provide further support to the development of reliable assessment methods.

Some adults with complex mental health needs come under the auspices of the Care Programme Approach (CPA, introduced in 1991; DOH 2008). This is designed to strengthen good practice by attending to assessment, care planning, the appointment of a key worker and regular review.

## Community Care

Nationally there were six key objectives for community care, as set out by *The National Health Service and Community Care Act (1990)*:

- Promote domiciliary, day and respite care services to enable people to live in their own homes wherever it is feasible and sensible.
- Make practical support for carers a high priority.
- Provide community care on the basis of careful assessment of individuals' needs and the co-ordination of services by the agencies involved.
- Work closely with the voluntary and independent sector in providing a comprehensive, high quality service.
- Clarify who is responsible for what and to ensure that we all account for our performance.
- Secure better value for taxpayers' and community charge payers' money.

Under this legislation certain agencies have a responsibility to assess needs for services, specify what services are required and commission an appropriate organisation to provide them (Roberts and Griffiths 1993). There are several pieces of legislation which determine current service provision. These are often statements of good intentions and are rarely accompanied by extra resources. As a result the intentions of legislation are not always translated into practice. Such an example is the above-mentioned *NHS and Community Care Act* (DOH 1990) and associated guidance on issues such as care management which continues to provide much of the over-arching legislative and organisational framework within which services are commissioned and provided.

*Care Management*    National policy is clear that services should be based on the assessed needs and wishes of individuals, rather than individuals being fitted into pre-planned services. Local authorities have been given the lead role in this, through the *Children Act (1989)* requirement for children and through the assessment process for adults. However NHS Trusts are required to contribute to these processes. A commonly used approach is 'person-centred' assessment and planning, where systems focus on developing the positive aspects of a person's life and abilities. One consequence of this approach is that people are likely to receive services from a wide range of providers, including non-professional or 'natural' supports, rather than be dependent upon one organisation for all aspects of their needs.

*Fair Access to Care Services* (DOH 2003) provided a framework for setting eligibility criteria for adult social care based on individuals' needs and associated risks to independence. This was developed to provide councils with a mechanism for allocating limited resources fairly and consistently nationally. The decision to help or not was strongly influenced by the resources locally allocated to adult social care.

In 2010 this was replaced by new guidelines following an independent review by the Commission for Social Care Inspection (DOH, 2010b). Retaining the four eligibility bands used to categorise immediate needs and also needs that would worsen for the lack of timely help (critical, substantial, moderate and low), the new guidelines provide clarity on fairness, transparency and consistency of application and also reflect the increased focus on prevention and personalisation of services.

## Commissioning Health and Social Care

Commissioning is the strategic activity of assessing needs, resources, and current services at population level, and developing a strategy to make best use of available resources to meet identified needs. Joint Commissioning is the process by which two or more commissioning agents act together to co-ordinate their commissioning, taking joint responsibility for the translation of strategy into action. It is now generally considered inappropriate for a healthcare provider to become substantially involved in non-healthcare provision.

Although Joint Commissioning (between health and social services) of services for people with intellectual disabilities was regarded as desirable, if not essential in the 1990s, the Department of Health guidance was not prescriptive on how it should be developed. As a consequence the rhetoric of joint commissioning was often greater than the reality across the country. National policies resulted in contradictory imperatives for different statutory organisations, such as to simultaneously collaborate and compete with each other, and to be engaged in prevention work while simultaneously prioritising short-term waiting lists. Such contradictory imperatives were exacerbated by different organisational cultures across agencies, which influenced the way in which they worked and the speed at which change was made. These difficulties prevented joint commissioning from having a beneficial impact on the services received by people with intellectual disabilities and their carers (Hattersley 1995).

Partnership boards were the means by which such difficulties were addressed for services for people with intellectual disabilities. The *Valuing People* strategy set a deadline of October 2001 for the establishment of Learning Disability Partnership Boards (LDPB) in NHS trusts (in addition to existing structures for inter-agency planning for intellectual disability funding). LDPB were required to operate within the framework of the *Health Act* (DOH 1999). Section 31 of the *Health Act* permits the NHS and local authorities to pool their resources, delegate functions and transfer resources from one organisation to another. One key aspect of *Valuing People Now* (DOH, 2009a) was its plans to make local LDPB stronger through setting up regional boards to oversee them, and to increase user and carer involvement in shaping local services. The boards are responsible primarily for:

- developing and implementing the joint investment plan;
- overseeing the planning and commissioning of comprehensive, integrated and inclusive services that provide people in their local community with a genuine choice of services;
- ensuring that people are not denied access to local services by a lack of skill and experience;
- the use of flexibilities under the *Health Act* (DOH 1999);
- ensuring that there are arrangements to help young people with intellectual disabilities to make a smooth transition to life as an adult.

The White Paper *Our Health Our Care Our Say* (DOH 2006) addressed the perennial issue of how to achieve greater coordination between health and social care services and confirmed the vision of high quality support meeting people's aspirations of independence and greater control over their lives, making services flexible and responsive to individual need.

It continued the trend towards integrated care and promoting independence in the community and had four main goals:

• To provide better prevention services with early intervention.
• To give people real choices and a stronger voice.
• To tackle local inequalities and improve access to community services.
• To provide more support for people with long-term needs.

This White Paper proposed that the introduction of Practice Based Commissioning (PBC) would develop services that are safe, high quality and closer to home, in the community. It was hoped PBC would provide the incentive for the health service to move services from secondary to primary care. In social care this White Paper contributed to the modernisation of services, setting of national minimum standards, developing more choice of provider, investing in workforce training and regulation, supporting people to remain active and independent in their own homes, integrating of social care services for children with other local authority services, and establishing of Directors of Children's Services to ensure a strong co-ordinated focus.

This was further strengthened and implemented through the Government's launch of its *Vision for Adult Social Care Capable Communities and Active Citizens* (DOH, 2010c) which placed personalised services and outcomes centre stage, and the consultation *Transparency in outcomes: a framework for adult social care* (DOH 2010) which outlined a framework to place outcomes at the heart of social care, improve quality in services and empower citizens to hold their local councils to account for the services they provide.

## The Personalisation Agenda

The journey towards the Personalisation of services started with the NHS and Community Care Act (DOH 1990) which realised the implementation of the White Paper *Caring for People* (DOH 1989). Central to its vision was the principle that when people needed ongoing support, they did not cease to be citizens or members of their local community. The services they used should therefore help them to retain or regain their roles and the benefits of community membership, including living in their own homes, maintaining or gaining employment and making a positive contribution. One way of promoting Personalisation was the introduction of Direct Payments in 1997, whereby people who were eligible for social care chose to receive a cash sum in lieu of services. Individual budgets brought together a range of different funding streams – in addition to social care expenditure – to support independent living. Adult social care was encouraged to provide higher quality support and to be more responsive to people's needs and wishes – to personalise their care as well as being more cost effective. This was taken one step further in the White Paper *Our Health, Our Nation, Our Care, Our Say* (DOH 2006) which announced the piloting of Individual Budgets. Its aims were to:

- allocate budgets to eligible people through self-directed support and providing the opportunity to have choice and control over purchased services, whether council managed or otherwise provided;
- make a strategic shift in care and support away from intervention at the point of crisis to a protective and preventative model centred on improved well being and maintaining independence;
- commission strategies which balance intensive care and support for those with high-level complex needs, with investment in prevention and early intervention;
- gain the active involvement of communities and individuals in the development and delivery of services;
- ensure universal services, including information, advice and advocacy are easy to find and available to everyone, regardless of who is paying,
- increase emphasis on treating people with dignity and respect, with a clearer understanding of what that means;
- actively manage the market to ensure high-quality care which can respond to choices made by individuals purchasing their own care directly or through self directed support.

These objectives provided a considerable challenge and the change required was fundamental. In services for people with intellectual disabilities person-centred planning has provided a means for some individuals to achieve personalised services, and good practice guidance has been developed (DOH, 2010d).

## The Future of Health Service Commissioning

The White Paper *Equity and Excellence: Liberating the NHS* (DOH, 2010a) has a number of supporting papers including a consultation paper regarding its plans for commissioning health services (DOH, 2010e). In order to shift decision making as close as possible to individual patients, the Department of Health will devolve power and responsibility for commissioning most health services to groups of GP practices (consortia). Consortia will have a duty to promote equalities and to work in partnership with local authorities, for instance in relation to heath and adult social care, early years services and public health. Consortia will need to engage patients and the public on an ongoing basis as they undertake their commissioning responsibilities, and will have a duty of public and patient involvement.

*The Health and Social Care Bill* was introduced into Parliament on 19 January 2011. The Bill proposes monumental changes to the UK National Health Services. Following on from *Equity and Excellence: Liberating the NHS* (2010) and *Liberating the NHS: legislative framework and next steps* (2010), which require primary legislation, the Bill proposes new commissioning arrangements as well as drastic cuts to existing health bodies:

- Establish an independent NHS Board to allocate resources and provide commissioning guidance.
- Increase GPs' powers to commission services on behalf of their patients.
- Strengthen the role of the Care Quality Commission.
- Develop Monitor, the body that currently regulates NHS foundation trusts, into an economic regulator to oversee aspects of access and competition in the NHS.
- Cut the number of health bodies to help meet the Government's commitment to cut NHS administration costs by a third, including abolishing Primary Care Trusts and Strategic Health Authorities.

At the time of writing there was apprehension within the public sector about whether the Bill can achieve the goals it sets out of improved services, empowering patients, services users and staff, and make financial savings in the longer term. The vital details of the UK government's plans and their impact on services, including for people with intellectual disabilities are yet to be specified.

## Public Health

There is a government commitment to giving higher priority and dedicating resources to public health which is made in the White Paper *Healthy Lives, Healthy People: Our strategy for public health in England* (DOH 2010). This is a response to Sir Michael Marmot's *Fair Society; Healthy Lives* (2010) report and adopts its life course framework for tackling the wider social determinants of health. The aim is to build people's self-esteem, confidence and resilience right from infancy – with stronger support for early years. It complements *A Vision for Adult Social Care: Capable Communities and Active Citizens* (DOH, 2010c) in emphasising more personalised, preventative services that are focused on delivering the best outcomes for citizens. The goal is a public health service that achieves excellent results, and enhanced professional leadership. This white paper builds on *Equity and Excellence: Liberating the NHS* (DOH, 2010a) to set out the overall principles and framework for making this happen.

## SERVICE PROVISION – THE CURRENT PICTURE

Services for people with intellectual disabilities are in a state of flux, with many innovative services springing up and many not so innovative services being given innovative new labels. Given this changing picture, any typology of service 'models' is likely to be incomplete and somewhat reductionist. Nevertheless, such a typology can be useful in illustrating the range and extent of services currently existing in the UK.

### Housing (Residential Services)

People with intellectual disabilities and their families have few options about where they live. *Valuing People* states one objective is to enable people and their families to have greater choice and control over where and how they live. In a report of the publically available data from English local authorities for April 2009 to March 2010, 136,450 adults with intellectual disabilities were living in some form of accommodation, including non-residential service settings (Emerson *et al*. 2011). The main types of accommodation were settled mainstream housing with family or friends (41,825 people), short term with family or friends (745 people), registered care homes (25,795 people), nursing homes (1,870 people) and healthcare residential facilities or hospitals (1,330 people). A further proportion of people were living in supported accommodation or group homes (17,965 people). There were also people with tenancies, either with local authorities or other organizations (13,620 people) or with private landlords (3,765 people). Fewer people were living in owner-occupied or shared ownership accommodation (2,695 people) or adult placement schemes (2,675 people). Small numbers of people were also living in less settled accommodation (Emerson *et al*. 2011).

Housing support services are varied geographically across the UK, with different regions and local authorities providing very different numbers and types of services (Emerson *et al*. 2011). Taking these trends into account, the major models of residential provision include:

*Care homes and private hospitals (village or residential communities)* are managed by the voluntary or private sector, are diverse in physical characteristics and outlook. They are usually large (50+ places) and rural, but can be smaller and urban, with numbers probably stable. These communities are sometimes guided by spiritual or religious values, and tend to offer services to people with more skills and fewer complex needs. There is almost no information regarding the quality of residential or village communities or the lifestyle they offer to residents (Hatton and Emerson 1996).

*Hostels*   typically managed by social services, rather than health or independent sector services, segregated, medium-sized (10–25 places), can be purpose-built or converted large houses, and located in urban settings, with numbers probably falling. Research evidence suggests that hostels are of substantially higher quality than institutions, but they fall some way short of ordinary life principles (Emerson and Hatton 1994; 1996).

*Group homes or staffed houses*   historically managed by health and social services, but transferred to the independent sector, segregated, relatively small (2–8 places), usually 'ordinary' houses (sometimes with conversions) in urban locations, with numbers rising. Staffed housing services can successfully support people with complex needs. Research evidence suggests that staffed houses are generally of higher quality than hostels and mental handicap hospitals and offer a more independent and valued lifestyle to residents. However, in some respects (especially poverty and choice) staffed housing services still fall short of 'ordinary life' principles or normative social standards, and vary widely in quality, with some houses offering a lifestyle similar to that offered by institutions (Emerson and Hatton 1994; 1996).

*Supported living*   A number of diverse approaches to providing residential supports to people with intellectual disabilities can be subsumed under this label. The basic principles of supported living are the separation of housing and support, person-centred planning, and the use of 'natural' supports (Howard 1996; Simons 1995). Prototypically, this involves a person living alone as a named tenant in an ordinary flat or house, although it could also involve life sharing arrangements (where a person shares a flat with a person or family without intellectual disabilities). This sector appears to be expanding. It is claimed that supported living services can successfully support all people with intellectual disabilities, although there is as yet no research evidence concerning the lifestyle afforded by supported living beyond individual success stories (Simons 1995).

*Independent living*   By definition, this 'model' involves people with considerable skills living independently of support, except for some support by social workers. People living independently usually live in urban, rented accommodation. There is little research evidence concerning independent living (Flynn 1989; Hatton and Emerson 1996), although that which exists suggests that the positive and valued aspects of independent living are often accompanied by poverty, unemployment and victimisation by people in local communities.

*Specialist residential services*   providing support to people grouped on the basis of particular characteristics or needs. These usually involve people with complex needs, such as offenders, people with challenging behaviour, people with multiple disabilities and people with mental health problems, where routine residential services are perceived to be absent or inadequate. Specialist services come in a range of sizes, locations, philosophies and managing agencies, although a substantial proportion is managed by health and voluntary sector providers. There is no available evidence concerning the number of people in such services, although it is probable that this sector is expanding. Research evidence tends to focus on specific examples of such services (e.g. Clare and Murphy 1993; Hatton *et al*. 1995; Mansell 1997), with varying results.

*Long-stay 'mental handicap' hospitals* were NHS managed, segregated, usually large (50+ places), and located in rural or semi-rural areas. Extensive research suggests that mental handicap hospitals were of poor quality and provided a materially and socially impoverished lifestyle to their residents (Emerson and Hatton 1994; 1996). The closure of long-stay hospitals started in the 1980s when people with intellectual disabilities were moved to residential care homes in the community. Since then numbers of people living in long-stay hospitals have fallen rapidly (Emerson and Hatton 1994; 1996). By 2007 almost all the long-stay hospitals were closed with about 700 people with complex needs, including challenging behaviours, remaining (Mansell 2007). *Valuing People* (DOH 2001) had set a target date of 2004, for closure of all 'mental handicap' hospitals, which was achieved in April 2009.

## Day Services

Since the 1970s, the purpose-built social services day centre has been the dominant form of day service. Adults are typically brought to centres in segregated transport between the hours of 9.30 and 4.00, Monday to Friday. As with residential services for people with intellectual disabilities, the purpose and usefulness of predominant patterns of day service provision has been called into question (Mental Health Foundation 1996; Wertheimer 1997, Mencap 2002). The extent, range and quality of activities offered by day centres vary greatly (Mental Health Foundation 1996; Mansell 2007). On normalization and integrationist grounds (not to mention the potential cash saving), there is an argument to move away from building-based services to more flexible daytime support, where individual support workers spend time with people with intellectual disabilities outside their home, enjoying a range of activities in integrated community settings. There has been a steady decline in the number of adults with intellectual disabilities using them from more than 200,000 people in 1995 (Department of Health Statistics Office 1995) to fewer than 58,000 in 2008/2009 (Emerson *et al*. 2011).

A national survey of people with intellectual disabilities found that 39 % of all people attended a day centre, two-fifths of whom attended five days a week (Cole *et al.* 2007). It was concluded that:

- day centres are still the main daytime service for people with intellectual disabilities;
- some places have smaller units or resource centres which people use as a base for activities in the community;
- in some newer projects, staff work individually with people so that they can choose their own activities on different days of the week;
- more could be done to improve day services for people with learning disabilities.

Person Centred Planning is considered of primary importance in the modernization of day services. It can provide an opportunity for people using day services to express their individual wishes and to come to decisions about what they want to do with their days and their lives. It is also an appropriate way for people to identify support needs and how they can best be met (Mencap 2002). In recent years the availability of Direct Payments has helped some individuals personalize their support services. In 2008/2009, there were 13,700 adults with intellectual disabilities using local authority-funded direct payments. From 2005/2006 to 2008/2009, there has been a rapid increase in the number of adults with learning disabilities using local authority-funded direct payments (annual percentage change +49.9%; Emerson *et al.* 2011).

On this model, adults with intellectual disabilities can experience the range of further education, work and leisure activities experienced by people in society generally. Further education schemes for people with intellectual disabilities do exist, but are geographically patchy, often unclear in their purpose, and are under considerable resource pressure (Mental Health Foundation 1996). Supported employment schemes, where adults with intellectual disabilities are employed with support and training from job coaches, are increasing, although complexities regarding benefit and prevailing economic conditions often make the provision of full-time jobs for people with intellectual disabilities problematic (Wertheimer 1997).

## Family and Individual Support Services

In addition to residential and day services, there are a range of services which aim to provide additional support to carers, individuals with intellectual disabilities, or both simultaneously.

As with family support services for children, there is a range of respite (or short-term break) services provided for families containing an adult with intellectual disabilities. The most common form of respite service is provided in specialist respite units (Flynn *et al.* 1995); however, such services are variable in the quality of experience they offer for users and are less likely to be used by families from ethnic minorities (Azmi *et al.* 1996). Other types of long-standing short-term breaks include domiciliary services (often called 'sitting' or 'befriending' services) and holidays for users (often organised through social services day centres). More recently there has been an expansion in short-term family placements, which are thought to provide a better experience for users and to be more accessible to people from ethnic minorities (Orlik *et al.* 1991). However, the need to provide a better short-term break experience for users has to be balanced against the wish of carers to have reliable respite services with trained staff (Stalker and Robinson 1994).

Community-based professional support is also available to people with intellectual disabilities and their carers. This support is usually in the form of multi-disciplinary community-based community learning disability teams, which can include input from clinical psychology, psychiatry, nursing, speech therapy, occupational therapy, social work and other professions. Such teams vary widely in terms of their size, professional membership and purpose, with some evidence that they have contributed towards the establishment of more co-ordinated services focused on the needs of individuals (Brown and Wistow 1990; McGrath and Humphreys 1988). However, the tensions of multi-disciplinary working can reduce the efficacy of community support teams. In addition to these general teams, specialist challenging behaviour teams designed to provide additional support to individuals, services and families have expanded considerably in recent years, although evidence for the efficacy of these teams is somewhat equivocal (Emerson, Forrest, Cambridge, & Mansell, 1996).

## Advocacy

Although often not conceptualised as a service, advocacy schemes including people with intellectual disabilities do exist, although they are geographically patchy and often somewhat marginal within service structures, operating on small and unstable budgets. Citizen advocacy aims to provide additional (usually non-professional) support to a person with intellectual disabilities, to help people to express their views and to ensure that people's rights and aspirations are respected. Self-advocacy (a somewhat curious term) aims to encourage self-determination and political action, on both an individual and group level, by people with intellectual disabilities. The most widespread self-advocacy organisation in the UK is People First which is consulted and involved in the processes of service planning and provision, and quality assurance.

There is an increasing growth of user-led organisations nationally. User-led organisations (ULOs) are led and controlled by disabled people. They provide a range of services including information and advice, advocacy, peer support, support in using direct payments and individual budgets and disability equality training. Backed by the UK Department of Health, and through working with local authorities, they are important in both delivering personalisation and achieving independent living for disabled people (DOH, 2009b).

## CONCLUSIONS: WHAT ABOUT THE LIVES OF PEOPLE WITH INTELLECTUAL DISABILITIES?

The Prime Ministerial foreword to the White Paper *Valuing People* explicitly stated that it set out the Government's commitment to improving the life chances of people with intellectual disabilities. It also stated that the challenge for us all is to deliver the vision set out in this document so that the lives of many thousands of people with learning disabilities will be brighter and more fulfilling. However, the bulk of activity seems to have been concerned with organisational structures, systems and processes, rather than with outcomes for service users and carers which lay at the heart of the White Paper's overt policy objective. The traditional range of domiciliary, day and institutional provision still prevails. This remains the case and few local authorities or health services are yet attempting to use improved outcomes for users and carers systematically as the main criteria against which their services are judged. The first National Survey of adults with intellectual disabilities was carried out in 2003/2004. The findings illustrated that people were socially excluded, had little control over their lives, had few opportunities to be independent, and were more likely than the general population to experience adverse life events (Emerson, Malam, Davies and Spencer 2005).

It will be interesting to see if the recent Government proposals in its *Vision for Adult Social Care: Capable Communities and Citizens* (DOH, 2010c) with its accompanying consultation paper *Transparency in Outcomes: a framework for adult social care* (DOH, 2010f) serves to change this picture. This will be complimented by the White Paper *Our Strategy for Public Health in England* (DOH, 2010g) in emphasising more personalised preventative services that are focussed on delivering the best outcomes for citizens and that help to build the 'Big Society'.

It remains to be seen whether the radical changes proposed do change services radically in the foreseeable future and, if they do, whether they will result in similarly radical improvements in the lives of people with intellectual disabilities. Indeed, the main planks of community care, particularly at a time when resources for people with intellectual disabilities are unlikely to increase, can be seen as a return to the philosophy of care underlying the poor laws 250 years ago.

# References

Andrews, J. (1996) Identifying and providing for the mentally disabled in early modern London. In *From Idiocy to Mental Deficiency: Historical perspectives on people with learning disabilities* (ed. Wright, D. and Digby, A.). Routledge: London.

Azmi, S., Hatton, C., Caine, A. and Emerson, E. (1996) *Improving Services for Asian People with Learning Disabilities: The views of users and carers.* Hester Adrian Research Centre, University of Manchester: Manchester.

Bradley, V. and Knoll, J.A. (1995) Shifting paradigms in services for people with developmental disabilities. In *The Community Revolution in Rehabilitation Services* (ed. Karan, O.C. and Greenspan, S.). Andover: Andover MA.

Brown, S. and Wistow, G. (1990) (eds) *The Roles and Task of Community Mental Handicap Teams.* Avebury: Aldershot.

Clare, I.C.H., and Murphy, G.H. (1993) M.I.E.T.S. (Mental Impairment Evaluation and Treatment Service): A service option for people with mild mental handicap and challenging behaviour and/or psychiatric problems. *Mental Handicap Research*, **6**, 70–91.

Cole, A., Williams, V., Lloyd, A., Major, V., Mattingly, M., McIntosh, B., Swift, P. and Townsley, R. (2007) *SCIE Knowledge review 14: Having a good day? A study of community-based day activities for people with learning disabilities.* Social Care Institute for Excellence: London.

Cox, P. (1996) Girls, deficiency and delinquency. In *From Idiocy to Mental Deficiency: Historical perspectives on people with learning disabilities* (ed. Wright, D. and Digby, A.). Routledge: London.

Day, K., and Jancar, J. (1991) Mental handicap and the Royal Medico-Psychological Association: A historical association, 1841–1991. In *150 Years of British Psychiatry, 1841–1991* (ed. Berrios, G.E. and Freeman, H.). Gaskell: London.

Department of Health (1989) *Caring for People: community care in the next decade and beyond.* HMSO: London.

Department of Health (1995) *Continuing NHS Care.* HMSO: London.

Department of Health (1990) *NHS and Community Care Act.* HMSO: London.

Department of Health (1999) *The Health Act.* TSO: London.

Department of Health (2000) *The NHS Plan: A plan for investment, a plan for reform.* TSO: London.

Department of Health (2001) *Valuing People: A New Strategy for Learning Disability for the 21st Century.* TSO: London.

Department of Health (2003) *Fair Access to Care Services.* London: TSO.

Department of Health (2006) *Our Health Our Care Our Say.* TSO: London.

Department of Health (2008). *Refocusing the Care Programme Approach: Policy and Practice Guidance.* TSO: London.

Department of Health (2009a) *Valuing People Now: a new three-year strategy for people with learning disabilities.* London: Department of Health.

Department of Health (2009b) *Putting People First: Working Together with User-Led Organisations.* TSO: London.

Department of Health (2010a) *Equity and Excellence: Liberating the NHS.* TSO: London.

Department of Health (2010b) *Prioritising need in the context of Putting People First: a whole system approach to eligibility for social care – guidance on eligibility criteria for adult social care, England 2010.* TSO. London.

Department of Health (2010c). *A Vision for Adult Social Care: Capable Communities and Active Citizens*. TSO: London.

Department of Health (2010d). *Personalisation through Person - Centred Planning*. TSO: London.

Department of Health (2010e). *Liberating the NHS: Commissioning for patients: A consultation on proposals*. TSO: London.

Department of Health (2010f). *A consultation on proposals – Transparency in outcomes: a framework for adult social care*. TSO: London.

Department of Health (2010g). *Healthy lives, Healthy People: Our strategy for public health in England*. TSO: London.

Department of Health (2011) *Health and social care bill 2011*. TSO: London.

Department of Health and Social Security (1971) *Better Services for the Mentally Handicapped*. HMSO: London.

Department of Health and Social Security (1977) *National Health Service Act*. HMSO: London.

Department of Health Statistics Office (1995) *Statistical Bulletin 95/6*. Department of Health: London.

Disability Discrimination Act (1995) London: HM Government.

Disability Discrimination Act (2005) London: HM Government.

Digby, A. (1996) Contexts and perspectives. In *From Idiocy to Mental Deficiency: Historical perspectives on people with learning disabilities* (ed. Wright, D. and. Digby, A.). Routledge: London.

Disability Rights Commission (2006) *Equal Treatment: Closing the Gap. A formal investigation into physical health inequalities experienced by people with learning disabilities and/or mental health problems*. Equal Treatment Investigations Publications: Manchester: Disability Rights Commission.

Emerson, E. (1992) What is normalisation? In *Normalisation. A reader for the nineties* (ed. Brown, H. and Smith, H.). Routledge: London.

Emerson, E. and Baines, S. (2010) *Health inequalities and people with learning disabilities in the UK: 2010*. Lancaster: Improving Health and Lives Learning Disabilities Observatory.

Emerson, E., Forrest, J., Cambridge, P. and Mansell, J. (1996) Community support teams for people with learning disabilities and challenging behaviours: Results of a national survey. *Journal of Mental Health*, **5**, 395–406.

Emerson, E. and Hatton, C. (1994) *Moving Out: The impact of relocation from hospital to community on the quality of life of people with learning disabilities*. HMSO: London.

Emerson, E. and Hatton, C. (1996) *Residential Provision for People with Learning Disabilities: An analysis of the 1991 Census*. Hester Adrian Research Centre, University of Manchester: Manchester.

Emerson, E. and Hatton, C. (1997) Regional and local variations in residential provision for people with learning disabilities in England. *Tizard Learning Disability Review*, **2**, 43–6.

Emerson, E., Hatton, C., Bauer, I., Bjorgvinsdottir, S., Brak, W., Firkowska-Mankiewicz, A., Haroardottir, H., Kavaliunaite, A., Kebbon, L., Kristoffersen, E., Saloviita, T., Schippers, H., Timmons, B., Timcev, L., Tossebro, J. and Wiit, U. (1996) Patterns of institutionalisation in 15 European countries. *European Journal on Mental Disability*, **3**, 29–32.

Emerson, E., Hatton, C., Robertson J., Roberts, H., Baines, S. and Glover G. (2011). *People with Learning Disabilities in England 2010: Services and Supports*. Durham: Improving Health and Lives: Learning Disability Observatory, 2011.

Emerson, E., Malam, S., Davies, I. and Spencer K. (2005). *Adults with Learning Difficulties in England 2003/2004. National Statistics*. NHS Health social care information centre.

England and Wales Court of Appeal (Civil Division) Decisions (1999) *The Coughlan Judgement*. Royal Courts of Justice: London.

Equality Act (2010) London: HM Government.

Equality and Human Rights Commission (2010a) *Equality Act 2010 Guidance for English Public Bodies (and non-devolved bodies in Scotland and Wales). Volume 1: The Essential Guide to the Public Sector Equality Duty*. Manchester: EHRC.

Equality and Human Rights Commission (2010b) *Equality Act 2010 Guidance for English Public Bodies (and non-devolved bodies in Scotland and Wales). Volume 5: Your Rights to Equality from Healthcare and Social Care Services*. Manchester: EHRC.

Felce, D. (1989) *Staffed Housing for Adults with Severe and Profound Handicaps: The Andover Project*. BIMH Publications: Kidderminster.

Felce, D. (1996) Changing residential services: From institutions to ordinary living. In *Changing Policy and Practice for People with Learning Disabilities* (ed. P. Mittler and V. Sinason). Cassell Education: London.

Flynn, M. (1989) *Independent Living for Adults with Mental Handicap: 'A Place Of My Own'*. Cassell: London.

Flynn, M., Cotterrill, L., Hayes, L. and Sloper, P. (1995) *A Break With Tradition: The findings of a survey of respite services for adult citizens with learning disabilities in England*. National Development Team: Manchester.

Giraud-Saunders, A. (2009) *Equal Access? A practical guide for the NHS: Creating a Single Equality Scheme that includes improving access for people with learning disabilities*. London: Dept of Health.

Gladstone, D. (1996) The changing dynamic of institutional care: The Western Counties Idiot Asylum, 1864–1914. In *From Idiocy to Mental Deficiency: Historical perspectives on people with learning disabilities* (ed. D. Wright and A. Digby). Routledge: London.

Government Equalities Office (2010) *Equality Act 2010: What do I need to know? A summary guide for public sector organisations*. London: HM Government.

Gray, G. (1996) Changing day services. In *Changing Policy and Practice for People with Learning Disabilities* (ed. P. Mittler and V. Sinason). Cassell Educational: London.

Hattersley, J. (1995) The survival of collaboration and co-operation. In *Services for People with Learning Disabilities* (ed. N. Malin). Routledge: London.

Hatton, C. and Emerson, E. (1996) *Residential Provision for People with Learning Disabilities: A research review*. Hester Adrian Research Centre, University of Manchester: Manchester.

Hatton, C., Emerson, E. and Kiernan, C. (1995a) Trends and Milestones: People in institutions in Europe. *Mental Retardation*, 33, 132.

Hatton, C., Emerson, E., Robertson, J., Henderson, D., and Cooper, J. (1995b) The quality and costs of residential services for adults with multiple disabilities: A comparative evaluation. *Research in Developmental Disabilities*, **16**, 439–60.

Healthcare Commission (2007) *A life Like No Other: A national audit of specialist inpatient healthcare services for people with learning disabilities in England*. London: Healthcare Commission.

Health Service Ombudsman for England (2003) *NHS Funding for Long Term Care of Older and Disabled People*. TSO: London.

Howard, J. (1996) A home of your own: moving from community residential services to supported living for people with learning disabilities. *Tizard Learning Disability Review*, **1**, 18–25.

Jackson, M. (1996) Institutional provision for the feeble-minded in Edwardian England: Sandlebridge and the scientific morality of permanent care. In *From Idiocy to Mental Deficiency: Historical perspectives on people with learning disabilities* (ed. Wright, D. and Digby, A.). Routledge: London.

Joint Committee of Human Rights (2008) *A Life Like Any Other? Human rights and adults with learning disabilities*. TSO: London.

King's Fund (1980) *An Ordinary Life: Comprehensive locally-based services for mentally handicapped people*. King's Fund Centre: London.

Lowe, K. and de Paiva, S. (1991) *NIMROD: An overview*. HMSO: London.

Mansell, J. (2007) *Services for People with Learning Disability and Challenging Behaviours or Mental Health Needs*. Department of Health: TSO: London.

Marmot, M., Allen, J., Goldblatt, P., Boyce, T., McNeish, D., Grady, M. and Geddes, I. (2010). *Fair Society, Healthy Lives: Strategic review of health inequalities in England post 2010: the Marmot Review*.

McGrath, M. and Humphreys, S. (1988) *The All Wales CMHT Survey*. University College of North Wales: Bangor.

Mencap (2002) *A Life In the Day: A report on the past, present and future of day services for people with a learning disability*. Campaigns: London.

Mencap (2007) *Death by Indifference*. London: Mencap.

Mencap (2010) *Getting It Right: A campaign guide*. London: Mencap.

Mental Health Foundation (1996) *Building Expectations: Opportunities and services for people with a learning disability*. Mental Health Foundation: London.

Michael, J. (2008) *Healthcare For All: report of the independent inquiry into access to healthcare for people with learning disabilities*. TSO: London London: Department of Health.

Mittler, P. and Sinason, V. (1996) (ed.) *Changing Policy and Practice for People with Learning Disabilities*. Cassell Education: London.

Neugebauer, R. (1996) Mental handicap in medieval and early modern England: Criteria, measurement and care. In *From Idiocy to Mental Deficiency: Historical perspectives on people with learning disabilities* (ed. Wright, D. and Digby, A.). Routledge: London.

O'Brien, J. and Tyne, A. (1981) *The Principle of Normalisation: A foundation for effective services*. The Campaign for Mentally Handicapped People: London.

Orlik, C., Robinson, C. and Russell, D. (1991) *A Survey of Family Based Respite Care Schemes in the United Kingdom*. Norah Fry Research Centre, University of Bristol: Bristol.

Parliamentary and Health Service Ombudsman and Local Government Ombudsman (2009) *Six Lives: the provision of public services to people with learning disabilities*. London: The Stationery Office.

Race, D. (1995) Historical development of service provision. In *Services for People with Learning Disabilities* (ed. N. Malin). Routledge: London.

Roberts, G. and Griffiths, A. (1993) *What Can We Do? The legal framework of community care services for adults with learning disabilities.* MENCAP/National Development Team: Manchester.

Rushton, P. (1996) Idiocy, the family and the community in early modern north-east England. In *From Idiocy to Mental Deficiency: Historical perspectives on people with learning disabilities* (ed. D. Wright and A. Digby). Routledge: London.

Ryan, J. with Thomas, F. (1987) *The Politics of Mental Handicap* (2nd edn). Free Association Books: London.

Scheerenberger, R.C. (1983) *A History of Mental Retardation.* P.H. Brookes: Baltimore.

Seebohm F. (1968) *Report of the Committee on Local Authority and Allied Personal Social Services.* London HMSO

Simons, K. (1995) *My Home, My Life: Innovative approaches to housing and support for people with learning difficulties.* Values Into Action: London.

Stalker, K. (1996) (ed.) *Developments in Short-Term Care: Breaks and opportunities.* Jessica Kingsley: London.

Stalker, K. and Robinson, C. (1994) Parents' views of different respite care services. *Mental Handicap Research,* **7**, 97–117.

Thomson, M. (1996) Family, community, and state: The micro-politics of mental deficiency. In *From Idiocy to Mental Deficiency: Historical perspectives on people with learning disabilities* (ed. D. Wright and A. Digby). Routledge: London.

Trent, J.W. (1995) *Inventing The Feeble Mind: A history of mental retardation in the United States.* University of California Press: Berkeley CA.

Wertheimer, A. (1997) *Changing Days: Developing new day opportunities with people who have learning difficulties.* King's Fund: London.

Wolfensberger, W. (1972) *The Principle of Normalization in Human Services.* National Institute of Mental Retardation: Toronto.

World Health Organization (2010) *European Declaration on the Health of Children and Young People with Intellectual Disabilities and their Families.* Regional Office for Europe.

Wright, D. and Digby, A. (1996) (ed.) *From Idiocy to Mental Deficiency: Historical perspectives on people with learning disabilities.* Routledge: London.

Chapter 3

# SOCIAL CONTEXT

## Eric Emerson and Rupa Gone

### SOCIO-ECONOMIC POSITION

All societies are hierarchically structured, with key institutions (e.g., the labour market, education and legal systems) helping to determine an individual's socio-economic position (SEP) within this hierarchy. SEP is important as it determines, in part, peoples' access to and control over key resources (e.g., power, wealth, social connections, health, skills, access to educational, health, and welfare services) that play an important role in shaping life experiences (Graham 2007). Low SEP is associated with high risk of experiencing poverty; being unable "due to lack of resources, to participate in society and to enjoy a standard of living consistent with human dignity and social decency" (Fabian Commission on Life Chances and Child Poverty 2006).

Across their lifespan people with intellectual disabilities are more likely than others to occupy low SEP and experience poverty (Emerson 2007, in press; Emerson and Hatton 2010). These *social gradients* in the prevalence of intellectual disability are likely to result from a combination of factors.

- In young children, exposure to adversity (prenatally and in the early years) impedes cognitive development and consequently increases the risk of intellectual disability (Shonkoff, Boyce and McEwen 2009).
- In later childhood, these social gradients may also reflect the impact of the child's intellectual disability on family SEP as a result of the direct and indirect costs associated with care (Tibble 2005). However, it appears that in the UK these effects may be small (Emerson 2007; Emerson and Hatton 2010; Emerson Shahtahmasebi, Berridge and Lancaster 2010; Shahtahmasebi, Emerson, Berridge, and Lancaster 2011).

*Clinical Psychology and People with Intellectual Disabilities*, Second Edition. Edited by Eric Emerson, Chris Hatton, Kate Dickson, Rupa Gone, Amanda Caine and Jo Bromley.
© 2012 John Wiley & Sons, Ltd. Published 2012 by John Wiley & Sons, Ltd.

- In adulthood, the exclusion of people with intellectual disabilities from the labour market is likely to play an important role in exacerbating social gradients.

Why is socio-economic position important in understanding the life experiences of people with intellectual disabilities? Two issues are important here, one rather general, and one very practical. The general point is that exposure to low SEP and poverty *for all of us* are associated with reduced social mobility, increased social exclusion and poorer physical and mental health (Fabian Commission on Life Chances and Child Poverty 2006; Graham 2007; The Marmot Review 2010; World Health Organization 2008). As a result, *some* of the adverse life experiences faced by people with intellectual disabilities may simply reflect their status as poor people (rather than being the result of intellectual disability *per se*). Recent studies have suggested that the increased risk of exposure to low SEP/poverty among people with intellectual disability accounts for: 20–50% of the risk of poorer mental and physical health among children with intellectual disabilities (Emerson and Einfeld 2010; Emerson and Hatton 2007a, 2007b, 2007c); and most or all of the risk of poorer mental health and low rates of well-being among mothers of children with intellectual disabilities (Emerson, Hatton, Blacher, Llewellyn and Graham 2006; Emerson *et al.* 2010).

So, when thinking more broadly about the determinants of the health and social inequalities faced by people with intellectual disabilities, we need to think considerably beyond the cognitive impairments associated with intellectual disability to the social conditions that both help create these impairments and (independently) reduce the life chances and opportunities of disabled people (Emerson *et al.* 2009). While in everyday clinical practice there is little we can do to alter the chances of exposure to low SEP/poverty, we do have the opportunity (and probably responsibility) to highlight them in our research and professional advocacy.

The more practical issue is that, if clinical psychology is not to *increase* health and social inequalities associated with SEP *among* people with intellectual disabilities, we need to ensure that our services are as effective for hard pressed families living in hard pressed communities as they are for the powerful and affluent. Equal access and uptake would mean that, in any locality, more service activity should be delivered in relatively more deprived neighborhoods (where the need will be greater); an issue that can be easily monitored through routine service audit. Achieving equity is likely to involve addressing inequalities in access to information about what is available and in referral pathways. It is also likely to involve ensuring a 'good fit' between the services and support that we offer and the practical realities and concerns of people living in difficult circumstances. Unfortunately, there is a long history of interventions that, while increasing health overall, also widen inequalities in health (White, Adams and Heywood 2009), and good evidence that some currently popular psychological interventions may have the same effect (Lundahl, Risser and Lovejoy 2006). We need to take care that our professional activity does not widen the gap in the life chances of people with intellectual disabilities from different backgrounds.

## GENDER

Gender refers to the characteristics of men and women that are socially determined and thereby is distinct from the biologically determined sex of a person, which refers to whether an individual is male or female. There are differences in the social context of men and women's lives which influence many aspects of their psychological wellbeing, including the manifestation of psychological distress. Gender is a recognised determinant of health across the life span for the general population (Walsh 2002).

There are different social and behavioural norms and expectations for men and women, which vary across cultures. In Western societies gender roles are bound to expectations about men and women's participation in work and care-giving. For men traditional gender roles relate to their ability to earn wages and their position in the labour force. Similarly traditional gender roles for women emphasise child-rearing and domestic labour as being their domain. In recent decades these stereotypes have been challenged by men and women and roles within Western society have changed, affording greater opportunities to men and women to hold different roles than that of previous generations. Over the last three decades there has been a marked increase in the number of employee jobs performed by women in the UK, and the employment rate for women (70%) was close to that of men (78%) (Office for National Statistics 2008). Persisting different gender roles may systematically benefit one group over another, and these inequalities can result in significant inequities between men and women. For instance, child care arrangements and undervaluing the types of jobs typically held by women (e.g. in the caring, cleaning and catering sectors) have given rise to inequities. Women were more likely to be employed in low paid, part-time work and had substantially lower incomes than men (Office for National Statistics 2009). One in every five women in the United Kingdom was living in poverty (Office for National Statistics 2009).

Gender inequalities also affect women with intellectual disabilities, for example, they were less likely to be in employment than men and earned less money (Julius, Wolfson and Yalon-Camovitz 2003; Olson, Cioffi, Yovanoff and Mank 2000). Moreover, paid employment levels among adults with intellectual disabilities were low at 17% (Emerson, Malam, Davies and Spencer 2005).

Men and women with intellectual disabilities are affected by the gender issues and inequalities in wider society, yet struggle to be recognised as gendered individuals. Often they are treated as a homogenous group of gender-neutral persons who are characterised by their disability and as service users (Umb-Carlsonn and Sonnader 2006; Walsh 2000). Hence, the gender aspirations of men and women with intellectual disabilities over their life span go largely ignored, for instance to have intimate relationships, to become parents, and to be employed. There are also social and cultural barriers to sexual expression for people with intellectual disabilities despite a recent ideological shift towards the recognition of their sexual autonomy (Healy, McGuire, Evans and Carley 2009).

Many psychiatric disorders, including depression, anxiety, panic attacks, obsessions, phobias, eating disorders, and self-harm, are twice as common in women compared to men (Kessler *et al.* 1994). Women with intellectual disabilities report higher levels of depressive symptoms than men with intellectual disabilities (Lunsky 2003) and are believed to be particularly at risk of developing mental health problems (Kohen 2004; Taggart, McMillan and Lawson 2008). The underlying psychosocial risk factors were found to be in common with women from the general population (Lunsky 2003). In a review of the literature, Taggart and colleagues identified that some of the social risk factors women faced were social deprivation and poverty, single parenthood, holding multiple carer and complex roles, social isolation, inequities in the workplace and unemployment, different societal expectations of women and stigma, discrimination, and a lack of opportunities and power in a male dominated society (Taggart *et al.* 2008). Many of these risk factors were also identified for women with intellectual disabilities (Lunsky 2003).

Violence and abuse are forms of adversity that can lead to mental health problems (Kohen 2004). In the majority of cases domestic violence occurs against women and women with intellectual disabilities are believed to experience high levels of domestic violence, which is under-reported (Walsh and Murphy 2002). It is estimated that the rates of sexual, emotional and physical abuse against women with intellectual disabilities are higher than in the general population (Sobsey 1994).

Clinical psychologists can identify gender specific risk factors for future mental health problems for people with intellectual disabilities, and be proactive in the early recognition, assessment and intervention of these, and in promoting opportunities for men and women to improve their self-esteem and self-efficacy. They can develop inter-agency collaborations with gender specific services such as Women's Aid, and promote the use of these by people with intellectual disabilities. Clinical psychologists are in a strong position to contribute to the development of gender sensitive services, ensuring that men and women with intellectual disabilities are not considered as gender-neutral by specialist or mainstream services, and advocating for their gendered needs in wider society.

# ETHNICITY

Ethnicity is used to refer to a group of individuals who share a common heritage that is distinct from other communities. Aspects of ethnicity include physical appearance, ancestry, geography, nationality and language (Karlsen and Nazroo 2002). In the 2001 UK population census, 7.9% of the population identified as non-White ethnicities. This constituted of 4% Asian (Pakistani, Indian, Bangladeshi); 2% Black (Caribbean, African); 0.4%, Chinese; 0.4% other ethnic groups, and 1.2% identified as mixed ethnicity (Office for National Statistics, 2004).

Substantial health differentials between minority ethnic communities and the general population exist (Department of Health, 2006). Identification of the underlying mechanisms has focused on the wider social context in which people from minority ethnic communities live, and their experiences of inequalities, discrimination and disadvantage (Hatton and Emerson 2001).

Two per cent of the adult population of England is estimated to have an intellectual disability (Emerson and Hatton 2004a). An increased prevalence of severe intellectual disabilities among South Asian children and young adults has been reported (Emerson *et al.* 1997; Emerson and Hatton 2004b), a difference that persists when differences in family and neighbourhood deprivation are taken into account (Emerson, in press). The causes of these differences in the prevalence of intellectual disabilities are currently unknown (Hatton and Emerson 2001).

Much of the variation in self-reported health between and within minority ethnic groups can be explained by differences in SEP (Karlsen and Nazroo 2002), rather than ethnicity *per se*. People from minority ethnic communities have higher unemployment rates, and are much more likely to live in low income households and have incomes below half the national average compared to people of White ethnicity groups (Office for National Statistics 2004), and thus were at higher risk of poverty. The findings for households that include a person with intellectual disabilities replicate this pattern. For instance, children and young people with intellectual disabilities from South Asian communities were living in circumstances of material disadvantage, high unemployment and low income (Emerson and Robertson 2002).

People with intellectual disabilities from minority ethnic communities experience the social stigma of having intellectual disabilities and pervasive racism. Racism stems from the belief that people should be treated differently because of their perceived race. It can manifest as individual or group acts and attitudes or institutional processes that lead to disparities (McKenzie 2003). Experiences of abuse, violence and discrimination are common for people from minority ethnic groups in the UK (Chahal and Julienne 1999). For people with intellectual disability, discrimination was reported from people in their neighbourhood, and in service settings from other people with intellectual disabilities and staff, and was associated with higher social isolation (Azmi, Hatton, Emerson and Caine 1997). In addition to the acute stress of direct racial harassment, the damaging impact of racism is cumulative, as people may live in fear of racial harassment and discrimination (Gee, Ro, Shariff-Marco and Chae 2009; Karlsen, 2007; Karlsen and Nazroo 2002, 2004; Mays, Cochran and Barnes 2007; Nazroo, 2003; Pascoe and Richman 2009; Williams and Mohammed 2009).

Inaccessible and inadequate services form another layer of social disadvantage. The barriers to universal and specialist services experienced by people with intellectual disabilities from minority ethnic communities and their carers are:

- *Communication*. There is a lack of accessible information about the services available, and a lack of interpreters or same-language staff (Mencap 2006; Nadirshaw and Sowerby 2009).
- *Cultural and religious needs*. Services may be culturally insensitive in terms of the meals and activities available, staff gender, wash and toilet facilities (Hatton, Azmi, Caine and Emerson 1998).
- *Racism and distrust*. Perceived racial discrimination within services based on past experience, experiences of discriminatory practice, and direct racism *(Hatton et al.* 1998; Mencap 2006).
- *Cultural stereotypes and misperceptions*. There is heterogeneity within ethnic groups, as aspects of culture vary across families and over generations. An over-reliance on ethnically or religiously-focused information in considering the needs of individuals and their families is unhelpful (O' Hara 2003). For instance, there is a belief that people from minority ethnic communities receive support from within their informal or familial social networks yet there is little evidence that these are available to them in practice (Hatton, Emerson, Azmi and Caine 1997).

Culturally sensitive intellectual disability services have yet to become a priority (Caton, Starling, Burton, Azmi and Chapman 2007). Consequent low service up-take is misattributed to the cultural characteristics of different minority ethnic communities rather than the institutional barriers and culturally inappropriate support (Gregory 2010).

With regard to the social context for people with intellectual disabilities from minority ethnic communities, clinical psychology can offer:

- Research and professional advocacy to identify the aspects of ethnicity which are relevant to health inequalities.
- Involvement in service design and improvement to increase the cultural sensitivity of mainstream and specialist services. This may involve advocating some very practical measures regarding food, activities,

staff gender, washing and toilet facilities. Further measures involve ensuring there is monitoring of service uptake by minority ethnic communities and that accessible information and skilled interpreters (trained in intellectual disabilities) are available.

• In clinical practice, clinical psychologists must make use of collaborative therapeutic approaches and work within the cultural framework of the person with intellectual disabilities and their family, and attend to the impact of contextual factors on the lives of people.

## DISABLISM

People with intellectual disabilities are at risk of experiencing discrimination associated with their disability (disablism). The impact of disability discrimination on health and well-being is likely to be mediated by multiple processes:

• First, the existence of systemic or institutional disability discrimination in the operation of key social institutions may prevent people with intellectual disabilities gaining access to timely, appropriate and effective health care (Disability Rights Commission 2006; Michael 2008).

• Second, discriminatory systems and practices contribute to the social exclusion of people with intellectual disabilities. As a result, they are more likely than their peers to be exposed to living conditions (poverty, unemployment, social adversity, low control, low status, poor housing) associated with poor health outcomes (Fabian Commission on Life Chances and Child Poverty 2006; Graham 2007; The Marmot Review 2010).

• Finally, as we have seen in the previous section exposure to and fear of racism have negative impacts on mental and physical health (Gee *et al.* 2009; Karlsen 2007; Karlsen and Nazroo 2002, 2004; Mays *et al.* 2007; Nazroo 2003; Pascoe and Richman 2009; Williams and Mohammed 2009). Similarly, direct exposure to disablism (e.g., through bullying) is likely to have a negative impact on the person's mental and physical health (Emerson 2011; Krieger 1999; Pascoe and Richman 2009).

Why is disablism important to clinical psychology? As with SEP, two issues are important, one general, one practical. The general point is that *some* of the adverse life experiences faced by people with intellectual disabilities will result from their exposure to disablism and, while in everyday clinical practice there is little we can do to alter the chances of exposure to disablism, we do have the opportunity and responsibility to foreground these issues in our research and professional advocacy.

The more practical issue is that clinical psychology is in an excellent position to: (1) help health care organisations make 'reasonable adjustments' in light of the specific needs of people with intellectual disabilities (and thereby reduce discrimination); and (2) help people with intellectual disabilities (and their families) address the psychological consequences of exposure to disablism (McGrath, Jones and Hastings 2010).

## References

Azmi, S., Hatton, C., Emerson, E. and Caine, A. (1997) Listening to adolescents and adults with intellectual disabilities from South Asian communities. *Journal of Applied Research in Intellectual Disabilities*, **10**, 250–63.

Caton, S., Starling, S., Burton, M., Azmi, S. and Chapman, M. (2007) Responsive services for people with intellectual disabilities from minority ethnic communities. *British Journal of Intellectual Disabilities*, **35**, 229–35.

Chahal, K. and Julienne, L. (1999) *'We Can't All Be White!': Racist victimization in the UK*. York: York Publishing Services Ltd.

Department of Health. (2006) *Health Survey for England 2004: Health of Ethnic Minorities – full report*. London: Information Centre for Health and Social Care.

Disability Rights Commission. (2006) *Equal Treatment – Closing the Gap*. London Disability Rights Commission.

Emerson, E. (2007) Poverty and people with intellectual disability. *Mental Retardation and Developmental Disabilities Research Reviews*, **13**, 107–13.

Emerson, E. (in press) Household deprivation, neighbourhood deprivation, ethnicity and the prevalence of intellectual and developmental disabilities *Journal of Epidemiology and Community Health*.

Emerson, E. (2011) Self-reported exposure to disablism is associated with poorer self-reported health and well-being among adults with intellectual disabilities in England: Cross sectional survey. *Public Health*, **124**, 682–9.

Emerson, E., Azmi, S., Hatton, C., Caine, A., Parrott, R. and Wolstenholme, J. (1997) Is there an increased prevalence of severe learning disabilities among British Asians? *Ethn Health*, **2**(4), 317–21.

Emerson, E. and Einfeld, S. (2010) Emotional and behavioural difficulties in young children with and without developmental delay: A bi-national perspective. *Journal of Child Psychology and Psychiatry*, **51**, 583–93.

Emerson, E. and Hatton, C. (2004a) *Estimating the Current Need/Demand for Supports for People with Learning Disabilities in England*. Lancaster: Institute for Health Research, Lancaster University.

Emerson, E. and Hatton, C. (2004b) Response to McGrother *et al.* (Journal of Intellectual Disability Research, 46, 299–309) 'The prevalence of intellectual disability among South Asian communities in the UK'. *Journal of Intellectual Disability Research*, **48**(2), 201–2.

Emerson, E. and Hatton, C. (2007a) The contribution of socio-economic position to the health inequalities faced by children and adolescents with intellectual disabilities in Britain. *American Journal on Mental Retardation*, **112**(2), 140–50.

Emerson, E. and Hatton, C. (2007b) The mental health of children and adolescents with intellectual disabilities in Britain. *British Journal of Psychiatry*, **191**, 493–9.

Emerson, E. and Hatton, C. (2007c) Poverty, socio-economic position, social capital and the health of children and adolescents with intellectual disabilities in Britain: a replication. *Journal of Intellectual Disability Research*, **51**(11), 866–74.

Emerson, E. and Hatton, C. (2010) Socio-economic position, poverty and family research. In Glidden, L.M. and Seltzer, M.M. (eds), *On Families: International Review of Research on Mental Retardation*. New York: Academic Press.

Emerson, E., Hatton, C., Blacher, J., Llewellyn, G. and Graham, H. (2006) Socio-economic position, household composition, health status and indicators of the well-being of mothers of children with and without intellectual disability. *Journal of Intellectual Disability Research*, **50**(12), 862–73.

Emerson, E., Madden, R., Robertson, J., Graham, H., Hatton, C. and Llewellyn, G. (2009) *Intellectual and Physical Disability, Social Mobility, Social Inclusion and Health: Background paper for the Marmot Review*. Lancaster: Centre for Disability Research, Lancaster University.

Emerson, E., Malam, S., Davies, I. and Spencer, K. (2005) *Adults with Learning Difficulties in England 2003/4*. Leeds: Health and Social Care Information Centre.

Emerson, E., McCulloch, A., Graham, H., Blacher, J., Llewellyn, G. and Hatton, C. (2010) The mental health of parents of young children with and without developmental delays *American Journal on Intellectual and Developmental Disability*, **115**, 30–42.

Emerson, E. and Robertson, J. (2002) *Future Demand for Services for Young Adults with Learning Disabilities From South Asian and Black Communities in Birmingham*. Lancaster: Institute for Health Research, Lancaster University.

Emerson, E., Shahtahmasebi, S., Berridge, D., and Lancaster G. (2010). Factors associated with poverty transitions among families supporting a child with intellectual disability. *Journal of Intellectual and Developmental Disability*, **35**, 224–34.

Fabian Commission on Life Chances and Child Poverty. (2006) *Narrowing the Gap: The Final Report of the Fabian Commission on Life Chances and Child Poverty*. London: Fabian Society.

Gee, G.C., Ro, A., Shariff-Marco, S. and Chae, D. (2009). Racial Discrimination and Health Among Asian Americans: Evidence, Assessment, and Directions for Future Research. *Epidemiologic Reviews*, **31**, 130–51.

Graham, H. (2007) *Unequal Lives: health and socioeconomic inequalities*. Maidenhead: Open University Press.

Gregory, C. (2010) *Improving Health and Social Care Support for Carers from Black and Minority Ethnic Communities. A Race Equality Foundation Briefing Paper. Better Health Briefing*, **20**. London: Race Equality Foundation.

Hatton, C., Azmi, S., Caine, A. and Emerson, E. (1998) People from the South Asian communities who care for adolescents and adults with intellectual disabilities: family circumstances, service support and carer stress. *British Journal of Social Work*, **28**, 821–37.

Hatton, C. and Emerson, E. (2001) Ethnicity and intellectual disabilities. In L.M. Glidden (ed.), *International Review of Research on Mental Retardation, Vol 25*.

Hatton, C., Emerson, E., Azmi, S. and Caine, A. (1997) Lost in translation. *Community Care, July*, 30–1.

Healy, E., McGuire, B.E., Evans, D.S. and Carley, S.N. (2009) Sexuality and personal relationships for people with an intellectual disability. Part I: service user perspectives. *Journal of Intellectual Disability Research*, **53**, 905–12.

Julius, E., Wolfson, H. and Yalon-Camovitz, S. (2003) Equally unequal: gender discrimination in the workplace among adults with mental retardation. *Work* (20), 205–13.

Karlsen, S. (2007) *Ethnic Inequalities in Health: the impact of racism. A Race Equality Foundation Briefing Paper, Better Health 3*. London: Race Equality Foundation, UK.

Karlsen, S. and Nazroo, J. (2002) Relation between racial discrimination, social class, and health among ethnic minority groups. *American Journal of Public Health*, **92**, 624–31.

Karlsen, S. and Nazroo, J. (2004) Fear of racism and health. *Journal of Epidemiology and Community Health*, 1017–18.

Kessler, R.C., McGonagle, K.A., Zhao, S., Nelson, C.B., Hughes, M., Eshleman, S., *et al.* (1994) Lifetime and 12 month prevalence of DSM-III-R psychiatric disorders in the United States: Results from the national comorbidity survey. *Archives of General Psychiatry*, **51**, 8–19.

Kohen, D. (2004) Mental health needs of women with learning disabilities: services can be organised to meet the challenge. *Learning Disability Review*, **9**, 12–19.

Krieger, N. (1999) Embodying inequality: a review of concepts, measures, and methods for studying health consequences of discrimination. *International Journal of Health Services*, **29**, 295–352.

Lundahl, B., Risser, H.J. and Lovejoy, M.C. (2006) A meta-analysis of parent training: Moderators and follow-up effects. *Clinical Psychology Review*, **26**, 86–104.

Lunsky, Y. (2003) Depressive symptoms in intellectual disability: does gender play a role?. *Journal of Intellectual Disability Research*, **47**, 417–27.

Mays, V.M., Cochran, S.D. and Barnes, N.W. (2007) Race, race-based discrimination, and health outcomes among African Americans. *Annual Review of Psychology*, **58**, 201–25.

McGrath, L., Jones, R.S.P. and Hastings, R.P. (2010) Outcomes of anti-bullying intervention for adults with intellectual disabilities. *Research in Developmental Disabilities*, **31**, 376–80.

McKenzie, K. (2003) Racism and health: Antiracism is an important health issue. *British Medical Journal*, **326**, 65–6.

Mencap. (2006) *Reaching Out: working with black and minority ethnic communities*: Royal Mencap Society, Midland Mencapo.

Michael, J. (2008) *Healthcare for All: Report of the Independent Inquiry into Access to Healthcare for People with Learning Disabilities*. London: Independent Inquiry into Access to Healthcare for People with Learning Disabilitieso.

Nadirshaw, Z. and Sowerby, B. (2009) Avoiding a colour blind approach. *Learning Disability Today*, **9**, 36–7.

Nazroo, J. (2003) The structuring of ethnic inequalities in health: Economic position, racial discrimination and racism. *American Journal of Public Health*, **93**(2) 277–84.

O' Hara, J. (2003) Intellectual disabilities and ethnicity: achieving cultural competence. *Advances in Psychiatric Treatment*, **9**, 166–76.

Office for National Statistics. (2004) *Focus on ethnicity and identity*. London: Office for National Statisticso.

Office for National Statistics. (2008) *Focus on gender*. London: Office for National Statisticso.

Office for National Statistics. (2009) *Gender Pay Gap*. London: Office for National Statisticso.)

Olson, D., Cioffi, A., Yovanoff, P. and Mank, D. (2000) Gender differences in supported employment. *Mental Retardation*, **38**, 89–96.

Pascoe, E.A. and Richman, L.S. (2009) Perceived discrimination and health: A meta-analytic review. *Psychological Bulletin*, **135**, 531–54.

Shahtahmasebi, S., Emerson, E., Berridge, D., and Lancaster, G. (2011) Child disability and the dynamics of family poverty, hardship and financial strain: Evidence from the UK. *Journal of Social Policy*, **40**, 653–73.

Shonkoff, J.P., Boyce, W.T., and McEwen, B.S. (2009) Neuroscience, molecular biology, and the childhood roots of health disparities: Building a new framework for health promotion and disease prevention. *JAMA*, **301**, 2252–9.

Sobsey, D. (1994) *Violence and Abuse In the Lives of People With Disabilities: the end of silent acceptance?* Baltimore: Paul H. Brookes.

Taggart, L., McMillan, R. and Lawson, A. (2008) Women with and without intellectual disability and psychiatric disorders: an examination of the literature. *Journal of Intellectual Disabilities*, **12**, 191–211.

The Marmot Review (2010) *Fair Society, Healthy Lives: Strategic Review of Health Inequalities in England Post-2010*. London: The Marmot Review.

Tibble, M. (2005) *Review of existing research on the extra costs of disability*. London: Department of Work and Pensionso.

Umb-Carlsonn, O. and Sonnader, K. (2006). Living conditions of adults with intellectual disabilities from a gender perspective. *Journal of Intellectual Disability Research*, **50**, 326–34.

Walsh, P.N. (2000) Rites of passage: life course transitions for women with intellectual disabilities. In D. May (ed.), *Transition and Change in the Lives of People with Intellectual Disabilities*. London: Jessica Kingsley.

Walsh, P.N. (2002) Women's health: A Contextual Approach. In Walsh, P.N. and Heller, T. (eds), *Health of Women with Intellectual Disabilities*. Oxford: Blackwell Publishing.

Walsh, P.N. and Murphy, G.H. (2002) Risk and vulnerability: dilemmas for women. In Walsh, P.N. and Heller, T. (eds), *Health of Women with Intellectual Disabilities*. Oxford: Blackwell Publishing.

White, M., Adams, J. and Heywood, P. (2009). How and why do interventions that increase health overall widen inequalities within populations? In Babones, S. J. (ed.), *Social Inequality and Public Health* (pp. 65–82). Bristol: Policy Press.

Williams, D.R. and Mohammed, S.A. (2009) Discrimination and racial disparities in health: evidence and needed research. *Journal of Behavioral Medicine*, **32**, 20–47.

World Health Organization. (2008) *Closing the Gap In a Generation: health equity through action on the social determinants of health. Final report of the Commission on the Social Determinants of Health*. Geneva: World Health Organisation.

Chapter 4

# COGNITIVE ASSESSMENT

Isobel Lamb

## HISTORY OF COGNITIVE ASSESSMENT

Cognitive assessment in the field of learning disabilities has had a history of negative associations. Such assessment often led to labelling of people as different, which had negative consequences for the individual. At its extreme, during the late nineteenth and early twentieth century, the eugenics movement suggested that 'mentally defective' individuals were a threat to society, which led to the detention and/or sterilisation of people with learning disabilities. This movement argued that society needed to be protected from such individuals, and that the human race could be improved by actively preventing adults with learning disabilities from having children (Kempton and Kahn 1991).

Secondly, the principles of social role valorisation (SRV) and normalisation (Wolfensberger 1983) still today underpin modern day social policy and services for adults with learning disabilities such as Valuing People (DOH 2001) and the development of individualised approaches such as person centred planning. Concepts of normalisation and SRV challenged the eugenics movement and related policy, by promoting the human rights of individuals with learning disabilities to be equally valued and accepted in society as individuals. Within services reluctance developed from professionals and carers of people with learning disabilities to refer to difficulties or differences. Consequently, cognitive assessment was viewed by some to be in contradiction with the principles of normalisation, as it emphasised individual's differences and weaknesses.

Thirdly, the assessment process itself continues to be viewed by some psychologists to be a negative experience for adults with a learning disability, exposing them to failure. Some argued that undertaking a cognitive

*Clinical Psychology and People with Intellectual Disabilities*, Second Edition. Edited by
Eric Emerson, Chris Hatton, Kate Dickson, Rupa Gone, Amanda Caine and Jo Bromley.
© 2012 John Wiley & Sons, Ltd. Published 2012 by John Wiley & Sons, Ltd.

assessment potentially interferes with the development of a therapeutic relationship for future work between the clinician and their client.

## COGNITIVE ASSESSMENT WITHIN A PERSON CENTRED FRAMEWORK

This chapter will argue that with certain safeguards in place and if a sensitive and flexible approach is used, it can be of benefit to people with learning disabilities to understand the nature of their strengths and weaknesses. Only then can the environment be engineered to maximise an individual's strengths and provide the support they need for areas of their functioning that cause them difficulty. By understanding their difficulties we can then provide information in a way that can maximise an individual's decision making in a meaningful way and ensure truly 'person centred' support. La Vigna and Willis (1996) have argued that often values and choice have been used as an excuse not to provide a service and/or to dismiss interventions and approaches such as behavioural technology which could provide improvements in quality of life. However, La Vigna and Willis (1996) and Emerson and McGill (1989) argue behavioural technology can be used in support of values. I would argue neuropsychological assessment can be used likewise. Without such assessment we are in danger of making errors of judgment about a person's level of disability, due to assumptions being made about their level of impairment, which are not evidence based. Research has shown that carers and potentially professionals do make such errors about the communication level of adults with learning disabilities (Banat, Summers and Pring 2002). It is likely that similar misinformed assumptions are made about other aspects of information processing and/or the overall level of intellectual functioning of many adults with learning disabilities. Therefore, in order to provide individualised, person centred, psychological intervention, it is critical that we understand the nature of a person's learning disability and particular information processing difficulties, based upon standardised psychometric assessment. This can be a useful intervention in itself or an essential component of a more detailed and complex holistic assessment. An example of the latter might be completing cognitive assessment to aid understanding of the person within their environment, and how this may contribute to the development and maintenance of challenging behaviour, as recommended by clinical practice guidelines for psychological interventions for severely challenging behaviours shown by people with learning disabilities (BPS 2004).

This chapter will also discuss how cognitive assessment information needs to be treated with care, and understood by those it is shared with, so it is not used to exclude people from services, or elements of an assessment used out of context to limit people's rights and choices, particularly in light of the increase in requests for 'capacity to consent' assessments as a result of the Mental Capacity Act (DOH 2005). The difference between assessment that leads to a formulation and understanding of a client, and that providing a score which may be poorly understood, such as IQ, is highlighted. Moreover, this chapter will differentiate IQ assessment (an outcome) from cognitive assessment as a qualitative process.

## DEFINITION OF LEARNING DISABILITY

There are a number of definitions of learning disability depending on the classification system used, e.g. Diagnostic and Statistical Manual of Mental Disorders – DSM-IV-TR (American Psychiatric Association 2000) and International Classification of Diseases – ICD-10 (World Health Organisation 1992). However, there is general acceptance by most professional groups that three core criteria are needed for an adult to be identified with a learning disability (BPS 2001).

The person shows

1. Significant impairment of intellectual functioning.
2. Significant impairment of adaptive social functioning.
3. With an age of onset before adulthood.

Whilst this chapter will focus on cognitive assessment to assess the degree and nature of impairment of intellectual functioning, it is important that this is balanced with the person's social functioning in determining if a person has a learning disability.

Historically distinctions have been made between mild, moderate, severe, and even profound learning disability (DOH 1999; ICD –10 1992; DSM-IV-TR 2000). The British Psychological Society (BPS 2001) states that sub-classification based on IQ scores below 50 cannot be carried out reliably as there are no valid and reliable psychometric tests to accurately assess this level of learning disability. This does not mean that adults with severe disabilities should not be assessed, but that lower IQ scores, will not be reliable or meaningful. However, qualitative information from cognitive assessment can provide useful information for intervention. In terms of classification by the BPS (2001), intellectual functioning was classified in terms of **significant impairment** (i.e. between two to three standard deviations below the general population mean or IQ score between 55 and 69 as measured by the WAIS-III; Wechsler, 1999a) and **severe impairment** (more than three standard deviations below the population mean or IQ score below 55). In terms of the Mental Health Act (1983), there is a distinction between mental impairment and severe mental impairment, the distinguishing factor being the level of impairment of intelligence and social functioning (i.e. significant or severe impairment).

## WHAT IS COGNITION AND CAN IT BE MEASURED?

There are a number of models of intelligence and cognition that exist in the research literature. They can largely be divided into three general groups: developmental approach, psychometric approach, and those that go beyond this approach to adopt non-psychometric evidence (O'Reilly and Carr 2007).

The dominant developmental theory is that of Piaget which outlines concepts and stages of child development at different ages. Such models provide useful information on developmental concepts of physical development, language and social understanding to name a few. The underlying premise of such theory is that all children progress through the same stages, but that the rate of progress varies, the level of ability or disability is determined by the stage reached (Weisz and Ziegler 1979). Caution is needed in using mental age as this can be misconstrued by others. However, such concepts do provide useful information to help explain why a person has difficulty with a task. This can aid carers to develop realistic expectations of an individual and understand their difficulties and behaviour, and provide better support strategies.

Psychometric theories of intelligence suggest this concept can be measured. There are a number of theories, which suggest different factors, which can be measured; leading to different models and structures of intelligence being argued for in the research literature. For example, Spearman (1904) identified two distinct factors; 'g' a general factor which effects all tasks of intelligence and 's' more specific factors required for some tasks. Much debate in the literature exists regarding what loads onto each factor including a number of primary mental abilities such as verbal ability, perceptual speed, and memory (Thurstone 1938 cited in O'Reilly and Carr 2007). Others classify intelligence as fluid ability 'Gf' and crystallised ability 'Gc' (Catell 1943 and Horn 1986 cited in O'Reilly and Carr 2007). Fluid intelligence is the type of reasoning used to problem solve, which is seen to draw on organic neurological concepts. Crystallised intelligence is that which has been acquired through experience, i.e. acquisition of knowledge. Other factors identified are short term memory ('Gsm') and processing speed ('Gs').

The final group of models of intelligence go beyond psychometrics in an attempt to explain intelligence, e.g. Sternberg's triarchic model of intelligence (Sternberg 2002, cited in O'Reilly and Carr 2007) and description of information processes underlying all intelligence, (Sternberg 2005, cited in O'Reilly and Carr 2007). The main difference is that these consider the environment, as well as processes internal to the person. Sternberg argues that how a person adapts to the environment and the mediation between internal and external processes needs to be considered. However, as yet such models have little research evidence to support their validity (O'Reilly and Carr 2007), but if supported could have considerable relevance to the field of learning disability.

Within academic psychology there is debate regarding what constitutes cognition or intelligence, and about the concept of 'g', how it can be measured, or if it even exists or reflects how we perform in the real world. However, most global assessments of intelligence argue that their measures of IQ are based on 'g'. Consequently there is a fundamental problem with the measurement of IQ as potentially we do not know what it is measuring or if this reflects the use of intellectual ability in the real world.

## GENERAL PRINCIPLES WHEN USING GLOBAL ASSESSMENTS OF INTELLIGENCE

There is debate about what constitutes intelligence and what is desirable and possible to measure with psychometric tests. However, it is evident that individuals do have strengths and weaknesses with information processing, which can be compared with the general population. Measurement of components of information processing can provide useful clinical information.

Providing we are cautious about what they predict, formal psychometric assessments such as Wechsler Adult Intelligence Scale – 3rd Edition (WAIS-III; Wechsler, 1999) can provide useful information. The majority of tests have been standardised for the general population, therefore any adult with a learning disability can be compared with the general population. However, often the observations made while carrying out such tests are more useful than the actual scores obtained. Scaled scores and index scores on the WAIS-III can provide useful clinical information about an individual's relative strengths and weaknesses, by comparing sub-tests. This can provide useful evidence for carers on the type and level of learning disability that an individual experiences on a daily basis, e.g. if a person has a visuo-spatial problem or executive type problem such as planning or sequencing. Observation during the psychometric assessment of how the person does a task can inform the type of support they need with everyday living tasks. Therefore, the process of noticing what helps a person perform better on a task, and understanding where in the neuropsychological system information processing is breaking down, can provide even more useful information. Indeed there is always a balance to be struck between the standardised administrating of a test to ensure the different scores that can be derived (scaled scores, index scores and IQ) are the most reliable, and gaining more useful clinical information. It is vital to ensure that the assessment prevent process is not a negative experience for the client.

Psychometric assessment is not the only source for gaining a neuropsychological understanding of a client's disability. Some of this information could be gained from observations and interviews with the client and their carers. However, formal psychometric assessment does provide reliable evidence based on data which can be compared with the general population in a time efficient way.

## PSYCHOMETRIC ASSESSMENT OF GLOBAL INTELLECTUAL FUNCTIONING

A number of assessments are available to assess global intellectual functioning. It is not possible here to review all the tests available, but a few tests are considered to illustrate some general principles. The tests that have normative data available for the UK population include the British Abilities Scales 2nd Edition (BAS-II; for age range 2 years and 6 months to 17 years 11 months; Elliott 1997); Wechsler Preschool and Primary Scale of Intelligence 3rd Edition (WPPSI-III; for age range 2 years and 6 months to 7 years 3 months; Wechsler 2003); Wechsler Intelligence Scale for Children 4th Edition (WISC-IV; for age range 6 years to 16 years 11 months; Wechsler 2004); and Wechsler Adult Intelligence Scale 3rd Edition (WAIS-III; age 16 to 89 years; Wechsler 1999a). Of these, the WAIS-III is the only test with UK norms for an adult population. None of the tests have normative data available for adults with a learning disability. This is partly due to this group being such a heterogeneous group.

Comparing the performance of an adult with a learning disability using general UK population data can be useful. However, for some people the WAIS-III is too difficult given their general level of ability. Administering this test to someone with an IQ below 45 would generate scaled scores of one on each subtest (thus making the IQ unreliable), along with a sense of failure for the client, no matter how you administered it. One alternative is to use the tests developed for children. The person's scores can be compared with the highest age norms available, which will give an indication of their level of ability and/or developmental level. Depending on the level of severity of disability pre-school versions may be used of the WPPS-III or BAS.

Other tests available, which have US norms rather than UK norms, include the Leiter – International Performance Scale Revised (LIPS-R; Roid and Miller 1997). This test is particularly useful as it is a non-verbal test, so it can be used with adults with limited communication and where the WAIS-III or WISC-IV may be too difficult. However, its administration can be arduous for the clinician, confusing for the client, and it is expensive to purchase. A practical limitation is that this test is not physically robust. Many of the items are made from card or felt, which is easily damaged. The LIPS-R provides age equivalents on individual sub-tests, which if used with caution, can be helpful for carers. This can aid staff/carer's understanding as to the level of the person's difficulties and point them in the direction of the type of activities they need to identify or purchase to engage clients, in terms of developmental level. However, it needs to be clearly explained to carers that mental age is specific to that task, and does not mean that the client generally functions at the level of a five year old, or should be treated like one in general terms. If the LIPS-R is unavailable, similar qualitative information can be found by using magazines, jigsaws, and/or coloured shapes but this needs a bit more creativity, and obviously does not have normative data for comparison.

Finally, a short form of the WAIS-III is available, the Wechsler Abbreviated Scale of Intelligence (WASI; Wechsler 1999b). This test requires the administration of two or four subtests only to gain an IQ. However, it needs to be used with caution as this can miss an unusual cognitive profile. Even with four subtests it can be difficult to predict rep-resentative of the person's overall functioning this may be. It potentially can miss if people have particular strengths or weaknesses, which may have been identified by administering the full WAIS-III and/or give a false mean for the person's full scale, verbal and performance IQ. I would advise caution in use of the WASI with adults with learning disabilities. The IQ gained based on two or four scaled scores may be inaccurate, and not identify strengths or weaknesses within the wider profile of a person's pattern of intellectual functioning. Consequently, a mean based on such limited information may be unreliable.

## WHY USE GLOBAL ASSESSMENTS OF GOGNITIVE FUNCTION?

It could be argued that knowing someone's individual pattern of information processing problems and/or their overall level of functioning does not help predict a person's ability to carry out certain tasks. Evidence from good practice in capacity assessment (BPS; 2006) would support this notion in that no one should predict someone's ability to make a decision based on level of cognitive functioning alone.

Good practice guidelines on the assessment of capacity to make decisions recognise that a person's overall level of cognitive ability impacts on how they may make a decision and how information should be presented to them. In addition, the qualities of the information provided to the person regarding a specific decision are as equally important to consider as the cognitive assessment findings. A functional approach to assessment, as opposed to a diagnostic approach, requires a deeper understanding of factors impacting upon the decision making process. Likewise cognitive assessment, I would argue, has developed from a model of gaining an IQ as an end in itself or diagnostic outcome, towards gaining a profile of a person's information processing difficulties in a range of different environments. In other words a more functional understanding of how a person copes with different tasks and decisions is gained by thorough neuropsychological assessment.

Murray and McKenzie (1999) illustrate the risks of focusing on IQ score rather than a person's overall functioning through assessing the same person on two different days, either side of her birthday. She gained four IQ points due to the age cut-off for scaled scores. One would hope any clinician would take such information into account, when making decisions on capacity by using standard errors of measurement and confidence intervals, i.e. the range of scores at different confidence levels, e.g. 95% confident that a person's measured IQ of 54 is between 51 and 59. However, it does demonstrate again that IQ scores taken out of context can be unreliable and misinterpreted.

Accepting these limitations of psychometric assessment, we can use a profile of a person's information processing to best support a person on a daily basis. Indeed to help adults with a learning disability to learn a new skill, or know how to best offer them choice in a meaningful way, on their next meal, or what to do that day, we need to know how they process this information. Therefore, we need to understand how they attend to information, how they visually perceive things, the level of language, or any alternative means of processing information that has meaning, how they process information into their memory and how much for how long, etc. In a world where we are constantly surrounded by information we need to understand this for our clients, so that we can understand them and begin to provide any intervention, whether direct psychological therapy and/or indirect work through educating carers. This approach is moving away from using WAIS-III and similar assessments as a means of gaining an individual's IQ to using a model of neuropsychological assessment and hypothesis testing. Clinical neuropsychologists in the field of brain injury have used this approach for many years. For more information on neuropsychological assessment and interpretation of assessment information, Lezak, Howieson and Loring (2004) are a useful resource. Similarly developmental psychology and clinical child neuropsychology has developed for children particularly for children with Autistic Spectrum Disorder, developmental dyspraxia and Attention Deficit Hyperactivity Disorder (cf Denkla 1996, Spreen 2001; Ozonoff, Pennington, and Solomon 2006). These approaches have relatively recently been embraced as useful for adults with learning disability.

# A FEW NOTES OF CAUTION WHEN CARRYING OUT COGNITIVE ASSESSMENT

This chapter so far has described a shift in clinical practice from using global assessments of cognitive functioning to simply gain an IQ, to using tests to identify neuropsychological processes through hypothesis testing. Consequently IQ is one piece of the information gained, rather than the end result of the assessment process. Concerns about how such information may be used, for instance for screening and clarifying eligibility for services, are outlined by The British Psychological Society (2001), which highlights that completing cognitive assessments purely to gate-keep services is not good practice. I would agree with this position stating that it is not appropriate to test adults with learning disabilities to enter or exclude them from services. Clearly if such information is already available from previous clinical intervention, this can be used. Similarly, to help inform staff of the nature of an individual's disability it may be appropriate to carry out a cognitive assessment, from which an IQ may be gained. However, it seems inappropriate to set out to complete a cognitive assessment solely for the purpose of deciding if an individual adult should gain access to a specialist learning disability service. Instead such decisions can usually be made based on historical information and previous assessments, including school reports.

Cognitive assessment completed for this purpose is likely to be a negative experience for the client and misuses the valuable resources of a clinical psychology service, which could be better used for other forms of assessment and psychological intervention.

In addition because of the unreliability of short form measures such as the WASI, it is not a satisfactory solution to use such assessments for the purpose of assessing eligibility to services. They may require less time in administration but may also be far less reliable. Mistakes of exclusion or over-inclusion to learning disability services could result.

Finally, one needs to be aware of the cultural bias of standardised psychometric assessment. Many tests may disadvantage and provide inaccurate scores for people from ethnic minority groups, especially for individuals whose first language is not English. One cannot safely assume that non-verbal tests can overcome the language and cultural barriers. It has been argued that tests such as and Vocabulary Scales do overcome these barriers (Raven, Ravens, & Court, 1998). Ravens Progressive Matrices have been used in many countries as a means of measuring IQ. However, the nature of the test situation itself and the testing materials have been criticised for not providing culturally unbiased information. The most useful series to use with adults with learning disability are the Standard Progressive Matrices or Ravens Coloured Matrices. These allow an IQ to be calculated; however, this measures only non-verbal reasoning ability so the implications for global information processing must be made with caution.

## HOW TO USE GLOBAL ASSESSMENTS OF COGNITIVE FUNCTION TO GAIN MORE USEFUL INFORMATION

This section will provide guidance on how to administer the WAIS-III, to gain more useful information than just an IQ. A focus on the WAIS-III is useful to illustrate key points that can be generalised to any psychometric test to gain information to aid the clinician in their work. It will hopefully make the experience of undergoing a cognitive assessment more positive too. WAIS III has 14 sub-tests of which half are verbal sub-tests and half are performance sub-tests, providing separate IQ for performance and verbal abilities, from which a full scale IQ may be calculated. Firstly, I would not advocate attempting with any adult with a learning disability, to complete the WAIS–III, or similar lengthy psychometric assessments, in one session. It is helpful to complete a few sub-tests each session, spending more time on each one, mixed among other forms of assessment, e.g. family and personal history, or talking about a person's life now and the support they receive. It is important to give the individual plenty of positive feedback and encouragement, and warn the person that no-one can do all the tests, and that often they keep going until a person fails, so they will feel like they are unable to do lots of things, but that that is the nature of the test and how it is set up. It is important to remind about this on different subtests and in a genuine way acknowledge that some of the questions are quite hard, particularly when needing to ask questions that the clinician is fairly sure the person will not know, to reach the six consecutive failures needed on some tasks. The clinician must use their judgment about whether to persist to the defined cut-off criteria. What can seem like a painful process at times may allow a person to surprise and get one or two items correct after several failures.

Prior knowledge, or that gleaned about the person from sub-tests completed earlier, can help the clinician mix the sub-tests to avoid administering all the ones the person finds most difficult at the end of the final session. Similarly the clinician may explain a bit about each test and ask which the person would prefer to do this week or next week.

Another important point is that there is always the potential for adults with a learning disability to be suggestible, and/or interpret any prompts automatically as if they had got the question wrong. It is therefore necessary to stray sometimes from the strict manualised approach, to gain more qualitative information, and indeed sometimes even to get an accurate score. One has to also be sensitive in not leading the person to an answer by what we say, or our body language. Many people with learning disabilities become adept at searching for social cues from carers and professionals about which is the desired response, for instance, the clinician's facial expression may convey cues, whilst the person's hand hovers over a choice of several responses. Similarly, the simple prompt of 'tell me a bit more' as required on the vocabulary sub test can be interpreted by someone with a history of failure academically as 'that was the wrong answer so try again'. This can be avoided by warning the person that sometimes they give a one point answer but you suspect they may know more and could get two points. With some clients making reference to game shows they watch can help with this concept, but for others this would not help and may increase their anxiety, or simply not be meaningful or of interest.

Another move away from the standardised manualised approach is to start at the first item on most psychometric tests rather than employing the reverse rule, which many clinicians already are reported to do (McKenzie and Wright 2004). I would argue that this allows the person to gain a rhythm and help the person get used to the new task. It also seems less aversive than presenting a hard task which a person struggles with, and then presenting simpler tasks some of which a person may pass (or perhaps even fail because they are now unsure what is being asked of them or have lost confidence) and then potentially return to hard items, which both the clinician and the client know, that the client can't answer correctly. However, whilst many experienced clinicians will use this approach, it has not been acknowledged by the test compilers for the WAIS-III among many assessments (Leyin 2006).

It would seem unwise for clinical psychologists, to present a test to measure competence in a way that goes against academic theory on what works best in a teaching situation, namely 'errorless learning', if the aim is to measure the potential of individuals rather than catch them out. Leyin (2006) argues that for most people the principle of 'errorless learning' applies covertly with standard WAIS-III administration, namely we start within a level of competence and progress throughout each sub-test gaining confidence and skill on that task, but people with learning disabilities who fail at the starting point (with standard administration) would not have the chance to learn the skill at all, and the reverse rule would confuse further.

Similarly, taking the principle of 'errorless learning' further, we need to provide the support for clients to learn what the task is asking. We can only then accurately observe why they are unable to do a task, and be sure we are measuring the right neuropsychological process. For example, in block design, one of the WAIS III performance subtests, a person is required to look at a pattern created by coloured blocks or in a picture, and recreate the same pattern using their own set of identical blocks within a set time. A person may be able to complete block design, that is to say, they are able to perceive the visuospatial design, and spatially organise blocks, and orientate them in the correct way, and plan and organise an effective strategy to do this. However, they may fail this task for a number of other reasons, for example they may not understand the verbal instructions, or are confused by the demonstration (modelling of what to do). Alternatively they may not have the time to process this information and complete the design in the allotted time. Finally, they may give up before time has run out on later items. If standardised administration has been followed and the person was stopped at the end of the allotted time on earlier items, they may have learned there is no way they can solve the problem in 30 seconds (as it is not explained that they are now allowed more time). However, many of these problems can be overcome if we approach administration of neuropsychological tests, in the way we would approach any other psychological situation, i.e. hypothesis test and formulate, gather evidence and re-formulate accordingly. This can be done without compromising reliability and validity too much, if a score is needed. For instance, a clinician can simplify and vary the instructions to make the test more meaningful, e.g. with the WAIS III block design sub-test, if a person does not understand 'watch me and make one like this' pointing at the demonstration blocks or picture and saying 'same' may be more helpful for a person with limited receptive language. Likewise one can record the pattern or design the person has created at the time limit but allow the person to continue unassisted to complete the task to see how long it takes. Clearly clinical judgment is needed here, about whether the person is likely to complete the task. Moving further away from standardised administration, one can hypothesize what it would take to pass an item. In the block design sub test, the clinician may ask the client if their design looks the same as the picture and if not can they pinpoint where it differs. Alternatively, if shown two designs can the person pick the one that matches the picture. Finally, one can note what kind of help is needed to help them problem solve, and if this is given on complex tasks, can they then complete them. Such prompts may help distinguish an executive problem from a spatial perception problem (Lezak et al. 2004) and/or help identify the type of support that will help a person complete other multi-element tasks such as cooking or cleaning in their home particularly if executive function is an issue, which it often is.

Whilst this section has focused on the WAIS-III, and in particular on block design, the ideas about hypothesis testing and remaining focused on an information processing model and trying to understand what is working, and what help is needed can be generalised to any other test, or indeed observation of a client completing a task. A useful exercise can be to think what processes are needed to carry out a routine task. If we can understand the processes involved, we can then observe, or gather information from carers, about why an individual may find similar tasks difficult. This can be a useful strategy for staff employed to care for adults with learning disabilities. Developing understanding in this way can powerfully change the attributions held by staff about a client they care for, for instance from the person is being 'lazy' or 'manipulative' to empathising, with the difficulty faced on a daily basis, and the effort it may take to carry out such tasks, as well as increasing knowledge and skill in providing support and information in a way that is the most beneficial for the individual in their care.

## OTHER SPECIFIC NEUROPSYCHOLOGICAL TESTS THAT MAY BE OF USE

There are numerous neuropsychological tests on the market for testing a range of specific neuropsychological processes and functions, e.g. memory, perception, executive functioning to name but a few. However, none of these tests have UK normative data available for adults with learning disability, with the exception of some tests for assessing dementia.

The majority of neuropsychological tests currently available can be purchased by clinical psychologists and do not require the person to be a qualified neuropsychologist, or additional specialist training. However, as with all psychological assessments, clinicians must operate within the limits of their own skill and competence. Supervision should be sought in administration and in interpretation of such tests if it is felt to be beyond an individual's competence.

Listed below are some of the neuropsychological tests widely used in the UK and already available in most Psychology departments. Hopefully, this should hearten clinicians (and their managers holding the budget) that spending a fortune on a cupboard full of neuropsychological tests is not essential.

### Communication

The British Picture Vocabulary Scale – BPVS 2 (Dunn, Dunn, Whetton and Burley 1997) is a useful test of hearing vocabulary ability, however this is all it tests. Some people have a good range of vocabulary but limited use of vocabulary in terms of complexity. The opposite can also be true, i.e. limited vocabulary but can understand complex grammar or amount of information. This test can be given in a non-threatening way, and requires non-verbal responses, so is a more reliable evaluation of receptive vocabulary (what the person understands) that does not rely on expressive communication. As with the LIPS-R it provides age equivalents, which can help carers understand, as long as it is made clear that this only applies to their understanding of single words and not overall understanding or ability.

The Test of Reception of Grammar – TROG 2 (Bishop 2003) is also useful and this or something similar should always be used alongside the BPVS-2. It is useful to identify the level of complexity of sentences people understand, and components within a sentence. It provides a useful demonstration for staff, on the amount of information in verbal instructions people can understand. It also provides evidence of whether clients understand concepts such as negatives, nouns, adjectives, verbs, and plurals. As with the BPVS-2 it requires a non-verbal response, so does not rely on expressive verbal communication.

## Memory

The Wechsler Memory Scale 3rd Edition (WMS-III, Wechsler 1999c) can be useful with more able clients. However, as with WAIS-III do not attempt all of it one session. Clinicians will need to ensure they have tasks to do in between immediate and delayed recall, and ensure that delayed recall is carried out before the person has lost concentration. It helps to have only a few tasks that require a delayed recall. Clinicians need to be aware that the vocabulary in the story recall may be too complex. However, it is useful to look at delayed recall compared with immediate recall, compare verbal and non-verbal processing and free recall and recognition. Information gained will provide clues about relative strengths and weaknesses within the memory system providing there isn't a floor effect.

The Rivermead Behavioural Memory Test may also be considered (RBMT or RBMT -II, Wilson, Cockburn, Baddeley, and Hiorns 1985, 2003; RBMT-E, Wilson, Clare, Baddeley Cockburn and Tate 1999). The RBMT or RBMT-II are better than the extended version, as lower ability is required particularly on face recognition and object recognition sub tests. Pictures of objects in the extended version are presented all at once, rather than one at a time (serial presentation). Some clients may not employ a useful strategy to attend and memorise information. This may be examined by re-testing with serial presentation of the items, but caution is needed of the learning effect. The most appropriate version to use depends on the ability of the person. The behavioural elements of the test can provide useful feedback to staff. However, some clients may be worried or upset by being asked to hand over a personal belonging, as required for one of the sub tests.

The Attention and Memory Battery (AM) of the Leiter International Performance Scale Revised (LIP-R) can be used with clients who do not communicate verbally. However, as outlined earlier it can be difficult to administer and is expensive.

Sometimes it is better for the clinician to develop memory tests specifically for an individual, based on the level of language assessed previously, for instance presenting a story with the words and level of grammar that the person understands. This makes findings more valid. It is also important to make sure before attempting memory tasks using pictures, that a person can recognise the pictures.

## Attention

The Test of Everyday Attention (TEA, Robertson, Ward, Ridgeway and Nimmo-Smith 1994) is only useful with more able clients, as many people with learning disabilities will reach a floor effect. Some sub-tests are deeply frustrating for clients, if they do have problem with attention. There is a child version (TEACh; Manley, Robertson, Anderson and Nimmo-Smith 1998), which can be administered fully or at least some relevant sub-tests selected. Child psychology colleagues may be more familiar with this test.

## Executive Functioning

Some of the sub-tests of the Behavioural Assessment of Dysexecutive Functioning (BADS, Wilson, Alderman, and Burgess 1996) may be useful to explore problem solving ability, ability to follow rules, sequencing, and distractibility. The action program, key search, and zoo map sub tests are considered the most useful. Many of the other BADS sub tests require complex instructions, or involve complex tasks, which are unsuitable for people with learning disabilities.

The Frontal Systems Behaviour Scale (FrSBe; Grace and Malloy 2001), examines behavioural syndromes, associated with frontal lobe damage, e.g. apathy, disinhibition, and executive dysfunction. There is a self-rater version and carer version available. This test can be quickly administered and can provide useful information to carers. It can be completed retrospectively (before a certain event), currently if a change is suspected, and repeated in future to monitor change. This test may also help to formulate a problem, as many behavioural elements of executive problems are identified, which cognitive testing often does not.

## USING A NEUROPSYCHOLOGICAL MODEL WHEN YOU CAN'T FIND THE RIGHT TEST IN THE CUPBOARD

For some individuals with more severe intellectual impairment formal tests are of little use due to floor effects, that is to say a person is unable to do the task because it is too hard. Sometimes due to the nature of the person's difficulties, even if the person does the task there is uncertainty that it is testing the neuropsychological system as intended, and is thereby difficult to interpret. For example, a test of verbal memory such as 'logical memory' in the WMS-III will not be testing memory if the vocabulary and language in it is too complex. Subtests require recall of information from a story immediately (immediate recall) or after a delay (delayed recall);

however an individual's ability to understand the language used in the story has a huge impact.

In such cases observation of the client in different environments, can glean useful information. For example, observing an individual's response to communication used by carers can give evidence of what a person does understand, and equally important what a person does not understand or respond to. Video of sessions or activities can also be useful to view with staff as a training tool. Where video is not practical, detailed descriptions of observations are almost as good. Involving support staff in trying out communication strategies and to demonstrate and coach clients can be beneficial too.

Observation of the client with their staff during activities, using different levels and types of communication, and support, can be useful to understand a person's difficulties and further inform the type and level of support needed. Modelling different approaches for carers with the client can provide evidence to carers of the difference modifying communication and other support strategies can make.

Observing a person carrying out a routine and/or new task can provide useful clinical information about a person's ability for instance to solve a problem, or sequence information. Similarly, observation of a person and the type of support needed to learn a new task can also give useful clinical information.

As with any observation it is important not to make assumptions but to apply a neuropsychological or information processing model to the situation, and hypothesis test each component, and identify where in the system it might be breaking down. Perhaps more important is observing for the type of support that helps, and understanding within a neuropsychological model why this helps, so that similar strategies can be generalised to other situations. Some creativity is needed to do this, detailed observation and engaging with clients in a range of activities can provide such information.

## SUMMARY AND CONCLUSION

Hopefully this chapter has outlined that neuropsychological assessment and interventions can be of benefit to adults with a learning disability and is not inevitably a negative experience. To support people well we need to understand their cognitive processes and to provide information regarding their cognitive functioning in the most meaningful ways. We need to understand this, in order to ensure effective psychological interventions for direct work with individuals, and to help inform families and carers and support services with evidence based strategies and recommendations for a wide range of needs, including how to communicate, how to teach new skills and maintain existing ones, how to meaningfully occupy, offer choices and help make decisions. Cognitive assessment must not be used to limit peoples lives further, but to widen their experiences, and provide them with greater opportunities, choices and individualised support, in a truly 'person centred' way.

Few adults with learning disabilities have recorded information explaining the nature of their learning disability or the impact of this intellectual impairment upon how they function and understand the world. In my clinical experience carers and sometimes professionals supporting these people often make misattributions about an individual's behaviour due to a lack of understanding about the nature of their difficulties. Indeed in many cases inaccurate opinions and information may be available about the nature and level of an individual's intellectual impairment. This inaccurate information forms an additional barrier to that person's quality of life. Consequently, it could be argued that we have an ethical and professional duty to provide detailed neuropsychological or cognitive assessment for all adults with learning disability. This can be a useful assessment and initial intervention on its own or used as part of a wider assessment integrating a neuropsychological approach with other psychological approaches.

# References

American Psychiatric Association (2000) *Diagnostic and Statistical Manual of Mental Disorders (4th Ed- Text Revision, DSM-IV-TR)*. Washington DC: APA.

Banat, D., Summers, S. and Pring, T. (2002) An investigation into carers' perceptions of the verbal comprehension ability of adults with severe learning disabilities. *British Journal of Learning Disabilities*, **30**, 78–81.

British Psychological Society (2001) *Learning disability: definitions and contexts*. Leicester: British Psychological Society.

British Psychological Society (2004) *Challenging Behaviours: psychological interventions for severely challenging behaviours shown by people with learning disabilities. Clinical Practice Guidelines*. Leicester: British Psychological Society.

Birtish Psychological Society: Professional Affairs Board (2006). *Assessment of Capacity in adults: interim guidance for pyschologists*. Leicester: British Psychological Society.

Bishop, D.V.M. (2003) *Test for Reception of Grammar – version 2*. London: Psychological Corporation.

British Psychological Society Professional Affairs Board (2006) *Assessment of Capacity in Adults: interim guidance for psychologists*. Leicester: British Psychological Society.

Catell, R.B. (1943) The measurement of adult intelligence. *Psychological Bulletin*, **40**, 153–93.

Denkla, M.B. (1996) Biological correlates of learning and attention: what is relevant to learning disability and attention-deficit hyperactivity disorder? *Journal of Developmental and Behaviour Paediatrics*, **17**(2), 114–19.

Department of Health (2001). *Valuing People: A New Strategy for Learning Disability for the 21st century*. TSO: London.

Department of Health (2005) *Mental Capacity Act*. London: TSO.

Department of Health (1999). *Once a Day*. NHS Executive.

Dunn, L.M, Dunn, L.M., Whetton, C.T. and Burley, J. (1997) *The British Picture Vocabulary Scale* (2nd edn). National Foundation For Education Research: Nfer Nelson.

Elliott, C.D. (1997) *The British Abilities Scales* (2nd edn). London Nfer Nelson.

Emerson, E. and McGill, P. (1989) Normalisation and applied behaviour analysis: Values and technology in services for people with learning difficulties. *Behavioural Psychotherapy*, **17**(2), p101–17.

Grace, J. and Malloy, P.F. (2001) *Frontal Systems Behaviour Scale*. Florida: Psychological Assessment Resources Incorporated.

Horn, J. (1986) Intellectual ability concepts. In R.J. Sternberg (ed.), *Advances in the Psychology of Human Intelligence*. New York: Macmillan.

Kempton, W. and Kahn, E. (1991) Sexuality and people with intellectual disabilities: A historical perspective. *Sexuality and Disability*, **9**, 93–111.

LaVigna, G.W. and Willis, T.J. (1996) Behavioural Technology in support of values. *Positive Practices*, **1**(4), 6–16.

Leyin, A.A. (2006) Don't know if I'm coming up or down....: The WAIS-III and people with learning disabilities. *Clinical Psychology Forum*, **163**, 26–9.

Lezak, M.D., Howieson, D.B. and Loring, D.W. (2004) *Neuropsychological Assessment* (4th edn). New York: Oxford University Press.

Manly, T., Robertson, I.H., Anderson, V. and Nimmo-Smith, I. (1998) *Test of Everyday Attention for Children*. Bury St Edmonds: Thames Valley Test Company.

McKenzie, K. and Wright, J. (2004) Adaptations and accommodations: The use of the WAIS-III with people with a learning disability. *Clinical Psychology Forum*, **43**, 23–6.

Murray, G.C. and McKenzie, K. (1999) What a difference a day makes: A cautionary tale in the use of the WAIS-R in assessing mental impairment. *Clinical Psychology Forum*, **130**, 27–8.

O'Reilly, G. and Carr, A. (2007). Evaluating intelligence across the life-span in Carr, A., O'Reilly, G., Noonan Walsh, P. and McEvoy, J. (eds). *The Handbook of Intellectual Disability and Clinical Psychology Practice*. London: Routledge Taylor and Francis Group.

Ozonoff, S., Pennington, B.F. and Solomon, M. (2006) Neuropsychological perspectives on developmental psychopathology in Cicchetti, D. and Cohen, D.J. (2006) *Developmental psychopathology, Vol 2: Developmental Neuroscience* (2nd edn). New Jersey: John Wiley and Sons, Inc.

Raven, J., Ravens, J.C. and Court, J.H. (1998) *Raven's Progressive Matrices and Vocabulary Scales*. London: Psychological Corporation.

Roid, G.H. and Miller, L.J. (1997) *Leiter – International performance scale revised*. Wood Dale IL: Stoelting Co.

Robertson, I.H. Ward, T., Ridgeway, V. and Nimmo-Smith, I. (1994). *Test of Everyday Attention*. Bury St Edmonds: Thames Valley Test Company.

Spearman, C. (1904) 'General intelligence', objectively determined and measured. *American Journal of Psychology*, **15**, 201–93.

Spreen, O. (2001) Learning Disabilities and their neurological foundations, theories and subtypes in Kaufman, A.S. and Kaufman N.L. (2001) *Specific learning disabilities and difficulties in children and adolescents: Psychological assessment and evaluation*. New York: Cambridge University Press.

Sternberg, R.J. (2002) Intelligence is not just inside the head: The theory of successful intelligence. In J. Aronson (ed.), *Improving Academic Achievement: Impact of Psychological Factors on Education*. New York: Academic Press.

Sternberg, R.J. (2005) *The triarchic theory of successful inteligence*. In D.P. Flannagan and P.L. Harrison (eds), Contemporary Intellectual Assessment: Theories, tests and Issues (2nd edition). New York: The Guilford Press.

Thurstone, L.L. (1938) Primary mental abilities. *Psychometric Monographics*, No.1.

Wechsler, D. (1999a) *Wechsler Adult Intelligence Scale^UK 3rd Edition*. London: Psychological Corporation.

Wechsler, D. (1999b) *Wechsler Abbreviated Scale of Intelligence – WASI*. London: Psychological Corporation.

Wechsler, D. (1999c) *Wechsler Memory Scale^UK 3rd Edition*. London: Psychological Corporation.

Wechsler, D. (1999) *Wechsler Abbreviated Scale of Intelligence – WASI*. London: Psychological Corporation.

Wechsler, D. (2003) *Wechsler Preschool and Primary Scale of Intelligence 3rd Edition*. London: Psychological Corporation.

Wechsler, D. (2004) *Wechsler Intelligence Scale for Children^UK 4th Edition*. London: Psychological Corporation.

Weisz, J.R. and Ziegler E. (1979) Cognitive development in retarded and nonretarded persons: Piagetian tests of the similar sequence hypothesis. *Psychological Bulletin*, **86**, 831–51.

Wilson, B.A., Alderman, N. and Burgess, P.W. (1996) *Behavioural Assessment of the Dysexecutive Syndrome*. Bury St Edmonds: Thames Valley Test Company.

Wilson, B.A., Cockburn, J. and Baddeley, A. (1985) *Rivermead Behavioural Memory Test*. Bury St Edmonds: Thames Valley Test

Wilson, B.A., Cockburn, Baddeley, A. and Hiorns, R. (2003) *Rivermead Behavioural Memory Test – II*. London: Harcourt Assessment.

Wilson, B.A., Clare, L, Baddeley, A., Cockburn, J. and Tate, R. (1999). *Rivermead Behavioural Memory Test – extended version*. Bury St Edmonds: Thames Valley Test

Wolfensberger (1983). Social role valorisation: A proposed new term for the principle of normalisation. *Mental Retardation*, **21**, 234–9.

World Health Organisation (1992) *ICD-10Cclassification of Mental and Behavioural Disorders: Clinical description and diagnostic guidelines*. Geneva: World Health Organisation.

Chapter 5

# COMMON LEGAL ISSUES IN CLINICAL PRACTICE

A.J. Holland

## INTRODUCTION

The law and associated policy is relevant with respect to a number of issues including: individual rights, the roles and responsibilities of professionals and carers in terms of their duty of care, the complex issues that can arise when balancing respect for individual autonomy and the risk of the exploitation and abuse of people who may be vulnerable, and it provides additional protection and alternative means of response, where appropriate, when a person with intellectual disability is arrested, charged and/or convicted of an offence. For those working in community teams for people with intellectual disabilities, when faced with complex clinical situations that raise legal and ethical concerns, the framework of the law and policy should guide the response and may also provide the legal means for helping to resolve such issues.

The focus of the chapter is clinical and specific clinical situations, where legal issues may be of particular importance and where a legal perspective may help in decision making, are discussed. Listed below are three areas in which those working in health and social care services may face difficult dilemmas yet are expected to make decisions, some of which may be against the wishes of the person him/herself and/or his/her family. They are:

1. Decision making by adults with intellectual disabilities and the balance between risk versus an adult's right to autonomy;
2. The management of suspected abuse, exploitation, or neglect of people with intellectual disabilities living in the community.

*Clinical Psychology and People with Intellectual Disabilities*, Second Edition. Edited by Eric Emerson, Chris Hatton, Kate Dickson, Rupa Gone, Amanda Caine and Jo Bromley.
© 2012 John Wiley & Sons, Ltd. Published 2012 by John Wiley & Sons, Ltd.

3. Suspected offending behaviour by a person with an intellectual disability and the special provisions in law if someone with an intellectual disability is arrested charged and/or convicted.

The cases described below are examples of situations that illustrate the topics listed above. They are included to set the principles discussed in this chapter into the context of day-to-day clinical and social care practice. Consider the specific questions at the end of each scenario as well as the following questions: What are the key ethical, clinical and legal issues in each case? How would you seek to resolve the problems described? These examples are chosen as consideration of specific legislation is required in each of these cases. The focus in the chapter will be on the law as applied to England and Wales but some of the principles may apply to the jurisdictions of Scotland, Northern Ireland, and of other countries, even if the legislation is different.

## Case Scenarios

Mr P is aged 46. He lives with his widowed mother and attends a work experience programme for people with intellectual disabilities. He is able to make his wishes known with difficulty because of his limited speech although he can use some signs to indicate his views. He has always indicated he wanted to continue to live at home with his mother. However, recently he has become increasingly distressed and has been mumbling to himself about death. He has lost weight and is sleeping poorly. He now says he wants to leave home. In conversation he says his mother does not love him any more, something she says is certainly not true. What are the key issues to be considered? What should the response be to him wanting to leave home? Can he and should he be prevented from leaving home and if so how? What are the responsibilities of services?

Ms S is aged 19 and has recently left her local special school and now attends an adult education course at her local college. She was diagnosed as having Prader Willi Syndrome when aged 5 years. The severe tendency to over-eat, which has resulted in severe obesity in the past, has been managed by her parents by keeping tight control on her access to food. Now she is more independent and has her own money she has been obtaining extra food and her weight has increased by 10 kilograms in three months. She is now severely obese and is suffering from physical complications. She does not accept she has a problem. Her parents are concerned she might die. Can her access to her benefits and her food be controlled? Can and should her over-eating be stopped – if so how? Is she making a decision having understood the consequences of such a decision?

Mr V is 48 years of age. He has severe ID. He can make his basic needs known through some spoken language, the use of gesture, and some signs. He is also said to have autism and does not like changes in routine. Since his parents died he has lived in a small group home run by a local voluntary organisation. He has no other relatives. Over a few days he is noticed to have become listless and a blood test to check for anaemia shows that he is very likely to have a serious form of leukaemia. The staff are advised that treatment has a reasonable chance of leading to a remission of his illness, however, they are of the opinion that he would find treatment very difficult. It is considered very unlikely that he would have the ability to consent to what is a complex course of treatment with significant side effects. Should he receive treatment for the leukaemia? What are the responsibilities of his support staff and the community team? Is he making a decision having understood the consequences of such a decision? What are the responsibilities of services?

Mr T is now aged 23 and lives in a housing association flat with an hour each day of support. He has Asperger's syndrome and has filled his flat with magazines on his favourite subject, model trains. He has difficulty planning and organising his life and spends money meant for food on magazines. He has severe debts. Recently he has being going to a 'friends' house where he obtains money to buy more magazines. There is increasing concern that he is being sexually abused. What responsibilities do services have under these circumstances? How might he be protected from abuse? Is he making a decision having understood the consequences of such a decision? What are the responsibilities of services?

Mr R is aged 32 and lives at a group home run by a local branch of a voluntary organisation. He has a moderate intellectual disability. Returning home one evening he tells the care staff that he has set a fire at a local college. He has a history of setting fires in the past and also has periods when he becomes irritable and threatening. He has adequate living skills but he easily wanders into potentially risky situations and has been assaulted himself. He is described as being easily led. Should the staff inform the police? If the police are involved what else does the staff need to consider?

Ms F is 24 years of age. She has lived apparently happily in a small privately run home for five years since her widowed mother died. She has attended a local college three days a week. Ms F has severe intellectual disabilities and has caused occasional concern because of her problematic behaviour and she is also considered, by those who support her, to be particularly at risk for exploitation and abuse by others. It is noticed that she hasn't attended college for several weeks and on enquiry it would appear that she is no longer allowed out of her care home. Her care manager visits and is unable to gain access and is concerned that Ms F is being kept in her room most of the time. The carers say that she has been very disturbed and it is in her best interests that she doesn't go to college for the moment and does not receive visitors. What is the responsibility of the care manager? How should the community team respond?

## BACKGROUND

The support of people with intellectual disabilities, such as those people described above, takes place within a framework that has developed through the evolution of general principles and the setting of such principles within policy and practice and in national legislation (most recently Department of Health 2001; 2009). Outlined below is a brief summary of how such policy and practice has emerged over time. Sometimes such policy has followed the belated recognition that the abuse and neglect of vulnerable groups of people, including people with intellectual disabilities, has taken place. There are also examples in history where such action has been sanctioned by the government of the country concerned.

### International Conventions and Declarations

There have been remarkable changes and advances in the recognition of the rights of minority groups, such as those with disability, particularly through the United Nations Conventions and Declarations. Cooper and Vernon (1996) have succinctly summarised the roles of different generations of rights from the 'civil and political', to the 'economic, social and cultural' and the more recent 'development' rights. These different 'generations' of rights, starting with the Universal Declaration of Human Rights (Secretary General, UN, 1948) include a statement of the basic rights to life, as well as the rights to freedom of opinion, to a fair trial, and to freedom from torture, slavery and violence. They are followed by rights reflecting quality of life, including working in favourable conditions, an adequate standard of living, the best possible mental and physical health, education, and the right to enjoy the benefits of cultural freedom and scientific progress. These should be enjoyed by all without discrimination. Finally, the more complex and contested area include the rights to peace and security, economic autonomy, and the right to development itself. These concepts are outlined in greater detail in subsequent Covenants that have a legal standing in those countries where they have been accepted (e.g., International Covenant on Civil and Political Rights and the International Covenant on Economic, Social and Cultural Rights, Secretary General, UN 1976). Subsequently, the specific issues concerning people with 'mental retardation' (General Assembly, UN 1971) or with disabilities (General Assembly, UN 1975) have been addressed through 'declarations'. Essentially these 'declarations' outline certain principles that have been agreed by the member states of the United Nations. These include statements relating to having, as far as meaningfully possible, the same rights as others, the right to security, to a decent standard of living, to freedom from exploitation and abuse, etc. In 1993 the General Assembly of the UN adopted the standard rules on the equalization of opportunities for persons with disabilities and, in 2007, the UN Convention on the Rights of People with Disabilities was past by the UN General Assembly. In 2008 this was finally ratified when sufficient countries had formally recognised the Convention. The emphasis has now moved clearly towards the importance of positive rights – in line with the Disability Discrimination Act 2005, people with disabilities have a right to expect reasonable adjustments to remove those barriers preventing their full inclusion as citizens.

## National Legislation, Policies and Practice

Historically a distinction had been made between those with impairments present from childhood (now referred to as 'intellectual disability') and those whose mental disability is acquired later in life (mental illness). Later, different Acts of Parliament (e.g., Mental Deficiency Act, 1913 and Lunacy Act, 1890) were enacted to meet the then perceived needs of these two groups of people. The passing of the Mental Deficiency Act, 1913 was influenced by the beliefs of the eugenics movement and their concerns about the effects on society as a whole of people considered 'feeble-minded' or 'moral imbeciles'. The definitions of the various 'labels' used in the Act were imprecise and the behaviour of individuals was a major determining factor as to whether someone met the specific criteria and could or could not be detained. This policy in the England of segregation and institutionalisation was officially reversed with the publication of the 1971 White Paper 'Better Services for the Mentally Handicapped' (DOH 1971).

Mental health legislation and the treatment of people with mental disorder was extensively reviewed by the Percy Commission and resulted in a new approach leading to the Mental Health Act (MHA), 1959. The advent of effective medications were beginning to change the outlook for people with serious and debilitating mental illnesses such as schizophrenia, depression or bipolar disorder and for this, and other reasons, a new approach to hospitalisation and care was required. The principle was accepted that people in need of treatment, because of a mental disorder, should have the option of informal admission and not always have to be admitted compulsorily, as had previously been the case. The MHA, 1959 continued to enable compulsory admission for assessment or treatment of a mental disorder (including people with intellectual disabilities) to take place under specific circumstances if considered necessary.

The 1959 MHA was superseded by the 1983 MHA, which included changes in definitions and powers of appeal. There have now been further developments in mental health legislation with changes in Scottish and then English and Welsh legislation that have resulted in new laws or amended legislation in these countries that are now, in their underlying principles, very different. For England and Wales the amended 1983 MHA 2007 brings a number of changes. There is a widening of definition of what is meant by 'mental disorder' and, unlike the new Scottish mental health legislation, the concept of 'impaired decision-making' or 'mental capacity' has not been included. Also, community treatment orders, which can follow a period of treatment in hospital, have been introduced, and the approved social work previously required to instigate a section has been replaced by the *'approved mental health practitioner'*, and the *'responsible medical officer'* replaced by a *'responsible clinician'*. From the perspective of people with intellectual disabilities, the use of the amended MHA is still limited to people with intellectual disabilities and associated problem behaviours. It could also apply if the person with intellectual disabilities had a co-morbid mental illness.

These changes in mental health legislation (at least in England and Wales) have been contentious and have been seen as a lost opportunity to bring such legislation in line with current ethical and legal thinking (e.g. Zigmond and Holland 2000; Szmukler and Holloway 2000). It is, however, developments in 'capacity-based' legislation that are perhaps the most significant for people with intellectual disabilities.

## Recent Developments in Policy and Practice

Policy developments relevant to the lives of people with intellectual disabilities are covered in greater detail elsewhere in this book but it is important to have a perspective on such developments when considering legal issues. In terms of service provision the NHS and Community Care Act 1990 placed a statutory duty on social services to undertake 'needs-led assessments' for those with special needs. It is this assessment that is the route into social care provision but not necessarily the guarantee that individual needs will be met (this has led to the development of *access* and *eligibility criteria*). Service structures and the way services are delivered have been subject to further change through, in England and Wales, the creation of Learning Disability Partnership Boards that are social service led. The funding systems are also changing with a move from residential care models to *'supported living'* through *'direct payments'* and brokerage arrangements. The individual needs of people with intellectual disabilities should be identified through the process of *'Person Centred Planning'*, thereby ensuring that a holistic and person specific system of support is provided according to need (Robertson *et al.* 2007).

Given this move towards the person with intellectual disabilities having control over his/her own budget and managing his/her own affairs, issues of choice and risk, and how these are balanced and managed are likely to become even more prominent. The concern is that a person's apparent 'choice' to live in a particular place or to engage in, or not to engage in, a particular activity will always be taken at face value. The cases of S, V and T above illustrate such issues – are each making a decision having understood the consequences of such a decision? Is Mr V's apparent dislike of hospitals a statement that he doesn't wish for treatment for his leukaemia and would prefer to die? Whilst individuals recognised as vulnerable may have the capacity to make such decisions, there is a responsibility to explore any apparent risky decision further. It may not necessarily be an issue of a person's understanding (and therefore possibly his/her lack of capacity), rather it may be that there are problems of coercion by others, or of a person not being able to respond or know who to turn to for help and therefore is being exploited. Matters relating to the potential inherent and situational vulnerabilities of people with intellectual disabilities and, how services respond to risk, is likely to be increasingly important as new and unregistered systems of support become more commonplace.

### Safeguarding Adults

People with intellectual disabilities may lead very dependent lives and may require intimate care and be unable to describe their experiences or likes and dislikes. The fact that both physical and sexual abuse occurs is beyond doubt even if the exact scale is difficult to establish (see Brown *et al.* 1995 for example). Hospital scandals in which physical and/or psychological abuse took place have been reported (e.g., Merton and Sutton, and Cornwell), as has abuse in community settings (e.g., Buckinghamshire). A further strand of Government policy is relevant to this issue. The publication of '*No Secrets*' in 2000 was the Governments response to such concern. In this context 'vulnerable adults' were seen as those needing statutory services. As has been considered by Dunn *et al.* (2008), '*No Secrets*' emphasised a person's 'inherent vulnerability' recognising the need to have mechanisms in place to deal with the various types of abuse in the context of the situations in which they occurred.

There are a number of major difficulties which can contribute to an unsatisfactory outcome in such situations. In the first instance, the possibility of abuse has to be suspected. Secondly, it may be difficult to collect sufficient evidence to proceed with criminal charges, and finally, depending on where they are living, there may be limited powers available to remove someone from an alleged abusive environment. Following the publication of '*No Secrets*' procedures were proposed to address such problems and to establish a framework for recording and managing those cases where there are concerns. These '*Protection of Vulnerable Adult*' (POVA) or '*Safeguarding Adults*' procedures (now referred to as Safeguarding of Vulnerable Adults – SOVA) bring together the relevant agencies and provides a forum to facilitate action to protect the person concerned and to seek a long term resolution of the problem. The agencies involved are likely to be social services, health (GP and intellectual disability services) and the criminal justice agencies. Legal advice may also be required. These issues are considered again later in the chapter in the context of the earlier examples.

Whilst abuse may be generally seen as an active process – something being done to someone – it is also about neglect or about the failure to act when such action was required. In the review undertaken by Sir Jonathan Michael (Michael 2008) following the publication of 'Death by Indifference' (Mencap 2007) he identified examples of good practice but also identified systemic and fundamental problems in the delivery of health care to people with intellectual disabilities. He proposed action at various levels from the Department of Health, to commissioners and providers, and inspectors and regulators.

*Decision-Making and the Concept of 'Mental Capacity'*

Mental health legislation, as described above, has a limited place to play in the context of the lives of people with intellectual disabilities and in the day-to-day work of community teams. It is the effects of a person's intellectual disability on his/her ability to manage his/her own affairs, and to protect him/herself from the risk of exploitation and abuse that is often a major concern. There can be a tension between respect for the principle of autonomy and the protection from harm or from neglect or abuse of those deemed to be vulnerable. In the cases quoted in some reports there almost seems to be have been a sense of paralysis affecting those concerned when someone has a significant intellectual disability lacks the capacity to consent to a health intervention. There would also appear to have been a disregard of the principles set out in human rights legislation – such as the right to life. This is illustrated in the Mencap Report 'Death by Indifference' (Mencap 2007) and also in cases that have come before the High Court for judicial decisions, such as requests for sterilisation (see Stansfield *et al.* 2007). High Court hearings to determine health decisions, when someone has not wished to consent and their capacity to consent is in question, such as illustrated in the cases of *Re: C*; and *Re: MB*, highlighted a gap in the law that had its origin in the passing of the 1959 Mental Health Act and the subsequent repeal of the powers of 'parens patriae' – the power and duty originally invested in the monarch to care for those unable to care for themselves. Such cases highlighted the absence of an established process for substitute decision-making for those adults who lacked the capacity to consent. High Court cases, such as those above emphasised the central importance of consent and the principle of autonomy or self-determination and the pivotal role of a person's 'mental' or 'decision-making' capacity. In the case of healthcare the following: informed consent, the provision of adequate information, a person's capacity to consent, and the fact that consent should be voluntarily given (free from coercion) were all very clearly established as important principles. *Re: F* (1990) had also set out the principles of 'necessity' and 'best interests' that apply, when someone is considered to lack the capacity to make the decision in question. Subsequent cases refined the process that needed to be followed when making decisions on behalf of people who lacked the capacity to make such decisions for themselves (see Wong *et al.* 1999 for review). Thus, the Adults with Incapacity (Scotland) Act 2000 and the Mental Capacity Act 2005 (for England and Wales) came into being to bring into statute the necessary framework for substitute decision-making for adults who were unable to make decisions for themselves.

A further case was also important, that of *Mr L vs Bournewood NHS Trust*, as this case highlighted the vulnerability of people with severe disabilities to potential injustice, as they themselves may not have the capacity to both recognise and to challenge what might be an injustice and, in the absence of appropriate statute, there was no ready means for others to challenge what, in the case of Mr L, was his de facto detention in hospital under common law. In this case, the European Court finally ruled that the UK Government had been at fault, as Mr L had, in effect, been

**Table 5.1** Principles of the mental capacity act 2005.

1. A person must be assumed to have capacity unless it is established that he lacks capacity.
2. A person is not to be treated as unable to make a decision unless all practicable steps to help him to do so have been taken without success.
3. A person is not to be treated as unable to make a decision merely because he makes an unwise decision.
4. An act done, or decision made, under this Act for or on behalf of a person who lacks capacity must be done, or made, in his best interests.
5. Before the act is done, or the decision is made, regard must be had to whether the purpose for which it is needed can be as effectively achieved in a way that is less restrictive of the person's rights and freedom of action.

**Table 5.2** Highlights of the definition of decision-making capacity MCA 2005 (see act for full details).

**2(1)** For the purposes of this act, the person lacks capacity in relation to a matter if at the material time he is unable to make a decision for himself in relation to the matter because of an impairment of, or a disturbance in the functioning of, the mind or brain.

**3 Inability to make decisions**
For the purposes of section two, a person is unable to make a decision for himself if he is unable –
a) to understand the information relevant to the decision.
b) To retain that information.
c) To use or weigh that information as part of the process of making the decision, or
d) To communicate his decision (whether by talking, using sign language or any other means)

deprived of his liberty as the hospital concerned had total control over his life and he had had no ready means of appeal. This has now led to further legislative changes in England and Wales referred to as the 'Deprivation of Liberty' safeguards (DoLS).

The MCA 2005 sets out the principles (Table 5.1) that should guide in such situations and states the necessary functional test (Table 5.2) that should be applied where, because of such *an impairment of, or disturbance in the brain or mind'*, the person's capacity to make that decision is in question.

Under the MCA 2005, it is for the person requiring the decision to be made to have *'a reasonable belief' 'on the balance of probabilities'* that the person concerned lacks the capacity to make the decision that is required to be made, given that appropriate effort has been made to help the person reach an understanding and to communicate a choice. Carers may wish to involve psychologists and others in the community health team for people with intellectual disabilities in advising about such issues (Murphy and Clare 1995). The person's advocate may also be involved. Documenting the outcome of a particular course of action and the reasons for it is important. Where someone lacks capacity to consent to a particular decision the person requiring the decision to be made can act in his/her best interests. This is considered later in the chapter.

*Independent Mental Capacity Advocates (IMCAs)*

The MCA 2005 also sets out circumstances when an 'Independent Mental Capacity Advocate (IMCA)' must be appointed. Mr R, whose summary is at the beginning of the chapter, is such an example as he has 'no family or friends' and a decision is having to be made about 'serious medical treatment'. For the first time there is a statutory duty to appoint an IMCA in such circumstances as it is recognised that particular situations carry with them heightened risks and there needs to be additional safeguards. Thus, IMCAs provide this where people may be particularly vulnerable and the decision in question is potentially serious or life changing. There is also the discretionary option of involving IMCAs in 'safeguarding adult' proceedings even if they have family and friends.

*Restraint and Deprivation of Liberty*

The MCA 2005 and the Code of Practice recognise the fact that some people who lack the capacity to make specific decisions may behave in a manner that requires restrictions on their freedom or the occasional use of restraint (defined as the use or threatened use of force). For example, the person with severe intellectual disabilities, who has a limited sense of the danger of traffic or who would get lost if out by him/herself, may wander out of the front door of the house. How then to justify such restrictions – the key principles are those of *'proportionality'* and the *'risk of harm'*. Such action can be justified providing it is a proportionate response to the risk and seriousness of harm. Whilst an immediate response may be required when some particular behaviour happens for the first time, if a behaviour is likely to occur again and restraint may then be necessary, it would be appropriate for those providing support to seek advice as to how this risky behaviour might be prevented and managed in a less restrictive way, and if restraint is occasionally needed, the staff are trained so that such restraint can be undertaken safely and in a manner that is respectful of his/her dignity.

As described earlier, following the ruling in the European Court with respect to the case of *Mr L v Bournewood NHS Trust*, the Government have had to introduce new safeguards if a person who lacks the capacity to make such decisions for him/herself is having their liberty restricted to the extent that it amounts to 'a deprivation of liberty'. The framework of the MCA 2005 by itself cannot be used to justify deprivation of liberty and had to be amended to include these new safeguards and also an additional Code of Practice. The distinction between 'restriction' and 'deprivation' must be judged with respect to the individual concerned, bearing in mind the whole range of factors that might be relevant – this distinction is one of degree or intensity, not one of nature or substance (see Deprivation of Liberty Code of Practice, Ministry of Justice 2008). Essentially it is about the extent to which staff have complete control over that person's life. Does he/she ever go out? Is he/she allowed visitors? Are they under continuous supervision and control? The same principles of *'proportionality'* and *'risk of harm'* apply as they do with the use of restraint.

*Deprivation of Liberty Safeguards* require that six different assessments are undertaken and that authorisation is given by what is referred to as the *'supervisory body'* established by the Local Authority and/or Primary Care Trust. The social care providers (referred to as *'managing authorities'*) have a duty to refer people for such assessments and authorisation ideally when they anticipate that such deprivation is likely to be necessary and he/she lacks the capacity to consent to such a course of action. Where a person's behaviour is such that deprivation of liberty is a possibility then this should be considered as part of the care planning process. Some *Deprivation of Liberty* assessments can be done by the same people but there must be a minimum of two assessors. Some are relatively straight forward (e.g., age assessment) others are more critical such as the 'best interest' assessment (see Deprivation of Liberty, Code of Practice 2008). To deprive someone of his/her liberty in the absence of formal approval would be unlawful. If there is a possibility that someone may be being deprived of his/her liberty in the absence of the DoLs process this should be reported to the relevant authority (PCT or LA).

*Criminal Justice System*

If a person with an intellectual disability is alleged to have offended there are a number of potential dilemmas which need to be faced. There is a general wish to protect people with intellectual disability from the criminal justice process but this course of action does not allow the facts of the case to be properly investigated by the experts (i.e., the police), the alleged perpetrator may not have the benefits of the case being heard by a jury and the rights of the victim may also not be met. The concern is that summary justice can occur and individuals held in de facto detention (see Gunn 1997) or detained under a civil section of the MHA but without the due process of law. In contrast, however, the criminal justice process is likely to be traumatic and people with intellectual disabilities may be particularly vulnerable and open to abuse and at risk in settings such as police cells or prisons. They may not understand what is being asked of them and they may find court proceedings both threatening and incomprehensible. Past miscarriages of justice have also highlighted the potential vulnerability of people with intellectual disabilities when being interrogated. It is also recognised that people with intellectual disabilities may not be able to understand the legal process and may not have been aware that what they were alleged to have done was wrong (absence of mens rea).

There are different points in the criminal justice process at which reports might be requested and where diversion from the criminal justice system might take place (Murphy and Holland, 1993). When the person is clearly mentally ill and suffering from abnormal mental beliefs (e.g., delusions) and/or abnormal mental experiences (e.g., auditory hallucinations), then rapid admission to hospital may well be indicated. However, in the absence of co-morbid mental illness this course of action has its limitations, particularly when there is no specific treatment likely to result in a significant and sustained improvement. Those Acts of Parliament that are particularly relevant to people with intellectual disabilities suspected of offending are outlined below.

*Police and Criminal Evidence Act (PACE 1984)*

At the time of arrest the police inform the suspect of his or her rights. This is in the form of the 'caution' and the 'notice to detained persons', which gives details of legal rights, for example, to consult a solicitor. If the police have reason to believe that a person has a mental disorder or intellectual disability they should arrange for a third party to be present (appropriate adult), usually a carer or social worker. This person has the responsibility to advise the person, to observe the interview is being conducted fairly and to facilitate communication. If these guidelines are not adhered to, the defence can ask the Judge at the time of the trial to rule that part of the evidence, for example, a confession, be ruled inadmissible. The defence may well seek expert advice as to the person's intellectual ability, suggestibility and the reliability of interview evidence. Fenner *et al.* (2004) have demonstrated that the current version of the caution is poorly understood, even by the general population. The potential for people to incriminate themselves inadvertently is therefore considerable. For this reason it is important for services to ensure that people with intellectual disabilities, whose behaviour is such that they may well come into contact with the criminal justice system, are helped to be made aware of what should happen and who should be with them if such an occasion was to arise.

*Criminal Procedure (Insanity) Act 1964 (amended 1991)*

This Act of Parliament was intended to divert those recognised as being 'unfit to plead' or 'to stand trial' by reason of disability. Under the original Act those found unfit to plead or not guilty by reason of insanity had to be detained indefinitely in hospital without trial and therefore without the facts of the case being determined. The person may, of course, have been innocent of the offence and there have been cases in which people have been detained for long periods of time. For those who were mentally ill at the time, treatment may well result in them becoming fit to plead and therefore a trial could take place. However, for those found unfit due to 'arrested or incomplete development of mind' the likelihood of marked change is small. Furthermore, the criteria for being unfit were such that many, regardless of intellectual level, could be considered unfit.

The Act was amended as a result of a Private Member's Bill in 1991. It is now possible for a trial of the facts to take place and if found unfit to plead the person will not automatically be detained in hospital. A range of options are available to the court, from the use of hospital orders to discharge. Expert evidence, such as psychological evidence, may be called to guide the court as to whether the person concerned understands the concept of being 'guilty' or 'not guilty', can follow the proceedings in court and can instruct his or her lawyers. These conditions for determining 'fitness to plead' have their origins in common law. It is possible that the courts will wish to take an approach that is more based on the concepts of mental capacity in the future.

The Act was further amended in 2004 so that the question of fitness to plead is considered by the court (not by a jury). The facts of the case (trial of the facts) are subsequently considered by a jury if he/she is found unfit to plead. If the 'act' (actus reus) is proven the court can determine sentence, perhaps following further expert evidence. The circumstances are then similar to those which pertain when the use of the MHA is being considered when a person with a mental disorder has been convicted of a crime (see below).

*Mental Health Act 1983 and Hospital Orders*

The MHA offers the possibility of diverting people who have or may have a mental disorder from custody in the criminal justice system to hospital for the purposes of assessment and/or treatment. This is undertaken through the use of 'hospital orders' (such as a Section 37), which are similar to the civil orders of the MHA, but are imposed by the courts following expert evidence. The task of services on these occasions is to try and understand the reasons for the offending behaviour which has been alleged, to support the person through the criminal justice process and to advise the courts as to possible sentence if convicted. If assessment in hospital is indicated either before or after conviction, sections 35, 36 and 38 can be used. The advantage of such assessment is that it enables a more complete picture to be established and for advice to be given to the court which is well informed. As with anyone else, the court has a range of sentencing options (e.g., fine, Probation Order, imprisonment) as well as other possible options (e.g., admission to hospital using a hospital order, Section 37 Guardianship Order, Probation Order with condition of treatment). In the case of very serious offences a Crown Court may also wish to impose in addition to a Section 37 a Section 41 order which places major restrictions on leave and discharge. When a Section 41 has been imposed the power to grant leave and to discharge, along with other responsibilities, lies with the Ministry of Justice. The 2007 amendment to the MHA 1983 introduced *Community Treatment Orders* (CTOs). These are available for use in the cases of those who have been detained in hospital and in which additional legal safeguards are considered necessary on discharge.

*Advice to Courts*

Psychologists and psychiatrists may well be asked to advise the prosecution or defence lawyers or act as experts on behalf all concerned to advise about the reliability of confession and other evidence obtained at time of police interview. The intellectual ability, comprehension, suggestibility and potential acquiescence of a person with an intellectual disability in the context of police interrogation may require thorough evaluation. The purpose of such assessments may be to advise on fitness to plead but more usually is concerned with either mitigation or sentencing in the event that the person pleads guilty or is found guilty or, in the case of those found unfit to plead, the 'act' is found to have taken place. Reports can appropriately highlight the circumstances of the offence, the nature of the person's disability and other relevant information that might help the Judge decide on sentencing. This might include whether or not the use of the MHA is appropriate or not.

## LEGALLY SIGNIFICANT DECISIONS IN CLINICAL PRACTICE

In this section of the chapter each of the above developments in law and in policy and practice are considered in a clinical and social care context, with particular reference to the examples given at the beginning of the chapter.

### Where a Person is Found to Lack Decision-making Capacity for a Particular Decision

Several of the cases described at the beginning of the chapter are concerned with adults – people who are 18 years or older – in which decisions have been made or are required to be made and acts have been undertaken or are required to be undertaken. In such situations it would normally be for the person him/herself to decide for him/herself what to do and to accept the consequences. In some of these scenarios described there are potentially adverse consequence that would follow having made a decision on way or other – severe obesity (Ms S), neglect and/or abuse (Mr P; Mr T; Ms F) and death (Mr V). – What are the responsibilities of services?

As described earlier, the courts, through case law, have clearly established the right of adults to take decisions that affect their lives. In the case of healthcare decisions the responsibility of the treating health professional is to appropriately advise and to then support the person concerned in the decision that the person concerned makes. Except under very specific situations (e.g. use of the MHA), it would be unlawful to force treatment on any one in the absence of their consent. Consent is what renders intervention lawful. It is where a person is found to lack the capacity to make the decision in question that 'capacity' legislation becomes relevant.

In the examples given at the beginning of the chapter each of the people concerned has an intellectual disability and would be considered to have *'an impairment of, or disturbance, in brain or mind'* – the term used in the MCA 2005. Whilst the MCA states that there is a presumption of capacity (see principles) it is possible that he/she may lack the capacity to take the decision that is required to be made. Where a person's capacity to make a decision may be in doubt this should be assessed. Capacity is 'decision-specific' and a judgement about a person's capacity to make a particular decision requires that the information about the decision in question (including information on other options) be given to him/her in a manner that is likely to optimise his/her understanding. The person is then asked to give an account, using the most appropriate means for the person concerned, of the relevant issues and the reasons for his/her decision. In the case of emergency situations, it may not be possible to take time over this process and it is in that person's best interests to respond quickly, perhaps to save his/her life or to relieve suffering. However, where time allows, it may be appropriate to present information in small junks; to go through the information on several occasions; use signs, symbols and or pictures; and/or involve a speech and language therapist to help in the communication process. Structuring this process (see MCA Code of Practice; British Psychological Society guidance, GMC guidance) helps to ensure a reliable assessment but, as with many things, it is a judgement, and there may be disagreements that require resolution through discussion. The Court of Protection is the final arbiter of a person's capacity and also of their best interests, if there are disagreements on either of these matters.

When determining what is in a person's best interests there is a requirement to seek the views of the person him/herself and to consider other relevant factors such as his/her previously expressed views, and his/her values and beliefs as well as the views of relevant others. A judgment has to be made by the person requiring the decision to be made, as to how to balance conflicting views and what weight to place on the views of the person him/herself, and that of others, etc. The requirement is to act in someone's best interests bearing in mind all relevant issues. If someone has made a valid advanced refusal of treatment or appointed a donee of a Lasting Power Attorney (LPA) these are likely to take precedence. In the case of Mr V the fact he might find treatment difficult is not in itself an indication that he should not be treated as he may not understand the consequences of saying 'no'. He has a *right to life* and that *right* is going to be a major factor in determining what action to take. The task of staff may well be to help make treatment possible and acceptable to him.

In the case of Ms S, with Prader Willi Syndrome (PWS), the issues are complex. Crucial to resolving this issue will be to try and engage with, and encourage the person, to accept supervision. If she refuses is this because the she lacks the capacity to make such a decision for herself? If she lacks capacity to make this decision, should she live in supported accommodation specifically for people with PWS on the grounds that it is in her best interests? Such an example indicates that often such situations are a complex process moving from trying to work with someone in a collaborative way in a manner that optimises his/her autonomy, to eventually determining that the person does not have the capacity to decide what course of action is appropriate and in her best interests. The MCA 2005 requires that every effort is made to optimise a person's capacity – in this case it may include allowing the person to follow a particular course of action so that the person has the opportunity to learn by experience. If this then fails, does he/she have the capacity to acknowledge this? If not, it may now be appropriate to argue that, despite the opportunity to learn, he/she does definitely lack capacity to make this particular decision.

The MCA 2005 does not give the power to intervene in the same way as the Mental Health Act 1983 does, rather it sets out the duties to act in a person's best interests (where he/she lacks capacity) and freedom from liability if subsequently challenged, providing the correct process has been followed. The MCA 2005 provides the justification for acting in such circumstances. All those acting in a professional capacity must have regard to the MCA 2005 and its Code of Practice when someone is found to lack the capacity to make the decision that is required to be made.

## Where Abuse, Exploitation, or Neglect is Suspected

The decision in such situations is whether or not to intervene and, if so, how and when? Whilst a public law framework for intervening may be limited in some situations and, in others, criminal proceedings may flounder due to lack of evidence, there are powers which may be helpful. These include the fact that social care homes have to be registered and the registration officers have the right to do announced and unannounced visits and can withdraw registration, an approved social worker can seek a warrant from a Magistrates Court to gain entry to premises and remove a person to a place of safety for up to 72 hours (section 135, MHA) and the police may also seek a warrant, if criminal behaviour is suspected. There is also the power of Guardianship included in the MHA. The potential value of a Guardianship Order in these circumstances is that it can determine where someone should live. The problem with such an Order is that it requires the consent of the nearest relative (unless a court agrees that he/she should be removed from that role) and does not give the power to remove someone from one place and take him/her to the designated place.

The MCA 2005 may also be helpful. In the person lacks the capacity to determine for him/herself where he/she should live, then there is a duty to act in that person's best interests. What is in that person's 'best interests' may be a matter of disagreement and where such disagreements cannot be resolved and application may be made to the Court of Protection for a ruling. The MCA, 2005 has also created new criminal offences that of *'wilful ill-treatment or neglect'*. Where such criminal offences are suspected then the police would have the powers to intervene.

The involvement of the MCA hinges on the fact that the person concerned lacks the capacity to make the decision in question (e.g. whether to continue to live in an environment that is neglectful). If the person is making an apparent capacitous decision to remain living in such an environment the MCA cannot apply. The responsibility of services, when someone apparently has capacity to make these decisions for him/herself, is somehow to remain involved so that if there is a serious risk of harm other possible action can be considered. Interestingly, the High Court has recently considered three cases where those involved were seen as vulnerable and at potential risk but they had capacity to make the decision in question. In these cases (*Re: G; SK* and *SA*) the Court agreed that they fell within the inherent jurisdiction of the High Court (see Dunn *et al*. 2008 for discussion).

The policy developments following the publication of *'No Secrets'* required the establishment of 'Safeguarding adult procedures' and each area of the country will have such a policy and should have a designated officer that suspected abuse should be reported to. As described earlier this process provides the means whereby concerns can be expressed and other agencies can become involved. The duty in such cases of suspect abuse is to report the matter and through the mechanisms in place seek to clarify and, where appropriate, to protect. Early on in the evaluation of the Independent Mental Capacity Advocacy (IMCA) pilot studies it was recognised that vulnerable individuals possibly lacking the capacity to make decisions about what to do, may require an advocate even though they have 'family or friends'. Those allegedly abusing the person concerned maybe those family members or 'friends'. There is now the option to appoint an IMCA in such a situation.

The advent of the Youth Justice and Criminal Evidence Act 1999 recognised that there also needed to be special provisions available for vulnerable adult who, as alleged victims, may need to give evidence, much like the special provisions available to children. This includes the use of screens or video-links as well as sign interpreters, and the option of visits to the courts for familiarisation.

A further development has been the clear demonstration that abuse (unsurprisingly) has significant psychological consequences for many of those subject to it (Murphy *et al.* 2007). The mental state, functional and behavioural changes seen in the months after abuse appear to be consistent and whilst they cannot be by themselves definitive indicators of abuse, they may well require treatment and when such behavioural changes are noted, at the least the question should be asked as to whether they could be a consequence of abuse.

## Where a Person with Intellectual Disabilities may have Committed an Offence or may Pose a Risk to Self or to Others

There is a growing realisation that approaches that have relied predominately on admission to hospital when offending or offending like behaviour is alleged are often inappropriate and may result in excessive long periods of incarceration in a secure setting, often some distance from home. A recent report from the Prison Reform Trust (No One Knows 2008) has highlighted concerns about people with intellectual difficulties or disabilities in prison and has begun to explore the types of community options that might exist (see also chapter on offending).

Where the behaviour is perceived to, or actually puts, others at risk then there is a decision that has to be made whether or not to call the police and seek the involvement of the criminal justice system in general. Whatever the risks (whether to self or others) the role of community teams is to determine the reasons for the behaviour and to seek a resolution through an informed intervention. Whilst in the majority of situations this is likely to be best done in the community settings, there may be times when admission to hospital or detention on remand may be considered appropriate. Whilst admission may be on a voluntary basis, if the person does not wish to consent to that course of action, mental health legislation maybe required to compulsorily admit the person to hospital. Mr P is an example where there is some indication that he has deteriorated in his mental state and behaviour and he may have a depressive illness. If such an illness led to neglect and there was a significant risk of suicide, admission either voluntary or compulsorily, might be considered. Mr R may be putting others at risk and the involvement of the police has the advantage of the facts being properly investigated, the 'suspect' has the right to legal representation and it gives the opportunity for the Court to consider various possible courses of action. This may include the use of a probation order or a period of assessment in hospital (e.g., Section 35) to determine whether treatment in hospital under a Section 37 is both possible (i.e., necessary criteria are met) and appropriate (i.e., there are treatment strategies which may diminish the risk of re-offending).

## SUMMARY AND CONCLUSIONS

There are a broad range of international, European and national laws and guidelines which are very significant for people with intellectual disabilities. In England and Wales the Mental Capacity Act 2005 and in Scotland the Adults with Incapacity (Scotland) Act 2000 have been very significant developments. Each provides the basic framework whereby decisions can be made on behalf of people who may not able to make particular decisions for themselves. This includes decisions about day to day life as well as decisions relating to health care. In the MCA 2005 the principles are set out at the beginning of the Act and the emphasis of the Act and its Code of Practice is that of empowerment as well as protection.

The examples given at the beginning of the chapter illustrate the complexity of such situations. In some circumstances the Law provides a framework that informs the subsequent action. However, these situations may involve difficult judgements requiring the balancing of competing principles. In this regard interdisciplinary teams can be of great value as they enable the sharing of different perspectives and the bringing together of different skills.

## References

Brown, H., Stein, J. and Turk, V. (1995) Report of a second two year incidence survey on the reported sexual abuse of adults with learning disabilities: 1991 and 1992. *Mental Handicap Research*, **8**, 1–22.
Cooper, J. and Vernon, S. (1996) *Disability and the Law*. London: Jessica Kingsley Publications.
Criminal Procedure (Insanity) Act (1964) (amended 1991, in force 1992) London: HMSO.
Department of Health (2001) *Valuing People: a new strategy for learning disability for the 21st century*. London: HMSO.
Department of Health (2009) *Valuing People Now: a new three year strategy for learning disabilities*. London: HMSO.
Deprivation of Liberty Safeguards, Mental Capacity Act 2005 New Schedule A1.
Dunn, M.C., Clare, I.C.H. and Holland, A.J. (2008) 'To empower or to protect? Constructing the 'vulnerable adult' in English law and public policy', *Legal Studies*, **28**(2), 234–53.
Fenner, S., Gudjonsson, G.H. and Clare, I.C.H. (2002) Understanding of the current police caution (England and Wales) among suspects in police detention, *Journal of Community and Applied Social Psychology*, **12**, 83–93.

General Assembly of the United Nations (1971) Declaration of the Rights of Mentally Retarded Persons. New York: United Nations.

General Assembly of the United Nations (1975) Declaration of the Rights of Disabled Persons. New York: United Nations.

Gunn, M. (1997) De facto detention. *Tizard Learning Disability Review*, **2**, 11–17.

Lunacy Act (1890) London: HMSO.

Mencap (2007) Death By Indifference. London: Mencap.

Mental Deficiency Act (1913) London: HMSO.

Mental Health Act (1959) London; HMSO.

Mental Health Act (1983) London: HMSO.

Michael, J. (2008) Healthcare for All. London: Michael's Inquiry.

Ministry of Justice (2008) Deprivation of Liberty Safeguards Code of Practice.

Murphy, G.H. and Clare, I.C.H. (1995) Adults' capacity to make decisions affecting the person: psychologists contribution. In *Handbook of Psychology in Legal Contexts* Eds; R. Bull and D. Carson, Chichester: John Wiley and Son, Ltd.

Murphy, G.H. and Holland, A.J. (1993) Challenging behaviour, psychiatric disorder and the law. In R.S.P. Jones and C.B. Eayrs (Eds) *Challenging Behaviour and Intellectual Disability: a psychological perspective* (pp195–223) Clevedon; BILD Publications.

Murphy, G.M., O'Callaghan, A.C.O. and Clare, I.C.H. (2007) The impact of alleged abuse on behaviour in adults with severe intellectual disabilities. *Journal of Intellectual Disability Research*, **51**, 741–9.

Police and Criminal Evidence Act (PACE), (1984).

Prison Reform Trust (2008) *No One Knows*.

Robertson, J., Emerson, E., Hatton, C., Elliott, J., McIntosh, B., Swift, P., Krinjen-Kemp, E., Towers, C., Romeo, R., Knapp, M., Sanderson, H., Routledge, M, Oakes, P. and Joyce, T. (2007) Person-centred planning: factors associated with successful outcomes for people with intellectual disabilities. *Journal of Intellectual Disability Research*, **51**, 232–43.

Secretary General, UN (1948) Universal Declaration of Human Rights. New York: United Nations.

Secretary General, UN (1976) International Covenant of Civil and Political Rights. New York: United Nations.

Secretary General, UN (1976) International Convenant on Economic, Social and Cultural Rights. New York: United Nations.

Stansfield, A.J., Holland, A.J. and Clare, I.C.H. (2007) The sterilisation of people with intellectual disabilities in England and Wales during the period 1988 to1999. *Journal of Intellectual Disability Research*, **51**(8), 569–79.

Szmukler, G. and Holloway, F. (2000) Reform of the Mental Health Act. Health or safety. *British Journal of Psychiatry*, **177**, 196–200.

Wong, J.G., Clare, I.C.H., Gunn, M.J. and Holland, A.J. (1999) Capacity to make health care decisions: Its importance in clinical practice. *Psychological Medicine*, **29**(2), 437–46.

Zigmond, A. and Holland, A.J. (2000) 'Unethical Mental Health Law; History Repeats Itself'. *Journal of Mental Health Law*, February, 49–56.

# Part 2
# GENERAL CLINICAL ISSUES

Chapter 6

# INTERVIEWING PEOPLE WITH INTELLECTUAL DISABILITIES

## Helen Prosser and Jo Bromley

### INTRODUCTION

Within clinical work, there are many worthwhile benefits to interviewing people with intellectual disabilities themselves rather than just relying on the views of carers or an interested third party. Primarily, one maximises the likelihood of obtaining valid information about a person's psychological sense of well-being, their physical and mental health, their particular needs and problems, their family and social relationships, and their satisfaction with the services they receive. Although people with intellectual disabilities can often experience difficulty in describing feelings and internal emotional states for example, maximising the opportunities for individuals to express themselves in interviews can enhance the quality of information elicited and minimise reliance on observable behavioural signs. While a third party is often a valuable source of information on describing observable behaviours, interviewing individuals themselves can provide a greater understanding of their subjective experiences and symptoms, attitudes and beliefs, etc. In addition, health care studies with the general population have shown that patient satisfaction is an important determinant of patients' compliance with treatment (Ley and Llewelyn 1995). As such, effective interviewing may also lead to improved compliance with beneficial treatment regimes (see also chapter on mental health). Thus, as a consequence of inclusive interviewing:

- clients are more likely to receive the help or treatment they need promptly;

*Clinical Psychology and People with Intellectual Disabilities*, Second Edition. Edited by Eric Emerson, Chris Hatton, Kate Dickson, Rupa Gone, Amanda Caine and Jo Bromley.
© 2012 John Wiley & Sons, Ltd. Published 2012 by John Wiley & Sons, Ltd.

- the knowledge and skills of health professionals are effectively put to use;
- clients are supported more successfully as their capacity for making choices about how they would like to live is enhanced;
- client satisfaction is increased.

Most of the principles involved in interviewing people with intellectual disabilities are straightforward enough and are not fundamentally different from those applicable to interviewing children or adults in the general population. The ground rules and foundations for good practice that you already know from your general training on communication are equally applicable when interviewing people with intellectual disabilities, and it is important to remain aware of the skills you already possess (refer to Shea 1988 for further reading).

However, because of cognitive disability and frequently associated limited communication skills, obtaining views or information from people with intellectual disabilities does pose particular difficulties. One such difficulty is that of response bias and, in particular, the proclivity of people with intellectual disabilities to acquiesce, especially to closed yes or no questions (Sigelman *et al.* 1981). Acquiescence is when the respondent gives an affirmative reply to contradictory prompts, i.e. replies yes to both questions 'Are you happy?' and 'Are you sad?', or when a person agrees with whatever statement has been given. The reasons that people are thought to acquiesce are basically due to two factors, impaired cognitive development and social desirability (Shaw and Budd 1982). Acquiescence is more common when the question is not understood or when respondents do not know how to answer the question, although it can also be a way of seeking social approval. The respondent may reply 'yes' even when he understands the question, but replies yes because he believes that a negative or other answer will displease the interviewer and/or the respondent will be looked upon unfavourably by the interviewer.

In clinical practice, minimising acquiescence and obtaining valid responses from people both with and without intellectual disabilities can be optimised by adopting particular interviewing techniques. Studies have shown how an interviewer's behaviour and the content and form of the interview, for example, the specific type of questions asked and the wording used, can determine the respondent's ability to respond validly. If inappropriate interviewing techniques are used, cooperation and reliable and valid information is threatened (Heal and Sigelman 1995; Schuman and Presser 1977; Shaw and Budd 1982; Sigelman *et al.* 1981). This chapter hopes to outline good practice that will minimise this risk and promote confidence in those interviewing people with intellectual disabilities.

## PROCEDURAL AND SETTING CONSIDERATIONS

As with any clinical session, an interview with a person with intellectual disabilities is best conducted in private in order to safeguard confidentiality. There are, however, some situations in which a third party may be present, such as when the respondent specifically requests it or if they have communication problems they require help with. The respondent may have difficulties with pronunciation, for example; English might not be their first language or they may prefer to augment verbal communication with a non-verbal form such as Makaton or PECS (Picture Exchange Communication System, Bondy and Frost 2002) which the interviewer might not be familiar with. In these cases, a third party, perhaps a carer or speech therapist, may act as an interpreter or may be helpful in avoiding any misunderstandings. However, the person accompanying the respondent should be asked to refrain from commenting or offering information and should only participate in the interview if directly asked to do so in order not to unduly influence the respondent's responses. It is also important to clarify that the respondent has given their consent to see you (Cea and Fisher 2003).

The interview should be created as a natural, relaxed and informal interaction through which individuals are able to express their views openly and with confidence. It may be helpful to conduct the interview in a setting that is familiar for the interviewee such as their place of work, school, day centre, or a local health centre. Putting the person at their ease, building trust and rapport and enhancing their confidence should be seen as a priority throughout the interviewing process. Clearly, the interview should be conducted as unthreateningly and sensitively as possible in order that the respondent does not feel they are under scrutiny, and to minimise any feelings of nervousness, anxiety or agitation that the respondent may have. It can take time to build rapport with someone, and in an ideal world it would be helpful to spend some time getting to know the respondent before the formal interview commences. For example, perhaps working alongside them or making an informal visit to see them before the interview. It may also be useful to talk to carers or relatives to gain some insight into the person. Another consideration, time allowing, is that it may be more apt to undertake more than one interview; not only because this approach can enhance rapport and trust, but also because people with intellectual disabilities may find two or three interviews easier to manage than one long interview.

## OPENING THE INTERVIEW

The attitude of anyone being interviewed, whether they have intellectual disabilities or not, is likely to be determined by their expectations of the interaction. People with intellectual disabilities may have had negative experiences in the past and be worried that something will happen to them as a result of the interview, such as changing residence, being given medication, or changing school/day care arrangements. People are likely to be concerned that information may be shared with others and are probably less likely to be compliant if they are worried about the consequences of disclosing information (Branston and Fogarty 2000). As in general practice it is therefore helpful to start by explaining what you intend to do with the information and the bounds of confidentiality. Take time to explain:

- what the purpose of the interview is;
- what questions will be asked;
- who and what the information is for;
- why the information is important;
- how long the interview will take;
- the limits on the interview's confidentiality.

It might also be important to take some time to reassure the respondent that there are no 'right' or 'wrong' answers and that they need not answer any questions they do not wish to. If the respondent is used to using visual timetables at school or in their place of work you may wish to incorporate a schedule into your session to let the respondent know what the stages will be.

After introducing the session, it is advisable to begin with relatively easy questions such as, 'Where do you live?' or 'What have you being doing at the centre today'. For children, you might ask about school or what the child likes to do. Respondents can usually accurately reply to these questions and this strategy makes respondents less anxious, develops a rapport between interviewer and respondent, and gives the respondent practice at answering. Potentially more probing and sensitive questions are best asked during the middle or towards the end of the interview. Various studies have shown that if respondents perceive themselves as incompetent and unable to answer questions they are more likely to be open to suggestibility (see Bull 1995) so the ordering of questions is an important issue. If people can be put at their ease and made to feel competent at the start of an interview the information elicited is more likely to be valid.

## THE CONTENT OF THE INTERVIEW

The type of questions asked and the phrasing and wording of questions are important elements of effective interviewing. When working with people with intellectual disabilities, the clinician must have an understanding of the cognitive ability of the individual and adapt their questioning accordingly. The expressive and receptive language skills of people with intellectual disabilities vary widely but it is useful to bear in mind that all individuals have a much greater understanding of language and the meaning of words than they regularly use. Someone with mild intellectual disabilities may have very good expressive verbal skills and respond appropriately to simple open-ended questions. On the other hand, someone with moderate intellectual disabilities may need more prompting and so respond better to closed type questions, with the interviewing using cross-questioning techniques as a means of assessing validity. A discussion of these various questioning styles is given below.

The points made apply not only to verbal interviewing but to written questionnaires and semi-structured interviews. Semi-structured interviews designed to assess mental health issues in the general population often do not have normative data and can be difficult to use with people with intellectual disabilities because of the demands imposed by the language used. However, there are some (e.g. the Psychiatric Assessment Schedule for Adults with Developmental Disability; PAS-ADD, Moss *et al.* 1996) which have been designed with this specific purpose in mind and have tailored questions accordingly.

## Open Questions

When starting the interview, it is a good idea to begin with an open question as this gives the respondent free rein to describe the situation as they see it. For example, if you were interested in finding out about someone's feelings about their current residential placement, you might start by asking an open question such as 'Tell me about your home?' or 'What is it like where you live?' Even if you feel the respondent is rambling off the point, it is often those problems or symptoms which are spontaneously mentioned that are more convincing than those elicited only by direct and closed questioning, such as 'Do you have any problems with your flat mate?'. This type of question only requires an answer of yes or no and does not require or necessarily encourage the respondent to elaborate. A surprising amount of relevant information can often be obtained by letting the person tell her or his own story with the questioner only interjecting occasionally, such as 'Can you tell me more about that?' or 'Can you explain what you mean by...?' By starting an interview in this way one also gains more understanding of the person's linguistic or communicative abilities. Consequently, the interviewer can then target questions more appropriately, and issues of response bias, such as acquiescence (the proclivity to answer 'yes' regardless of the question asked) can be side stepped.

However, although open questions are good ice-breakers and can provide very valuable information, they are often difficult for someone with intellectual disabilities to answer as they require quite a high level of cognitive and communicative skill. As such, open-ended questions achieve a lower response rate than closed questions, and so can be limited in their usefulness (Sigelman *et al.* 1982).

## Closed Questions

*Yes/No Questions*

Since there is more of a risk that a respondent will acquiesce when presented with a closed yes/no question such as, 'Are you usually happy?' or 'Do you have any friends?' the interviewer must pay close attention to monitoring the validity of respondents' responses to such questions. This can be done through additional probing and cross-questioning techniques or by seeking external validation from other sources. These methods allow inconsistencies to be assessed and the fullest answers possible obtained.

For example, if one wanted to find out about attitudes towards and satisfaction with current residential accommodation, the interviewer might ask, 'Do you like living here?' followed by 'Would you rather live elsewhere?' In addition to this, item-reversal techniques provide a check on the validity of the respondent's answers to closed questions. For instance, a closed question such as, 'Are you happy?' can be followed by its reverse question, 'Are you sad?' further into the interview. Obviously, the answers to each should not be contradictory. If you are going to use this technique, however, you may wish to explain to the respondent that you might be asking questions in different ways so they do not worry they are getting questions wrong (Rapley 1995).

*Multiple Choice Questions*

With multiple choice questions, it is worth noting that respondents may experience difficulty in remembering a choice of replies and some have a tendency to echo the last phrase of an interviewer. Multiple choice questions can also create tension and confusion as sometimes it is difficult for the respondent to understand what is really being asked.

However, multiple choice questions may still be used appropriately, if the interviewer takes time to explore whether the person can understand the question or if the question is supported by visual or written scales that might make it easier for the person to understand (see section on self report measures below).

*Either/Or Questions*

Either/or questions appear to provide more valid answers than multiple choice questions, and reduce the tendency for acquiescence with yes/no questions. Either/or questions offer a choice of no more than two responses. They are still susceptible to response bias in that people with intellectual disabilities do have a tendency to favour the last of the two options. However, Sigelman *et al*. (1981) found that oppositely worded either-or questions generated responses that were more consistent than answers to oppositely worded yes-no questions. As a general rule, if you are using either-or questions and the respondent echoes or repeats the last part of a question, further clarification is called for and it should be regarded as a request for help with understanding the question.

When there is no alternative to a closed question, the answer should be followed up with a request for an example. To assess someone's understanding of actual words and concepts that are used in the interview questions may be framed so as to allow the subject to reply by giving examples, rather than a definition, e.g. 'What do you do when you are in a bad mood?', or 'How do you show that you are happy?'. Open statements such as 'Tell me more about this?' are useful prompts to clarify and validate responses to closed questions. There is also no reason why pictures cannot be used to enhance understanding. When Sigelman and colleagues replaced verbal either-or questions with pictorial ones, more respondents were able to answer the pictorial than the verbal questions and fewer people contradicted themselves with the pictorial responses than with the verbal options.

## Questions to Avoid

What is the type of questions an interviewer might want to avoid when talking to someone with intellectual disabilities? One should be careful of using suggestive or leading questions. A common fault is to distort the person's own story to fit one's own preconceptions. Try not to ask questions in such a way that you make it clear the answers you are expecting, e.g. 'You're not sleeping very well, are you?' or 'You don't get on well with your sister, do you?' Pre-hand knowledge or information gained from a third partyabout the respondent k may lead you to think you know the answer to a question, but people often keep hidden their innermost thoughts. It is also important as an interviewer that you try not to challenge the respondent's answer (e.g., by saying, 'Do you really?' or 'Are you sure?') as this will only aggravate potential for acquiescence and can hinder, rather than help, clarify an issue.

In general, if you need to ask very direct questions, it is more helpful to be specific. It is best to avoid abstract questions and concepts such as, 'What is the extent of your problems?' or 'What do you expect to do in the future?'. This level of generality makes greater demands on the expressive language abilities of respondents, requiring them both to respond to abstract terms and to collate experience relevant to the issue in question and distil a summary position.

## Appropriate Vocabulary

Sophisticated vocabulary, difficult propositions and complex linguistics raise respondents' intellectual demands and increase the probability that someone with intellectual disabilities will either not respond or respond inappropriately. If a person does not understand the question you are likely to get no response, an unintelligible response, an irrelevant response, a 'don't know', 'don't remember' or 'not sure' response, a refusal to answer or an inadequate response. It is important, therefore, to let respondents know that they can request clarification or rephrasing of a question if they do not understand it. Likewise, the interviewer may want to seek clarification from the respondent that they have understood a question.

People with intellectual disabilities often do not know the meaning of words used by professionals and research indicates that professionals often fail to adjust their language in line with a person's communication skills (McConkey *et al.* 1999). Ideally, questioning needs to be simple, often repetitive and carefully explained in order to keep the respondent's attention. To simplify questioning, the following are useful guidelines:

- Use short words and short sentences. Simplify a sentence if the person does not seem to understand it.
- Use single clause sentences. Questions such as, 'How well do you know and like the staff?' should be avoided because they essentially contain two questions and might be quite difficult to follow. Try and introduce one idea at a time and avoid subordinate clauses. 'When you are at the centre, on a Thursday, and Jill's there, do you get angry?' is quite a long winded and confusing question to understand.
- Use active verbs rather than passive ones. For example, 'Did you make the bed?' is easier to follow than 'Was the bed made by you?'
- Use the present tense where possible. 'Are you upset?' is better than, 'Have you been upset?' It is appropriate, however, to use the present tense to introduce a concept, and then move to the past tense if you need to know more than the present, e.g. 'Were you upset before Christmas?'.
- Avoid questions regarding abstract consideration of future actions or attitudes, such as 'What do you expect to do in the future?' Such

questions are highly speculative and one might not get a very reliable answer. Stick with more concrete questions about the present or the past.

- Avoid double negatives. Also, use 'Can you sit still?' rather than 'Can't you sit still?'
- Avoid jargon and unexplained technical terms.
- Use concrete descriptions and avoid figurative language. For example, it might be better to ask 'What is your job?' rather than 'What do you do for a living?'.
- Prepare your questions in advance with the above principles in mind. If you are using a written questionnaire, apply the Flesch formula (1948) to assess readability.
- Try and monitor your own speech for colloquialisms. How many times do you normally say 'You know', 'O.K.?', 'It's like..'? These kind of statements might detract the person from the real question you would like them to answer.

## Anchor Events

Questions relating to time, number and frequency pose particular problems for people with intellectual disabilities. Accurate information regarding when events occurred or the time-course of problems is often essential, but can be difficult to obtain from respondents with intellectual disabilities. One way to help the respondent focus on time course is to get them to think about an event they can remember accurately and which has occurred in the recent past, e.g. their own birthday or a birthday of a close relative or friend, Christmas, parties, days out, etc. *'How have you been feeling since your birthday?'*

## Summarising

People with intellectual disabilities tend to have a relatively short span of attention. It is important, therefore, to recap and summarise what the respondent has said. As with any interview, there are a number of benefits to doing this. It re-engages and focuses the respondents' attention, giving them an opportunity to add more detail. It also provides the respondent with the opportunity to concur with or refute the interviewer's interpretation of what has been said.

## Use of Video

To check you are using appropriate questions and to monitor issues such as acquiescence it is helpful to record your session in some way so that you can review it after the respondent has left and adapt any future interviews accordingly. However, this might not be the best strategy if it is likely to make the respondent nervous and self conscious.

## Use of Self Report Measures

As part of your interview, you may want to include some kind of self report measure to assess a particular area of the respondents' subjective experience. In the last few decades a number of studies have examined the use of self report measures for people with intellectual disabilities. Starting with questionnaires designed to assess quality of life, self report measures for people with intellectual disabilities now exist to measure a range of internal states including happiness, stress and pain. Initially these measures often took the form of yes/no or either/or questions and were susceptible to the response biases we have already described. However, there has also been a growth in the development of likert type scales for use with people with intellectual disabilities.

Hartley and MacLean (2006) provide an excellent overview of the reliability and validity of likert scales as well as the factors that increase the ability of people with intellectual disabilities to complete these scales. They reviewed 51 studies and concluded that likert type scales were a useful way of configuring a self report measure; although they identified a number of factors that affected response rate. For example, they noted that having pictorial representation on the scale increased response rate. Allowing the interviewer to paraphrase or expand on the question also increased response rate and decreased response bias. However, it was noted that to maintain issues relating to standardisation these 'deviations or additions' should be ideally written into the measure as additional prompts.

Hartley and MacLean note that response rate to likert scales does tend to be higher in adolescents and adults with mild intellectual disabilities although using pre-tests is a useful way of increasing reliability and validity with people with more severe disabilities. An example of this can be seen in Cummins' 1997 paper exploring quality of life. To establish if participants could use a visual analogue scale (VAS) to indicate how important they thought certain activities were to them, Cummins initially asked participants to distinguish between smaller and larger sized blocks. If they could do this successfully he then asked people to put the different blocks on the scale, the largest at the top and the smallest at the bottom. Subsequently, he showed participants a VAS which had 'not important at all' at one end and 'very important' at the other and asked people to rate how important certain activities were for them by using this scale. If people could not distinguish the different sized blocks or could not put them correctly on the scale it was assumed that they could not use the scale in the correct way and would need to be asked the question in a different format. The same procedure was used by Bromley *et al.* (1997) to establish whether people with mild and moderate intellectual disabilities could use a 'pain ruler' to indicate different degrees of pain intensity.

In clinical practice there is nothing to stop an interviewer designing their own scale to access a certain opinion from a respondent with intellectual disabilities. However, there are a few points to consider. In general, when using a scale rather than a questionnaire, it is preferable to use either a three or five point scale people with intellectual disabilities tend to get the two middle points of the latter scales confused (Levine 1985). The main problem with three or five point scales, however, is that they limit a person's possible choice of responses, and sometimes suffer from ceiling effects. VASs which tend to have two anchor points marked out but no intermediate marks, are often seen as a less restrictive alternative. As noted above, you can include pictures and prompts to increase response rates but you should always try and find some way to measure the reliability and validity of the measure you have constructed.

## Interviewing People with More Profound Intellectual Disabilities

This chapter has largely concentrated on techniques for interviewing people with intellectual disabilities who have some verbal communication. Although we have talked about augmenting verbal communication by using non-verbal means, the assumption has been that the person can express a view verbally. There is a wider debate, outside the scope of this chapter, which looks at the complexities involved in trying to ascertain the views of people who have more profound disabilities and who may be non-verbal. Some researchers have argued that many of the methods of augmented communication that might be used to explore the views of this particular group, are not sophisticated enough to provide reliable and valid information (e.g. Ware 2004). Others note that using augmented communication takes time and an interviewer would need to spend a long time building up a communication system that could be used in interview (Cambridge and Forester Jones 2003). This is not to assume, of course, that augmented communication should not be tried and there are studies that have used these measures to help people with profound intellectual disabilities express a choice (e.g. cited in Ware 2004), however, the information sought may be of a different complexity than for people with less severe intellectual disabilities who are verbally more able.

## Be Creative!

Whilst the above guidelines should help you conduct an effective interview with someone with intellectual disabilities, it is worth remembering that each client is an individual and you may have to try more creative methods of engaging them in conversation than you would a member of the general population. There is nothing to stop you using drawings and photographs to help explain a certain concept or involve the person in the interview process. If the person feels more comfortable talking when walking it may be better to get to know them and ask certain questions whilst out on a walk. Work out what questions you would like to ask and perhaps discuss with someone who knows them well how you might best access their views.

## INTERVIEWING CARERS AND RELATIVES

This brings us to our final point; interviewing carers and relatives. Although we have noted the potential dangers of relying solely on third party interviews, it is still important to see either a care, relative or someone who knows the respondent well in addition to the respondent themselves. Carers may be able to give additional information or another view of a situation as well as validate the information told by respondents. For example, they are sometimes better able to date the onset of illness accurately, especially if it was gradual, or remember dates of events that are likely to be important to the respondent (e.g., the death of a close relative). A carer or relative can also give a useful indication of how disabling an illness is or how a behaviour affects other people. Interviewing carers or relatives also enables you to discern to what extent they are aware of the individuals' needs and problems. The caveat is, however, that if the carer's and respondent's answers are different, one should not automatically assume the carer's view is the correct one.

   Relatives, people with whom the respondent lives and care staff are all liable to have different information at their disposal The respondent may be more likely to open up to his or her parent, and talk about things which it would be more difficult for a stranger to gain access to. On the other hand, a key worker may have access to information which parents do not see, so in some cases it may be appropriate to talk with more than one informant. Nevertheless, it is important that the informant is someone who has known the person well for some time and has regular contact with him, or is used to observing and communicating with the respondent in the particular environment relevant to your area of interest. If the respondent is able to give informed consent, their opinion should always be sought before carers and relatives are interviewed and if possible one should check if there are any parts of your interview with the respondent that they would not like you to discuss.

## IN SUMMARY

Interviewing people with intellectual disabilities can seem daunting but with practice and preparation it will enrich the therapeutic experience of both the interviewee and the interviewer. We hope this chapter has given you ideas to take forward into clinical practice for as a clinician it is your responsibility that the voice of those with intellectual disabilities can be heard and understood.

# References

Bondy, A. and Frost, L. (2003) *The Picture Exchange Communication System.* Pyramidal Educational Systems: Newark.

Branston, P. and Fogarty, G. (2000) The assessment of emotional distress experienced by people with an intellectual disability: a study of different methodologies. *Research in Developmental Disabilities*, **21**, 487–500.

Bromley, J., Emerson, E. and Caine, A. (1998) The development of a self report measure to assess the location and intensity of pain in people with intellectual disabilities. *Journal of Intellectual Disability Research*, **42**, 72–81.

Bull, R.H.C. (1995) Interviewing people with communicative disabilities. In *Handbook of Psychology in Legal Contexts* (ed. R. Bull and D. Carson). John Wiley and Sons, Ltd: Chichester.

Cambridge, P. and Forester Jones, R. (2003) Using individualised communication for interviewing people with intellectual disabilities: a case study of user centred research. *Journal of Developmental Disabilities*, **21**(1), 5–23.

Cea, C. and Fisher, C. (2003) Health care decision making by adults with mental retardation. *Mental Retardation*, **41**, 78–87.

Children's Act (2004) DFES Publications.

Cummins, R.A., McCabe, M.P., Romeo, Y., Reid, S. and Waters, L. (1997) An initial evaluation of the comprehensive quality of life scale- intellectual disability. *International Journal of Disability, Development and Education*, **44**, 7–19.

Every Child Matters. (2003) Government Green Paper, DFES Publications.

Flesch R. (1948) A new readability yardstick. *Journal of Applied Psychology*, **32**, 221–233.

Hartley, S. and MacLean, W. (2006) A review of the reliability and validity of Likert-type scales for people with intellectual disabilities. *Journal of Intellectual Disability Research*, **50**(1), 813–27.

Heal, L.W. and Sigelman, C.K. (1995) Response bias in interviews with individuals with limited mental ability. *Journal of Intellectual Disability Research*, **39**, 331–40.

Levine, H.G. (1985) Situational Anxiety and everyday life experiences of mildly retarded adults. *American Journal of Mental Deficiency*, **90**, 27–33.

Ley, P. and Lewellyn, S. (1995) Improving patients' understanding, recall, satisfaction and compliance. In *Health Psychology: Process and Applications*. (2nd edn) (A. Broome and S. Lewellyn). Chapman and Hall: London.

McConkey, R., Morris, I. and Purcell, M. (1999) Communications between staff and adults with intellectual disabilities in naturally occurring settings. *Journal of Intellectual Disability Research*, **43**, 194–205.

Moss S., Goldberg, D., Patel, P., Prosser, H. Ibbotson, B., Simpson, N. and Rowe, A. (1996) *The Psychiatric Assessment Schedule for Adults with a Developmental Disability: PAS-ADD*. Hester Adrian Reseach Centre, University of Manchester and the Institute of Psychiatry.

Rapley, M. (1995) Black swans: Conversational analysis of interviews with people with learning disabilities. *Clinical Psychology Forum*, **84**, 17–23.

Schumann, H. and Presser, S. (1977) Question wording as an independent variable in survey analysis. *Sociological Methods and Research*, **6**, 151–70.

Shaw, J.A. and Budd, E. (1982) Determinants of acquiescence and nay saying of mentally retarded persons. *American Journal of Mental Deficiency*, **87**, 108–10.

Sigelman, C., Budd, E.C., Spaniel, C. and Schoenrock, C. (1981) When in doubt say yes: Acquiescence in interviews with mentally retarded persons, *Mental Retardation*, **19**, 53–8.

Sigelman, C., Schoenrock, C., Spanhel, C., Hromas, S., Winer, J., Budd, E. and Martin, P. (1981) Surveying mentally retarded persons: Responsiveness and response validity in three samples. *American Journal of Mental Deficiency*, **84**, 479–84.

Sigelman, C., Budd, E., Winer, J., Schoenrock, C. and Martin, P. (1982) Evaluating alternative techniques of questioning mentally retarded persons. *American Journal of Mental Deficiency*, **86**, 511–18.

Valuing People: A new strategy for Learning Disability for the 21st Century. (2001) Governement White Paper.

Ware, J. (2004) Ascertaining the views of people with profound and multiple learning disabilities. *British Journal of Learning Disabilities*, **32**, 175–9.

Chapter 7

# WORKING WITH PEOPLE: DIRECT INTERVENTIONS

## Nigel Beail and Andrew Jahoda

Clinical psychology has a long history of delivering indirect therapeutic interventions with people with intellectual disabilities. However, since around 1980 direct therapeutic approaches have been explored, developed and evaluated. During the 1980s and 90s case reports and accounts of direct individual and group interventions began to appear in the literature (Beail 1995; Kroese, Dagnan and Loumidis 1997; Sinason 1992; Waitman and Conby-Hill 1992).

To date two main approaches have been reported in the literature; cognitive behavioural therapy and psychodynamic psychotherapy. Other approaches such as systemic interventions are also being discussed and described (Baum and Lyngard 2006). However, evidence for effectiveness is limited and at present only exists for CBT and psychodynamic psychotherapy (Beail 2003; Beail, Warden, Morsley and Newman 2005; Rose, Loftus, Flint and Carey 2005; Taylor, Novaco, Gillmer, Robertson and Thorne 2005; Willner 2005).

We recognise that there is considerable variation in how psychotherapeutic approaches are being adapted and applied with people who have intellectual disabilities. At this early stage in the use of these interventions it is important to be imaginative. We also recognise that there may be real dilemmas around particular process issues such as including significant others alongside clients in treatment. Hence, what follows should be considered as a framework or guide for therapeutic work. Yet Safran and Segal (1990) make the point that innovating to accommodate individual needs in therapy should not mean abandoning the therapeutic model. Instead, the therapist requires a deeper understanding of the model

*Clinical Psychology and People with Intellectual Disabilities*, Second Edition. Edited by
Eric Emerson, Chris Hatton, Kate Dickson, Rupa Gone, Amanda Caine and Jo Bromley.
© 2012 John Wiley & Sons, Ltd. Published 2012 by John Wiley & Sons, Ltd.

to ensure that innovative or creative strategies remain faithful to the underlying principles of the approach.

## ACCESSING PSYCHOLOGICAL THERAPIES AND ASSESSMENT

A noteworthy difference between clients with intellectual disabilities and non-disabled individuals receiving psychological therapies from mainstream mental health services is that the non-disabled usually seek help for themselves, whereas others usually refer people with intellectual disabilities. Moreover, many people with intellectual disabilities are dependent upon the support of professional carers or family members if they are to attend an out patient clinic for treatment. Thus we cannot assume that clients with intellectual disabilities come voluntarily or are well informed about why they are attending. Although clients should be involved in the referral process, an appointment letter may be the first time they become aware that they are to see a psychologist. It is therefore important to establish from the outset whether it is the client or someone else who believes that treatment is needed. If it is possible to influence the referral process, then a good starting point is to ensure that the clients are informed that they are being referred for psychotherapeutic help. Otherwise, the information in the referral letters should be shared sensitively with clients. It is important to remember that whatever the wishes of the carer, treatment cannot be provided without the client's informed consent.

Obtaining consent for therapy does not mean that potential clients require a full grasp of the therapeutic model from the outset, as most people learn about what this entails from doing it rather than from explanations about it. Some beliefs that clients bring to therapy may prove helpful and others may cause confusion. For example, it may be important to make it clear to clients at the outset that you will not be giving them medication.

The therapist also has to inform the client about the positives and negatives of therapy. This includes telling them that the treatment may help reduce their symptoms and improve their quality of life with reference to their difficulties and possible outcomes. The negative aspects of therapy include the fact that it may be a difficult process involving talking about painful or upsetting things. The therapist needs to check that the client has retained and understood this, weighed the positives and negatives and made a choice. Some clients may not be able to do this. If the therapist believes that treatment is in the client's best interest and that they would assent, they should follow the legal procedures and guidance for their state or country for providing treatment for adults who cannot consent. Wherever possible clients should be enabled to make an active choice and enter the therapeutic relationship willingly.

The first phase of therapy aims to socialise clients into an understanding of the treatment model. Yet even the basic tenets of CBT or psychodynamic psychotherapy may prove quite difficult for some clients with intellectual disabilities to grasp. For example, there is a body of evidence pointing to the fact that the life experience of people with intellectual disabilities can leave them believing that they have limited control over their lives and feeling dependent on others to complete challenging tasks (Zigler 2002). One might imagine that this outlook would leave such clients sceptical about the notion of a time limited intervention like CBT that assumes they have the power to achieve positive change in their lives. For this reason, it may be important to ask clients explicitly at the outset if they are willing to come along to therapy and if they think it can be of any help to them. Alternatively, a psychodynamic approach with less explicit time limits and goals may prove more appropriate to enable the client to assimilate their problems. We do not want to exclude the sceptics from therapy, but for the therapist to be aware that this may be an important factor in the success of therapy and something that they should monitor and address explicitly.

Involving carers at the initial assessment can provide important insights into the client's situation. This allows the psychologist to hear at first hand about the issues or concerns of the referrer. The meeting may also serve to inform the psychologist about the client's social situation, the stability of their home life and their social supports. Moreover, the referrer could have helpful views concerning the client's ability and willingness to consent to an assessment. This information could prove useful in formulating whether psychotherapeutic work is indicated in any given case. Yet there has to be sensitivity about the involvement of carers. While some clients may be keen to have a carer present and to have a familiar person's support at their initial meetings to allay their anxieties, others may want to meet the psychologist in confidence.

## Suitability for Psychotherapy and Assessment

The psychotherapeutic literature contains various selection criteria concerning suitability for psychodynamic treatment. These include factors such as 'ability to enter an intensive treatment relationship', emphasising the importance of possessing psychological mindedness, motivation, and adequate ego strength. Some even suggest that the person should be of at least average intelligence (Brown and Pedder 1991: Tyson and Sandler 1971). The application of such criteria would exclude people with intellectual disabilities from treatment. However, the application of psychodynamic therapy with adults who has intellectual disabilities have shown that these factors may not be as relevant as claimed. Psychodynamic therapy was adapted and developed for use with children by Anna Freud and Melanie Klein. It is these approaches along with the ideas of Bowlby and Winnicott amongst others that have influenced the development of an age appropriate treatment approach for people who have intellectual and developmental disabilities.

Dagnan and Lindsay describe assessments devised to assess whether potential clients with intellectual disabilities are able to engage in the key therapeutic tasks of CBT. For example there are examinations of whether people can link their view of events with consequent thoughts, feelings and behaviour (Dagnan, Chadwick and Proudlove 2000). Whilst such assessments can prove an extremely helpful guide, they should not be used as the sole basis for deciding whether someone should or should not be included in therapy (Willner and Goodey 2006). The reason for this is that a client's inability to understand hypothetical situations does not necessarily reflect an inability to provide an account of their emotional difficulties. When people produce narratives about their everyday lives, the events that they describe may be intuitively linked to their thoughts, feelings and behaviour (Jahoda *et al.* 2006).

The ability of clients to enter into a dialogue with the therapist about such events is, in part, due to their communicative capacities. However, it is also about the ability of the therapist to facilitate communication. In the first instance, good communication requires shared understanding between those involved in dialogue. For example, one barrier to communication can happen if clients tend to assume that the therapist knows about the characters and events in their lives they are describing. This means that to avoid confusion or misunderstandings, the therapist has to allow time for clients to tell their stories, listen carefully and check that they have a shared understanding of the characters and events being described. It has been found that people with intellectual disabilities may believe that those in their dreams share their dreams (Kroese *et al.* 1998). Hence, therapists wishing to explore dreams with clients should be aware that they may conceptualise them differently.

## Contraindications

During the assessment phase the psychologist also considers reasons against using a therapeutic approach. As CBT and psychoanalytic interventions are talking therapies, potential clients require sufficient verbal understanding and expressive abilities to have a dialogue with the therapist. However, psychoanalytic play techniques have been used with clients who do not have verbal ability (Sinason 1992). Clinical judgement is required for each individual case, but common contraindications include where a person is abusing drugs or alcohol, and where the person is

experiencing an acute psychotic episode. In the case of a psychotic episode therapy can begin once the acute phase of psychosis has passed. It is
good practise to make such a decision in conjunction with both the client
and, where involved, a psychiatrist. People also find it difficult to engage
in therapy when the rest of their life is in chaos. A further contraindication
for therapy in mainstream service settings is where the client habitually
acts out distress in the form of significant violence to self or others. Therapy
may be offered in such cases in specialist settings that are equipped to
manage the risk of violence.

## Assessment and Establishing a Therapeutic Relationship

Prior to engaging a client in treatment the psychologist needs to assess
the client's problem, their circumstances and their treatment needs. This
process and the way therapy is delivered will involve adaptations to take
account of the client's developmental level and cognitive abilities. Willner
and Goodey (2006) has pointed out that the therapist has to take care to
avoid making the client feel inadequate by using complex techniques or
talking at a level of abstraction that the client finds confusing. At the
assessment stage, the psychologist may also have to help their clients to
label objects, feelings and behaviours. People who have intellectual disabilities often have difficulties in recalling the chronology of events in their
lives. Therefore, part of the work in assessment and treatment may
involve the construction of a clearer chronology of events. Pictorial
images, such as a 'time line' illustrating key moments in the client's auto-
biographical history, can be used to provide a concrete representation to
aid this process.

   The assessment phase is the beginning of the therapeutic relationship.
Whatever the approach taken, the process of psychotherapy is under-
pinned by the nature of the therapeutic relationship (Keijsers, Schaap
and Hoogduin 2000). Therapy is an interpersonal process and a range of
terms and theories are used to describe what constitutes an effective
therapeutic relationship or working alliance (Bugental 1987). Different
schools of psychotherapy emphasise different aspects of the alliance. The
basic premise of working cognitive-behaviourally with people is that
there is a collaborative relationship between the therapist and the client,
and that they work towards explicit goals. In psychodynamic psychotherapy the client and the therapist enter therapy with the intention to
allow their relationship to be therapeutic. So whatever happens between
them they seek to understand in terms that will serve the underlying aim
of therapy. The aims may be less explicit as psychodynamic psychotherapy is an exploratory approach and may be more appropriate for clients
who are not yet able to see or say what their difficulties are (Newman and
Beail 2005).

Key to the therapeutic alliance is that the client agrees to tolerate the difficulties, strains and frustrations of the relationship so that they stick with it and allow the therapist to guide the work. The factors identified by the client-centred school as 'necessary and sufficient conditions' for patient change are accurate empathy, positive regard, non-possessive warmth, congruence and genuineness. Today these are accepted as essential aspects of all psychotherapeutic endeavours. Clearly people with intellectual disabilities will have problems with comprehension and they might have additional expressive communication problems that will have an impact on the relationship. However, the factors affecting the therapeutic relationship will not merely arise from disability per se but, as with everyone, from their views of therapy and the therapist. Equally, the therapist's personality, attitudes and ability to relate to the client and communicate effectively will have an impact on the relationship. Above all, the success of the therapeutic relationship rests on the nature of the interaction between the client and therapist.

## The Physical Space

Psychodynamic therapeutic interventions require a safe and private space. The room needs to be free from intrusion and impingements from the outside world. The room should offer comfortable seating, be warm, have neutral decor and also be free of personal mementoes of the psychologist. The psychologist sits with their client in comfortable chairs, able to see each other, but not face to face. This aim is to create a less threatening situation where eye contact is reduced so that people do not feel under scrutiny. Whilst many of the same principles apply to CBT, there would be no concern about avoiding face to face contact. As some clients may have speech problems, face to face interaction can provide essential cues to assist the therapist's understanding of what the client is saying. Given the behavioural component of CBT, therapists may also engage in practical tasks with clients in everyday settings.

If undertaking weekly sessions, the same room should be used if at all possible. Appointments should be at the same time and day of the week. This routine seems to help clients who attend without support. Clients are offered a set time in terms of session duration – usually 50 minutes – for each session they attend. However, some people with intellectual disabilities find the 50-minute duration hard to tolerate and sessions lasting 30 or 40 minutes may be offered initially. Risks to personal safety for the therapist are usually low but still present. Therefore, prior to any session the psychologist should take into account risk issues. How you conduct the session will be informed by the outcome of the risk assessment. For example where there is a risk of the client acting out angry feelings in the session, then the psychologist should arrange the seating so that they are sat closest to the door or have a means of raising the alarm should their personal safety become compromised.

## PSYCHODYNAMIC PSYCHOTHERAPY

In psychodynamic work the therapist refrains from revealing anything personal about themselves. The safe setting, the clear boundaries and the therapeutic relationship are all designed to facilitate the client in exploring and clarifying their psychological reality. Furthermore, they function to contain the client and therapist in a manner whereby previously intolerable psychological states can become held within the session, clarified and where possible resolved and reintegrated in a tolerable form by the client.

In psychodynamic psychotherapy the therapist is concerned with the client's mental representation of themselves within the world and seeks to identify the origin, meaning and resolution of difficult feelings and inappropriate behaviours. The work entails making links between early life experiences and how these experiences influence unconscious and conscious expectations of relationships in the present day.

Psychodynamic sessions begin with the therapist providing the client with the space to free associate. This involves inviting the client to say whatever is in their mind and whatever comes to mind. The therapist will be interested in anything that the client says, including information on their current problems, circumstances, current and past relationships, dreams, fantasies and so on. The therapist resists giving the client information about them. The therapist presents him or her self as a type of screen on to which the client can project their imagined perceptions of the therapist or project intolerable aspects of themselves into the therapist.

The therapist uses a number of methods to enable the client to tell their story and then formulates interpretations aimed at accessing and making sense of unconscious content. It is important that the therapist works within the vocabulary and comprehension capacities of their client. The therapist may provide information giving responses about their treatment, reason for referral, and about matters such as the time left in the session and so on. However, advice and instruction are not usually within the remit of the psychodynamic model. The therapist will listen carefully to and observe the client's verbal and non-verbal communications. The therapist attends to the factual content of what the person says, the words used and also what is not said. The therapist also observes the client's mood, as communicated through what they say, the way they say it and how they behave. The client may talk about a range of things and the therapist does not interrupt. Whilst listening to the client the therapist monitors his or her own feelings, fantasies and reactions in response to the client's material. Theses are accepted as meaningful elements in the communications between client and therapist. How the client makes the therapist feel in the session may very likely reflect their impact on others outside of the session. This is referred to as the counter-transference.

At various times when the client is telling their story the therapist may reflect back, paraphrase or précis what the client has been telling them or acting out. Also, exploratory and information seeking responses attempt to draw out more information from the client. Theses are generated from hypotheses about what the client might not be saying in words but could be hinting at through behaviour or tone of voice. Information seeking responses are aimed at clarification, which helps sort out what is happening by questioning and rephrasing. When working with people who have intellectual disabilities there may be times when therapists need to help their clients communicate by helping them label objects, actions and feelings. Psychodynamic psychotherapists also make linking responses. Here, words and/or actions are linked together as a tentative interpretation to try and understand the nature of the client's anxiety in the session. These responses differ from the others in that they aim to elucidate unconscious feelings and ideas.

Psychodynamic therapists seek to understand with the client the latent or unconscious meaning of the client's communications. In order to do this they recontextualise the manifest content of the communications as transference (Smith 1987). Freud (1912) described transference as occurring when psychological experiences are revived and instead of being located in the past are applied to dealings with a person in the present. In psychodynamic psychotherapy the establishment, modalities, interpretation and resolution of the transference are, in fact, what define the cure (Laplanche and Pontalis 1988). Transference within therapy allows the therapist to identify interpersonal issues and deal with them as empirical data in the here-and-now. This process allows early traumatic experiences and empathic failures on the part of parents and other caregivers to be relived and corrected.

Psychodynamic psychotherapy also seeks to understand unconscious communications through models of the internal world. Most significantly, we all have an ego, which is the location of the anxiety caused by unconscious material. It is the ego that employs a range of defences to ward off anxiety. There are also a range of psychodynamic theories of development, which the therapist may employ to understand the origins or development of difficulties and conflicts, as well as coping styles. Clarkson (1993) highlights the reparative/developmentally-needed relationship and defines this as the internal provision by the therapist of a corrective/reparative or replenishing parental relationship (or action) where the original parenting

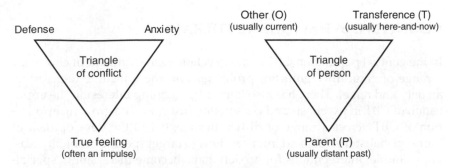

**Figure 7.1** Malan's triangles of conflict and the person.

was deficient, abusive or over- protective. Such a relationship modality is a further facet of the therapist's intervention and style.

Malan (1979) depicts the aim of psychotherapy in the form of the 'Two Triangles' (see Figure 7.1). The two triangles describe the process of psychodynamic psychotherapy. Each triangle stands on its apex. The aim of the therapeutic endeavour is to reach beneath the defence and anxiety to the true feeling. At this point, the true feeling can be traced back from the present transference location – the therapy room – to its origin in the past – usually to the relationship with parents or significant carers. For Malan (1979) 'The importance of these two triangles is that between them they can be used to represent almost every intervention that a therapist makes; and that much of the therapist's skill consists of knowing which parts of which triangle to include in his interpretation at any given moment' (p.91).

When making interpretations with people with intellectual disabilities it is preferable to make the links in parts, gradually developing it so that the client can retain what is being said. In psychodynamic therapy there is a dispute regarding whether interventions should be given when the client is in a state of negative transference. We would suggest that interpretations are made when transference is positive or negative for pragmatic reasons. First the client may have lost touch or can no longer recall the content of the dialogue later in a session or in later sessions. Also there is some evidence to suggest that people who have intellectual disabilities employ more primitive defence mechanisms, which can result in feelings and emotions being split off and disowned. However, when making any interpretations that aim to bring unconscious material into consciousness the therapist needs to assess that the client is emotionally able to hear it and begin to assimilate it. For illustrations of this process see Beail and Newman (2005) and Newman and Beail (2002). For an example of case formulation see Beail and Jackson (2008). Further case studies can be found in Sinason (1992) and Simpson and Miller (2004).

## COGNITIVE-BEHAVIOURAL THERAPY

In the general population CBT is the psychological treatment of choice for a range of clinically significant problems, and these include depression, anxiety and anger. There has also been a burgeoning interest in the application of CBT in psychosis and personality disorder. The growing application of CBT across a range of difficulties has led to the development of more specialist theories and interventions to target specific problem areas. For example, interventions for anxiety have become increasingly specialised as more elaborate cognitive models of such problems have developed (Clark and Wells 1995).

Cognitive-behavioural therapy for emotional problems is an approach that works essentially with the meaning that people attach to events or the nature of their self-evaluations (Beck *et al*. 1979; Ellis 1962). In other words, it works from the premise that people's perceptions of events influence their affect and behaviour. Therefore, beliefs and thinking styles contribute to clinically significant emotional problems and maladaptive patterns of behaviour. For example, depressed individuals may hold negative beliefs about their past present and future, and they are also likely to interpret events negatively even where there is little reason to do so. Low mood might also mean that they are unable to concentrate or gain pleasure from pastimes that they had previously enjoyed, leading to withdrawal and an increasing sense of hopelessness. Therefore, interventions usually consist of a package of approaches that work at a cognitive, emotional and behavioural level.

The growing literature about the use of CBT with people who have intellectual disabilities, along with evidence for its effectiveness, is discussed in Dagnan and Lindsay's chapter. They describe the attempts to adapt CBT and REBT interventions for people with intellectual disabilities that work with the meaning they attach to events. However, Dagnan and Lindsay also point out that many interventions with people who have an intellectual disability adopt a 'deficit' model. In other words it is assumed that people's cognitive deficits play a major role in their emotional difficulties. Hence, these deficits are addressed through educational or self-instruction type approaches dealing with topics like problem solving, assertiveness or anger management.

The basic premise of working cognitive behaviourally with people is that there is a collaborative relationship between the therapist and client, and that they work towards explicit goals. We have already discussed aspects of the relationship between client and therapist that are deemed necessary to engage in key components of the CBT process. Here we will consider the process of working towards changing people's patterns of thinking and beliefs. Then we will examine the 'outward focus' of therapy, and attempts to relate therapeutic work to real life and ultimately produce tangible change. Blackburn and Twaddle (1996) characterise this 'collaborative' process as being active and empirical in nature.

When CBT therapists work at a cognitive level they use techniques like Socratic questioning because they involve an active negotiation of meaning between the client and therapist. If the therapist adopts an educational or self-instructional type approach there may be less emphasis on a collaborative therapeutic relationship. Nevertheless, there remains an assumption that clients will have sufficient agency or sense of self-efficacy to be able to use the information they obtain to change the way they think, feel and behave. Findings from studies in the general population have shown that clients' level of motivation on starting CBT is the best predictor of positive outcome (Keisjers et al. 2000). It has been suggested that therapeutic techniques such as motivational interviewing, developed to help people with addictions, could be used with people who have intellectual disabilities at the outset to increase clients' motivation (Willner and Goodey 2006).

The main cognitive goal of CBT is to challenge or attempt to shift patterns of thinking or underlying beliefs that are maladaptive (Beck et al. 1979; Ellis 1962). For example, someone who is socially anxious may tend to believe that other people are laughing at her in public situations, despite being reassured that laughter has nothing to with her. The aim of the work would be to attempt to get her to become open to different possible interpretations of other people's laughter. If she becomes less sensitive in social situations and recognises that she is not always being picked on, then she should become less anxious. Yet challenging people to open up to different interpretations of their world does not mean that the therapist necessarily holds a more accurate or objective view of events. People with intellectual disabilities are likely to face stigmatised treatment. Hence, the aim may also be to work with the nature of clients' self and inter-personal beliefs that stem from such experiences. For example, the woman described above may have come to believe that she is going to be rejected by other people of her age group because they see her as 'stupid'.

CBT is a talking therapy, and people with intellectual disabilities may have difficulty discussing abstract thoughts and feelings. It is extremely important to recognise the limits of the approach and the fact that people require the ability to hold and articulate their views of events. Moreover, they need to be able to enter into a dialogue with another person and to realise that they may hold a different perspective from their own. There are growing attempts to systematically gather information about techniques that can be used to help people overcome communication problems or other difficulties arising from poor memory or concentration in therapy sessions (Whitehouse et al. 2006). These might include the use of flip charts to set out agendas and ways of using visual aids to bring points to life. For example, one can draw thought bubbles to represent different possible interpretations of the same events. Role-plays can provide an excellent way of exploring what happens in particular situations and how different interpretations can lead to different emotions and outcomes. Yet the purpose is not merely to increase understanding, but also to help clients play an active role in sessions. Thus, role-play should not be used to impose different views or ways of thinking but, as with Socratic questioning, to encourage clients to realise for themselves that there may be different interpretations of the same events.

For clients who are more likely to have an external locus of control, it is vital that the therapeutic process emphasises that they can play an active role in achieving positive change. To achieve this goal and in the empirical spirit of CBT, a considerable emphasis is placed on self-monitoring of thoughts, feelings and behaviour. However, many of the materials used in CBT for recording thoughts, feelings or behaviour require some level of literacy skills. Hence it is necessary to adapt existing materials or adopt new approaches in order to make them accessible for people with intellectual disabilities. For example, tape recorders or dictaphones can be given to people to use as personal diaries or simplified diaries with stickers can be adapted for recording purposes. Giving people a folder in which they can keep any materials that have been used in therapy, alongside homework tasks and recordings, can also help to instil a sense of engagement and control. In addition, keeping a record of therapy can also help to maintain continuity across sessions.

The other element likely to have an impact upon therapeutic work within sessions is the nature of the relationship or 'bond' between the client and therapist (Keijsers et al. 2000). CBT involves the therapist challenging the views and beliefs held by the client. Willner and Goodey (2006) have suggested that such challenges may be particularly uncomfortable for clients with intellectual disabilities. Yet this depends upon the emotional climate in which they are made. If the client likes, trusts and feels respected by the therapist then it would be fair to assume that the client would be reasonably tolerant of challenges, even if they evoked temporarily negative emotions. As an inter-personal process, it has been argued that one of the main routes of change in therapy sessions is through social influence (Safran and Segal 1990). Consequently, the therapist is going to have a greater impact if the client values their contribution.

The other key process issue concerns the 'outward' focus of CBT. In other words, CBT is about helping clients to make positive changes in their lives and not just in their heads. Hence, a key part of CBT interventions is the process of linking the work in sessions to clients' wider lives. This is achieved through the use of homework tasks where the clients are asked to seek empirical evidence to support the work being done in sessions. These homework tasks play a crucial role in both generalising the interventions to clients' everyday lives and in supporting the rationale for the work carried out in sessions. For example, the person described above who was socially anxious might be asked to go into a social situation between sessions to observe whether or not young people look in her direction when they are laughing or having fun. In other words, she is being asked to find out other reasons why young people laugh and joke in public settings. The B in the CBT package also means that interventions have a behavioural element, involving tasks such as graded exposure or scheduling pleasurable events. The difficulty for people with intellectual disabilities is that they may lack sufficient independence or confidence to follow through on these homework tasks. For example, someone might be unable to complete a graded exposure exercise or schedule pleasurable events without the support of staff or significant others in their lives.

The need to involve significant others in clients' lives taps into one of the strengths of psychological work with people who have intellectual disabilities, which is discussed in Dagnan and Lindsay's chapter of this book. Interventions have traditionally taken a psycho-social approach and worked both at an individual and systemic level (Clements 1997). Safran and Segal (1990) point out that people learn and change through experience in life rather than just in therapy. Therefore, being concerned with someone's employment status, social opportunities and relationships, or the autonomy that they are afforded, might all be crucial components of an intervention rather than long-term goals. For the anxious person described earlier, an important element of change could be to learn that she can enjoy relationships with others of her age group at a regular social activity. Rose et al. (2005) have also found that including staff alongside clients in cognitive-behavioural anger management groups leads to better outcomes than working with clients alone. It could be hypothesised that changing staff perceptions contributes to a shift in their relationships with the individuals concerned, which in turn reduces the level of conflict.

There are examples of cases in the literature where cognitive behavioural approaches have been adapted for people with intellectual disabilities presenting with a variety of emotional problems (Black et al. 1993; Lindsay et al. 1993; Willner and Goodey 2006).

## How Long Will Treatment Need to Be For?

There is no evidence base regarding the length of treatment required for successful outcomes with people with intellectual disabilities. Experimental research in the general population suggests that most people make most gains in eight to twelve sessions. Thereafter, there seem to be diminishing returns. The only study to evaluate this effect with people with intellectual disabilities found a similar effect (Beail, Kellett, Newman and Warden 2007). However, this was a naturalistic study with small participant groups. Psychoanalytic treatments are usually associated with longer-term interventions than time limited CBT approaches. However, published reports suggest that both psychoanalytic (Beail 1995; 2001; Beail *et al.* 2005) and CBT approaches (Willner, Jones, Tams and Green 2002, Taylor *et al.* 2005) show a range of treatment lengths from short to long-term. Research in the general population suggests that those with severe presentations tend to need longer treatment. Shorter-term interventions tend to be implicated when clients present with a single problem, which becomes the focus of work. Longer-term interventions, on the other hand, are not problem-focussed or goal-orientated and are more open-ended.

## Routine Evaluation of Outcomes

Whatever the length of treatment, we would encourage clinical psychologists to evaluate their clinical interventions through routine monitoring of outcomes (Beail 2004a; 2004b; Newman, Kellett and Beail 2003). Such assessments simply involve using a psychometric assessment tool relevant to the client's clinical problem as part of the assessment at intake and at termination. This could include a measure of problematic behaviours such as the Behaviour Problems Inventory (Rojahn *et al.* 2001), a single trait measure of Anger such as the Modified Novaco Anger Scale (Novaco and Taylor 2004; Taylor *et al.* 2005) or a multitrait measure such as the Brief Symptom Inventory (Kellett, Beail, Newman and Frankish 2003). Carefully developed single trait self-report measures such as the Glasgow Anxiety scales (Mindham and Espie 2003) may also prove helpful in formulating treatment and monitoring outcomes for the client. Psychodynamic psychotherapists also focus on interpersonal issues and so the Inventory of Interpersonal Problems has been used (Beail *et al.* 2005: Kellett, Beail and Newman 2005). Simple measures can also be tailored to assess changes in particular beliefs or behavioural goals that are the targets of intervention.

There are some counsellors and psychotherapists who object to the evaluation of outcome, as they believe that introducing an evaluative element into treatment has a negative impact on the therapeutic relationship. Others have no philosophical objection and just fail to make habitual use of such measures. However, at this early stage of adapting psychotherapeutic approaches for people with intellectual disabilities it is essential to develop an adequate evidence base to support their use. This is an area where the scientist practitioner model fits well, as our evidence base needs to be practice-based (Beail 2003, 2004a).

## CONCLUSIONS

This brief overview of process issues for psychodynamic psychotherapy and CBT with people who have intellectual disabilities needs to be treated with some caution, as there is a dearth of research evidence about establishing effective therapeutic relationships with this client group. Moreover, the issues may vary across problem areas and settings. For example, developing therapeutic relationships with people referred from the criminal justice system will be quite different from those seeking help for emotional problems in community settings.

Clinical psychologists who provide direct psychological interventions have also found that they sometimes have to adapt their working methods to involve significant others in people's lives and work with systems. People with intellectual disabilities are usually referred by someone else and then supported by them to access treatment. However, it is not the dependence but the interdependence of people with intellectual disabilities and their family or carers that has stimulated the use of systemic work alongside individual interventions. This represents an important shift from an intra-psychic model of CBT and psychodynamic psychotherapy towards a view that thoughts, beliefs and actions are socially embedded and negotiated. However, care has to be taken at all times to ensure that the individuals with intellectual disabilities do not become the junior partners in this negotiation. If this happens then it is likely to reinforce a sense of helplessness or a feeling that change can only be achieved through the actions of others. An external locus of control is a contra-indication of good outcome in psychological interventions (Foon 1987).

Willner and Goodey (2006) point to a number of possible barriers to working effectively with family members or support staff, including their psychological mindedness and motivation to change. There is also a danger that involving significant others in clients' lives may conflict with clients' own wish for a private therapeutic space, or leave them feeling that they are being talked about rather than to. The goal of providing clients with a therapeutic space to work on their difficulties is meant to be empowering. This is an important rationale for adopting a psychotherapeutic approach with a relatively disempowered group, who are rarely listened to or considered to have the potential to alter the direction of their lives. Moreover, many people with intellectual disabilities may have no one to confide in. For example, someone who is rather socially isolated and living at home with his parents may have no one with whom he can discuss his sexual concerns. From this point of view the confidential nature of the therapeutic relationship may be greatly valued by individuals with intellectual disabilities.

Significant difficulties may arise when clients feel trapped in an unhelpful therapeutic relationship, working with someone they do not relate well to. Given that people with intellectual disabilities usually find themselves in a relatively powerless position with figures in authority, it is quite easy to imagine how this could happen. Clients in the general population may be more likely to vote with their feet if they dislike their therapist. Even if the intellectually disabled client and therapist enjoy a good relationship, the client might still be reluctant to disagree with the therapist or raise concerns about the direction being taken. Once again, the therapist needs to be conscious of the wider social context of clients' lives and how this could affect the therapeutic communication and relationship, being careful to avoid making assumptions that the clients are on the same wavelength.

In addition to generating more data about process issues likely to affect outcome, it is also important to adopt a theoretical model for this work. Communication theory concerning dialogue (Linell *et al.* 1988) and the Assimilation Model promote analysis of dialogue as an interaction between communicative partners, rather than as the sum of each person's contributions. This enables analysis of the balance of power between the two communicative partners, and the ability of each to influence the direction and content of dialogue. Whilst helping to set a research agenda, these kinds of theoretical models can also guide practitioners in their work. Client and therapist variables are usually considered separately. On the one hand, there is concern to establish the kinds of abilities needed to engage constructively in psychotherapy. On the other, there have been efforts to adapt CBT and psychodynamic psychotherapy to make them more accessible. However, thought needs to be given to how these two elements can be combined. Research needs to examine how effective particular adaptations are in allowing people, with particular strengths or needs, to participate in psychodynamic psychotherapy and CBT. In the absence of evidence, practitioners need to think through how their adaptations foster or hinder the development of a good therapeutic relationship. Care should be taken to avoid over emphasis on technique, particularly at the outset of therapy. What remains paramount for non-disabled people receiving psychotherapy is that they feel they are listened to properly and understood (Keisjers *et al.* 2000). It seems reasonable to assume that this is also true for people with intellectual disabilities.

## References

Baum, S. and Lynggard, H. (2006) *Intellectual disabilities: A systemic approach.* London: Karnac.

Beail, N. (1995) Outcome of psychoanalysis, psychoanalytic and psychodynamic psychotherapy with people with intellectual disabilities: a review. *Changes*, **13**, 186–91.

Beail, N. (2003) What works for people with mental retardation? Critical commentary on cognitive-behavioral and psychodynamic psychotherapy research. *Mental Retardation*, **41**, 468–72.

Beail, N. (2004a) Method, design and evaluation in psychotherapy research. In E. Emerson, C. Hatton., T. Parmenter and T. Thompson, *International Handbook of Methods for Research and Evaluation in Intellectual Disabilities*. New York: John Wiley and Sons, Inc.

Beail, N. (2004b) Approaches to the evaluation of outcomes with work with developmentally disabled offenders. In W.R. Lindsay, J.L. Taylor and P. Sturmey (eds), *Offenders with Developmental Disabilities*. pp. 143–60, Chichester: John Wiley and Sons, Ltd.

Beail, N., Kellett, S., Newman, D.W. and Warden, S. (2007) The dose effect relationship in psychodynamic psychotherapy with people with intellectual disabilities. *Journal of Applied Research in Intellectual Disabilities*, **20**, 448–54.

Beail, N. and Jackson, T. (2008) Psychodynamic formulation. In P. Sturmey (ed.), *Varieties in Case Formulation*. New York: John Wiley and Sons, Inc.

Beail, N. and Newman, D. (2005) Psychodynamic counseling and psychotherapy for mood disorders. In P. Sturmey (ed.), *Mood Disorders in People with Mental Retardation*, pp. 273–92. New York: NADD Press.

Beail, N., Warden, S., Morsely, K. and Newman, D.W. (2005) A naturalistic evaluation of the effectiveness of psychodynamic psychotherapy with adults with intellectual disabilities. *Journal of Applied Research in Intellectual Disabilities*, **18**, 245–51.

Beck, A.T., Rush, A.J., Shaw, B.F. and Emery, G. (1979) *Cognitive Therapy of Depression*, New York, John Wiley and Sons, Inc.

Black, L. and Novaco, R. (1993) Treatment of Anger with a Developmentally Handicapped Man. In R.A. Wells and V.J. Giannetti (eds) *Casebook of the Brief Psychotherapies*. London: Plenum Press.

Blackburn, I.M. and Twaddle, W. (1996) *Cognitive Therapy in Action*. London: Souvenir Press.

Brown, D. and Peddar, J. (1991) *Introduction to Psychotherapy*, London: Methuen.

Bugental, J.E.T. (1987) *The Art of the Psychotherapist*. New York: W.W. Norton.

Clark, D.M. and Wells A. (1995) A cognitive model of social phobia. In R.G. Heimberg, M. Liebowitz, D. Hope, and F. Schcier (eds) *Social Phobia: Diagnosis, Assessment, and Treatment*, Pp. 69–93. Guilford: New York.

Clarkson, P. (1993) *On psychotherapy*. London: Whurr Publications.

Clements, J. (1997) Sustaining a cognitive psychology for people with learning disabilities. In Kroese, B.S., Dagnan, D. and Lumidis, E. (eds) *Cognitive Behaviour Therapy for People with Learning Disabilities*. London: Routledge.

Dagnan, D., Chadwick, P. and Proudlove, J. (2000) Toward an assessment of suitability of people with mental retardation for cognitive therapy. *Cognitive Therapy and Research*, **24**, 627–36.

Ellis, A. (1962) *Reason and Emotion in Psychotherapy*. New York: Lyle Stuart.

Foon, A.E. (1987) Locus of control as a predictor of outcome of psychotherapy. *British Journal of Medical Psychology*, **60**, 99–107.

Freud,. S. (1912) On Psychotherapy. In J. Strachey (ed.), *The Standard Edition of the Complete Psychological Works of Sigmund Freud* (Vol 12, p. 263).London: Hogarth Press.

Jahoda, A., Dagnan, D., Jarvie, P. and Kerr W. (2006) Depression, social context and cognitive behavioural therapy for people who have intellectual disabilities. *Journal of Applied Research in Intellectual Disabilities*, **19**(1), 81–9.

Keijsers, G.P., Schaap, C.P. and Hoogduin, C.A. (2000) The impact of interpersonal patient and therapist behavior on outcome in cognitive-behavior therapy: A review. *Behavior Modification*, **24**(2), 264–97.

Kellett, S., Beail, N. and Newman, D.W. (2005) Measuring interpersonal problems in adults with mild mental retardation. *American Journal on Mental Retardation*, **110**, 136–44.

Kellett, S., Beail, N., Newman, D. and Frankish, P. (2003) Utility of the Brief Symptom Inventory in the assessment of psychological distress. *Journal of Applied Research in Intellectual Disabilities*, **16**, 127–34.

Krose, B.S., Cushway, D. and Hubbard, C. (1998) The conceptualisation of dreams by people with learning disabilities. *Journal of Applied Research in Intellectual disabilities*, **11**, 146–55.

Kroese, B.S., Dagnan, D. and Loumidis, K. (1997) (eds). *Cognitive Behaviour Therapy for People with Learning Disabilities*. London: Routledge.

Laplanche, J. and Pontalis, J.B. (1988) *The Language of Psychoanalysis*. London: Karnac Books.

Lindsay, W., Howells, L., Pitcaithly, D. (1993) Cognitive therapy for depression with individuals with intellectual disabilities. *British Journal of Medical Psychology*, **66**, 135–41.

Linell, P., Gustavsson, L. and Juvonen, P. (1988) Interactional dominance in dyadic communication: A presentation of initative-response analysis. *Linguistics*, **26**(3), 415–42.

Malan, D.H. (1979) *Individual psychotherapy and the science of psychodynamics*. London: Butterworth.

Mindham, J. and Espie, C.A. (2003) Glasgow Anxiety Scale for people with intellectual disability (GAS-ID): development and psychometric properties of a new measure for use with people with mild intellectual disability, *Journal of Intellectual Disability Research*, **47**, 22–30.

Newman, D.W. and Beail, N. (2002) Monitoring change in psychotherapy with people with intellectual disabilities. The application of the Assimilation of Problematic Experiences Scale. *Journal of Applied Research in Intellectual Disabilities*, **15**, 48–60.

Newman, D.W. and Beail, N. (2005) An analysis of assimilation during psychotherapy with people who have mental retardation. *American Journal on Mental Retardation*, **110**, 359–65.

Newman, D.W., Kellett, S.C. and Beail, N. (2003) From research and development to practice based evidence: Clinical governance initiatives in a service for adults with intellectual disability and mental health needs. *Journal of Intellectual Disability Research*, **47**, 68–74.

Novaco, R.W. and Taylor, J.L. (2004) Assessment of anger and aggression in male offenders with developmental disabilities. *Psychological Assessment*, **16**, 42–50.

Rojahn, J., Matson, J.L., Lott, D., Esbensen, A.J. and Smalls, Y. (2001) The Behavior Problems Inventory: An instrument for the assessment of self-injury, stereotyped behavior, and aggression/destruction in individuals with developmental disabilities. *Journal of Autism and Developmental Disorders*, **31**, 577–88.

Rose, J., Loftus, M., Flint, B. and Carey, L. (2005) Factors associated with the efficacy of a group intervention for anger in people with intellectual disabilities. *British Journal of Clinical Psychology*, **44**, 305–18.

Safran, J. and Segal, Z. (1990) *Interpersonal Process in Cognitive Therapy*, New York: Basic Books.

Sinason, V. (1992) *Mental Handicap and the Human Condition: New Approaches from the Tavistock*. London: Free Associations.

Smith, D. (1987) Formulating and evaluating hypotheses in psychoanalytic psychotherapy. *British Journal of Medical Psychology*, **60**, 313–16.

Simpson, D. and Miller, L. (2004) *Unexpected Gains: psychotherapy with people with learning disabilities*. London: Karnac.

Taylor, J., Novaco, R.W., Gillmer, B.T., Robertson, A. and Thorne. I. (2005) Individual cognitive-behavioural anger treatment for people with mild-borderline intellectual disabilities and histories of aggression: A controlled trial. *British Journal of Clinical Psychology*, **44**, 367–82.

Tyson, R.L. and Sandler, J. (1971) Problems in the selection of patients for psychoanalysis: comments on the application of 'indications', 'suitability' and 'analysability'. *British Journal of Medical Psychology*, **44**, 211–29.

Waitman, A. and Conboy-Hill, S. (1992) *Psychotherapy and Mental Handicap*. London: Sage.

Whitehouse, R.M., Tudway, J.A., Look, R. and Stenfert-Krose, B. (2006) Adapting individual psychotherapy for adults with intellectual disabilities: A comparative review of cognitive behavioural and psychodynamic literature. *Journal of Applied Research in Intellectual Disabilities*, **19**, 55–65.

Willner, P. (2005) The effectiveness of psychotherapeutic interventions for people with learning disabilities: a critical overview. *Journal of Intellectual Disability Research*, **49**, 75–85.

Willner, P. and Goodey, R. (2006) Interaction of cognitive distortions and cognitive deficits in the formulation and treatment of obsessive-compulsive behaviours in a woman with an intellectual disability. *Journal of Applied Research in Intellectual Disabilities*, **19**, 67–74.

Willner, P., Jones, J., Tams, R. and Green, G. (2002) A randomized controlled trial of the efficacy of a cognitive-behavioural anger management group for clients with learning disabilities. *Journal of Applied Research in Intellectual Disabilities*, **15**, 224–35.

Zigler, E., Bennett-Gates, D., Hodapp, R., Henrich, C.C. (2002) Assessing personality traits of individuals with mental retardation. *American Journal on Mental Retardation*, **10**, 181–93.

# Chapter 8

# WORKING WITH FAMILIES

## Jo Bromley and Christine Mellor

## INTRODUCTION

It has long been recognised that having some knowledge of the
environment in which the referred client lives can be useful in formulating
hypotheses and deciding whether certain interventions will be viable or
acceptable. Functional analyses, for example, often take into consideration
where and with whom clients spend their time (see Chapter 11). From
a behavioural perspective, therefore, there are clear advantages to
interviewing families of clients with intellectual disabilities.

More recently, however, there has also been an upsurge of interest in the
application of systemic ideas and principles in working with families
where there is a member with an intellectual disability (see, e.g., Fiddell
2000). One of the basic premises of family therapy is that the family acts as
a self regulating, interdependent 'system'. This system can be described as
'an entity whose parts interact, co-vary and evolve with each other in
ways which maintain and protect existing patterns of living and adapt to
change by creating and promoting new patterns' (Burnham 1994). The
question such practitioners may ask is what function a particular behaviour
is serving for the whole family. The focus is firmly on examining how family beliefs and patterns of behaviour impact on the situation or behaviour
that is being defined as problematic.

## SHARING THE NEWS

One of the earliest points of contact a clinician may have with families
who have a member with an intellectual disability is shortly after that
family has been given a diagnosis. Various studies have shown that

*Clinical Psychology and People with Intellectual Disabilities*, Second Edition. Edited by
Eric Emerson, Chris Hatton, Kate Dickson, Rupa Gone, Amanda Caine and Jo Bromley.
© 2012 John Wiley & Sons, Ltd. Published 2012 by John Wiley & Sons, Ltd.

families are often dissatisfied with the manner in which this is done (e.g., Quine and Pahl 1986). Sloper and Turner (1993a) found that out of a sample of 107 parents of children with physical and/or intellectual disabilities, 52% were dissatisfied or very dissatisfied with how the news was broken. Factors related to higher levels of satisfaction included whether professionals disclosing the news had seemed sympathetic, had appeared to understand parental concerns, and were direct and open to questions. Greater satisfaction was also achieved if parents were allowed to come back and ask questions later. In a recent study looking at diagnosis of Autism, only 55% of parents were satisfied or very satisfied with the disclosure, with the manner of the professional remaining highly important, as well as parents being given written information (Brogan and Knussen 2003).

Parental dissatisfaction with how a diagnosis is given is certainly not inevitable (Hasnat and Graves 2000). A number of documents have now been produced that illustrate good practice when sharing the news to parents that their child has some kind of disability (e.g., Hedderly et al. 2003). These documents emphasise points such as seeing both parents together, giving enough time for a consultation, and having a time for follow up. Clinical psychologists may well have to share news around diagnoses such as Autism, but even if they are not involved directly, they may see a family shortly after the news has been given and should be sensitive to their needs at this point. There is also guidance as to how services should work together immediately after a diagnosis has been given so that a team is formed around a child to support that child and family (Together From the Start 2002).

Being told that your child has an intellectual disability and perhaps, some life threatening disorder, is something parents do not prepare for (for a personal account of this experience see Forrest 1992). The process of adjusting to a child's disability has often been compared to the stages outlined in grief and bereavement work. Cunningham has suggested that families go through four stages shock; reaction; adaptation and orientation (see Cunningham 1979; Cunningham and Davis 1985).

In the shock phase, parents are described as being confused and disbelieving. In the reaction phase, they begin to accept the diagnosis and start to recognise that their lives will need to change and adapt. Common emotions at this point can include anger, sorrow, disappointment, guilt and failure. In the adaptation phase, parents begin to ask about what can be done and how they can get help. Cunningham suggests this signals a move forward in that parents are seeking to gain a greater understanding of their child's condition and learn more about what they can do to support them. Whereas parents are still focused on the family at this point, by the orientation phase it is thought they are beginning to look outwards and start to develop routines for family life and make plans for the future.

As illustrated in Box 8.1; supporting parents through the assessment process and helping them express some of their hopes and fears at this time can be a valuable role for a clinician.

Formulating parents' responses according to stage theories can therefore be helpful in that it can help clinicians understand family reactions or family needs. However, it should not be forgotten that stage models only provide general guidelines. As indicated by the case study above, carers' responses are very individual and one carer may spend a lot longer in one stage than another. Parents' responses to their child's disability will depend greatly on their own beliefs about disability. These beliefs will have originated from their own experiences, from their family's views about disability and from societal and cultural indicators. As noted in Chapter 2 western society's views of disability have changed dramatically over the last century and it might therefore be expected that families might hold a number of different views on this issue. Families from other cultural groups may have different sets of beliefs although, as Shah (1992) points out, it should not be assumed that every family from an ethnic minority has one view of disability born of their primary culture.

With stage theories, it is also often assumed that all families pass through each stage smoothly and consecutively and will eventually reach a point where they will have resolved any conflict or distress (Blacher 1984). However, parents may move back and forth between stages and whilst they may be able to look to the future and plan ahead this does not mean they will necessarily have overcome feelings of loss. Similarly, just because the family may hear about a setback for their child and be temporarily shocked by this change, they may move quickly back to the orientation phase. Emotions that parents experience are often mediated by events in the family life cycle and by their own strategies for managing stress and coping with difficulties.

## LIFE CYCLE THEORY

In brief, life cycle theory (Carter and McGoldrick 1980) states that there are different stages that families usually go through as they grow and develop. The first stage involves two people becoming partners, then there is the birth of their first child, the birth(s) of subsequent children, children starting school, passing through adolescence to adulthood, leaving school and leaving home, retirement, death of parents/grandparents and children forming relationships. Movement to each new stage can be difficult for many families to negotiate, particularly if family members are at incongruent stages of the life cycle (e.g., if older children in the family have their own children close to the age of their youngest sibling).

## Box 8.1

Mr and Mrs F had three children aged 11, 7 and 3. Their youngest child, E, was referred to the Clinical Psychology service as he was displaying pica. During the assessment, Mr and Mrs F expressed concern that E seemed to be quite socially withdrawn compared to their other children. They noted that he tended to prefer playing by himself and made little eye contact with others, particularly strangers. E's speech was delayed quite significantly and they were currently seeing a speech and language therapist. Mr and Mrs F noted that E's paediatrician had mentioned that E might have 'autistic tendencies' but were unsure what this meant for E and whether, if he received more speech and language input, E might develop to a cognitive level that was similar to other children his age.

Whilst the initial referral had therefore been for behaviour management advice with regards to the pica, the issue which turned out to be more important for Mr and Mrs F was whether their son had a global developmental delay and/or features of autism. To clarify this issue, the psychologist instigated a multi agency assessment and supported the family through this process. When the family did receive a diagnosis of autism for their son; the clinical psychologist was able to offer some follow up to help parents understand more about their child's diagnosis.

During these follow up sessions, Mr and Mrs F explored their feelings about the word 'autism' and the images they had of their son growing up. Initially Mr F was unable to accept the possibility that there may be any long-term difficulties with his son. He was guilty about feeling embarrassed by his son's behaviour and since his daughters did not have any similar difficulties his initial thought was that it must have been something he had passed on genetically. Mrs F did not react in quite the same way as she said she had always felt something had been different about her youngest child. To some extent she said she was relieved that E was going to get extra help, however she was clearly confused and upset when she thought of his future and she was worried that she had contributed to his difficulties by continuing to work when he was a young child.

Both parents initially reported feeling quite alienated from their son and both had fears about what might happen if they decided to have any more children; would they have the same difficulties; how would E cope? Gradually, however, both parents came to realise that neither of them were to blame for E's difficulties. They still experienced periods of upset but they began to be more active about exploring different nursery placements for E and became more interested in joining the local branch of the National Autistic Society. They were also more able to see past the diagnostic label they had been given to look at the strengths and weaknesses of their child. All of these might indicate a move to the adaptation/orientation phases of Cunningham's model.

However, for families with a member with intellectual disabilities each stage will have slightly different meanings and may lead to increased family stress or conflict (Vetere 1993). When a child is ready to start school, for example, parents have to make the decision about whether they would like their child to be integrated into a mainstream school or attend a 'special' school. As the child with intellectual disabilities becomes a young adult, problems can arise if parents fail to renegotiate boundaries to give a young person more independence and allow them to take risks and have new experiences, or if they feel unable to let the person have a voice of their own (Konanc and Warren 1984). For the person with intellectual disabilities themselves, problems may arise at any point if they are prevented from completing different stages of the life cycle by other family members or by the state (e.g., if they wish to form a partnership or have children). At such points, families may need extra support to help the person or themselves negotiate that particular stage. Parker *et al.* (1987) describe an interesting group approach for helping families where there is a young adult with intellectual disabilities to discuss pertinent issues relating to the transition for that family member from child to adulthood.

How families cope at different stages of the life cycle will partly depend upon the stage each family member is at. If, for example, the child with intellectual disabilities is the youngest sibling and parents are older and have retired, there may be different pressures than in a family where the child with intellectual disabilities is the oldest sibling and parents are still expecting to care for younger children. Some studies (e.g., Selzer and Ryff 1994, cited in Floyd *et al.* 1996) have shown that parents might enjoy caring for an adult with intellectual disabilities as they view their child as a companion, someone with whom they can still share their life and maintain an important caring role. There may thus be a situation when an individual wishes to become more independent but is being hampered by their parents' caring role. When formulating any particular problem it can therefore be helpful to consider where the family is in its life cycle and what life cycle issues each member faces, and ask oneself why this particular family might have presented for help right now (see Box 8.2).

## STRESS AND COPING

Families with a member with intellectual disabilities do have certain issues to face that families without a member with intellectual disabilities do not. Often they experience very real economic and social restrictions that can lead to extra pressures being placed on their physical and mental health (Emerson and Hatton 2007). However, a common misconception is that all family members are more stressed just because they are living with someone with intellectual disabilities. Indeed, there is evidence to

## Box 8.2

N, a 16 year-old young man with moderate intellectual disabilities, was referred by his GP as his mother was concerned that he seemed to have become quite withdrawn. He attended the initial assessment with his mother, Ms D who spoke for most of the interview. She noted that N had been spending a lot of time on his own in his room rather than with her in the lounge. She also said that he no longer seemed keen to go out for walks with the family and was reluctant to go to the local after school club even though he used to enjoy it. Ms D noted that she was a single parent and had one daughter aged, 26 and another son aged 18. N had been very close to his sister who had just married and left home. Ms D said N's relationship with his brother was something of a 'love-hate' one as although they moments of being very close they also tended to fight and his brother would tease N. This was something that angered his mother, however, N's brother was about to go to university and she was hoping N's mood might improve when he was not around.

From a life cycle perspective; it could be hypothesised that N was actually feeling quite sad about his sister leaving and his brother's imminent departure. Perhaps their leaving highlighted his feelings of being 'different' and being left behind with his mother. This may have been the case with many young adults his age without a learning disability although one could hypothesise that they could establish some independence from their parents and may be allowed out with their friends as and when they wished. Could the fact that his siblings were leaving, lead N's mother to be more over protective than usual and less able to allow N his own space to develop? Given N's age and his developmental stage, would it not be normal for him to be spending more time in his room away from his mother? Subsequent discussions with the family revealed that N had very few social contacts outside his family although his brother and sister often had friends round. Another hypothesis was therefore that he was now at an age when he felt his disability more keenly and perhaps could be feeling quite depressed about his social life in comparison to his peers, as well as feeling low about his siblings leaving.

suggest that many families cope very well with the extra pressures placed on them (Byrne *et al.* 1988; Carr 2005). Where once it was assumed that parents of children with intellectual disabilities, particularly mothers, would have very high stress levels compared to mothers of children without intellectual disabilities, it is now recognised that the amount of stress any family member might feel is individual and will change over time (Byrne and Cunningham 1985). Undoubtedly some family members will be very distressed and experience high levels of stress at some times, but others seem to cope well and there seems to be a complex relationship between potential stressors, families' resources and individual thinking styles which can dictate levels of stress within individual family members.

What seems to make some families more vulnerable to stress than others? Vulnerability factors relating to the child include: severe levels of disability; extreme levels of activity; the existence of behaviour problems; poor sleep patterns; communication difficulties and the presence of physical health problems. Factors linked to the parents and family include: social isolation; economic difficulties; marital problems; lack of family closeness; and a high number of life events and the use of more passive coping strategies such as wishful thinking (i.e., wishing the situation was different) or avoidance. There is also evidence that, as with sharing the news, the attitude of professionals can either increase or lower family stress.

Factors which seem to promote resilience to stress include: having a supportive social network; meeting parents who are in similar situations; marital satisfaction; material wealth and resources; good health within the family; good communication between family members; ability to maintain a positive outlook whilst having a realistic view of their child's disability; and the use of good problem solving techniques and more active coping strategies, such as asking for help and support from services when it is needed (see, e.g., Dale 1996; Floyd and Gallagher 1997; Heiman 2002; Kelso et al. 2005; Quine and Pahl 1985; Sloper and Turner 1993b).

When considering how best to conceptualise stress and coping in families with a member with intellectual disabilities, many studies have explored the cognitive behavioural model described by Lazarus and Folkman (1984). According to this theory, when faced with a new situation, individuals will evaluate how important that event is to them and whether they have the resources to deal with it. The individual thus decides whether an event is potentially challenging (i.e., they have the resources to master it) or threatening (they do not have the resources and are in danger of losing something). Resources may mean financial backup or degree of social support or professional assistance. Whether a particular event is considered threatening and stressful at any one time therefore depends on many factors. These include an individual's perception of the support they have both inside and outside the family, their attributions about the resources needed to cope and the importance of the situation to them. Various questionnaires have been designed to measure stress and coping such as the Ways of Coping Questionnaire (Knussen et al. 1992) and it is important to consider family members' coping styles and attributions in assessment and formulation.

Hassell *et al*. (2005) explored parenting cognitions, self esteem and locus of control in relation to parenting stress. They found that having low parenting self esteem and a more external locus of control contributed to higher levels of parenting stress. Indeed, they suggested that these two factors together with the severity of a child's behaviour, accounted for over half the variance in parenting stress. Having positive wider support networks was also important but the relationship between parents stress and level of support seemed mediated by the locus of parenting control suggesting that family support was important in so much that it increased mothers' sense of having an internal locus of control. Research such as this emphasises the need to consider how parental cognitions fit into your formulation of a child's difficulties and it recognises that cognitive work with parents may be just as much a priority as behavioural work with the child (see section on CBT interventions).

## SIBLINGS

Just as the emotional well-being of parents may at times be compromised by the additional requirements of caring for a child with intellectual disabilities, the social and emotional adjustment of the child's siblings may also be expected to be disrupted. Shulman (1988) suggests the following possible mechanisms for this disruption:

- Changes in the parent–child interaction as the parent may be less available due to the demands and additional needs of the child with intellectual disabilities.
- Changes in family organisation as routines and activities may be altered in order to fit with the needs of the child with intellectual disabilities.
- Changes in the role the non-disabled child may be given in the family, e.g they may be given additional caring responsibilities.

In addition, where the child presents with challenging or unusual behaviours, the siblings may respond with feelings of distress or embarrassment, particularly with peers (Roeyers and Mycke 1995).

Several studies exploring the social and emotional adjustment of siblings of individuals with intellectual disabilities, have in fact produced findings suggesting overall good psychological adjustment and positive sibling relationships (Burton and Parks 1994; Heller and Arnold 2010; Rodrigue *et al*. 1993; Roeyers and Mycke 1995). From a meta-analysis of 25 studies, Rossiter and Sharpe (2001) however conclude there to be an overall small negative effect on children of having a sibling with intellectual disabilities. There is some evidence to suggest that the risk of negative outcomes, may be greater for siblings of children with autism than for siblings of children with intellectual disabilities alone (Fisman *et al.* 2000; Rodrigue *et al.* 1993), however other studies suggest there to be no difference (Kaminsky and Dewey 2002; Pilowsky *et al.* 2004).

Thus, it would appear that although many siblings of children with intellectual disabilities are well adjusted, in certain circumstances some may develop problems. Although studies of risk factors have produced contradictory findings, there is some suggestion that as with typical families, family characteristics such as parent stress, problem-solving and communication style, appear to be some of the most powerful influences on adjustment (Giallo and Gavidia-Payne 2006). Interventions aimed at addressing these factors may impact positively on siblings but in some cases, direct work with siblings is indicated.

Where direct work is indicated, it should be borne in mind that genetic factors related to certain disabilities and disorders, may be shared by siblings but expressed to a lesser degree. Siblings may present with cognitive limitations or particular behaviours that do not reach thresholds for clinical diagnoses, but that still impact on their social and emotional functioning, (Pilowsky *et al.* 2004). Intervention may therefore be required to address these needs directly. Where intervention offered focuses more on helping the child gain a better understanding of their sibling, such support may be provided on an individual basis or in a group format, with groups having the added advantage of providing contact with other children and young people with siblings with intellectual disabilities (Evans, Jones and Mansell 2001). Helpful books and resources specifically aimed at siblings are available through national organisations such as MENCAP or the the National Autisitc Society (NAS).

## THE FAMILY INTERVIEW

### Who to Invite?

Clearly, to assess some of the issues above there are going to be times when you want to interview different family members. One of the first points to consider is who to invite to a family session and when to invite them. If you have been seeing the person with intellectual disabilities as an individual client it may be that this is negotiated with them. Alternatively, when you receive a referral for a client you may decide to invite the whole family to come to the initial session and work individually with the named client at a later point. Basically, there are no hard and fast rules and you should negotiate with the client and family what seems most helpful.

## Joining Other Professionals

As families with children with disabilities have many appointments, it may be worth considering whether you can join any other professional for the first session (e.g. the speech therapist or paediatrician). Many families report feeling annoyed and stressed at having to repeat basic developmental and family information to different professionals over and over again and guidance from the National Service Framework and government supported projects such as the 'Early Support Pack' (Department of Education 2004) direct professionals to coordinate their appointments with others.

## Including the Person with Intellectual Disabilities

It is clearly important to ensure the person with intellectual disabilities is included in family sessions, wherever possible. If the person can speak or sign they then have an opportunity to comment on what they feel is happening within the family and can respond to comments others make. The therapist is also in a better position to observe how family members react to and communicate with this person. Does the person with intellectual disabilities have one particular advocate in the family? Do family members contradict each other in how they respond to the person with intellectual disabilities? Who interacts most/least with the referred person and who do they choose to interact with?

## Describing the Problem?

As with any interview it is useful to begin with questions about whatever the family feel they have a problem with. This will elucidate whether family members do have the same ideas and recognise a similar problem or whether their ideas are more diverse. If the 'problem' being described relates to the referred person's behaviour, a full behavioural assessment may be completed as usual. However, having all family members present does mean there is the chance to highlight any discrepancies in terms of how problematic behaviour is handled within the family, learn more about what functions that problem might be serving in the family, and discover family members' different beliefs and attributions about that problem. As Floyd et al. (1996) point out, families with a member with intellectual disabilities may be very used to accessing services for that family member. However, like any other family, those with an intellectually disabled member will still have crisis points and may have to cope with separation, divorce or the reconstitution of two families as parents remarry. These issues may be particularly pertinent and the initial goal of therapy may be to help families identify what part of the 'problem' is to do with disability and what is to do with other external or environmental issues. Some families who are still adjusting to the news that their child has a disability might come hoping that this can be 'fixed'. In this case, it may be one of the first goals of therapy to address this and help the family look at what exact difficulties they or their child is experiencing that together you might be able to modify.

## Systemic Interview Techniques

In meeting with the family as a whole, you may want to consider using assessment techniques appropriated from the systemic literature. For example, geneograms can be a useful way to elucidate recent life changes; gain some perspective on family life cycle issues and assess the degree of support a family might have available to them. The act of drawing up a geneogram is also one way to include the whole family, including the referred person.

When considering questioning style, it may also be useful to think about using circular questions. The aim of using circular questions is to encourage family members to think beyond linear causation, raise their awareness of family relationships and consider alternative ways of acting for the future (see Tomm 1985). By definition, a circular question has to refer to two or more entities that are external to the person being questioned.

Circular questions have been divided into various different categories (see Burnham 1994; Mason 1991; Tomm 1985). These include questions relating to relationship differences, classification or ranking questions, questions focusing on one behavioural sequence, hypothetical or future questions and diachronic (now/then) questions. Examples of each are given in Table 8.1. It is important to note that some questions can belong to more than one category. A question designed to produce change rather than just elicit information is sometimes referred to as a reflexive question (Tomm 1987).

To understand a circular question, one clearly needs the ability to conceptualise family relationships in some way and it may be thought that this would preclude the use of such questions with people with intellectual disabilities. However, recent articles by Fiddell (1996) and Salmon (1996) indicate that circular questioning and other systemic techniques can be used effectively with people with intellectual disabilities. Questions may simply need adapting and more visual aids and markers may need to be included in the session. Fiddell refers to a comprehensive paper by Benson (1991) which explores the use of circular questions with children. When discussing relationship differences Benson has tried using role plays to help elicit children's views about

**Table 8.1** Examples of some circular questions.

| Question type | Focus | Examples |
|---|---|---|
| Relationship differences | Aim is to explore different relationship patterns within a family group | Who gets most upset when Shamila doesn't talk to them; your mum or your dad? Who likes it best when A |
| Classification/ ranking | Respondent is asked to rank items in some way | Who do you think gets most upset in your family? Who would you argue with most? Who is most likely to agree with Nick? If your brother isn't there; who's most likely to agree with Nick? |
| Behavioural sequence | Encourage families to reflect on what happens when a particular behaviour occurs. These are the types of questions that might be asked in a functional analysis | What does your mum do when Steve hits your brother? What does your stepdad do then? What does Steve do when your stepdad responds like that? |
| Hypothetical/ future | Can help the family acknowledge ideas they already have about the future and consider alternative ideas and possibilities | Lets suppose David finds a place where he does want to live, who will be the first to celebrate with him? How will you know when Louis is feeling less sad? If you thought Louis was never going to feel any better, what would your mum have to do to make sure he had some happy times? |
| Diachronic | Encourage families to look at time differences; compare the past, present and future | Do you think your sister was more aggressive towards you before Dad moved out or after? What was different about Sarah before she started high school compared to now? |

other family members (e.g., by encouraging children to use props like hats and scarves to act as if they are someone else in the family). Benson also suggests videoing the family and then using the video with them to explore different patterns of interaction and ask behavioural sequence questions.

With regard to classification questions, Benson discusses the use of pictures of smiling and frowning faces and asking children 'Which one of these is most like what you and your brother have been like this week? As discussed in Chapters 7 and 15 there is evidence that people with intellectual disabilities can use rating scales. Thus there seems no reason why visual rating scales could not be used to back up classification or ranking questions in a session. Benson also discusses the use of pictures and cartoons to convey certain ideas. Again there seems to be no reason why similar ideas could not be used in family sessions where there is a person with an intellectual disability. People with intellectual disabilities are commonly talked over and about and it could be argued that circular questions might be seen to reinforce this practice if the question is not asked to all family members and if attempts are not made to hear the person with disability's views too. The challenge to the therapist is perhaps in seeing how inventive they can be. Questions taken from the field of Brief Solution Focused Therapy can also be helpful in conceptualising families' goals and ideals (Lloyd and Dallos 2006).

Questioning families will reveal certain patterns of relationships and reflecting on these patterns might provide valuable insights into the 'problem' that the family brings. Minuchin (1974) was one of the first to talk about family enmeshment and disengagement. In an enmeshed family one might see extreme closeness with enmeshed family members being unwilling to stand alone and act in an individual way. Disengagement represents under- rather than over-involvement in the family, with some members appearing distant to others. In enmeshed relationships, boundaries between the different roles of family members are likely to be blurred and diffuse, whereas in disengaged relationships they seem firm and inflexible. One parent might become particularly enmeshed with their child with intellectual disabilities, for example, which might make it harder for that family to negotiate life cycle stages where the child might have to become more independent (e.g., when they start school or leave home). Such an enmeshed relationship might also then impact on other siblings in the family, as noted earlier, and their relationship with their carer might be characterised more by disengagement. Whilst exploration of this and other systemic concepts and interventions (including an emphasis on narrative work) are outside the scope of this chapter, those interested should review Burnham (1994); Fidell (2000) or Baum and Walden (2006) and consider seeking some systemic supervision.

## BEHAVIOURAL AND COGNITIVE BEHAVIOURAL INTERVENTIONS

At some stage in your interaction with the family, as well as exploring family relationships in a systemic way and considering parental attributions, there will almost definitely be a point where behavioural programmes are considered. As behavioural assessment, formulation and intervention are covered in Chapter 11, we have kept this chapter more focused on systemic interviewing. However, behavioural theory still underpins much of the work completed with families who have a family member with an intellectual disability as the main cause of referral is often related to challenging behaviour.

There is considerable evidence to suggest that parents of people with intellectual disabilities can learn to use behavioural techniques effectively to better understand and manage challenging behaviours (Arndorfer et al. 1994; Baker 1996; Hudson et al. 2003; O'Reilly and Lancioni 2001). Behavioural intervention may focus on specific behaviours, e.g. sleep problems, or on learning general techniques which may be applied to a range of behaviours. In addition to helping to reduce the difficult to manage behaviour, positive outcomes of behavioural training with parents may include, reduction in parent stress and increased perception of control over the behaviour (Hudson et al. 2003; Wiggs and Stores 2001).

However, all interventions need to be collaborative (National Service Framework for Children Young People and Maternity Services, Department of Health, 2004) and the therapist will need to make some assessment of what internal and external resources the family have available to them in order to ensure the behavioural programme on offer can achieve maximum efficacy with minimum family stress (Allen 1999). Some families need extra respite and other social support to be available before a programme can be considered (Emerson 2003).

There is some evidence to suggest that parental stress may be a predictor of poorer outcome in behavioural programmes and that behavioural interventions may be more successful if parental stress is dealt with first (Baker et al. 1991; Rhodes 2003). As noted earlier, some of the mediators of parental stress are parental beliefs and cognitions about their child and their own parenting. Using cognitive behavioural therapy to try and address unhelpful attributions and cognitive biases can be an extremely helpful in decreasing parental stress and may well be a precursor to beginning behavioural work with the child (Hasting and Beck 2004; Turk 1998). As described below, there is some evidence for group as well as individual cognitive work with parents.

## PARENTING GROUPS

Behavioural training may be carried out with individuals or in groups and there would appear to be little difference in effectiveness between the two (Brightman et al. 1982; Chadwick et al. 2001). One of the advantages of

greater scope for focusing on
generally more cost-effective
vith greater social support and

conduct disorders who do not
ased on behavioural principles,
interest (e.g., Webster-Stratton
nce to support the use of these
ellectual disabilities and it could
uld need tailoring to meet the
because their focus is on the
to gain adult attention which,
population, is one that underes-
by challenging behaviour of
renting groups targeted at par-
luding some understanding of
more appropriate.
been various targeted group
erstand their child's diagnosis,
lenging behaviour and research
elpful and supportive (Shields

to group interventions which
le parental stress and negative
ducted a study with a group of

parents with children with intellectual disabilities who showed high levels of self-blame and guilt. Parents were seen in a group format and cognitive behavioural techniques were used to challenge commonly held negative assumptions about their children and their roles as parents, with the result that levels of depression in parents and incidence of guilty and negative automatic thoughts decreased (see Nixon, 1992 cited in Floyd et al. 1996, for details of how to obtain a treatment manual). In a review of a number of studies of group interventions, Hastings and Beck (2004) conclude there to be a 'reasonable evidence base' for the effectiveness of cognitive behavioural group therapy in reducing stress in parents of children with intellectual disabilities.

## INDIVIDUAL WORK

Involving family members invariably remains important even when engaging the person with intellectual disabilities in individual work. For example, in recent years there has been a growing acceptance that people with intellectual disabilities can engage in cognitive behavioural therapy (Stenfert-Kroese et al. 1997). When undertaking such work, family members can be enlisted to act as co-therapists providing support between sessions, for example by prompting and reinforcing the use of coping strategies in situ. In addition, evidence from research with typically-developing children suggests that involving family members also allows for addressing any issues the family have which may be serving to maintain the person's presenting problem, e.g. overprotective parenting style leading to reinforcement of anxious avoidant behaviour (Bogels and Siqueland 2006).

## ENDING THERAPY

Often, one of the most difficult questions to answer is when involvement with a family should end. Life cycle changes are constant and mean that fresh dilemmas will be faced by families as time passes. In general, it should help if clear goals are set at the beginning of therapy with regards to what specific tasks or difficulties the family want help with. It will then be easier to take baseline measures, monitor change and establish when the tasks of therapy have been completed. It is not always easy to find measures that have valid norms for children or adults with intellectual disabilities but being able to set some sort of goal with a family and measure the family's success in achieving this goal, even if it is only on a 10 point visual analogue scale, can be extremely useful. Part of the therapeutic role may also be to give families information about local self help and support groups, as well as advocacy services who can support them more appropriately in the longer term.

## References

Allen, D. (1999) Mediator Analysis: an overview of recent research on carers supporting people with intellectual disability and challenging behaviour. *Journal of Intellectual Disability Research*, **43**, 325–39.
Arndorfer, R.E., Miltenberger, R.G., Woster, S.H., Rortveldt, A.K. and Gaffaney, T. (1994) Home-based descriptive and experimental analysis of problem behaviours in children. *Topics in Early Childhood Special Education*, **14**, 64–87.
Baker, B.L. (1996) Parent training. In *Manual of Diagnosis and Professional Practice in Mental Retardation* (ed. J.W. Jacobson and J.A. Mulick). American Psychological Association: Washington DC.
Baker, B.L., Landen, S.J. and Kashima, K.J. (1991) Effects of parent training on families of children with mental retardation: Increased burden or generalised benefit? *American Journal on Mental Retardation*, **96**, 127–36.
Baum, S. and Walden, S. (2006) Setting up and evaluating a family therapy service in a community team for people with intellectual disabilities. In S. Baum & H. Lyngaard (Eds.) Intellectual disabilities: A systemic approach. London: Karnac.
Benson, M.J. (1991) Accessing children's perceptions of their family: Circular questioning revisited. *Journal of Marital and Family Therapy*, **4**, 363–72.

Blacher, J. (1984) Sequential stages of parental adjustment to the birth of a child with handicaps: Fact or artifact? *Mental Retardation*, **22**, 55–68.

Blacher, J., Neece, C. and Paczkowski, E. (2005) Mental Retardation and developmental disorders. *Current Opinion in Psychiatry*, **18**(5), 507–13.

Bogels, S.M. and Siqueland, L. (2006) Family cognitive behavioural therapy for children and adolecents with clinical anxiety disorders. *Journal of American Academy of Child and Adolescent Psychiatry*, **45**(2), 134–41.

Brightman, R.P., Baker, B.L., Clark, D.B. and Ambrose, S.A. (1982) Effectiveness of alternative parent training formats. *Journal of Behaviour Therapy and Psychiatry*, **13**, 113–17.

Brogan, C.A. and Knussen, C. (2003) The Disclosure of a Diagnosis of an Autistic Spectrum Disorder: Determinants of Satisfaction in a Sample of Scottish Parents. *Autism*, **7**, 31–45.

Burnham, J. (1994) *Family Therapy*. Routledge: London.

Burton, S.L. and Parks, A.L. (1994) Self-esteem, locus of control and career aspirations of college-age siblings of individuals with disabilities. *Social Work Research*, **18**(3), 178–85.

Byrne, E.A. and Cunningham, C.C. (1985) The effects of mentally handicapped children on families: A conceptual review. *Journal of Child Psychology and Psychiatry*, **26**, 847–64.

Byrne, E.A., Cunningham, C.C. and Sloper, P. (1988) *Families and Their Children with Down's Syndrome: one feature in common*. Routledge: London.

Carr, J. (2005) Families of 30–35 year olds with Dow's Syndrome. *Journal of Applied Research in Intellectual Disabilities*, **18**, 75–84.

Carter, E.A. and McGoldrick, M. (1980) *The Family Life Cycle: a framework for family therapy*. Gardner: New York.

Chadwick, O., Momcilovic, N., Rossiter, R., Stumbles, E. and Taylor, E. (2001) A randomised trial of brief individual versus group parent training for behaviour problems in children with severe learning disabilities. *Behavioural and Cognitive Psychotherapy*, **29**, 151–67.

Cunningham, C.C. (1979) Parent counselling. In *Tredgold's Mental Retardation* (12th edn) (ed. M. Craft). Tindall: London.

Cunningham, C.C. and Davis, J. (1985) *Working with Parents: frameworks for collaboration*. Open University Press: Milton Keynes.

Dale, N. (1996) *Working with Families of Children with Special Needs: partnership and Practice*. Routledge: London.

Department of Education and Skills (2002) *Together from the start*. London: DES. http://www.dfes.gov.uk/sen.

Department for Education (2004) Early Support Programme. http://www.education.gov.uk/childrenandyoungpeople/SEN/earlysupport.

Department of Health (2004) *National Service Framework for Children, Young People and Maternity Services*. http://www.dh.gov.uk/PolicyandGuidance.

Emerson E. (2003) Mothers of children and adolescents with intellectual disability: Social and economic situation, mental health status and the self assessed social and psychological impact of the child's difficulties. *Journal of Intellectual Disability Research*, **47**, 385–99.

Emerson, E. and Hatton, C. (2007) *The Mental Health of Children and Adolescents with Learning Disabilities in Britain*. Institute for Health Research, Lancaster University. Lancaster.

Evans, J., Jones, J. and Mansell, I. (2001) Supporting siblings: Evaluation of support groups for brothers and sisters of children with learning disabilities and challenging behaviour. *Journal of Learning Disabilities*, **5**(1), 69–78.

Fiddell, B. (1996) Making family therapy user friendly for learning disabled clients. *Context*, **26**, 11–13.

Fiddell, B. (2000) Exploring the use of family therapy with adults with a learning disability. *Journal of Family Therapy*, **22**, 308–23.

Fisman, S., Wolf, L., Ellison, D. and Freeman, T. (2000) A longitudinal study of children with chronic disabilities. *Canadian Review of Psychiatry*, **45**(4), 369–75.

Floyd, F.J., Singer, G.H.S., Powers, L.E. and Costigan, C.L. (1996) Families coping with mental retardation: Assessment and therapy. In *Manual of Diagnosis and Professional Practice in Mental Retardation* (ed. J.W. Jacobson and J.A. Mulick). American Psychiatric Association: Washington DC.

Floyd, F.J. and Gallagher, E.M. (1997) Parental stress, care demands, and use of support services for school age children with disabilities and behaviour problems. *Family Relations: Interdisciplinary Journal of Applied Family Studies*, **46**(4), 359–71.

Forrest, L. (1992) Dream on. *Learning Together Magazine*, **2**, 4–8.

Giallo, R. and Gavidia-Payne, S. (2006) Child, parent and family factors as predictors of adjustment for siblings of children with a disability. *Journal of Intellectual Disability Research*, **50**(12), 937–48.

Government's Annual Report on Learning Disability (2005). Valuing People: Making things better. http://dh.gov.uk/en/Publicationsandstatistics.

Harris, S.L. (1986). Parents as teachers: A four to seven year follow up of parents of children with autism. *Child and Family Behaviour Therapy*, **8**, 39–47.

Hasnat, M. J. and Graves, P. (2000) Disclosure of developmental disability: A study of parent satisfaction and the determinants of satisfaction. *Journal of Paediatric Child Health*, **36**, 32–5.

Hassell, R., Rose, J. and McDonald, J. (2005) Parenting stress in mothers of children with an intellectual disability: the effects of parental cognitions in relation to child characteristics and family support. *Journal of Intellectual Disability Research*, **49**(6), 405–18.

Hastings, R.P. and Beck, A. (2004) Practitioner review: Stress intervention for parents of children with intellectual disabilities. *Journal of Child Psychology and Psychiatry*, **45**(8), 1338–49.

Hedderly, T., Baird, G. and McConachie, H. (2003) Parental reaction to disability. *Current Paediatrics*. **13**, 30–5.

Heiman, T. (2992) Parents of Children with Disabilities: Resilience, Coping and Future Expectations. *Journal of Developmental and Physical Disabilities*, **14**(2), 159–71.

Hudson, A.M., Matthews, J.M., Gavidia-Payne, S.T., Cameron, C.A., Mildon, R.L., Radler, G.A. and Nankeris, K.L. (2003) Evaluation of an intervention system for parents of children with intellectual disability and challenging behaviour. *Journal of Intellectual Disability Research*, **47**, 238–49.

Kaminsky, L. and Dewey, D. (2002) Psychosocial adjustment in siblings of children with autism. *Journal of Child Psychology and Psychiatry*, **43**(2), 225–32.

Kelso, T., French, D. and Fernandez, M. (2005) Stress and coping in primary caregivers of children with a disability: a qualitative study using the Lazarus and Folkman Process Model of Coping. *Journal of Research in Special Educational Needs*, **5**(1), 3–10.

Knussen, C., Sloper, P., Cunningham, C.C. and Turner, S. (1992) The use of The Ways of Coping Questionnaire (Revised) with parents of children with Down's Syndrome. *Psychological Medicine*, **22**, 775–86.

Konanc, J.T. and Warren, N.J. (1984) Graduation: Transitional crisis for mildly developmentally disabled adolescents and their families. *Family Relations Journal of Applied Family and Child Studies*, **33**, 135–42.

Lazarus, R.S. and Folkman, S. (1984) *Stress, Appraisal and Coping*. Springer: New York.

Lloyd.H. and Dallos, R. (2006) Solution-focused Brief Therapy with Families who have a child with Intellectual Disabilities: A Description of the Content of Initial Sessions and the Processes. *Clinical Child Psychology and Psychiatry*, **11**(3), 367–8.

Mason, B. (1991) *Handing Over*. Karnac Books.

McConachie, H., Randle, V., Hammal, D. and Le Couteur, A. (2005) A controlled trial of a training course for parents of children with suspected Autism Spectrum Disorder. *The Journal of Paediatrics*. 335–40.

Minuchin, S. (1974) *Families and Family Therapy*. Tavistock: London.

National Institute for Health and Clinical Excellence (2006) *Conduct Disorder in children – parent-training/education programmes in the management of children with conduct disorders*. http://www.nice.org.uk.

Nixon, C.D. and Singer, G.H.S. (1993) Group cognitive behavioural treatment for excessive parental self blame and guilt. *American Journal of Mental Retardation*, **97**, 665–72.

O'Reilly, M.F. and Lancioni, G.E. (2001) Treating food refusal in a child with Williams syndrome using the parent as therapist in the home setting. *Journal of Intellectual Disability Research*, **45**(1), 41–6.

Parker, T., Hill, J.W. and Miller, G. (1987) Multiple family therapy: Evaluating a group experience for mentally retarded adolescents and their families. *Family Therapy*, **14**, 43–51.

Pilowsky, T., Yirmiya, N., Doppelt, O., Gross-Tsur, V. and Shalev, R.S. (2004) Social and emotional adjustment of siblings of children with autism. *Journal of Child Psychology and Psychiatry*, **45**(4), 855–65.

Quine, L. and Pahl, J. (1985) Examining the causes of stress in families with severely mentally handicapped children. *British Journal of Social Work*, **15**, 501–17.

Quine, L. and Pahl, J. (1986) First diagnosis of severe mental handicap: Characteristics of unsatisfactory encounters between doctors and patients. *Social Science and Medicine*, **22**, 53–62.

Rhodes, P. (2003) Behavioural and family systems interventions in developmental disability: Towards a contemporary and integrative approach. *Journal of Intellectual and Developmental Disability Research*, **28**, 51–64.

Roeyers, H. and Mycke, K. (1995) Siblings of children with autism, with mental retardation and with normal development. Child: Care, *Health and Development*, **21**, 305–19.

Rossiter, L. and Sharpe, D. (2001) The siblings of individuals with mental retardation: A quantitative integration of the literature. *Journal of Child and Family Studies*, **10**, 65–84.

Salmon, A. (1996) Family therapy and learning disabilities: A case discussion. *Context*, **29**, 42–5.

Shah, R. (1992). *The Silent Minority: children with disabilities in Asian families*. National Children's Bureau: London.

Shields, J. (2001) The NAS Early Bird Program: Partnership with parents in early intervention. *Autism*, **5**, 49–56.

Shulman, S. (1988) The family of the severely handicapped child: The sibling perspective. *Journal of Family Therapy*, **10**, 125–34.

Sloper, P. and Turner, S. (1993a) Determinants of parental satisfaction with disclosure of disability. *Developmental Medicine and Child Neurology*, **35**, 816–25.

Sloper, P. and Turner, S. (1993b) Risk and resistance factors in the adaptation phase of parents of children with severe physical disability. *Journal of Child Psychology and Psychiatry*, **34**, 167–88.

Stenfert Kroese, B., Dagnan, D. and Loumidis, K. (1997) (ed.) *Cognitive-Behaviour Therapy for People with Learning Disabilities*. Routledge: London.

Tomm, K. (1985) Circular questions. In *Applications of Systemic Family Therapy: The Milan Approach* (ed. D. Campbell and R. Draper). Academic Press: London.

Tomm, K. (1987) Interventive interviewing part II. Reflexive questioning as a means to enable self healing. *Family Process*, **26**, 167–83.

Turk, J. (1998) Children with learning difficulties and their parents. In: P. Graham (ed.) *Cognitive-Behaviour Therapy for Children and Families*. Cambridge University Press: Cambridge.

Vetere, A. (1993) Using family therapy services for people with learning disabilities. In *Using Family Therapy in the 1990s* (2nd edn) (ed. J. Carpenter and A. Treacher). Blackwell: Oxford.

Webster Stratton, C. (1991) Annotation: strategies for helping families with conduct disordered children. *Journal of Child Psychiatry and Psychology*, **32**, 1047–62.

Wiggs, L. and Stores, G. (2001) Behavioural treatment for sleep problems in children with severe intellectual disabilities and daytime challenging behaviour: Effect on mothers and fathers. *British Journal of Health Psychology*, **6**, 257–69.

Chapter 9

# WORKING WITH ORGANISATIONS OR: WHY WON'T THEY FOLLOW MY ADVICE?

Judith McBrien and Sue Candy

## INTRODUCTION

Most of your career as a clinical psychologist specialising in work with people with intellectual disability will not be spent face to face delivering 'psychology' to the client. Rather the majority will be spent working through third parties, asking them to collect assessment information, persuading them of the wisdom of your proposed intervention, providing them with advice and training. Recall the Tharp and Wetzel (1969) triadic model in which consultants are 'anyone with the knowledge', mediators are 'anyone with the reinforcers' and targets are 'anyone with the problems'. An approach that ignores the importance of the mediators is to be avoided. In this way, the lot of the clinical psychologist is to be 'an authority' rather than 'in authority', using persuasion rather than coercion. Contrast this with the position of, say, a head teacher or service manager who can insist that their advice is followed. Whilst working as an authority can bring a sense of status and worth and earn the respect and gratitude of others, it may conversely prove a surprisingly frustrating and disempowering experience if mishandled.

To avoid such a fate, the clinical psychologist needs two skills in addition to their core skills *qua* psychologist: those of giving advice and of working with other advice givers (i.e. colleagues from other professions, as part of multi-disciplinary teams and wider service networks). These skills are essential for a successful psychologist who wishes to be

*Clinical Psychology and People with Intellectual Disabilities*, Second Edition. Edited by Eric Emerson, Chris Hatton, Kate Dickson, Rupa Gone, Amanda Caine and Jo Bromley.
© 2012 John Wiley & Sons, Ltd. Published 2012 by John Wiley & Sons, Ltd.

influential with clients, carers and systems, but surprisingly, are not routinely taught on clinical training courses. Too often the clinical psychologist behaves as a 'one man band', failing to maximise their impact through joint approaches.

This chapter commences with a brief description of the working environment, then discusses avoiding the pitfalls involved in giving advice, and when working with the recipients of your advice. It is assumed that the reader has at their finger tips a range of skills in conducting assessment, functional analysis, making formulations, designing and delivering interventions.

## THE WORKING ENVIRONMENT

### The Range of Provision

People with intellectual disabilities are enmeshed in a web of caring agencies, individuals and bureaucratic organisations. The difficulties of effecting change in such complex situations were well described in the classic work of Georgiades and Phillimore (1975). They developed the 'myth of the hero-innovator: the idea that you produce, by training, a knight in shining armour who, loins girded with new techniques and beliefs, will assault the organisational fortress and institute changes in himself and others at a stroke … the fact of the matter is that organisations … will, like dragons, eat the hero-innovator for breakfast!'

To avoid being eaten, an understanding of the ways in which services for people with intellectual disabilities are provided and commissioned (paid for) is essential, together with at least a passing understanding of the attendant legislation and government policy. For children and most adults, parents have a life long role and stake in the care provided (see Chapter 14). In addition, the average community-based adult with moderate to severe intellectual disabilities may be living with staff in a group home or 'supported living' (run by an independent sector provider), attending part time two different day centres (perhaps run by the Local Authority) and occasionally spending time in a treatment unit (NHS run). People living with their parents will have a similar range of services with the possible addition of occasional respite care. They may have different aspects of their health care delivered by any number of health professionals (generic and specialist). More able people are likely to be in 'supported living' with a number of different staff providing help (more or less intensively), attending work or college placements. They will almost certainly have aspects of their life organised by the Local Authority's Adult Social Care team via a Care Manager. The Care Manager draws up a 'package' of care based on a 'care plan'.

## The Commissioning of Provision

The purchasers of this range of care will be the Local Authority (either the Child and Family services or Adult Social Care), and/or the local Primary Care Trust – the two organisations increasingly acting in partnership. Care packages for social care and their funding are dependent on the Local Authority's policies for access to care, which in turn are guided by government legislation. At present, this is 'Fair Access to Care Services' (2003), which provides guidance on eligibility criteria for adult social care. In the early years of the 21st century there was specific advice regarding how intellectual disability services should be provided, in the form of a Government White Paper Valuing People (2001) and its update Valuing People Now (2009).

The picture for children with intellectual difficulties is similar, with the all important addition of education providers (special schools, mainstream schools). Increasingly inclusion in mainstream schools is seen as the goal for children with special needs (DfES 2004).

## Broader Policies

At a broader level, there are policies concerning health and social care generally that are intended to impact on services for people with intellectual disability as well as other groups. The key elements for health and social care policy in recent years have been increased personalisation and choice for consumers of health and social care. For people with intellectual disabilities this can include Direct Payments (i.e. purchasing their own care) and this is due to be enhanced by a scheme of Individual Budgets. Commissioning a Patient Led NHS (2005) has been guiding NHS developments. This made the main role of Primary Care Trusts a commissioning one with the expectation that provision of services would be placed at arm's length. The White Paper Our Health, Our Care, Our Say (2006) set out a vision to provide people with good quality social care and NHS services in the communities where they live. This continues the trend towards integrated care promoting independence in the community. As a result of policy changes, in the coming years psychologists might find themselves working in a variety of new organisations. Within the NHS this might be in a Partnership Trust or a Foundation Trust; outside the NHS it might be in a new type of independent organisation, such as a privately run one or a Social Enterprise.

Some clients with complex mental health needs come under the auspices of the Care Programme Approach (CPA, introduced in 1991, See Department of Health, 2008). This is designed to strengthen good practice by attending to assessment, care planning, the appointment of a key worker and regular review. As the reader will know, mental health problems can be common in people with intellectual disabilities. When working with a client subject to CPA, the psychologist must take care to understand how this system works and their role in it.

Policies aside, unless there is a return to the days of the total institution, the provision of services for people with intellectual disabilities will always be shared across many provider agencies. These providers will have varying levels of expertise and maturity as organisations, reflected in the quality of their staff, their management arrangements and their protocols. Different providers will also hold differing philosophies of care and treatment. Understanding your own position within this complex scheme is an essential first step in becoming a useful and influential practitioner.

Question: do you know how intellectual disability services are organised and paid for in your area? Are there limits to the availability of certain services, set by current policies in either health or social care?

Question: do you know which organisations provide for adults and children in your area? Do you know the role, philosophy and policies of each, especially your own employer?

## GIVING ADVICE

This section addresses a number of issues related to giving advice to staff groups and provider organisations. It assumes that you have made your assessments, developed a formulation and are ready to draw up a plan for intervention which you wish others to implement. The most soundly based advice is only good advice if it can be and is implemented. An important but often neglected step is to plan to increase adherence to advice alongside the development of the actual intervention. Making a plan for implementation is as important as making a good assessment, formulation and plan of intervention. This section looks at some of the stages of doing this.

### Presenting Your Formulation and Plan

The aim in presenting your formulation is two fold – to gain agreement and to gain commitment to implementation. The recipients of your advice will need to reach a consensus that your formulation of the presenting problem is the right one or at least worth pursuing. An effective way to do this is to present the data from your baseline assessments/risk assessment and the options for intervention or risk management and then facilitate the care staff to identify the salient issues. This can be done through brain storming at a staff meeting or with a smaller group of key worker and manager/s. This will foster a joint responsibility for the success of the plan. The data should be presented in as creative a fashion as possible using video tapes or graphs of baseline information, role-play, comparative case studies, evidence from the literature and so on, as appropriate.

## Making the Plan Clear to All

Once agreement is reached on the nature of the intervention or risk management, it is important that everyone understands their role in implementation. Do not assume that gaining agreement means that everyone has a clear understanding of their role in the plan or that expectations are similar. Always check this out. This can be done informally or more formally through the use of a written intervention agreement that clarifies who will do what, when and for how long, what constitutes success or progress, when to seek further advice or a change and how the plan will be monitored and evaluated. Such an agreement will clarify expectations for all stakeholders and avoid misperceptions or confusion as the plan unfolds. In some situations, such a formal approach may adversely affect rapport, so its use should be carefully judged. A rule of thumb is that the more carers and settings there are, the more likely it is that an agreement of some sort will be useful. An alternative is the circulation of clear minutes of each meeting with actions carefully noted.

Front line staff, in particular, need the plan and its rationale explained first hand. This can be time consuming, especially when it involves a large staff group and a range of shift patterns, but it is time well spent. Without this, you are at the mercy of the organisation's own communication system and the Chinese whispers that may involve.

If your plan necessitates expenditure by the recipients, it will help to be realistic about the level of resources available and to try to understand the organisation's constraints. When resources are required, especially if this is long term, this must be presented to those who hold the budget as soon as possible in a way that is well argued and clear. If funding is not possible then your plan will need adjusting or even abandoning in favour of a different course of action.

## The Advice Itself

The advice should be written down in a simple to follow way. You should avoid jargon or abbreviations, which may not be understood by all. If the advice is genuinely lengthy or complex there should be a step by step summary to act as an *aide mémoire*. Written instructions are not always sufficient to ensure compliance as they may not be understood. Role-playing complex intervention programmes or video-taping someone carrying it out effectively is useful.

## Follow Through

It is this stage of an intervention that is most often neglected, the psychologist moving on to new referrals and failing to provide adequate follow up. Assuming an intervention has commenced and the carers are enthusiastic, remember that maintenance over time will be affected by your commitment to monitoring it, refining it and providing summarised feedback on progress. Initial advice compliance may be good, especially if the advice works immediately, but may then drift. Any records which you have asked staff to make should be regularly collected, analysed, summarised and fed back to the carers. Explain when carers should contact you during implementation. Keep other key stakeholders informed, for example the Care Manager. Instigate follow up reviews, preferably chaired by the Care Manager but failing that chair them yourself. Give positive feedback, including to managers, praising staff for compliance and enthusiasm. Keep monitoring. Identify when to let the recipients stop the programme or modify it. Listen to carers' views and any objections or practical difficulties that arise. Modify the plan to overcome these where possible. Keep set backs and problems in perspective, referring back to the original baseline data and targets.

More can be achieved by a ten minute telephone call at frequent intervals (even daily) in the early stages than by setting a review date a month ahead, by which time the intervention may already have faltered. The literature on advice adherence is relevant here (e.g. Ley 1981; Stanton 1987). Ley's model suggests that compliance follows if patients were satisfied with the consultation process.

## Good Housekeeping

Keeping your own records in order and up to date is essential. There will be quality standards for this, set by your own organisation, which need to be followed. Make sure that all your contacts with the carers and client are recorded and dated, and that relevant others are copied in to your reports (e.g. Care Manager, GP, head teacher), ensuring that the circulation list is clearly noted.

To cope with complaints against your practice and with potential or actual litigation, make sure that all your records and reports are observation specific and do not stray into generalisations which go beyond the evidence. For example, write 'I saw Mrs Jones pick up John Smith by the arm and shake him on Tuesday June 12th at 12.30 p.m.' rather than 'care staff in this home are aggressive towards clients'. If you feel it necessary to report third party information, then note your source. For example, write 'Mr Hopkins told me on Wednesday June 13th that he had seen

Mrs Jones ...'. In writing a conclusion, you can say, for example, 'given the data collected there is some evidence that clients in this home are not being given adequate quantities of food. This is based on a limited number of direct observations. More data are needed to substantiate the suspicion'.

A final point on reports is to be careful about their distribution. Make it clear if it is not to be copied on to others without your permission, particularly the Courts.

## Problems in the Psychologist

Some of the common pitfalls are lack of background information, on your part, about the setting or about previous interventions with the same client; a failure to listen to the carers' points of view; an over theoretical approach which lacks practicality for the setting/s; an over-complex, and hence misunderstood, presentation of your advice; and failure to follow through.

Sometimes, when advice has not been followed, the psychologist looks to blame the setting, the staff or the management, rather than the quality of their own advice or the way it is delivered. This can lead to an array of problems, with the psychologist perceived as a 'hit and run' professional who does not really understand the day to day struggles faced by staff. The relationship suffers and it becomes harder to gain commitment and co-operation from the setting. This can make the psychologist adopt a 'take it or leave it' attitude to their own advice. At best, this might result in a half-hearted attempt to follow it or at worst it would be sabotaged from the start.

Psychologists do not always enjoy a good reputation amongst colleagues. Osborne-Davis (1996) in a small survey of attitudes to clinical psychologists amongst nurses and occupational therapists in the same service, found that clinical psychologists were a virtually unknown group in the eyes of other health care staff. Psychologists were perceived as 'remote' and 'aloof' and playing a 'minimal or no role in providing a service'. They were seen as occupying well-paid, well-resourced and privileged positions.

The 'we know best' attitude coupled with the ability to walk away from a difficult case has long been tolerated but this is rapidly changing in a world which is ever more accountable for both quality and costs. Since the Layard report (2004) psychological therapies are increasingly delivered by non-psychologists. Consequently, psychologists need to refine their core skills and ability to work at multiple levels to ensure 'added value' in what they offer. It is the additional attention to detail, focusing not just on the inter or intra personal but considering the system, context and culture that will ensure the psychologist continues to offer value for money.

## WORKING WITH THE RECIPIENTS OF ADVICE

The previous section looked at how advice can be enhanced by attention to its delivery. Amongst a group of carers, such as in a staffed home, a number of difficulties may present themselves. This section looks at difficulties from which the recipients of your advice may be suffering which militate against advice being followed.

### Staff Stress

It is worth remembering that sometimes staff are simply coping as best they can and the psychologist needs to be sensitive to identifying the problems in a way that facilitates change rather than de-motivates staff. There is increased understanding of the role of burnout and stress amongst staff (see for example Robertson *et al*. 2005; Rose, Horne, Rose and Hastings 2004) and a recognition that the best way to manage staff emotional responses to clients is through effective staff support. The psychologist designing their intervention should ensure they have a sense of the staff group and individual staff coping and stress levels. These may require specific attention to enhance the success of an intervention.

### Poor Communication

Poor communication bedevils nearly all teams at some time either between the managers and the staff or between the staff themselves. This is usually exacerbated by shift systems, especially those that have dedicated night staff. Supported living teams are particularly at risk here. For example a man placed in a one person tenancy may have a dozen different staff visiting him to provide support, on a rota system. It can be extremely difficult to bring these staff together for discussion of the client's needs. Most psychological interventions require consistent application by all staff and accurate record keeping and this means relying on good communication between carers.

### Lack of Staff

A team may be short staffed for any number of reasons, resulting in overload for those who remain at work and a reduced capacity to implement new approaches.

## Weak Links

There may be one weak link in a team who is disaffected or incompetent and whose effect is to disrupt attempts at consistency in an intervention. This type of problem should be tackled by the management team rather than the psychologist.

## Lack of Experience/Knowledge

The staff in a team may be inexperienced in working with people with intellectual disabilities and may lack basic knowledge or information, which you might have taken for granted. See the example of Joe.

### Joe

The local respite unit for children aged 5–15 years referred a 15 year old boy with Down syndrome. Joe lived at home with his parents and had been excluded from the unit because he was beyond their control. The parents and his special school experienced no difficulties, although he could be moody and distressed. The respite unit had a large staff team (more than 20) who, with the exception of the manager, were all young women, newly recruited, many into their first jobs. They had no qualifications and no in-service training beyond induction. Moody adolescents were a very different proposition to endearing five year olds. Staff were divided about their feelings for Joe. Some felt he should not attend and some were fond of him and felt he should. Staff inconsistency was high and previous psychological advice had been unsuccessful.

*Approach taken*: the manager was asked to identify a core group of staff who were fond of Joe. The psychologist worked solely with this group for the next few months to devise and implement a workable approach to Joe's behaviour. The manager's cooperation was crucial in that he had to alter the staffing rota to ensure that whenever Joe was in for respite, then staff from the core group were on duty. As the new approach was seen to work, other staff were gradually rota'd to work alongside members of the core group until each gained the confidence and skills necessary to work with Joe.

## Management Style

There may be a management style in a home or day centre which is not conducive to the implementation of a new way of working with a client. For example, a culture of fear and suspicion against a background of allegations and dismissals will not lend itself to frank discussion of a client's needs. A disorganised or *laissez-faire* management style is also counter-productive. The management style is an important factor in the culture within an organisation. In turn, culture affects performance by influencing the behaviour of staff and managers. Certain organisational cultures can increase users' vulnerability to abuse (White, Holland, Marsland and Oakes 2003).

## Attitudes, Beliefs and Theories

The staff team or parent carers may hold, individually or collectively, beliefs about the client or about all people with intellectual disabilities, which are in conflict with your own or indeed with the available evidence. They may have espoused a particular theory of behaviour or a particular 'therapy' or approach, which would have to be dropped if your recommendations were to be followed. It is important to understand the underlying philosophy of a provider. For example, a group home which sees itself as a family may hold the view that 'these people cannot change, they just need tender loving care'. A variation on this is the attitude that 'this is their home – they must not be made to do anything they do not want to' (and therefore we must not keep records, help them to change their behaviour, etcetera). Such teams will view client need and how to meet it differently from a home which has a philosophy of staff as support workers.

Allen (1999) provides an excellent review of research on carers (parents and paid carers) supporting people with intellectual disability. He demonstrates how behavioural programmes can be effective but how implementation and compliance are often poor. Allen's review encompasses studies on carer attributions, mediator beliefs and emotions. Parental beliefs and views need to be incorporated into any implementation plan to ensure parental stress is minimised and when necessary beliefs gently challenged (see Hassall, Rose and McDonald 2005).

Erroneous theories of behaviour can be an obstacle, particularly when working to reduce challenging behaviour. The apparently unassailable logic of your functional analysis may meet with resistance. There is a small body of research in this area now (see for example, Weigle and Scotti 2000; McCausland, Wester and McClean 2004).

## Hidden Agendas

It may be that the staff team or their manager has an ulterior motive in referring a client to you. For example, it is not uncommon for a residential setting to request an assessment to support an application for further funding or to use your advice to have a client removed from a setting on the grounds that they are too difficult to manage or that their needs are not properly met in that setting. See the example of the Group Referral. Less common but still possible is an agenda that sets out to use your expertise to assist in building evidence against an incompetent or dangerous member of staff.

### Group Referral

All the residents in a privately run residential home were referred to clinical psychology by Adult Social Care for an assessment of their needs. Enquiry showed that the Local Authority, who funded the home, were overspent and had poured additional funding into the home for some years. The reason for the referral, while not unreasonable, was to gain information as to whether the fees paid to the home could be reduced whilst still meeting client need.

*Approach taken*: The reason for referral was discussed with the referrer, who was asked to make this explicit to the residential home before the referral was accepted. After discussion, it was felt more appropriate that the local community nurse, linked to the home, should undertake the assessment task using the regular assessments for placing clients in residential care.

## Difficulties Between Providers

A group of care staff, whilst in themselves well organised, may be receiving advice contradictory to yours from another quarter, perhaps from another professional or organisation. Such advice may have been given in the past or may be occurring contemporaneously with yours. A particular problem may occur if different advice has been given by another clinical psychologist. See the example of Duncan.

## Duncan

A 14 year old boy on the autism spectrum with profound intellectual disabilities was referred to clinical psychology because of aggression to others. He attended a school for children with Severe Learning Difficulties, where he was taught in a class of eight by a teacher and classroom assistant. During assessment, it was clear that the parents believed that the teacher did not understand or teach their son adequately. The school expressed confidence in the teacher, but the Speech and Language Therapist felt that the teacher was poor. The parents had close links with a local support group for parents of children with autism and drew on their advice, which directly contradicted the psychologist's.

*Approach taken*: there was little alternative here but to gather firm data on the problems by observation in class of the teaching content and style and the management methods and by listening to the parental views. This information was then presented at a series of meetings: parents with psychologist; psychologist with head teacher; psychologist with head teacher and class teacher; psychologist with local support group representative; a meeting of all parties. It proved possible to iron out differences with the support group so that there was no further conflict of advice for the parents. The head teacher, recognising that the particular class teacher was failing, began a process of setting clear performance targets and requiring compliance with outside advice, but was not prepared to move the boy to another class (which the parents were requesting). It was not until the following school year that the boy moved to a different class and no further problems with aggression were experienced. Whilst meeting the reason for referral, the process of working in this way helped the parents to clarify what they desired for their son and helped the head teacher tackle a sensitive staff management problem. It also brought about a better relationship between the psychologist and the local support group.

## Whose Problem Is It?

The client may have been referred because the carers perceive that his behaviour or lack of it is a problem. Analysis may reveal however that this is not a problem to the client but presents difficulties for the carers. You may feel it unethical to change the client to suit the needs of the carers. Conversely, you may decide that a client definitely needs help with a particular behaviour or life style, but the carers are content to allow the situation to continue. This too raises an ethical dilemma. How do you bring pressure to bear in the interests of the client? See the example of Diana.

## Diana

During therapy, a woman with a mild learning disability became distressed and disclosed that she had been told not to masturbate at home. Her keyworker explained that Diana would masturbate in the lounge and that other residents were complaining. The psychologist suggested installing a lock on her bedroom door. This was against the home's policy. To overcome this, the psychologist suggested a sign that she could place on the outside of her door to signify that no-one should enter. The idea was dismissed by the home.

*Approach taken*: the home seemed unable to support the ethical solution to this problem and it was not possible for the psychologist to recommend or support a more aversive strategy. At this point, the involvement of the Care Manager was invaluable. She was able to force the home to comply and facilitate privacy for the client. Whilst this solved the difficulties experienced by the client, and to a large extent the home itself, it did have a knock-on effect on the relationship between the psychologist and the home. The home began to feel suspicious of the psychologist's involvement and extra work had to be undertaken to mend the rift, which ultimately was successfully achieved.

## Knowing Your Audience

As soon as you become involved in a setting or with carers whom you do not know, you will need to assess their strengths and weaknesses. In particular the skills and attitudes they possess, the available resources, the level of commitment and the nature of any constraints. In residential or day care settings, it is important to do this at all levels, from the front line carers through to the manager/s.

How to assess staff strengths and weaknesses? The extent to which care staff have completed baseline records and kept appointments with you is a guide to their motivation to follow advice. Further, the accuracy of such records and competence at filling them in are a guide to their ability to follow advice.

A useful method to ascertain a staff team's capabilities is to seek the opinions of other members of the multi-disciplinary team who are familiar with working there. Remember that the staff team's usual ways of working are more influential than formal policies - staff will believe they know the client best and generally advice and support from outside the staff team is unlikely to be highly valued (Whitworth, Harris and Jones 1999). See the example of Sanjay.

## Sanjay

Sanjay, a 20 year old man with severe physical and intellectual disabilities, had recently arrived in a residential home for 12 clients. Sanjay required help to eat, as he was unable to hold cutlery. He was referred for 'screaming at mealtimes'. Staff reported other clients being distressed by the noise. During initial assessment, the psychologist discovered there had been a successful intervention programme for distress at mealtimes at his previous home. This programme described the importance of Sanjay not having to wait for his food whilst other clients received their meal. The managers claimed the programme was still in use but the psychologist's observation suggested Sanjay and two other residents with physical disabilities waited until all other residents had eaten, and the plates had been cleared away before they were helped to eat. Staff complained that the managers had not listened to their point of view and it seemed that morale was low. They explained that they had always left helping the less able clients until last and Sanjay would soon get used to the new routine if they could just get on with it. They felt other residents would suffer if Sanjay had preferential treatment.

*Action taken*: although it was immediately obvious from observation and in the written programme what was causing Sanjay's distress, the psychologist set up a baseline recording system to help staff understand. It was quickly apparent that some staff had very few recording skills and little was being recorded. The psychologist attended the weekly staff meeting and used a video of several mealtimes to help staff learn how to record what was happening and to discuss how staff felt about the intervention plan. Those staff who missed the meeting were followed up during the week. It was clear that not only was there difficulty in knowing how to record but also a feeling that it was pointless and simply another chore. The psychologist gave the staff time to vent their frustration about staffing levels and encouraged them to complete the baseline records so that they would have a good case to put to management for more staff at critical times. This increased compliance, with the result that evidence was collected to indicate more staff were required. The managers agreed to an increase in staffing for a trial period. Staff understood the value of the programme and the monitoring and not surprisingly Sanjay's distress reduced almost immediately.

## Minimise Constraints

The most usual constraints and those that you should consider are: programmes with other clients in the same setting, staff holidays, other events due to take place (such as Christmas), staff burnout or turnover, inflexible staffing levels or rotas and differences of opinion. Some constraints can be worked round and your intervention still remain viable. Others will require a different approach such as staff training or reporting the difficulties to people who can effect more fundamental change. It may be that there is an issue to be dealt with but it may not be a priority, at that time, in comparison to other issues. Recognise that you may not be the right person or involved at the right time to be effective. See the example of Stuart.

### Stuart

Stuart was a young man with severe intellectual disabilities on the autism spectrum. Many of his behaviours were challenging and he was excessively aggressive to staff. Assessment suggested that keeping to a clear and structured routine significantly reduced the aggression. A new intervention plan was developed and the initial response was good. However as Christmas approached the staff began discussing Christmas arrangements. The manager said that the routine should be continued but the staff refused saying Stuart should have presents, a tree, decorations, crackers, etcetera. Emotions ran high and the manager asked the psychologist to attend the next meeting.

*Action taken*: the psychologist listened carefully to the staff views but reinforced the need to keep to the routine. He explained how Stuart had no concept of Christmas and would find the changes distressing. The psychologist helped staff to think creatively. Stuart was accustomed to art sessions and often put his work up on the walls. The psychologist suggested the art sessions used Christmas material. This worked well and the art work did help to make the unit look 'Christmassy', but did not upset Stuart's routine or increase his challenging behaviours. By giving the staff time to vent their feelings and seeking a compromise the psychologist had helped to keep the unit's intervention on track.

### Staff Training

In order for staff to follow your advice, it may be necessary to take a sideways step from meeting the needs of the referred client and set up some training. Staff training is most effective if delivered at the point when it addresses an immediate need for the staff group. Thus providing training directly to support an individual intervention is likely to be a worthwhile use of your time.

There is an enormous array of quality training materials available off the shelf. Sources of training packages include the British Institute of Learning Disabilities and Pavilion Publishers. Do not assume that any training needs must be met by you. In most places, the NHS Trust and/or the Local Authority will have local Training Officers (some generic and some dedicated to intellectual disability) and/or a local management development trainer. These people have a wealth of resources and expertise plus a remit to train staff. Skills and knowledge-based training founded in clinical psychology may appropriately fall to the clinical psychologist. Other topics may best be tackled with or by a colleague from another profession.

## When to Give Up and When to Blow the Whistle

There are times when despite your best efforts you are getting nowhere. You may reach a point when there is little or no compliance with your advice and apparently no constructive action left open to you. The important point here is not simply to walk away and discharge the client but to present a cogent report to the referrer and the stakeholders, which highlights the needs and the obstacles. The objective is to alert the relevant people who may be able to engineer change (having recourse to those 'in authority'). For example, you may recommend that the client's needs can only be served by a move from their residential home. In such a case, a referral to the Adult Social Care Care Manager is the best course of action. Clarify in your reports the conditions which would need to obtain before psychological advice would be useful.

If you believe the risks to the client are significant and need to be acted upon, then you must make a report to the authority who can take action. To do this you will need to be familiar with the relevant legislation. In April 2009 the Care Quality Commission became the new regulator for health and social care for England, replacing the separate bodies of the Healthcare Commission, Commission for Social Care Inspection and the Mental Health Act Commission.

There is important legislation in place for protecting vulnerable people, for example the Children Act (1989) with the associated local Safeguarding Children Boards, the Mental Health Act (2007) (see also Chapters 4, 5 and 9) and procedures in each Local Authority for the protection of vulnerable adults. If you work in the NHS there will be lead managers for child protection and safeguarding vulnerable adults whose advice can readily be sought. Indeed, practitioners are obliged to advise these leads of any safeguarding concerns that they encounter. These are not only important for the safeguarding of clients when you perceive a risk but you can also use them to inform your interventions and to assist you in gaining compliance. See the example of Bill.

As discussed in the introduction, you should also be aware of the local arrangements for commissioning (i.e. paying for) different services and their associated contracts. Interventions or recommendations which require resourcing will need to come to the attention of the relevant commissioner. Contracts for services (whether set by Adult Social Care or Health) can serve as a lever on the provider for improving the quality of care and for ensuring that interventions are implemented in a setting.

Always share your information – do not work in isolation. Talk over your concerns with your immediate supervisor/manager. Keep comprehensive notes. Strength lies in working with others. Do not let spurious ideas about confidentiality being paramount cloud your judgement of when to pass on information. A chilling account of the failure to pass on clinical information to others can be found in Blom-Cooper, Hally and Murphy (1994).

A multi-disciplinary team working in many different residential homes and day settings will between them build up a considerable body of knowledge on the strengths and weaknesses of different providers. It is important to share this knowledge and be able to feed it back to the relevant people in an objective and co-ordinated way.

---

### Bill

A young man with severe intellectual disabilities who lived in one of a chain of small, private residential homes was excluded from his home following an aggressive incident with a passer-by, which had been adversely reported in the press. The home had not followed the clinical psychologist's advice, which involved guidelines that highlighted the risk of such an incident and a recording system.

*Approach taken*: the psychologist contacted Adult Social Care, who set a new contract in collaboration with their local CSCI inspector, which stipulated that the home managers were to seek and follow the advice of the local health professionals and keep adequate records. It had always been difficult to work collaboratively with this group of homes. The adverse press attention helped the manager of the organisation to realise how vulnerable their isolation made them. Consequently, they welcomed the changes to their contract and were receptive to the involvement of the psychologist. The psychologist used this to build a supportive relationship with the organisation.

## CONCLUSION

We have looked at some of the many variables that might explain why the 'mediators' (staff, carers or parents) might not follow your advice. Understanding these will help you cope with your own feelings of frustration, annoyance or helplessness. The important messages are first, not to work in isolation from other professionals, stakeholders, systems or rules, but to bring people together early on to make differences explicit, seek agreement (compromising if necessary) and clarify roles. Second, despite the ever-changing political and professional climate, hold on to your core skills as a clinical psychologist. Drawing on the full range of psychological theory and clinical practice and not just that relevant to people with intellectual disabilities is useful. Roth and Fonagy (1998) discuss how efficacy follows not from the type of therapy but from core consulting skills – attunement, engagement, rapport building, listening skills, reflection and summaries.

Clinical psychologists reading this book are likely to be in training, maintaining a faith in and enthusiasm for the profession and its capabilities – after all it was hard enough to get onto the training course – and that is certainly worth holding onto. However, not everyone out there has such a rosy view of us. Rapley and Clements (1996), in a light hearted but hard-hitting article, describe two alternatives for life as a psychologist. The less desirable alternative is to become one of the 'affluent, exotic and irrelevant'. This would mean spending your career feeling slightly hard done by, if superior and well paid and thus contributing to the eventual extinction of the profession. More useful, they recommend, is to adopt the role model of the 'psychologist as plumber'. The plumber comes when called, equipped with a range of useful skills. This means appreciating that a clinical psychologist working in complex organisational structures with vulnerable, devalued people is only needed (and only likely to be hired at all) if the skills they offer, the way they offer them and their ability and commitment to work with a range of ordinary, down to earth people, dealing with some of the most intransigent problems in individuals, staff teams and organisations are of the highest order. This approach can provide a truly rewarding experience of working life, which is entirely achievable if some of the basic advice we suggest in this chapter is adopted.

## References

Allen, D. (1999) Mediator analysis: an overview of recent research on carers supporting people with intellectual disability and challenging behaviour. *Journal of Intellectual Disability Research*, **43**, 325–39.
Blom-Cooper, L., Hally, H. and Murphy, E. (1994) *The Falling Shadow: One Patient's Mental Health Care*. London: Duckworth.
British Institute of Learning Disabilities www.bild.org.uk.

Care Quality Commission http://www.cqc.org.uk/.

Department for Education and Science (2004) Removing Barriers to Achievement. The Government's Strategy for SEN.

Department of Health (2000) The NHS Plan.

Department of Health (2001) Valuing People.

Department of Health (2005) Commissioning a Patient Led NHS.

Department of Health (2006) Our Health, Our Care, Our Say.

Department of Health (2008) Refocusing the Care Programme Approach.

Department of Health (2009) Valuing People Now: a new three-year strategy for people with learning disabilities.

Fair Access to Care (2003)

Children Act (1989)

Department of Health (1983) The Mental Health Act.

Georgiades, N.J. and Phillimore, L. (1975) The myth of the hero-innovator and alternative strategies for organisational change. In: Kiernan, C.C. and Woodford F.R. (eds) *Behaviour Modification with the Severely Retarded*. Amsterdam: Associated Scientific Publishers.

Hassall, R., Rose, J. and McDonald, J. (2005) Parenting stress in mothers of children with an intellectual disability: the effects of parental cognitions in relation to child characteristics and family support. *Journal of Intellectual Disability Research*, **49**(6), 405–18.

Layard, R. (2004) *The Layard Report: Increasing Access to Evidence Based Psychological Treatment?*

Ley, P. (1981) Professional non-compliance: A neglected problem. *British Journal of Clinical Psychology*, **20**, 151–4.

McCausland, D., Wester, G. and McClean, B. (2004) Effects of functional versus non-functional explanations for challenging behaviour treatment acceptability. *Journal of Learning Disabilities*, **8**(4), 351–69.

Osborne-Davis, I. (1996) Awareness and attitudes of other healthcare professionals towards clinical psychologists. *Clinical Psychology Forum*, **91**, 10–15.

Pavilion Publishers www.pavpub.com.

Rapley, M. and Clements, J. (1996) Go to the Mirror! Thoughts on the future development of applied psychology. *Clinical Psychology Forum*, **89**, 4–7.

Robertson, J., Hatton, C., Felce, D., Meek, A., Carr, D., Knapp, M., Hallam, A., Emerson, E., Pinkney, L., Caesar, E. and Lowe, K. (2005) Staff stress and morale in community-based settings for people with intellectual disabilities and challenging behaviour: a brief report. *Journal of Applied Research in Intellectual Disabilities*, **18**, 271–7.

Rose, D., Horne, S., Rose, J.L. and Hastings, R.P. (2004) Negative emotional reactions to challenging behaviour and staff burnout: two replication studies. *Journal of Applied Research in Intellectual Disabilities*, **17**, 219–23.

Roth and Fonagy (1998) *What Works for Whom? A critical review of psychotherapy research*. London. The Guildford Press.

Stanton, A.L. (1987) Determinants of the Adherence to the Medical Regimes by Hypertensive Patients. *Journal of Behavioural Medicine*, **10**(4), 377–94.

Tharp, R.G. and Wetzel, R.J. (1969) *Behavior modification in the natural environment*. New York. Academic Press.

Weigle, K.L. and Scotti, J.R. (2000) Effects of functional analysis information on ratings of intervention effectiveness and acceptability. *Journal of the Association for Persons with Severe Handicaps*, **25**, 217–28.

White, C., Holland, E., Marsland, D. and Oakes, P. (2003) The identification of environments and cultures that promote the abuse of people with intellectual disabilities: a review of the literature. *Journal of Applied Research in Intellectual Disabilities*, **16**, 1–9.

Whitworth, D., Harris, P. and Jones, R. (1999) Staff culture in a residential setting for people with learning disabilities and challenging behaviour: a qualitative analysis. *Mental Health Care*, **21**, 376–8.

Chapter 10

# REFLECTIONS ON 25 YEARS WORKING IN THE NHS

Ian Fleming

## AN INTRODUCTION: SOME STOPS IN A CAREER

My career in the National Health Service (NHS) started in 1978 when I was accepted on to a British Psychological Society (BPS) Diploma course in Clinical Psychology. I had a strong interest in working with people with learning disabilities generated through my previous experience in research posts and although the generic training allowed and required me to work with different client groups my first post was in the specialism.

Upon qualifying in the autumn of 1981 I started working full time in a large district clinical psychology department. My post was one of two clinical psychology posts making up the learning disability service, based in a small mental handicap hospital, situated rather unusually in the middle of an urban area near to shops, banks, bus stops and public houses. I worked with individuals with learning disabilities who lived in that hospital and those who lived outside. During the eight years I was there the specialism grew to five full time posts, and together we were able to carry out developmental work as well as to manage a large caseload; there was collaboration on projects, research, staff development work, leading to some real innovations in the local services and a feeling that the contribution of clinical psychology was valued. However, this productive situation changed when posts that became vacant were not filled. The exact reasons for this were unclear.

Clinical Psychology remains a small profession in the NHS. In 2006 there were reported to be 7122 Clinical Psychologists in the NHS; a rise of 29% since 2001 and 69% since 1997. Learning Disabilities has always been

*Clinical Psychology and People with Intellectual Disabilities*, Second Edition. Edited by
Eric Emerson, Chris Hatton, Kate Dickson, Rupa Gone, Amanda Caine and Jo Bromley.
© 2012 John Wiley & Sons, Ltd. Published 2012 by John Wiley & Sons, Ltd.

a small specialism within the profession. In 1994 the BPS recommended that there should be four qualified clinical psychologists working with people with learning disabilities per 250,000 population area; at this time the vast majority of areas do not achieve this (e.g. Rose *et al*. 2001; Fleming 2008). One reason for the variation in posts is historical: posts were dependent on local hospital provision more than later community service developments.

In 1989 I moved to work in an innovative service in a nearby large city in the North West. This service also had a number of clinicians (four at its peak) and had been commissioned to play the lead role in reconstructing appropriate services in the city after critical reports. Developing new services was a major and 'ideological' thrust of our work, and this was complemented by more 'traditional' clinical work with individuals.

Three years later I moved to another service and worked into a specialist team that, I was to realise, had not been commissioned with any apparent coherence and which failed to function effectively. In all three of these posts I worked with both adults and children, and worked into or as part of a Community Team for People with Learning Disabilities.

In the late 1990s I moved to an urban area in the North West to my current post within a large, longstanding 'district' psychology department that had provided a continuous service to adults and children with learning disabilities for 30 years. The post is part time and is generalist; I have a colleague who works with children and there is a post (currently vacant) committed to working with people in transition, making a total establishment of 2.3 whole time equivalents. The specialism nationally has suffered from periodic recruitment problems resulting in unfilled posts, and retention can also be an important issue, especially if posts are single handed or supported inadequately for CPD and supervision. It appears that recruitment difficulties are not evenly spread geographically, change over time, and are influenced by a range of factors including personal reputations. A recent survey of posts in the NW of England showed great variation in establishment and a vacancy rate in qualified posts of around 12% (Fleming 2008).

I have regularly supervised trainee clinical psychologists during my career and benefited hugely from this. I also owe a huge debt to the support from peers, whether as work colleagues, through formal supervision or from the local special interest groups. Currently I receive regular supervision from a colleague in a neighbouring NHS Trust.

I have therefore experienced most of the possible roles, and team working and management arrangements that clinical psychologists will encounter. These are:

- generic team workers managed by one team manager;
- team member but managed by clinical psychologist;
- consultant to the team/service.

## CLINICAL ACTIVITY – AN EVOLUTION?

There are no current data available as to the work of clinical psychologists in learning disabilities, but it is my impression that historically individuals to a large degree defined their own activity. Arguably, this was a reasonable response to working single-handed, a desire to implement one or more of the important research led initiatives, and an awareness of the lives of people with learning disabilities. Local commissioners', services' and colleagues' expectations of clinical psychologists varied enormously and there was more than enough psychological work to be done.

In my career developments in clinical activity seemed to mirror those in the profession as a whole: an initial, required and limited focus on assessment as an aid to diagnosis developed into specific psychological interventions, and this in turn led to a self-declared role in research, training and service development (cf Leyin 2001). Another major influence at that time was the dominant influence of a radical environmentalist perspective that emphasised the role that the environment played in influencing behaviour. This resulted in work that was focused more on changing the environments in which people lived and less on changing individuals per se as exemplified in more traditional therapy. In the early 1980s behavioural approaches had been shown to have considerable success in increasing the competencies of individuals, and in reducing less functional behaviours. It was in this role providing behavioural management advice that many of us were involved in initiatives including, increasing Engagement, Goal Planning (Houts and Scott 1975), Individual Programme Planning (Blunden 1980) and Room Management and contained a focus on active engagement in meaningful activity. It is unfortunate that these innovative forms of practice often were not effectively implemented and maintained, despite the promising initial research (e.g. that carried out by the Wessex research team), and discarded in favour of the next innovation. Other directions range from Constructional approaches to functional analysis of behaviour (Goldiamond 1974), to developing supported employment (Wertheimer 1992). Despite their early origins, it is telling that many of these issues remain in 2007 pertinent to the practice of Clinical Psychologists in 2007. (see Chapter 11). For example, Positive Support has many elements in common with some of the procedural innovations such as increasing Engagement, and Goal planning referred to above. Indeed the origins of Active Support (Felce et al. 2002) in the research carried out in South Wales (e.g. Porterfield et al. 1977) and Wessex in the 1980s are acknowledged.

In the North West at least, a shared experience was that despite the effectiveness of such approaches individuals' lives were determined by the way in which services were delivered. This realisation lead to many clinical psychologists becoming involved in staff training and the promulgation of normalisation and Social Role Valorisation as a value base/philosophy for the delivery of services (Flynn and LeMay 1999; Wolfensberger 1999). Specific examples of activities derived from this approach included developing Circles of Friends (Forest and Lusthaus 1989), Getting To Know You (Brost and Johnson 1982), and linked initiatives included Person-Centred Planning mechanisms (e.g. Ritchie *et al.* 2003) and Quality Assessment (e.g. IDC1986; NWRMHAG 1989).

In the 1980s I was fortunate to work in an area of the UK that was in the forefront of operationalising the changes devolved from the adoption of a clear values base to local services. Over time the balance in my own work has shifted with an increase in work that follows a more traditional model of therapy, and this is reflected in some of the discussion below. Such a change may be typical of the profession as a whole, and there has been a definite expansion in the use of individualised therapeutic approaches to working with individuals with learning disabilities. I hesitate to endorse the view that the change has represented a retreat for clinical psychology (Clements and Hassall 2008) but the reasons underlying such a change are worthy of investigation.

Although only a minority of clinical psychologists are research active, many have been active in *disseminating* research findings and have prioritised work aimed at service change and development.

## SOME ISSUES CONCERNING DIRECT CLINICAL WORK

Here I want to review issues that from my experience seem pertinent to working directly with individuals. Working more indirectly will be discussed later, and there is a more extensive review in Chapters 9 and 10.

### Establishing Effective Venues for Working

The nature of the work means that individuals are seen in a variety of settings. This can present its own challenges. I have personal experience of attempting to interview individuals with the television on in the same room or 'friendly' Dobermans jumping up into my lap; of resistance to my request that neighbours leave while I try to interview about sensitive topics, and so on.

It is recognised that psychological therapy requires a comfortable, quiet, private room free from interruptions and that this is critical to establishing an effective therapeutic relationship (one that has clear boundaries and that values the client (see Chapter 7).

Recent changes towards team-working and practising 'in the community' appear to assume that offices are less necessary and, implicitly, that therapeutic work is done *somewhere else*. In practice this is likely to mean venues that make it difficult to ensure any of the essential requirements listed above.

This assumption may be related to misunderstandings about the nature, content and process of *therapeutic work*, and perhaps extend to a failure to understand the particular work carried out by a Clinical Psychologist Challenging it may be difficult because Clinical Psychologists can be perceived as being precious or protectionist requiring 'special' working conditions or because such a discussion implies a critical commentary on others, work practices and implicitly, on the quality and content of that work.

Although these points are more relevant to direct clinical work than that involving service change, this has its own requirements, such as space for uninterrupted thought and concentration, resources for writing and presentation, etc. (see Chapter 9).

## Using Different Psychological Approaches

Clinical Psychologists currently draw on different psychological models in their work with people with learning disabilities. Historically, work was derived commonly from the *applied analysis of behaviour* with its emphasis on observed behavioural events and the systematic application of assessment and interventions derived from learning theory. One result of this was the development of robust experimental methodologies that created an extensive research literature identifying the effects of applied psychology. Another, referred to above, was an emphasis on changing environments.

A third was the under-appreciation of the importance to effective work of the therapeutic relationship (see Lovett 1985 for a critique of the behavioural approach).

Clinical experience and the recognition of the importance of relationships have led to the adoption and adaptation of other psychological approaches. These have made a significant contribution to practice including *systemic* and *psychotherapeutic* approaches, both of which place greater emphasis on the transforming qualities of the relationship between the clinician and the individual with learning disabilities. There have been important reviews of the using of systemic approaches (Baum and Lyngaard 2006) that have been particularly important for working with clients and their families and carers, for instance placing emphasis on the number and qualities of relationships surrounding the individual. Psychotherapeutic approaches (such as Cognitive Behaviour Therapy) have become more widely used and a number of reviews of the research have been carried out (see Chapter 9).

In my experience power relations in therapy must be acknowledged and are particularly important when working with people with learning disabilities. People with learning disabilities continue to lack power in their lives over both everyday and major decisions in their lives.

I think that engaging in and using individual psychotherapy can be particularly difficult for learning disabled people. One reason is that in my experience the language of therapy may be very different from the pre-dominant command discourse that many individuals experience. Another reason lies in the presumption in therapy that the person can be an *agent* of change. This may run counter to the person's 'real life' experience and affect their ability to participate in the therapy. These may present particular difficulties in therapeutic work that attempts to help an individual identify their thoughts or feelings, to talk about these, and to make links between aspects of their experience. A result can be behaviour that we typically describe as acquiescent. It can also contribute to the feelings of being 'stuck' in therapy. It may be important to prioritise the validation of the individual's experience especially as a way of acknowledging and building resilience.

## Assessment

Once a defining feature of our practice, assessment remains important, and ranges from skilled interviewing through careful use of non-verbal strategies to more formalised psychometric instruments. During the 1980s many clinicians (including myself) turned away from requests for 'IQ assessments', and there was a period when skills assessments appeared to become a functional replacement. However, I have returned to this area with a renewed interest in making any psychometric assessments functional and constructive. Continuing to maintain competence in all these areas of assessment skills can remain a challenge (see later discussion on Continuing Professional Development). This may be a particularly pertinent issue with regards to neuropsychological assessment and associated interpretation of the results. It remains the case that there are fewer standardised assessments for this client group compared with others and idiosyncratic forms are widely used. In my experience gaining informed consent to carry out assessment is often not easy and the experience of 'failure' for the client needs to be carefully considered.

In my experience most Clinical Psychologists are characterised by an enquiring approach, and their ability to draw on different models and perspectives. This means we are in a unique position to assess an individual (using historical, psychological and physiological information) within their social context. I have found that such an assessment leading to a psychological formulation provides the basis for valued, person-centred work to take place.

## Addressing Complexity in Evaluation

Although careful evaluation of our work is a sine qua non we have not always gathered routine outcome data. Throughout my career we have struggled with and debated various means of measuring the effectiveness of our interventions. There are a number of reasons for this. It is often complex and needs to incorporate changes at different levels, and may take longer than that of the modularised interventions used by other clinicians. Current developments of 'broad-brush' evaluation tools in the NHS do not always seem to fit with our clients' experiences. These considerations mean that it is not always possible to use structured, validated measures of change to evaluate our work. The task is to develop valid measures to demonstrate the effectiveness of an intervention (see Chapter 14).

The focus on observed behaviour and absence of necessity for standardised psychometric assessments of mental states can make it easier to evaluate interventions derived from applied behavioural analysis. Within this tradition there developed considerable experience of 'idiosyncratic' measures and utilising experimental methodologies suitable for single case design and group comparisons as exemplified for example, in the *Journal of Applied Behaviour Analysis* and the *Journal of Applied Research in Intellectual Disabilities* (see below). The nature of such interventions requires the evaluation of a number of domains if it is to be valid. For example, the evaluation of an intervention to reduce 'challenging behaviour' would require not only an analysis of the target behaviours but also might measure changes in alternative, appropriate behaviours, changes in the behaviour of others (carers, colleagues, staff), changes in medication, and increases in the use of a wider range of more valued activities and resources. This poses issues for evaluation that are very different to those facing colleagues working with other client groups, although similarities may also exist in work with older adults for example.

For a while in the 1990s value was seen to lie in *Quality of Life* measures, for this was seen to be an entity that psychologists' work was seen to effect. However, the problems with these measures were identified and widely debated (e.g. Hatton, 1998). I think that we will continue to wrestle with this issue and it may be that we need to use multiple methods of measurement.

## Mode of Working

Traditionally Clinical Psychologists in the UK receive referrals made by others; rarely are there self-referrals. Because this work is within a health system these referrals are defined predominantly in terms of *problems* that require resolution. During my time working in the NHS it seems as if a symbiotic relationship has developed in which Clinical Psychologists have increasingly extended the list and range of problems that they are able to offer help with – I hesitate to say 'cure'. This may, in part, reflect the change in practice towards helping individuals to change.

Working with people with learning disabilities offers real opportunities to move away from this referral driven, *pathological* model. The experience of working at different levels, of utilising a broad range of psychological knowledge and of addressing environmental change in addition to that of mentalistic factors combine to suggest that an alternative model of practice is possible and likely to be effective. Aspects of *community psychology* practice (e.g. Prilleltensky and Nelson 1997) could be utilised and learned from. Teaching about community psychology models, has used the experience of a colleague who worked in Learning Disability in the NW of England to illustrate alternative practices (Fleming and Burton 2001).

Such a model would not exclude problem-defined referrals. However, it would introduce more proactive interventions with individuals, carers and services that utilised broad psychological knowledge to develop individuals' resilience and quality of life. Features of this approach have been present historically, for example the central role of clinical psychologists in the introduction, support and maintenance of planning processes that were *not* defined by problems. I believe it is time to learn from, modify, and return this form of proactive work. Unfortunately, this may be underrepresented in the typical data collected to quantify performance in the NHS. The implications of such a narrow conception of professional work for commissioning are self-evident. Such a change in our activity will require a different set of data to be collected.

## ISSUES INVOLVED IN WORKING IN TEAMS

My experience has allowed me plenty of opportunity to reflect on working in teams and as a result I would like to make the following points.

### Origins of Community Teams for people with Learning Disabilities (CTLDs)

Most Clinical Psychologists are based in, or work into Community Teams for People with Learning Disabilities (CTLD). These Teams vary on almost every count: size and membership, organisation, style, definitions, although they would probably all claim allegiance to their original historical origin.

CTLDs originated 40 years ago in the development of community based services that were recommended in the White Paper *Better Services for the Mentally Handicapped* (DHSS 1971). The National Development Group (1976) proposed them as the cornerstone of community services to replace the predominant existing hospital based services. They were to be managed by Health Services, to comprise a core of Nurses and Social Workers and to work with a population figure of around 80,000 meaning three teams in a typical Borough/Health District; furthermore they were initially to work with both children and adults. Teams were to have the following functions: to act as the first point of contact for parents and to provide specialist advice and help with problems related to mental handicap; to coordinate access to services; to establish close working relationships with voluntary organisations.

## Organisational Features

Clearly this arrangement had massive potential: it was explicitly multi-disciplinary; it had an emphasis on early intervention; through the course of its work it 'got to know' literally hundreds of individuals with learning disabilities locally.

Teams also had weaknesses: they didn't hold budgets and possessed no formally recognised planning function. Also, the organisational basis for the formation and maintenance of team-working was rarely prioritised. Some teams struggled to have a shared value base and purpose, to understand and effectively utilise the different areas of knowledge and expertise in their ranks, and to work in the way that best used their skills.

CTLDs have outlived many innovations: for example *Individual Programme Planning, Room Management, Sexuality and Personal Relationships Training, PASS and PASSING, Supported Employment*. Individual CTLDs may have led, responded to, or remained largely unaffected by these developments. Such a heterogenous response by local services to these developments is indicative of the arbitrariness that has characterised service development. It also points to a potential role for Clinical Psychology in scrutinising research evidence to identify and evaluate innovation (see below).

The recent change with the transfer of resources from Heath to Social Services (see Chapter 5), is likely to have important implications for CTLDs (e.g. the role of *care management*), but so far seems to have had little impact on the issues identified here.

## Clinical Psychology Within Teams

Clinical Psychologists always a small profession (see above) rarely achieved a critical mass in local services and were often single-handed within a Team. This had implications for our role and our ability to influence the development of the CTLD. The experience for Psychologists was variable. At best, teams were milieu in which individuals thrived and professionally developed; where initiatives were followed through, and the team worked effectively to enable its value to be recognised in contributing to or leading local service developments. However this was not always the case.

Opportunities are missed because of the lack of attention paid to the organisation of teams. Ovretveit (e.g. 1993) has produced a canon of valuable research into team organisation (in the NHS) that is rarely utilised. He emphasises the need to have clarity about the purpose and functions of a Team before addressing issues of membership and organisation.

It is interesting that there has been little evaluation of CTLDs in the 30 years of their existence. Perhaps the best paper is Brown *et al*. 1992. In the 2001 White Paper *Valuing People* (DOH 2001) CTLDs are referred to but not discussed. It is important that Clinical Psychologists develop practice that enables them to effectively employ their particular contribution to team working.

## Clarification About Practice and Overlapping Roles

The ignorance of Ovretveit's work can result in Teams in which all members claim to do broadly the same thing This can result in an apparent consensus on generic roles with any questioning resulting in disharmony.

Clearly, roles overlap and since much therapeutic work involves applied psychology then a lot of people do '*do psychology*'. However, closer examination of this work may identify the presence of some but not all elements of a psychological approach. Thus, assessments both written and observational (particularly of skills) are common, and behavioural interventions are also routine and often carefully evaluated. However, a Formulation may often be absent and with it the ability to identify and prioritise the range of tasks that are necessary to bring about sustained change.

There may be a role for Clinical Psychologists in developing these competencies in members of other professions, and in the supervision and management of resulting practice.

At this point I recognise that the reader may feel I am unduly critical of CTLDs and/or team-working. I must be clear that this is not the case. In my career I have worked in good, bad and indifferent teams. My view is that we need to use the research that exists as well as our own professional reflection to enable us to work as effectively as possible. It is not enough to accept uncritically an ill thought out organisational form. Recently, there is some evidence (Onyett 2007) that the profession of clinical psychology appears to be taking more interest in these issues. The related issue of the role of leadership is discussed below.

## ISSUES INVOLVED IN RESEARCH

### A Preserve of Specialists?

It is well known that few Clinical Psychologists are active researchers after qualification despite an emphasis on the acquisition of research skills during clinical training, and the Learning Disabilities specialism is not an exception.

In the UK the small number of leading researchers are associated with particular Universities and there appears to be less research being carried out and published by clinicians in the NHS than in the past, although clinicians may be carrying out research that remains unpublished. It is clear that field clinicians are working in interesting and innovative ways to meet the needs of their learning disabled clients and in the process also developing their own Continuing Professional Development. Of importance may be the lack of support from colleagues (especially if working as isolated clinicians) and a lack of priority given to research and development by their employing organisation.

The need to tie in research carried out during clinical training to existing research in University departments may provide fewer opportunities for trainee clinicians to do research into aspects of Learning Disabilities and thus fruitful experience that might be maintained and extended is not gained.

Historically, research concentrated on the effectiveness and practical implications of initiatives that were derived from functional analysis. Some of these initiatives seem to have been discarded or replaced before they were properly assessed and it is interesting to consider their current forms. There certainly seem to be many issues that would benefit from assessment and evaluation. Developments in the use of cognitive behavioural therapy and psychotherapies with people with learning disabilities (see Chapters 9 and 19 for a discussion of this) will benefit from research into their effectiveness and general validity.

## ISSUES INVOLVED IN SERVICE DEVELOPMENT AND LEADERSHIP

### Do Services Have a Clear Values Base?

I was fortunate to work in the NW of England during a period when services were changed and planned according to an explicit model defined in various documents such as the *Model District Service* (NWRHA 1983) which was derived from the principles of normalisation. With hindsight this perspective had shortcomings, one of which was the inadequate process for monitoring the practices of services. However these were overshadowed by its strengths in describing a clear vision/direction for services and some of the standards by which services could be evaluated.

It seems now as if services are being developed with less attention to explicit statements about purpose, process and outcomes; as a result expediency and a lack of evaluation to guide further development ensue. It is interesting to ask whether local services are being analysed and planned according to operational statements derived from *Valuing People* (DOH 2001) (see Burton 2004 for an interesting criticism of Valuing People).

## What is the Potential Contribution of Clinical Psychology?

It can be argued that Clinical Psychology provides a major constituent of any coherent clinical leadership to services for people with Learning Disabilities. This is because applied psychology is central to the research that has increased knowledge and effective interventions for individuals, including the understanding of the crucial importance of environmental factors to an explanation of behaviour. This statement does not preclude the contribution of other professions.

There are however few clinical psychologists leading local services. One factor is the profession's small numbers, and in particular the dearth of teams of psychologists working together. Another factor may be the lack of evidence that clinical psychologists can be effective leaders-managers; this is a problem that does not affect our colleagues in the Nursing and Medical professions. Another reason may lie in a reluctance to take on this role, partly prompted by a preference for a purely clinical role and partly by a lack of confidence in leading services.

This may imply a need for training clinical psychologists in leadership and management skills. This has been a concern of the CPD scheme in the North West of England that has recently developed and ran a training course in leadership skills. CPD for LD specialists is discussed further below.

## Staff Training

Two things follow from the suggestion that important therapeutic and service innovations for people with learning disabilities are derived from applied psychology. First, the small numbers of clinical psychologists are inadequate to meeting all of the therapeutic need and therefore others need to be helped to acquire and use (at least some of) these skills. Second, as professionally trained psychologists we have a responsibility to be actively involved in this enterprise. This is the context for staff training and development that is a well-established activity with a long history in this specialism (these issues are discussed further in Chapter 11).

Staff training is regularly asked of Clinical Psychologists, and has become a core activity. Although there may be a superficial satisfaction from thinking that training can change both staff and client behaviour, the reality is more complex and we should be using the research to develop best practice. The research evidence for the effectiveness of staff training is equivocal (Ziarnik and Bernstein 1982; Cullen 2000), perhaps the reason many choose to ignore it. This is unfortunate because the research is actually more promising when read alongside that into staff management and organisation. The literature indicates that acknowledging the service context and identifying the resources to manage and maintain change are crucial. A failure to do so result in the training having minimal effect, an outcome described pithily by Stokes and Baer (1977) as 'train and hope'.

In summary, the work of most clinical psychologists can be characterised as an attempt to manage in a person centred way a significant caseload of problem-defined referrals and to introduce research based methodologies into local services.

It is this combination of tasks, requiring the clinician to draw on their total knowledge of psychological theories and their experience, that I find so stimulating. Working with people with LD requires the clinician to work at many different levels and to draw on a range of psychological models, perhaps more so than working with other client groups.

## SUPERVISION

### Recent Developments in Supervision

Historically the profession has focused on the supervision of its own members (especially those in training) more than on members of other professions. In the past, Qualification implied that one has competence to supervise members of other professional groups, although now more attention is paid to articulating and developing supervisory skills.

Increased opportunities for Clinical Psychologists to gain competence in supervisory skills are accompanied by developments towards *accreditation* (Fleming and Golding 2007), as already exists in other health professions (e.g, Physiotherapy). This recognition that supervisory skills span prequalification training and post-qualification Continuing Professional Development (CPD) has implications for ensuring that all clinical psychologists are competent in bringing about the changes implied by 'working through others'.

This is of importance precisely because working through others is an important part of the activity of clinical psychologists in the learning disabilities specialism. This is discussed more extensively in Chapter 11.

I would argue that effectively and professionally 'working through others' to bring about the use of techniques based in applied psychology implies a degree of supervision.

## Obtaining Agreement About the Supervisory Activity

Good supervision requires clarification and agreement about its practice. The supervisee may prefer to use a different term to describe the activity and these may include: 'consultation', 'a brief chat', 'some advice', 'a few words if you have a moment'. There may be all sorts of reasons for this reluctance to name an activity as supervision, and confusion may be more common within multidisciplinary supervision, where individuals can feel that seeking supervision is tantamount to inadequacy or fault or weakness.

None of these should prevent us from being clear about what is supervision. We should attempt to develop a relationship that utilises our knowledge and experience to foster clinical activity of the highest quality, and that includes continuity and accountability. Implicitly we need to assert that supervision is not a semantic choice but a valuable professional activity that benefits individuals. The alternative can result in a laissez-faire and selective approach by the supervisee to our provision of information and advice, and possibly an unintended misinterpretation of it. This does not assure a professional use of our time.

## BOUNDARY ISSUES IN WORK

Clinical psychologists rightly prioritise working in an ethical manner, including recognising and working within appropriate boundaries. When working with people with learning disabilities are there different factors to consider? In the following discussion some of the factors affecting boundaries are considered.

It is imperative that certain issues are recognised at the outset of any therapeutic work with an individual. Many clients will not have asked to see a clinical psychologist, and will have been referred by someone else. Best practice will involve an informed consent. Real life will mean that the decision will have been made somewhere on a continuum from informed consent through informed acquiescence through to being uninvolved. Thus their expectations of the first meeting may be unformed.

Achieving consent may be further complicated by difficulties in explaining the process of therapy and gaining understanding of this (see 'Some Issues Concerning Direct Clinical Work' above). Clients may attend therapy with all sorts of expectations and agendas that may present difficulties for clarification and agreement. Furthermore, there may be very different expectations of therapy between the client and the referrer that may lead to future pressures on the therapist.

I have found that validating the experience of individuals is of crucial importance. Therapy may be one of the few occasions in which an individual has been listened to uncritically. The past experience may have contributed to feelings of hopelessness that will influence the individual's ability to participate actively and define outcomes for therapy – however skilful the therapist (Bandura 2006).

Such experience may also foster dependence and increase the likelihood of *transference* and fantasies about the ability of the therapist.

Confidentiality is an important issue. It can be affected by a person's historical experience, the need to share information with others and issues about seeing a person alone or with other carers present. It is commonplace for many people to know personal information about individuals with learning disabilities, and there may be good reasons for a therapist sharing information with others. People who may be used to being accompanied in therapy may presume that this should happen. All of these factors will influence the boundaries around therapeutic work.

The *venue* for clinical work may be much more varied than with other client groups (see above). This poses particular concerns for confidentiality, but also for consent. It is difficult to not attend if someone turns up at your home to see you. Furthermore, working with someone in their own home, while giving access to information that might be unavailable otherwise, can also put pressure on the clinician's professional boundaries.

Often individuals will ask us about ourselves. When asked in an appropriate way this signifies a degree of social skill, although confounded perhaps by an absence of recognition of some of the rules of behaviour towards professionals. I have found it unhelpful to ignore these requests and have used discussion of things that are relevant to me as part of assessment.

Specific assessment techniques, such as *Getting To Know You* (op cit.), imply a degree of information exchange to be effectively administered. The clinician may well give out personal information about herself that would be seen as irresponsible in other areas of work. Such an assessment requires placing ourselves in a variety of venues and substituting for example, cafes and newspaper advertisements for therapy rooms and stopwatches.

This means that we need to carefully consider boundaries. Indeed, precisely because the listening, attention and validation in our therapeutic work can be so important it is essential that we are clear about our role and do not allow it to become fused or confused with the idea of being *a friend*. In particular, there are implications for careful consideration of ending therapeutic work with a person.

## CONTINUING PROFESSIONAL DEVELOPMENT

Continuing Professional Development (CPD) is now rooted in our profession (Golding and Gray 2006). Clinical Psychologists in this specialism have significant CPD needs because of their *generalist* status. Thus their expected competencies will range across the administration and interpretation of psychometric assessment (including that of ASD and Asperger's Syndrome); using different psychological models in therapy; in the use of creative strategies to engage people with differing and multiple disabilities; in perfecting skills in supervising, teaching, service development and Court work. A further challenge has been to find where this CPD can be obtained.

There are limited opportunities. One important annual event has been the annual *Advancing Practice Conference* organised by the BPS LD Faculty. Local groups of the Faculty have also provided a venue for more informal CPD and support. The growing take-up of regular supervision (see above) also plays a part.

Inspection of professional journals, conference programmes and publishing flyers however indicates that there is not a great deal offered to meet CPD need in this specialism. Courses and conferences may be less relevant to working with adults with LD than to other client groups. One response to this in the North-West of England was to develop a bespoke training programme consisting of 12 days training over two years (Fleming and Golding, 2007). This Programme covered topics including *Neuro-psychological assessment, Assessing Capacity and Risk,* and *Applying an analysis of social context to work with people with intellectual disabilities* and 46 local clinicians with varying degrees of experience registered for the programme.

Developing the means to enable clinical psychologists to participate in high quality CPD will be an important issue in the future. Local initiatives, supported by good supervision are most likely to be practical.

## CURRENT CHALLENGES

### Can We be Effective Instruments of Change?

Let us begin by agreeing that despite 30 years of community-based care, there remains the need for huge changes in the lives of people with learning disabilities. Earlier in this chapter we considered the potential leadership role of Clinical Psychologists.

Working with individuals with Learning Disability requires a clear understanding of the person's social context (see Chapter 3 for a fuller discussion). More than many other areas of work Clinical Psychologists have focused on an assessment of the role that environmental (rather than intra-psychic) factors play in the behaviour of individuals. One result of this form of analysis is that resulting interventions will require the clinician to work with carers and services, and perhaps agencies not currently involved, as well as direct work with the individual concerned. There is a clear understanding of the *secondary* handicaps that are environmentally determined.

This means that we are informed by our clinical work of the lives and experiences of people with learning disabilities which often provides a clear impetus for change in the way services are provided. This knowledge has been and will continue to be extremely useful in informing our leadership roles.

There have been and are a number of individual Clinical Psychologists who have been effective in changing services. Clinical Psychologists possess important relevant skills, such as an ability to evaluate research, familiarity with psychological models and knowledge of group processes. The Clinical Psychology qualification does not in itself provide the skills to lead *organisational change*. Particular qualities may be insufficient and individuals may benefit from training in these skills (see CPD discussion above). An example of an initiative relevant to this is the *Introduction to Clinical Leadership and Management Programme* developed by the North-West Clinical Psychology CPD Scheme.

A number of questions remain: How realistic is this? What are the possibilities and the limitations? Also, how is this being enacted given the scarcity of Clinical Psychologists in acknowledged positions of service leadership? Might this require a conscious shift back from therapy work to shaping and changing environments (cf. Clements and Hassall 2008; Hassall and Clements 2011)? These will continue to inform our practice as Clinical Psychologists and hopefully some of the reflections in this chapter will mean that we can learn from the past in order to contribute to the future.

## What are the Current and Next 'Big Issues'?

The Learning Disabilities world has experienced many initiatives in the last 40 years and much change. There are a number of issues that in future will continue to be important to clinical psychologists working with people with learning disabilities. Some involve returning to issues not fully resolved earlier.

One of these concerns staff training and management, and the planning and organisation of services. These are critical to the employment of tried and tested applied psychological interventions. Despite injunctions for *Clinical Governance* and the introduction of North American franchised versions of innovation/management (such as MAGNET and LEO), too often services remain ignorant of applications that will improve the quality of life of those they care for or they are organisationally incapable of ensuring consistent good practice.

Another concerns the development of practical interventions for common psychological distress suffered by people with LD. This may well involve adaptations of Cognitive Behavioural Therapy that is now used widely with the non learning- disabled adult population and for which a burgeoning evidence base is now reported (see Chapter 19). Other therapeutic approaches must not be forgotten and it will remain important to fully acknowledge issues common to people with learning disabilities that may impinge on therapeutic work and limit their ability to benefit from it.

As well as interventions aimed at individuals diagnosed with specific forms of psychological distress (usually DSM-IV categories but see Cooper, 2004), there are still far too many services that fail to develop learning environments. The application of psychology to accurately assess, understand learning difficulties and then to develop procedures to manage or overcome these remain of paramount importance.

Working with service users to enable them to influence services remains an under-developed area and psychological skills can be important in enabling this to move beyond being merely an aspiration within localities.

The development of work based in a perspective from community psychology would appear to be congruent with both the historical environmentalist approach and that which prioritises empowerment through the establishment of therapeutic relationships that can enhance a sense of agency (cf Bandura 2006). It can be argued that this legacy has required clinical psychologists working with this client group to have a more political basis to their work when compared to colleagues in other specialisms. This is derived from practice that emphasises changing individuals (and by extension ideologies) rather than individuals (and cognitions). Care must be taken not to exaggerate this however, and the recent research (Emerson and Hatton 2007) demonstrating the relationship that social inequalities have to psychological issues in people with learning disabilities will require us to review our practice and the philosophy underlying this.

## CONCLUSIONS

This chapter has described some important factors influencing the practice of a Clinical Psychologist working with adults with learning disabilities. It is a personal account that has considered experience against the general factors affecting the profession.

Clinical Psychology has grown rapidly in the last 30 years but remains a small profession, closely tied to the National Health Service that remains its major employer. Currently, the expansion of Clinical Psychology numbers seems to have slowed, and Government initiatives to expand availability of psychological therapies appear to be based on assumptions that Clinical Psychologists are not the main provider of this service. It remains to be seen how this might translate to individuals with learning disabilities. People who often have very complex psychological needs and who have largely failed to benefit from any consistent, large-scale transference of research into practice.

*Valuing People* signalled a transfer of Learning Disability leadership and service provision away from the NHS. It has been pointed out that Clinical Psychologists can find themselves facing two opposing sets of demands. On the one hand as predominantly NHS employees they need to meet the demands of waiting times, throughput, CPA (developed for other client groups); on the other hand there is a local authority context that prioritises eligibility, Vulnerable Adults, and returning individuals from expensive out of area placements.

The shift towards Local Authorities as being lead commissioners of services adds to the complexity of Clinical Psychologists' work. The move is likely to be accompanied by a reduction in influence and a requirement to work into services that have a different set of priorities.

*Valuing People* contained little detail about some of the main issues relevant to the work of Clinical Psychologists, e.g. mental health and challenging behaviour. This difficulty is compounded by the greater power (and therefore on NHS services) contained in National Service Frameworks and the absence within NICE guidelines of much reference to people with learning disabilities. Other initiatives add to the complexity of understanding and commissioning clinical psychology services for people with learning disabilities.

Market driven policies in the NHS appear to emphasize, more than ever before, the need for a profession to demonstrate its value and worth. Readers may feel that in this chapter the value of Clinical Psychology has been presumed rather than proven. Two areas point to the continuing value of clinical psychology. The first is the ability to draw on and synthesize a range of psychological (and non-psychological) models and sources of information in developing means of understanding psychological distress. Another is the commitment, outlined above, to looking beyond pathology in the identification of futures for individuals. Furtherance of these activities will ensure the contribution of Clinical Psychology to the lives of individuals with LD.

## References

Bandura, A. (2006) Towards a Psychology of human agency. *Perspectives on Psychological Science*, **1**, 164–80.

Baum, S. and Webb, J. (2002) Valuing People: what will it mean for clinical psychology services for people with learning disabilities. *Clinical Psychology*, **14**, 20–4.

Baum, S. and Lynggaard, H. (eds) (2006) *Intellectual Disabilities: a systemic approach*. London, Karnac Books.

Blunden, R. (1980) Individual Programme Plans for mentally handicapped people: a draft procedural guide. Cardiff, Applied Research Unit Ely Hospital.

Brost, M.M. and Johnson, T.Z. (1982) *Getting to Know You. One approach to service assessment and planning for individuals with disabilities*. LaCrosse, Wisconsin, Wisconsin Coalition for Advocacy.

Brown, S., Flynn, M. and Wistow, G. (1992) *Back to the Future. Joint work for people with learning disabilities*. London, National Development Team.

Burton, M. (2004) *Policy analysis and Inequalities: the case of valuing people*. Paper presented at the UK Community Psychology Conference, Exeter, October.

Clements, J. and Hassall, R. (2008) The lost patrol? Will clinical psychology make any worthwhile difference to the lives of children with learning disabilities and their families? *Clinical Psychology Forum*, **191**, 15–19.

Cooper, R. (2004) What is wrong with the DSM? *History of Psychiatry*, **15**, 1–25.

Cullen, C. (2000) *A Review of Some Important Issues in Research and Services for People with Learning Disabilities and Challenging Behaviour*. Edinburgh, Scottish Executive review of services for people with a learning disability.

Department of Health (2001) *Valuing People: A new strategy for learning disability for the 21st century*. London: The Stationary Office.

DHSS (1971) *Better Services for the Mentally Handicapped*. London, HMSO.

Emerson, E. and Hatton, C. (2007) Contribution of socio-economic position to health inequalities of British children and adolescents with intellectual difficulties. *American Journal on Mental Retardation*, **112**, 140–50.

Felce, D., Jones, E. and Lowe, K. (2002) Active support: planning daily activities and support for people with severe mental retardation. In S. Holbourn and P.M. Vietze (eds) *Person–centred Planning: research, practice and future directions*. Baltimore, Paul H. Brookes.

Fleming, I. and Burton, M. (2001) Teaching about individual and society links on the Manchester Clinical Psychology Training Course' *Clinical Psychology*, **6**, 28–33.

Fleming, I. and Steen, L. (eds) (2011) *Supervision and Clinical Psychology* (2nd edn) Hove, Brunner-Routledge.

Fleming, I. and Golding, L. (2007) Organising CPD for learning disability specialists in the North West of England. *Clinical Psychology Forum*, **176**, 31–5.

Fleming, I.R. (2008) An analysis of the establishment for clinical psychologists working with people with learning disabilities in the North West of England. *Clinical Psychology and People with learning Disabilities*, **6**, 31–9.

Flynn, M. and LeMay, R. (eds) (1999) *A Quarter Century of Normalisation and Social Role Valorisation: evolution and impact*. Ottawa, University of Ottawa Press.

Forest, M. and Lusthaus, E. (1989). Promoting educational equality for all students: Circles and maps. In S. Stainback, W. Stainback, and M. Forest (eds), *Educating All Students in the Mainstream of Regular Education*. Baltimore, MD: Paul H. Brookes.

Goldiamond, I. (1974) Toward a constructional approach to social problems. *Behaviorism*, **2**, 1–84.

Golding, L. and Gray, I. (eds) (2006) *Continuing Professional Development for Clinical Psychologists: a practical handbook*. Oxford, BPS Blackwell.

Hassall, R. and Clements, L. (eds) (2011) Clinical psychology getting lost? Special edition. *Clinical Psychology Forum*, 217.

Hatton, C. (1998) Whose quality of life is it anyway? Some problems with the emerging quality of life consensus. *Mental Retardation*, **36**, 104–15.

Houts, P.A. and Scott, R.A. (1975) *Goal Planning with Developmentally Disabled Persons: Procedures for Developing an Individualised Client Plan*. Pennsylvania, Pennysylvania State University.

Independent Development Council for People with a Mental Handicap (1986) *Pursuing Quality*, London, IDC.

Leyin, A. (2001) The evolution of psychological approaches in working with people with learning disabilities. *Clinical Psychology Forum*, **148**, 12–17.

Lovett, H. (1985) *Cognitive Counselling and Persons with Special Needs*. Westport, Ct, Greenwood Press.

National Development Group for the Mentally Handicapped (1976) *Mental Handicap: Planning Together*. Pamphlet Number 1. London, HMSO.

North West Regional Health Authority (1983) *Services for People Who Are Mentally Handicapped: a model district service*. Manchester, NWRHA.

North West Regional Mental Handicap Advisory Group (1989) *A Guide to Quality Assessment*. Manchester, NWRMHAG.

Onyett, S. (2007) *New Ways of Working for Applied Psychologists in Health and Social Care-Working Psychologically in Teams*. Leicester, BPS.

Ovretveit, J. (1993) *Coordinating Community Care: multidisciplinary tams and care management*. Milton Keynes, Open University Press.

Porterfield, J., Blunden, R. and Blewitt, E. (1977) *The Organisation of an Activity Period for Profoundly Handicapped Adults*. Cardiff, Mental Handicap in Wales – Applied Research Unit.

Prilleltensky, I. and Nelson, G. (2002) *Doing Psychology Critically: making a difference in diverse settings*. New York, Palgrave Macmillan.

Ritchie, P., Sanderson, H., Kilbane, J. and Routledge, M. (2003) *People Plans and Practicalities – achieving change through person centred planning*. Edinburgh, SHS.

Stokes, T.F. and Baer, D.M. (1977) An implicit technology of generalization. *Journal of Applied Behavior Analysis*, **10**, 349–67.

Rose, J., Simmons, S., Hughes, K. and Smith, M. (2001) Establishment and function of clinical psychology services for people with learning disabilities. *Clinical Psychology*, **5**, 9–12.

Wertheimer, A. (1992) *Changing Lives: supported employment and people with learning difficulties*. Manchester, National Development Group.

Wolfensberger, W. (1999) A brief overview of social role valorisation. *Mental Retardation*, **38**, 105–23.

Ziarnik, J.P. and Bernstein, G.S. (1982) A critical examination of the effect of inservice training on staff performance. *Mental Retardation*, **20**(3), 109–14.

# Part 3
# WORKING WITH …

## Chapter 11

# WORKING WITH PEOPLE WHOSE BEHAVIOUR CHALLENGES SERVICES

### Alick Bush

## WHAT DO WE MEAN BY 'CHALLENGING BEHAVIOURS'?

Since its inception in the USA (Blunden and Allen 1987), the term 'challenging behaviour' has undergone many corruptions, such that its current usage often deviates significantly from the original definition. The term was developed in order to shift the requirement to change away from the *individual* and towards the *environment* around the person. The challenge was for services was to understand why the person was behaving as they were, to find effective ways to support them in order that the behaviour no longer needed to fulfil the same function, and hence to diminish the occurrence of the behaviour.

Increasingly, the term 'challenging behaviour' has been corrupted and is being used as a label or description of the person, and is sometimes even used as a quasi diagnosis. Thus people may be referred to as 'having challenging behaviour' or 'living in the challenging behaviour house'. The intention in this chapter is to revert to the original use of the term that views challenging behaviour as being socially constructed. Behaviour develops, and is maintained, through the interaction of both individual factors (e.g. the person's experiences, disabilities, communication difficulties, mental health etc) and environmental factors (how the person is supported, quality of the environment, opportunities to engage in activities, etc).

*Clinical Psychology and People with Intellectual Disabilities*, Second Edition. Edited by
Eric Emerson, Chris Hatton, Kate Dickson, Rupa Gone, Amanda Caine and Jo Bromley.
© 2012 John Wiley & Sons, Ltd. Published 2012 by John Wiley & Sons, Ltd.

The definition of challenging behaviour that is adopted here is: *Behaviour can be described as challenging when it is of such intensity, frequency or duration as to threaten the quality of life and/ or the physical safety of the individual or others, and is likely to lead to responses that are restrictive, aversive or result in exclusion'* (Royal College of Psychiatrists, British Psychological Society and Royal College of Speech and Language Therapists 2007). Behaviours that are likely to have such an impact may include those that are self injurious, aggressive and threatening, destructive or anti-social.

## HOW DO WE UNDERSTAND BEHAVIOUR THAT CHALLENGES?

Behavioural and neurobiological/psychiatric approaches to understanding challenging behaviour have predominated the literature. Although the focus of this chapter is upon understanding challenging behaviour from the perspective of behavioural psychology, it is important to do so within a broad understanding of other models. Integrated models that are operationalised within multi-disciplinary settings are likely to provide the most constructive approach to support people's complex behaviour.

### Neurological Models

Neurological theories have focussed upon the role of endogenous neurotransmitters in the development and maintenance of challenging behaviour. Specific mechanisms include:

- Opioid peptides such as the neurotransmitter β-endorphin may be released when a person self-injures. β-endorphin has an analgesic property and may act as an automatic reinforcer for the self-injury.
- Abnormalities in the dopamine receptor systems, such as those that occur in Lesch-Nyhan syndrome, appear to be implicated in some self-injury.
- There may be a link between the serotoninergic system and aggression, and possibly with obsessional forms of self-injury.

Integrated diagnostic and treatment models for self injury have been developed based upon assessing the specific operant functions and clinical characteristics of the behaviour (Mace and Mauk 1995).

### Communication-based Models

Challenging behaviours typically increase in frequency, intensity or duration as communication difficulties (Feldman and Griffiths 1997) and degree of cognitive impairment (McClintock *et al.* 2003) increase. Challenging behaviour can be conceptualised as having a 'communicative function' (Carr and Durand 1985), and such an interpretation can lead to a very different way of understanding why a behaviour is occurring. For example, a behavioural analysis of an excess behaviour may demonstrate that it is followed by social attention. A potential consequence of this analysis could be a recommendation to use an extinction contingency, by removing the social attention. However, if the function of the behaviour is to communicate a need, then applying an extinction procedure is not likely to be a successful intervention unless the person could generate an alternative way of expressing what they need/want. If this is not possible there is a high probability that the person will develop an even more undesirable behaviour in order to get their need met.

In addition to the link between expressive communication skills and challenging behaviour, the role of understanding is also crucial. Many staff-client communication acts are outside the level of understanding of the people they support, and a common function of challenging behaviour is 'escape motivated' (Kevan 2003). One factor that could contribute to a situation being perceived as aversive, and hence lead to 'escape motivated' behaviour, is if the expressive communication used by others is pitched at a level that is beyond the person's understanding. Escape from demands or social situations is a common function of challenging behaviour (Hanley et al. 2003).

## Psychiatric Models

There is a long tradition of behavioural excesses being interpreted within a psychiatric model. This framework often leads to pharmacological interventions as the treatment of choice (Deb et al. 2006). There are a number of ways in which psychiatric disorders may be associated with behaviours that present a challenge (Emerson et al. 1999; RCPsych et al. 2007; Allen, 2008). However, pharmacological interventions are often used to manage behaviours, rather than to proactively treat underlying psychiatric causes of the behaviour (McGillivray and McCabe 2004), despite the lack of an evidence-base for the effectiveness of many such interventions (Tyrer et al. 2008).

## Behavioural Models

Within a model of Applied Behavioural Analysis, challenging behaviours are seen as examples of 'operant behaviour'. Viewed in this way, challenging behaviours can be seen as *functional* and *adaptive*; they have been shaped through the person's interaction with their physical and social environment.

The operant approach to understanding behaviour is concerned with:

- the discovery of *functional relationships* between behaviours and environmental factors;
- an emphasis on the importance of the *context* in which the behaviour occurs;
- considering the behaviours shown by a person as the product of a *dynamic system.*

This is sometimes referred to as the Antecedent–Behaviour–Consequences (or A–B–C) model. See Sturmey *et al.* (2007) for a detailed review.

## Functional Relationships

Within applied behaviour analysis, consequences that shape or maintain behaviour are termed 'reinforcers'. These are defined functionally in terms of the impact which their presentation or withdrawal has upon subsequent behaviour. Positive reinforcement refers to those stimuli which increase the rate of a behaviour when *presented* contingently. Negative reinforcement refers to stimuli that increase the rate of a behaviour when they are *withdrawn* contingently. Conversely, positive punishment refers to stimuli that decrease the rate of a behaviour when they are contingently presented, while negative punishment has the effect of decreasing the rate of a behaviour as a consequence of contingent withdrawal of a stimulus.

Until a particular stimulus can be shown to increase or decrease the rate of a behaviour, it can not be classified as a 'reinforcer,' or 'punisher'. Thus food, smiles, praise, gentle contact, money, etc, are not defined as being positive reinforcers unless their presentation increases the rate of a specific behaviour.

## Contextual Factors

The context in which a behaviour occurs is an essential component of applied behaviour analysis. Contextual factors are important in two ways:

- *Establishing the motivational basis within which the behaviour occurs.*
  Biological and environmental contexts may influence the motivational basis of behaviour. For example, if someone is tired, in pain, frightened or in a noisy, uncomfortable environment, and is approached by a familiar member of staff with a request to do something, this may set the conditions for the staff member to become a negatively reinforcing

stimulus (positive punisher). In this set of circumstances the likelihood of the person carrying out the request will reduce. In a different context (e.g. the person is comfortable and relaxed in an environment that is peaceful and pleasant), the same request may be met by the person carrying out the behaviour, i.e. the staff member has become a positive reinforcer. Similarly, food is only likely to become a positive reinforcer if the person is hungry and does not have free access to it. When a person is satiated, food is more likely to operate as a negative reinforcer or positive punishment.

Increased attention is being given to the concept of *establishing operations* (EO). These are the factors such as reinforcer satiation and deprivation that alter the relationships between the antecedent events, the subsequent behaviour, and its maintaining consequences (Kennedy and Meyer 1998; McGill 1999).

- *Acting as discriminative stimuli for behaviours.*

Aspects of the context in which behaviour occurs may provide cues to the person concerning the probability of particular behaviours being reinforced. For example, the behaviour of 'knocking on an office door' is likely to lead to a positive outcome (a manager attends to the person's knocking) if there is a notice on the door indicating they are available, or if the door is ajar. However, if a notice reads 'engaged', the same behaviour is likely to lead to a negative outcome. The sign is a discriminative stimulus that determines whether the behaviour (knocking) is more or less likely to result in the consequence of the manager attending to the person.

It is important to consider the relationship between genetic syndromes and particular topographies of challenging behaviour, including self injury. There is a growing awareness of the status of certain genetic syndromes as significant risk markers for the development and maintenance of self injury (McClintock, Hall and Oliver 2003), and the development of models of gene-environment inter-play that enhance the understanding of the relationship between social interactions and behaviour (Langthorne and McGill 2008). A number of studies have explored the association between environmental events and challenging behaviours in people with different phenotypes, suggesting that gene-environment interactions may govern the presentations of these behaviours. This has important implications for understanding how a genetic predisposition to experience social or other stimuli as significantly rewarding in some syndromes can have an influence on the social reinforcement paradigm that underpins the development of challenging behaviours (Richman 2008). This understanding could lead to possible early interventions (Taylor and Oliver 2008).

**Table 11.1** Characteristics of positive behavioural support (Allen *et al.* 2005).

Positive Behavioural Support (PBS) has a number of characteristics:

- The goal of achieving enhanced community inclusion, choice, independence and respect, rather than simply behavioural change in isolation.
- Using functional analysis, it establishes what purposes the behaviours serve.
- It focuses on the triggers for the behaviours and how they can be altered in order to change the behaviours.
- It employs skills teaching as a central intervention.
- Improvements in quality of life are seen as both an intervention and an outcome measure.
- Reductions in behaviour are achieved as a side-effect of positive interventions.
- It has a long-term focus, recognising that challenging behaviours are often of a long-term nature and interventions need to be maintained over long periods.
- Challenging behaviours are often multiply determined, so interventions require a multi-component focus.
- Punishment approaches are reduced or eliminated.
- Risk management strategies include both proactive strategies for developing new behaviours and reactive strategies for managing behaviour when it occurs.

## Positive Behavioural Support

ABA has sometimes been portrayed as representing a technology for intervention that is devoid of a guiding value-base governing how it should be used, with the consequence that it could foster abusive practices (Emerson and McGill 1989). In contrast, the normalisation (social role valorisation) philosophy provides a positive value-base, but has been criticised for lacking the accompanying technology to translate these values into practice. These approaches have been combined to create a values-led approach to achieving behavioural change – Positive Behavioural Support (Allen *et al.* 2005). The characteristics of PBS are summarised in Table 11.1.

Interventions that utilise such approaches can be effective at addressing severe challenging behaviour, show long-term maintenance of improvements, generalise across settings, and are most likely to be effective if interventions are based upon a functional analysis (Carr *et al.* 1999; McClean *et al.* 2007).

## ASSESSMENT AND FORMULATION OF CHALLENGING BEHAVIOUR

Assessment is an essential stage in the development of interventions for challenging behaviour, and the results of several meta-analyses (Scotti *et al.* 1991; Didden *et al.* 1997, 2006; Grey and Hastings 2005) indicate that a pre-intervention experimental functional analysis is associated with the most effective behavioural treatments. Assessment serves three main purposes (BPS 2004):

- To collect sufficient information to lead to a coherent psychological formation.
- To enable the development of an intervention plan which fits theperson and their environment ('goodness of fit').
- To establish a baseline so that the effectiveness of the intervention can be evaluated.

A number of detailed guides to the assessment of challenging behaviour are available (Carr *et al.* 1994; Meyer and Evans 1989; Miltenberger 1998; O'Neill *et al.* 1997). Some of the steps in the process and available methods will be explored further in this section and are summarised in Figure 11.1.

### Step 1: Identify the Problem and Select the Target Behaviour

The first step in assessment is to obtain information about:

- what the behaviour is that is of concern;
- where and when it occurs;
- the impact (level of risk) on the person and others.

The selection of the 'target behaviour' should be of social significance and relevance to the person, so that a change in the behaviour will have a meaningful outcome. This requires a wider assessment beyond the topography of the specific behaviour. Factors may include:

- short- and medium-term physical harm to the person, the environment and others;
- limitations on their access to functional age-appropriate community-based activities;
- exclusion from their family or community-based services;
- stress and burnout experienced by carers and care staff;
- quality of relationships with other people;
- service responses that include restrictive practices (seclusion, restraint, locked doors, etc);

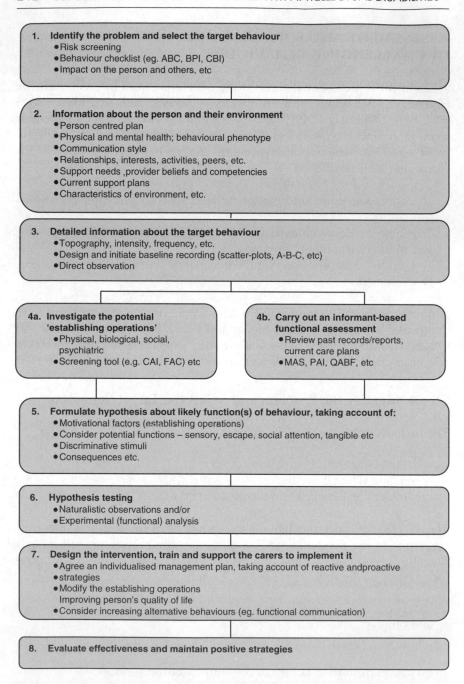

**Figure 11.1** Steps in the assessment and formulation of challenging behaviour.

- interventions that may be abusive or overly restrictive, involve inappropriate prescribing of medication, punitive interventions, or rely on risk avoidance rather than risk management (RCPsych *et al.* 2007).

This information is likely to be gathered through interviews with staff and carers who have the most direct contact with the person. Validated check-lists such as the *Aberrant Behaviour Checklist* (Aman *et al.* 1995), the *Behaviour Problems Inventory* (Rojahn *et al.* 1989), and the *Challenging Behaviour Interview* (Oliver *et al.* 2003) are useful tools that may help to clarify which behaviours are causing the greatest concern to the safety of the person and their environment. They are also useful as a repeated measure to evaluate the impact of any intervention.

If the behaviours are of low frequency, but have a high impact (e.g. assault, violence, fire setting), opportunities for direct observation are likely to be limited. In these circumstances there will be a heavy reliance on past information gathered from care plans, reports, incident forms, etc. Such retrospective information may be unreliable, and may not contain the detail required to be able to develop a functional assessment.

Increasingly within services, challenging behaviour is being reviewed within a framework of 'risk'. Effective risk assessment is at the centre of the process, with some services using frameworks such as the Care Programme Approach (Department of Health 1999) to ensure that risks to the individual, staff and the community are adequately identified and prioritised, and that plans are in place to manage the risks.

Risk assessments can sometimes become an excuse for services to adopt a 'risk averse' stance that severely restricts a person's life further, with the potential consequence of inadvertently increasing their level of risk. A framework for *therapeutic risk taking* (Allen 2002) will be considered later in the chapter.

## Step 2: Information About the Person and Their Environment

Any assessment to establish the function of a person's challenging behaviour must gather detailed information about the person and the environment in which they live. To focus solely on the topography of the behaviour will lead to an incomplete understanding of the behaviour, and of the factors that have shaped and maintain the behaviour.

Individual factors should already be detailed in their *person centred plan* and may include:

- physical and mental health problems;
- genetic syndrome that may have an implication for gene-environment interaction;
- how much they understand about what is said to them, how they make their needs known, and any specific communication or sensory difficulties;

- their likes, dislikes and aspirations – 'what makes a good day for the person?';
- their personal history of relationships and experiences;
- how much support does the person need to carry out a variety of activities, etc.

Environmental factors will include characteristics of the person's immediate support and of the service providing that support (McAtee *et al.* 2004):

- Availability of staff, their skills, values and working relationships.
- Quality and comfort of the material environment.
- Ability of the service to understand and respond to the unique needs of the individual and to form positive relationships.

## Step 3: Detailed Information About the Target Behaviour

There are a variety of different methods that can be used to gather direct information about the form, frequency and intensity of the behaviour, and the relationships between the stimuli and consequences. Frequently, an individualised recording system will be designed for care staff to gather detailed information about the behaviour. The method of data collection, and the complexity of the information being sought, will be influenced by the competency of the staff to carry out the observations, the time they can devote to it, and the availability of suitable technologies (e.g. use of hand-held computers, or video recording). These factors will also influence the reliability and validity of the information that is gathered by such approaches.

## A–B–C analysis

One of the most frequently used observational approaches to descriptive analysis of behaviour and its function, is the *Antecedent Behaviour Consequence* (ABC) chart. This method usually involves care staff completing a recording sheet of specific information about the occurrence of antecedent events (A) and consequent events (C) in relation to a defined target behaviour (B). Many variations of the chart exist (see Table 11.2), depending on the specific use to which it is put (Desrouchers *et al.* 1997; Groden and Lantz 2001). A common factor in their application is that staff who are completing the observations and recording the information, require a level of training to be able to make sufficiently detailed observations and interpretation of the relevance of the antecedents and consequences (Emerson 1995).

**Table 11.2** Example of an A–B–C chart.

| Name: | | Date: | |
|---|---|---|---|
| Target behaviour: | | | |
| Please complete the chart each time the target behaviour occurs | | | |
| Time: | | Location: | |
| What was (s)he doing in the 20 minutes leading up to the behaviour? | What was said/done to her/him immediately before the behaviour? | What was the immediate response by people around? | What was the impact on the behaviour following this? |
| | | | |

The data that is generated from the ABC records is typically used to provide information about:

- the frequency, context and pattern of when the behaviour occurs;
- factors in the environment (e.g. whether demands are being made of the person, noise, presence/absence of certain stimuli) that may be common antecedents of the behaviour;
- the impact that the behaviour may have upon other people in the person's environment (e.g. withdrawal by others, staff discontinue making requests of the person, comfort and attention provided by staff).

From this data, provisional hypotheses can start to be developed for further investigation.

## Sequential Analysis

More complex approaches to recording and analysis can address some of the limitations of A–B–C charts (Hall and Oliver 2000). Hand-held computers (Thompson *et al.* 2000) have been used for time-based lag sequential analyses in order to identify relationships in real time between behaviours and environmental factors.

## Scatter Plots

Scatter plots (Touchette *et al.* 1985) provide a relatively straightforward approach to investigate the temporal characteristics of a target behaviour (see Table 11.3). Observers record the presence/absence of the

**Table 11.3** Scatter plot – simplified version.

| Period | Mon | Tue | Wed | Thurs | Fri | Sat | Sun | Total |
|--------|-----|-----|-----|-------|-----|-----|-----|-------|
| Name: | | | | | Week commencing: | | | |
| Target behaviour: | | | | | | | | |
| Please enter X on the chart each time the target behaviour occurs | | | | | | | | |
| 7.00 – | | | | | | | | |
| 7.30 – | | | | | | | | |
| 8.00 – | | | | | | | | |
| 8.30 – | | | | | | | | |
| 9.00 – | | | | | | | | |
| 9.30 – | | | | | | | | |
| 10.00 – | | | | | | | | |
| 10.30 – | | | | | | | | |
| 11.00 – | | | | | | | | |
| 11.30 – | | | | | | | | |
| 12.00 – | | | | | | | | |
| 12.30 – | | | | | | | | |
| 13.00 – | | | | | | | | |
| 13.30 – | | | | | | | | |
| 14.00 – | | | | | | | | |
| 14.30 – | | | | | | | | |
| 15.00 – | | | | | | | | |
| 15.30 – | | | | | | | | |
| 16.00 – | | | | | | | | |
| 16.30 – | | | | | | | | |
| 17.00 – | | | | | | | | |
| 17.30 – | | | | | | | | |
| 18.00 – | | | | | | | | |
| 18.30 – | | | | | | | | |
| 19.00 – | | | | | | | | |
| Etc. | | | | | | | | |
| **Total** | | | | | | | | |

behaviour within specified blocks of time. Over time, patterns may emerge that show a relationship between the behaviour, time of day, activities, etc.

## Step 4: What is the Function of this Behaviour for the Person? (Functional Assessment)

The purpose of assessment is to establish the processes that contribute to an understanding of *why* the behaviour is important to the person, i.e. what function does it serve the person? Functional assessment is a specific behaviour-analytic procedure, which employs structured observation and other methods of assessment (e.g. interviews of people who are in frequent contact with the person, or the use of standardised questionnaires) to generate hypotheses about the challenging behaviour, antecedents which may be acting as discriminative stimuli for the behaviours and consequences which may be reinforcing and maintaining it.

The terms *functional assessment* and *functional analysis* are used interchangeably by some clinicians, but there is an important distinction. *Functional assessment* is a more general term that includes a variety of approaches that contribute to establishing the function of the behaviour. *Functional analysis* is a more specific term that refers to structured techniques, such as analogue assessment (Iwata *et al.* 1994) that may include manipulating antecedents and consequences in order to establish their functional relationships.

There is a correlation between the use of a functional assessment and successful outcomes, as measured by reduced levels of challenging behaviour (Grey and Hastings 2005). Pre-intervention functional assessment should therefore be adopted as one part of the process for intervention in challenging behaviour. Miltenberger (1998) reviews some of the different methods for conducting a functional assessment, with emphasis on the antecedents to the behaviour.

## Step 4a: Investigate Potential 'Establishing Operations'

The information gathered from the various assessments can be combined with other information about the person's bio-behavioural state, the context of the behaviour and the environment, to generate hypotheses about the processes that may be maintaining the person's challenging behaviour. Instruments such as the *Contextual Assessment Inventory* (McAtee *et al.* 2004) and *Functional Analysis Checklist* (Van Houten *et al.* 1989; Sturmey 2001) can be helpful in structuring the investigation of potential establishing operations.

## Step 4b: Informant-based Functional Assessment

Although direct observation is the foundation of the functional analytic approach, there are practical limitations to its use in the context of where the person is living and how they are being supported. Indirect methods such as informant-based assessments are therefore also used to generate hypotheses about the function of a behaviour. For low frequency behaviours, these may be the most practical way to obtain the information required for a functional assessment. For high frequency behaviours they may provide useful initial information that will help guide a more comprehensive observational or experimental approach as part of the hypothesis development stage of the assessment.

Typically, informant-based assessment tools aim to identify the possible function(s) of the person's challenging behaviour, by means of structured interviews with staff or carers who know the person well. They are designed to elicit detailed information about when, where and how the behaviour occurs, and what events may influence its occurrence. Potential functions that this approach may identify include:

- *Sensory* – obtaining sensory stimulation as a consequence of the behaviour.
- *Escape* – avoiding an undesired situation or task.
- *Attention* – obtaining social reinforcement that is otherwise not available.
- *Tangible* – obtaining a desired object or activity that is not available.

There is conflicting evidence about the reliability and validity of many of the informant-based assessment tools and some caution should be exercised in their use (Toogood and Timlin 1996; Sturmey 2001). It would not be appropriate to use them as the sole basis for the development of a formulation, but they can provide a useful insight into staff beliefs about the causes and possible functions of the person's behaviour, which will help to inform the assessment and subsequent intervention (Hastings 1996). Zimbelman (2005) provides a review of several instruments. Some of the more commonly used tools include:

- *Motivational Assessment Scale – MAS* (Durand and Crimmins 1988).

  A 16-item questionnaire that asks the respondent to rate the likelihood of the behaviour occurring in specific situations using a 7-point Likert scale (e.g. 'Does the behaviour occur following a request to perform a difficult task?').

- *Functional Analysis Interview – FAI* (O'Neill *et al.* 1997).

  Open-ended questions about features of the behaviour, events that are likely to trigger it and consequences that may maintain it. It provides a framework for carrying out an extended interview with informants.

- *Questions About Behavioural Function – QABF* (Matson *et al.* 1999).

  A 25 item rating scale, where each item is rated on a 4-point Likert scale. Five subscales address five maintaining variables. Like the MAS, it has been developed as an alternative or adjunct to the use of analogue baselines. The QABF has been demonstrated to have predictive validity, and interventions based on functions identified following use of the QABF have been shown to have greater decreases in behaviour than non-function based interventions.

## Step 5: Formulate Hypothesis About Likely Function(s) of the Behaviour

Having completed the investigations of potential establishing operations and informant-based functional assessments, the clinician should be in a position to draw up hypotheses about the likely function or functions of the behaviours and what maintains them. Within the framework of Applied Behavioural Analysis, this is the 'formulation'.

## Step 6: Hypothesis Testing

Events that are hypothesised to be maintaining the behaviour can be manipulated in order to assess whether they influence the behaviour. If it can be demonstrated that the interventions bring about changes in aspects of the challenging behaviour, then it may be concluded that the formulation has validity and a systematic intervention can be designed based on the functional assessment.

Broadly, there are two main approaches to testing out the hypotheses before proceeding to the intervention stage:

- *Naturalistic observations (or structural analysis)* involve manipulating events in the person's natural environment that are thought to be maintaining the behaviour. Detailed observations are employed to evaluate the effect of the changes on the occurrence of the behaviour. The conclusions from the observations should enable the clinician to confirm the function of the behaviour (i.e. under what conditions is the behaviour likely to occur most frequently, hence what contingencies maintain it, and what interventions might bring about change?). Statistical techniques such as lag sequential analysis may be incorporated into the methodology as a means of verifying the conclusions from the observations (Emerson *et al.* 1996). In clinical practice in community settings, naturalistic observations are the most likely approach that would be used.
- *Experimental (functional) analysis* can be conceptualised as a series of 'mini-experiments', in which antecedents and/or consequences

that are hypothesised to influence the behaviour, are systematically manipulated. A functional relationship is demonstrated if the frequency or intensity of the behaviour changes in relation to the different contingencies. Interventions based upon the functional relationships, can then be instituted. Analogue analyses are the best known method of functional analysis (Iwata *et al*. 1982).

This hypothesis testing process can best be considered as a variety of different single case experimental design approaches (Barlow and Hersen 1984) as a means to demonstrate the contingencies that are influencing the behaviour (Didden *et al*. 2006; Vollmer and Van Camp 1998). At the conclusion of this process, the clinician should have confirmed or amended the formulation that will subsequently guide the design of the intervention.

## Step 7: Design the Intervention, Train and Support Carers to Implement It

Within an ABA model, interventions are based upon addressing the identified functions of the behaviour. There are many examples of guidelines for interventions within a framework of positive behavioural support (BPS 2004; Scotti and Meyer 1999; Lucyshyn *et al*. 2002; Condillac 2007). It is beyond the scope of this chapter to review the full range of approaches that are described in the literature, and the remainder of this section will address the key principles to be considered when designing an intervention.

## Reducing Challenging Behaviour by Modifying Establishing Operations

*Establishing operations* (EOs) are factors that alter the relationship between antecedent events, the subsequent behaviour, and the consequences that maintain it. By identifying the EOs that influence the likelihood of the behaviour occurring, it is possible to design interventions that effectively reduce the motivational basis underlying the challenging behaviour. For example, a functional assessment may indicate that a person's self-injury is maintained by escape from social demands. A detailed analysis may identify some of the EOs that lead to social demands being an aversive stimulus for that person. Potentially these could include such factors as tiredness, hunger, pain or sedation (bio-behavioural state); complexity of language used, repetition of tasks, previous experiences (preceding activities); ambient noise, presence or absence of key staff or peers, levels of demand, etc (current context).

It is likely that a common factor in their effectiveness is that they reduce the potency of the reinforcers that are responsible for maintaining the challenging behaviour (Emerson 2001). Thus, in the example of the person whose self-injury is maintained by escape from social demands, if it is shown that the behaviour is more likely to occur when the person is asked to perform an activity by a staff member whom the person finds intimidating (i.e. staff demands are aversive and evoke escape motivated self-injury) then by changing the staff member, or improving the way they interact with the person, it is likely that the person will show less self-injury.

One of the implications of an approach based on the modification of EO's is that challenging behaviours can be significantly reduced by taking account of the person's preferences. In a situation where a person's challenging behaviour is associated with the presence of particular people, activities or settings, it is likely that the required intervention may merely be to change the opportunities available to the person (Meyer and Evans 1993; Saunders and Saunders 1998). Interventions that take full account of a person's physical needs, and a well developed person centred plan are therefore essential foundations for any interventions (Department of Health 2007).

A theme identified in several studies is that low rates of reinforcer quality or density in the environment operate as setting events for challenging behaviour (Grey and Hastings 2005). Quality of life outcomes following behavioural interventions are rarely reported, suggesting that this dimension is not routinely measured. Resources such as Positive Goals (Fox and Emerson 2002) can assist practitioners to identify socially valid interventions that enhance the quality of life of the person, while at the same time providing the means to evaluate the effectiveness of the interventions by measuring outcomes against agreed goals.

## Increasing Alternative Behaviours

The incidence of challenging behaviour can be reduced by reinforcing (and thereby increasing the rate of) other behaviours. Two approaches can be employed to achieve this aim: the principle of *functional displacement* involves replacing challenging behaviour with a more appropriate behaviour from within the same response class (Carr 1988); *differential reinforcement* of other behaviours involves replacing challenging behaviour with a new behaviour.

- *Functional displacement.*

  Interventions based on functional displacement seek to introduce a new behaviour (or increase the rate of an existing, but low frequency behaviour), which will tap into the existing contingencies of reinforcement and thus displace the challenging behaviour. Carr and Durand (1985) conceptualise challenging behaviours as having a 'communicative function'. Rather than being maladaptive, challenging behaviours can be viewed as adaptive, given that they often bring about environmental change (e.g. staff go away when the person shouts in response to being asked to complete a difficult task). If challenging behaviour is interpreted as an attempt by a person with limited communication skills to communicate a message such as wanting to obtain attention, rejecting activities, or requesting something tangible, then functional communication training (FCT) may effectively reduce the likelihood of challenging behaviour occurring.

However, FCT does not automatically reduce challenging behaviours in settings other than those in which FCT is taught, and explicit generalisation strategies may be required (Schindler and Horner, 2005). Staff training initiatives are required to foster appropriate communication interactions between staff and adults who challenge services (Duker *et al.* 2004; Smidt *et al.* 2007).

In order for functional displacement to be effective, the replacement response must be equivalent to the challenging behaviour and relatively more 'efficient' in achieving the outcome for the person (Carr 1988). From this, it follows that factors such as the rate and quality of reinforcement, the response effort required by the person, and the immediacy of reinforcement, will all impact on the likelihood of success of functional communication training. It may also be necessary to combine functional communication training with more traditional reactive strategies such as extinction or differential reinforcement of the avoided task (Hagopian *et al.* 1998; Fisher *et al.* 2004).

• *Differential reinforcement*.

It is possible to reduce the incidence of challenging behaviour by reinforcing (and thereby increasing the rate of) other behaviours. There are variations on the principle:

– *Differential reinforcement of other (DRO)* behaviours – this is sometimes also referred to as omission training, and involves the delivery of a reinforcement, contingent upon the non-occurrence of the target behaviour. The 'other' can be any behaviour, so for example in a classroom situation where a child disrupts lessons by shouting, reinforcement will be provided for any other activity that occurs during a specified time period.
– *Differential reinforcement of incompatible (DRI)* behaviours – this is a more specific approach, in which the differentially selected alternative behaviour is incompatible with the challenging behaviour.

The evidence-base for the effectiveness of approaches that are based on differential reinforcement is mixed, and appears to be less effective when it is used alone to reduce severely challenging behaviours (Emerson 2001). Approaches such as *Active Support* (Stancliffe *et al.* 2008) provide structures that enable carers to enhance the quality of a person's environment, and there is some evidence that this can have an impact on the frequency of challenging behaviours (Toogood *et al.* 2009).

## Altering the Consequences of Behaviours

The focus of this chapter has been on *antecedent control* of behaviour, rather than on the relationship between the specific behaviour and the consequences that may be maintaining it. However, it is important to have an understanding of the techniques that result from this relationship, as they can have powerful influences on the occurrence of behaviour, and are still utilised in many services, often being implicated in investigations of abusive practice (e.g. Commission for Healthcare Audit and Inspection 2006). Clinical psychologists may be asked to advise on their use.

• *Extinction.*

If the functional analysis demonstrates that a particular behaviour occurs because it is being reinforced by consequences that are positive for the individual, then removal of the reinforcer should stop the incentive for the behaviour and reduce the likelihood of its future occurrence. This approach is *extinction*.

There is an evidence base (Scotti *et al.* 1991) that extinction can be an effective intervention. However, most of the reviewed studies were carried out under very controlled conditions in highly structured settings. Practical difficulties with applying this technique in community settings include the need to apply the approach consistently, the temporary increase in behaviour frequency during the early stages of the extinction process (extinction burst), ethical issues of withholding reinforcing activities when a person may already be in an impoverished environment and so may have little access to sources of reinforcement, the limited generalisation of effects to new situations, and the possible increase of other collateral behaviours. Care staff also describe the dilemmas they can face in community settings when they are expected to ignore a behaviour that the public may find unacceptable.

It is therefore generally inappropriate to implement extinction procedures on their own, but they may be included as one component of a complex package of interventions.

• *Punishment.*

*Punishment* is the application of a response which reduces the frequency of a behaviour. Punishment may be *positive* (in the technical sense of *adding* a stimulus), for example when a person is reprimanded, or physical pain, discomfort or psychological distress is applied. Alternatively, it may be *negative* (by *removing* a stimulus), for example by using time out, fines or withdrawal of attention. There is an evidence base that punishment-based procedures may be effective in reducing behaviour. However, Adam *et al*. (2004) have demonstrated that non-aversive procedures are equally effective in the treatment of such behaviours as pica. Punishment-based procedures are generally viewed as being ethically unacceptable (Evans and Meyer 1990), and high rates of negative outcomes such as increases in non targeted challenging behaviours have been reported. There is poor generalisation of the effects to other situations.

Procedures that are based upon punishment should *not* be used in general clinical practice. Any proposed interventions should be subjected to rigorous multi-disciplinary scrutiny that will involve careful consideration of the legal framework and Human Rights legislation, the person's access to effective advocacy, and a full exploration of alternative positive approaches.

## Individualised Management Plans

Challenging behaviour is frequently conceptualised within a framework of risk management, in which the behaviour may present a risk to either the person with a learning disability or to others in their environment. This approach therefore places requirements upon services to operate within the appropriate legislative framework for health and safety. One consequence of this can be a tendency by some services to adopt a culture that is risk averse. This in turn can lead to reduced opportunities for active participation, reduced quality of life and an increase in the very conditions that become the setting events for challenging behaviour.

Allen (2002) provides a 13-step model for the development of a risk management plan that encourages an approach of *positive risk management*. Core to the framework are functional assessment, proactive (or preventative) strategies to reduce the future probability of the behaviour occurring, and reactive strategies (which may include physical interventions) to provide clear direction for staff on how to respond when the behaviour occurs. Table 11.4 provides a summary example of such a plan.

Clinicians are often placed in a dilemma as to how to prioritise their work with someone who presents significantly challenging behaviour – the imperative to act quickly to institute reactive strategies that reduce the immediate risk of harm, whilst also needing to carry out a thorough functional assessment to ensure that longer term preventative strategies will be effective. LaVigna and Willis (2005) provide a model for supporting people who challenge using strategies that encourage social and community inclusion, whilst including both reactive and proactive strategies. They recommend a number of reactive strategies for managing crises that

**Table 11.4** Individualised risk management plan (adapted from Allen, 2002).

**Name:** John Smith                     **Date completed:** 4 July 2007

### 1. Behaviour of concern?
John hits his forehead against the wall- usually one or two sharp blows, but at times in bursts of 10–15 hits. The frequency of episodes varies from zero times per day to a maximum of 30 times. This pattern has been the same throughout the 5 years he has lived here.

### 2. Who is at risk and how?
John is at risk of serious injury. He has permanent scarring and a raised bump on his forehead. He often bleeds from the wound.

### 3. When is this most likely to occur?
Initial functional assessment suggests that it is most likely to occur when staff ask him to do something, particularly when he is already doing something else or when his preferred schedule is interrupted. There are periods when he appears to be depressed and he is withdrawn, has little appetite and a disturbed sleep pattern. He is even more likely to self-injure at these times.

### 4. Primary preventative strategies
  a. Closely monitor for early signs of John becoming depressed and re-refer to psychiatrist.
  b. Wait until he has finished an activity before asking him to do something else.
  c. Consistently use his pictorial communication board to ensure he understands what he is being asked to do.
  d. Follow the daily Active Support plan to ensure he is offered his preferred activities from his person centred plan.

### 5. Behavioural indicators that his behaviour may be increasing
*Green* – John smiles when interacting; will initiate self care, obtaining snacks/drinks, and takes an interest in his environment. He will participate in most activities identified in his support plan, and will push objects or staff away if he does not want the activity.
*Amber* – John smiles less and requires 2–3 prompts to do things. He does not watch T.V. and appears to be in a world of his own, requiring a lot of encouragement to eat and drink. When asked to do something he does not want, he may rock his body vigorously.
*Red* – John does not smile, is withdrawn and rarely participates in any activities. He sometimes requires physical prompts to eat and drink, and this prompting can lead to him banging his head.

*(Continued)*

**Table 11.4** (*cont'd*)

### 6. Secondary preventative strategies if he shows 'red' behaviours
a. Ensure the mental health monitoring sheets are completed, and that John is reassessed by his psychiatrist. Administer prescribed medication.
b. Familiar staff to offer him meals and drinks, spending more 1:1 time with him.
c. Sit between him and wall.
d. If he pushes food and drink away, wait 10 minutes before re-offering.

### 7. Reactive strategies to be used if required
a. Follow the procedures that are detailed in John's 'Reactive Management Care Plan' in any situation when he starts to bang his head against the wall.
b. Ensure all staff who work with John have received training in these procedures.

### 8. Unmanaged risks
a. Other tenants can become upset and may require re-assurance.
b. Additional staffing may be required.
c. Closely monitor daily food and drink intake.
d. Refer for specialist assessment if the behaviour persists.

### 9. Staff response following incident of banging his head
a. First aid to forehead as detailed in care plan.
b. Avoid offering another activity for 10 minutes.

### 10. How does the plan support community access?
a. Use the flexible staffing agreement to increase staff cover when he shows 'red' behaviours.
b. Follow procedure for accessing mental health team input.
c. Continue to encourage him to sit in the garden, even if he does not want to access wider community.

### 11. Recording and reviews
a. Scatter plot and ABC recording of each incidence.
b. Care plan entry for each 'red' behaviour.
c. Key worker to analyse forms and provide monthly summary at team meeting.
d. Follow Trust's serious incident reporting.

### 12. Agreement with the plan
A.Brown (Team Leader), R Green (Service Manager), Dr P White (Psychiatrist), Dr D Black (Psychologist), Mrs Smith (Mother)

### 13. Review process
Feedback at monthly team meeting with house staff and psychologist. Annual review at Care Programme Approach meeting.

do not involve physical interventions. These include diversion to a reinforcing or compelling event or activity, and strategic capitulation.

It is important that any plan addresses both reactive and proactive approaches and that these are developed in a way that ensures the safety of the person and others. The evidence base for the effectiveness of physical interventions is limited (McDonnell 2009), but if they are required, they must be developed in accordance with the current guidance (DH/DES 2002).

## Step 8: Evaluate Effectiveness and Maintain Positive Strategies

This chapter has emphasised the long term nature of challenging behaviour and the importance of environmental factors in its development and maintenance. The process of assessment, re-formulation and intervention is therefore an iterative one, and the clinician will need to ensure that interventions are effectively evaluated (BPS 2004). Factors such as the introduction of new support staff or changes in the person's daytime opportunities may have a significant impact on the person's behaviour. Specific steps will need to be taken to monitor the implementation and effectiveness of interventions. Explicit strategies are required to ensure that effective interventions can be maintained within 'capable environments' (RCPsych et al. 2007), despite possible changes in the person's support team.

## CONCLUSIONS

This chapter set out to describe the processes involved in the assessment of challenging behaviour in order to understand the function of the behaviour within the person's social context. This approach provides the basis for the development of socially valid interventions that can lead to significant outcomes that enhance the person's quality of life. The emphasis here has been upon the model of Applied Behavioural Analysis, and it is important that this is delivered within a multi-disciplinary framework.

Despite the evidence that interventions based upon a functional assessment are the most likely to bring about a positive change, their use within community settings is disappointingly low. When interventions exist, most are 'informal' and they frequently lack important elements such as input from a qualified professional, a written intervention plan, organised caregiver training and supervision, formal monitoring, and evaluations of their outcomes (Feldman et al. 2004).

Most people who present challenging behaviour now live in the community, often in small residential homes or supported living, with varying levels of support. Many of these services are insufficiently developed and organised to be able to provide the necessary levels of support (Broadhurst and Mansell 2007), resulting in placement breakdown and removal to accommodation out of area that may be a long way from the person's home (DoH 2007). A task for practitioners is to disseminate approaches such as positive behavioural support to front line support workers (Grey and McClean 2007).

If people are to be effectively supported in local communities, a comprehensive range of services is required. Rather than relying on attempts to alter a person's behaviour through individualised interventions alone, it is necessary to design services that can promote a person's quality of life *in spite* of the intensity or frequency of their behaviour. The rhetoric of 'treatment', in which challenging behaviour is seen as being located within the individual and amenable to psychological (and other multidisciplinary) interventions, can help to perpetuate unsophisticated support for individuals within various care arrangements. Clinicians, managers and commissioners need to be developing capable environments that are well organised, understand the needs of the individual, and support staff to deliver effective interventions that are based upon the principles of Positive Behavioural Support.

# References

Adam, D.B., Sherman, J.A., Sheldon, J.B. and Napolitano, D.A. (2004) Behavioural interventions to reduce pica of persons with developmental disabilities. *Behavior Modification*, **28**, 45–72.

Allen, D. (2002) Devising individualised risk management plans. In D. Allen (ed.) *Ethical Approaches to Physical Interventions: responding to challenging behaviour in people with intellectual disabilities*. Kidderminster: BILD.

Allen, D. (2008) The relationship between challenging behaviour and mental ill health in people with intellectual disabilities: A review. *Journal of Intellectual Disabilities*, **12**, 267–94.

Allen, D., James, W., Evans, J., Hawkins, S. and Jenkins, R. (2005) Positive Behavioural Support: Definition, current status and future directions. *Learning Disability Review*, **10**, 4–11.

Aman, M.G., Burrow, W.H. and Wolford, P.L. (1995) The Aberrant Behavior Checklist-Community: factor validity and effect of subject variables for adults in group homes. *American Journal on Mental Retardation*, **100**, 283–92.

Barlow, D.H. and Hersen, M. (1984) *Single Case Experimental Designs*. Oxford: Pergamon.

Blunden, R. and Allen, D. (1987) *Facing the Challenge: an Ordinary Life for People with Learning Disabilities and Challenging Behaviours*. London: Kings Fund Centre.

British Psychological Society (2004) *Challenging Behaviours: psychological interventions for severely challenging behaviours shown by people with learning disabilities*. Leicester: British Psychological Society.

Broadhurst, S. and Mansell, J. (2007) Organisational and individual factors associated with break down of residential placements for people with intellectual disabilities. *Journal of Intellectual Disability Research*, 51, 293–301.

Carr, E.G. (1988) Functional equivalence as a mechanism of response generalisation. In R.H. Horner, G. Dunlap and R.L. Koegel (eds) *Generalisation and Maintenance: life style changes in applied settings*. Baltimore: Paul H. Brookes.

Carr, E.G. and Durand, V.M. (1985) Reducing behavior problems through functional communication training. *Journal of Applied Behavior Analysis*, 18, 116–26.

Carr, E.G., Horner R.H., Turnbull, A.P., Marquis, J., McLaughlin, D., McAtee, M., et al. (1999) *Positive Behavior Support for People with Developmental Disabilities: a research synthesis*. Washington: AAMR.

Carr, E.G., Levin, L., McConnachie, G., Carlson, J.L., Kemp, D.C. and Smith, C. E. (1994) *Communication-based Intervention for Problem Behaviour: a user's guide for producing positive change*. Baltimore: P. H Brookes.

Commission for Healthcare Audit and Inspection (2006) *Joint Investigation into the Provision of Services for People with Learning Disabilities at Cornwall Partnership NHS Trust*. London: Commission for Healthcare Audit and Inspection.

Condillac, R.A. (2007) Behavioural intervention and intellectual disabilities. In I. Brown and M. Percy (eds). *A Comprehensive Guide to Intellectual and Developmental Disabilities*. Baltimore: Paul H. Brookes.

Deb, S., Clarke, D. and Unwin, G. (2006) *Using Medication to Manage Behaviour Problems Among Adults with a Learning Disability*. University of Birmingham, Royal College of Psychiatrists, Mencap.

Department of Health/Department of Education and Skills (2002). *Guidance on Restrictive Physical Interventions for People with Learning Disability and Autistic Spectrum Disorder in Health, Education and Social Care Settings*. London: Department of Health.

Department of Health (1999) *Effective Care Co-ordination in Mental Health Services: modernising the care programme approach*. London: Department of Health.

Department of Health (2007) *Services for People with Learning Disabilities and Challenging Behaviour or Mental Health Needs (Revised Edition)*. London: Department of Health

Desrochers, M.N., Hile, M.G. and Williams-Moseley, T.L. (1997). Survey of functional assessment procedures used with individuals who display mental retardation and severe problem behaviours. *American Journal of Mental Retardation*, 101, 535–46.

Didden, R., Duker, P. and Korzilius, H. (1997) Meta-analytic study on treatment effectiveness for problem behaviours with individuals who have mental retardation. *American Journal on Mental Retardation*, 101, 387–99.

Didden, R., Korzilius, H., van Oorsouw, W. and Sturmey, P. (2006) Behavioral treatment of challenging behaviours in individuals with mild mental retardation: Meta-Analysis of single-subject research. *American Journal on Mental Retardation*, 111, 290–8.

Duker, P., Didden, R. and Sigafoos, J. (2004) *One-to-one Training: instructional procedures for learners with developmental disabilities*. Austin, TX: Pro-Ed.

Durand, M. and Crimmins, D.B. (1988) Identifying the variables maintaining self-injurious behaviour. *Journal of Autism and Developmental Disorders*, 18, 99–115.

Emerson, E. (1995) *Challenging Behaviour: analysis and intervention in people with learning difficulties*. Cambridge: Cambridge University Press.

Emerson, E. (2001) *Challenging Behaviour: analysis and intervention in people with severe intellectual disabilities* (2nd edn). Cambridge: Cambridge University Press.

Emerson, E. and McGill, P. (1989) Normalization and applied behaviour analysis: values and technology in services for people with learning disabilities. *Behavioural Psychotherapy*, **17**, 101–17.

Emerson, E., Moss, S. and Kiernan, C. (1999) The relationship between challenging behaviour and psychiatric disorder in people with severe developmental disabilities. In N. Bouras (ed.) *Psychiatric and Behavioural Disorders in Developmental Disabilities and Mental Retardation*. Cambridge: Cambridge University Press.

Emerson, E., Reeves, D., Thompson, S., Henderson, D. and Robertson, J. (1996) Time-based lag sequential analysis in the functional assessment of severe challenging behaviour. *Journal of Intellectual Disability Research*, **40**, 260–74.

Evans, I.M. and Meyer, L.H. (1990) Toward a science in support of meaningful outcomes: A response to Horner *et al*. *Journal of the Association for Persons with Severe Handicaps*, **15**, 133–5.

Feldman, M.A., Atkinson, L., Forti-Gervais, L. and Condillac, R. (2004) Formal versus informal interventions for challenging behaviour in persons with intellectual disabilities. *Journal of Intellectual Disability Research*, **48**, 60–8.

Feldman, M.A. and Griffiths, D. (1997) Comprehensive assessment of severe behaviour disorders. In N.N. Singh (ed.), *Prevention and Treatment of Severe Behaviour Problems: models and methods in developmental disabilities* (pp. 23–48). Pacific Grove, CA: Brooks/Cole.

Fisher, W.W., DeLeon, I.G., Rodriguez-Catter, V. and Keeney K.M. (2004) Enhancing the effects of extinction on attention-maintained behaviour through noncontingent delivery of attention or stimuli identified via a competing stimulus assessment. *Journal of Applied Behavior Analysis*, **37**, 171–84.

Fox, P. and Emerson, E. (2002) *Positive Goals: interventions for people with learning disabilities whose behaviour challenges*. Brighton: Pavillion.

Grey, I. M. and McClean, B. (2007) Service user outcomes of staff training in positive behaviour support using Person-Focussed Training: A control group study. *Journal of Applied Research in Intellectual Disabilities*, **20**, 6–15.

Grey, I.M. and Hastings, R.P. (2005) Evidence-based practices in intellectual disability and behaviour disorders. *Current Opinion in Psychiatry*, **18**, 469–75.

Groden, G. and Lantz, S. (2001) The reliability of the Detailed Behaviour Report (DBR) in documenting functional assessment observations. *Behavioural Interventions*, **16**, 15–25.

Hagopian, L.P., Fisher, W.W., Sullivan, M.T., Acquisto, J. and LeBlanc, L.A. (1998) Effectiveness of functional communication training with and without extinction and punishment: a summary of 21 inpatient cases. *Journal of Applied Behavior Analysis*, **31**, 211–35.

Hall, S. and Oliver, C. (2000) An alternative approach to the sequential analysis of behavioural interactions. In T. Thompson, D. Felce and F. Symons (eds). *Computer Assisted Behavioral Observation Methods for Developmental Disabilities*. Baltimore: Paul H. Brookes.

Hanley, G.P., Iwata, B.A. and McCord B.E. (2003) Functional analysis of problem behaviour: a review. *Journal of Applied Behavior Analysis*, **36**, 147–85.

Hastings, R.P. (1996). Staff strategies and explanations for intervening with challenging behaviour. *Journal of Intellectual Disability Research*, **40**, 166–75.

Iwata, B.A., Dorsey, M., Slifer, K., Bauman, K. and Richman, G. (1982) Toward a functional analysis of self-injury. *Analysis and Intervention in Developmental; Disabilities*, **2**, 3–20.

Iwata, B.A., Pace G.M., Dorsey, M.F., Zarcone, J.R., *et al.* (1994) The functions of self-injurious behavior: An experimental epidemiological analysis. *Journal of Applied Behavior Analysis*, **27**, 215–40.

Kennedy, C.H. and Meyer, K.A. (1998) Establishing operations and the motivation of challenging behavior. In J.K. Luiselli and M.J. Cameron (eds). *Antecedent control: Innovative Approaches to Behavioral Support*, pp. 329–46. Baltimore: Paul H. Brookes.

Kevan, F. (2003) Challenging behaviour and communication difficulties. *British Journal of Learning Disabilities*, **31**, 75–80.

Langthorne,P. and McGill, P. (2008) Functional analysis of the early development of self-injurious behaviour: Incorporating gene-environment interactions. *American Journal on Mental Retardation*, **113**, 403–17.

LaVigna, G.W. and Willis, T.J. (2005) A positive behavioural support model for breaking the barriers to social and community inclusion. *Learning Disability Review*, **10**, 16–23.

Lucyshyn, J.M., Dunlap, G. and Albin, R.W. (2002) *Families and Positive Behavior Support: addressing problem behavior in family contexts*. Baltimore; Paul H. Brookes.

Mace, F.C. and Mauk, J.E. (1995) Bio-behavioral diagnosis and treatment of self-injury. *Mental Retardation and Developmental Disabilities Research Reviews*, **1**, 104–10.

Matson, J., Bamburg, K., Cherry, K. and Paclawskyj, T. (1999) A validity study on the Questions About Behavioral Function scale. *Research in Developmental Disabilities*, **20**, 163–76.

McAtee, M., Carr, E. and Schulte, C. (2004) A Contextual Assessment Inventory for problem behaviour: Initial development. *Journal of Positive Behaviour Interventions*, **6**, 148–65.

McClean, B., Grey, I. and McCracken, M. (2007) An evaluation of positive behavioural support for people with very sever challenging behaviours in community-based settings. *Journal of Intellectual Disabilities*, **11**, 281–301.

McClintock, S., Hall, S. and Oliver, C. (2003) Risk markers associated with challenging behaviours in people with intellectual disabilities: A meta-analytic study. *Journal of Intellectual Disability Research*, **47**, 405–16.

McDonnell, A. (2009) The effectiveness of training in physical intervention. In Allen, D. (ed.) *Ethical Approaches to Physical Interventions. Volume 2.* (pp. 3–25). Kidderminster: BILD Publications.

McGill, P. (1999) Establishing operations: implications for the assessment, treatment and prevention of problem behavior. *Journal of Applied Behavior Analysis*, **32**, 393–418.

McGillivray, J.A. and McCabe, M.P. (2004) Pharmacological management of challenging behaviour of individuals with intellectual disability. *Research in Developmental Disabilities*, **25**, 523–37.

Meyer, L.H. and Evans, I.M. (1989) *Nonaversive Interventions for Behavior Problems: a manual for home and community*. New York: Teachers College Press.

Meyer, L.H. and Evans, I.M. (1993) Meaningful outcomes in behavioral intervention: Evaluating positive approaches to the remediation of challenging behaviors. In J. Reichle and D.P. Wacker (eds). *Communicative Alternatives to Challenging Behaviour*, pp. 407–28. Baltimore: Paul H. Brookes.

Miltenberger, R.G. (1998) Methods for assessing antecedent influences on challenging behaviours. In J.K. Luiselli and M.J. Cameron (eds) *Antecedent Control: Innovative Approaches to Behavioral Support*, pp. 47–66. Baltimore: P. H. Brookes.

Oliver, C., McClintock, K., Hall, S., Smith, M., Dagnan, D. and Stenfert-Kroese, B. (2003). Assessing the severity of challenging behaviour: psychometric properties of the Challenging Behaviour Interview. *Journal of Applied Research in Intellectual Disabilities*, **16**, 53–61.

O'Neill, R.E., Horner, R.H., Albin, R.W., Storey, K. and Sprague, J.R. (1997) *Functional Analysis and Program Development for Problem Behaviour*. Pacific Grove, CA: Brooks/Cole.

Richman, D.M. (2008) Early intervention and prevention of self-injurious behaviour exhibited by young children with developmental disabilities. *Journal of Intellectual Disability Research*, **52**, 3–17.

Rojahn, J., Polster, L.M., Mulick, J.A. and Wisniewski, J.J. (1989). Reliability of the Behaviour Problems Inventory. *Journal of the Multihandicapped Person*, **2**, 283–93.

Royal College of Psychiatrists, British Psychological Society, Royal College of Speech and Language Therapists (2007) *Challenging Behaviour: a unified approach. Clinical and service guidelines for supporting people with learning disabilities who are at risk of receiving abusive or restrictive practices*. Royal College of Psychiatrists.

Saunders, R.R. and Saunders, M.D. (1998) Supported Routines. In J.K. Luiselli and M.J. Cameron (eds). *Antecedent control: Innovative Approaches to Behavioral Support*, pp. 245–72. Baltimore: Paul H. Brookes.

Schindler, H.R. and Horner, R.H. (2005) Generalized reduction of problem behaviour of young children with autism: building trans-situational interventions. *American Journal on Mental Retardation*, **110**, 36–47.

Scotti, J.R., Evans, I.M., Meyer, L.H. and Walker, P. (1991). A meta-analysis of intervention research with problem behavior: Treatment validity and standards of practice. *American Journal on Mental Retardation*, **96**, 233–56.

Scotti, J.R. and Meyer, L.H. (1999) *Behavioral Intervention: principles, models and practices*. Baltimore: Paul H. Brookes.

Smidt, A., Balandin, S., Reed, V. and Sigafoos, J. (2007) A communication training programme for residential staff working with adults with challenging behaviour: Pilot data on intervention effects. *Journal of Applied Research in Intellectual Disabilities*, **20**, 16–29.

Stancliffe, R., Jones, E., Mansell, J. and Lowe, K. (2008) Active support: A critical review and commentary. *Journal of Intellectual and Developmental Disability*, **33**, 196–214.

Sturmey, P. (2001) The Functional Analysis Checklist: Inter rater and test-retest reliability. *Journal of Applied Research in Intellectual Disabilities*, **14**, 141–6.

Sturmey, P., Ward-Horner, J., Marroquin, M. and Doran, E. (2007) Operant and respondent behaviour. In P. Sturmey (ed) *Functional Analysis in Clinical Treatment*, pp. 23–50. Burlington, MA: Academic Press.

Taylor, L. and Oliver, C. (2008) The behavioural phenotype of Smith-Magenis syndrome: evidence for a gene-environment interaction. *Journal of Intellectual Disability Research*, **52**, 830–41.

Thompson, T., Felce, D. and Symons, F. (2000) *Computer Assisted Behavioral Observation Methods for Developmental Disabilities*. Baltimore: Paul H. Brookes.

Toogood, S. and Timlin, K. (1996) The functional assessment of challenging behaviour. *Journal of Applied Research in Intellectual Disabilities*, **9**, 206–22.

Toogood, S., Drury, G., Gilsenan, K., Parry, D., Roberts, K. and Sherriff, S. (2009) Establishing a context to reduce challenging behaviour using procedures from active support. *Tizard Learning Disability Review*, **14**, 29–36.

Touchette, P.E., McDonald, R.F. and Langer, S.N. (1985) A scatter plot for identifying stimulus control of problem behaviour. *Journal of Applied Behaviour Analysis*, **18**, 343–51.

Tyrer, P., Oliver-Africano, P.C., Ahmed, Z., *et al.* (2008) Risperidone, haloperidol, and placebo in the treatment of aggressive behaviour in patients with intellectual disability: a randomised trial. *Lancet*, **371**, 57–63.

Van Houten, R., Rolider, A. and Ickowitz, J. (1989) *Functional Analysis Checklist*. Unpublished instrument.

Vollmer, T.R. and Van Camp, C.M. (1998) Experimental designs to evaluate antecedent control. In J.K. Luiselli and M.J. Cameron (eds) *Antecedent Control: Innovative Approaches to Behavioral Support*, pp. 87–111. Baltimore: P.H. Brookes.

Zimbelman, K. (2005) Instruments for assessing behavioural problems. In J. Hogg and A. Langa (eds), *Assessing Adults with Intellectual Disabilities: a service providers' guide*, pp.179–91. Oxford: Blackwell.

# Chapter 12

# WORKING WITH OFFENDERS OR ALLEGED OFFENDERS WITH INTELLECTUAL DISABILITIES

## Glynis H. Murphy and Isabel C.H. Clare

## INTRODUCTION

Throughout most of the last century, most work relating to people with intellectual disabilities who have, or are alleged to have, committed criminal offences was focused on the putative association between intellectual disability and crime and other social problems (Trent 1994; Fennell 1996). In contrast, in recent years, there has been increasing interest in evidence-based approaches to the characteristics of this group of men and, to a lesser extent, women, and to their assessment and treatment (Murphy and Mason 2007).

## RELATIONSHIPS BETWEEN CHALLENGING BEHAVIOUR, ALLEGED OFFENDING, AND OFFENDING

Strictly speaking, the terms 'offence' and 'offender' can only be justified if a person has committed a criminal act and has been convicted by a court (in England and Wales, a Crown Court or, much more commonly, a magistrates' court). It is well known that many illegal behaviours are not reported to the police; and when they are reported, they may not be understood as a possible crime or investigated. Even when an alleged perpetrator has been identified, and arrested as a suspect, he or she is not always charged, and the charge may not lead to a prosecution. Prosecutions lead

*Clinical Psychology and People with Intellectual Disabilities*, Second Edition. Edited by Eric Emerson, Chris Hatton, Kate Dickson, Rupa Gone, Amanda Caine and Jo Bromley.
© 2012 John Wiley & Sons, Ltd. Published 2012 by John Wiley & Sons, Ltd.

to court proceedings and, normally, to a court appearance by the alleged perpetrator, who is now known as a defendant; in any case, not all defendants are convicted. In the absence of such a conviction, the terms 'alleged offence' and 'alleged offender' are more accurate.

Of course, much 'challenging behaviour' (see Chapter 11), such as violent or destructive behaviour, is illegal and could constitute a criminal offence. However, in English law (i.e. the law in England and Wales), a crime is not defined simply by a behaviour or its consequence (*actus reus*). Other key 'ingredients' must be present. One of the most important is a guilty 'state of mind' (*mens rea*) relating to the behaviour (such as intention, recklessness and so on; see Carson and Clare 1997). Sometimes, it is clear that one or more of these aspects of *mens rea* is missing (for example, because the person did not know that the act was illegal, or was not aware of the possibility that harm would result, see Carson 1995).

The likelihood both of fulfilling the criteria for a crime (*actus reus* and *mens rea*) and of being involved meaningfully in criminal justice procedures is much greater for people with *mild* intellectual disabilities and it is this sub-group of men and women who are most likely to come into contact with the criminal justice system following illegal behaviour. It is important to reiterate that, while someone may be suspected of such acts, and there may be good reason for the suspicions, until he or she has been convicted by a court, that person is not an offender; his or her offending is only *alleged*. Service providers have a duty of care towards *all* service users, and whilst they need to protect the rights of alleged victims, it is also important that they do not assume prematurely that someone is an offender and impose informal sanctions. This is an area of considerable complexity: in England and Wales, for example, the *Human Rights Act 1998*, the Deprivation of Liberty provisions introduced into the *Mental Capacity Act 2005* under the *Mental Health Act 2007*, parts of the *Safeguarding Vulnerable Groups Act 2006*, and various policies and guidance, may all be relevant.

## SERVICE RESPONSES TO OFFENDING AND ALLEGED OFFENDING

Despite numerous research studies, the extent to which people with intellectual disabilities are alleged or convicted offenders remains uncertain; nor is it clear whether the type of crimes differ from those committed by the general population. The reasons for this confusion reflect a number of methodological problems, including variations in the way in which terms such as 'intellectual disability' and 'offending' are defined and established and the location of the sample from which prevalence is estimated (for reviews of this issue, see Holland, Clare and Mukhopadhyay 2002; Loucks 2007; Murphy and Mason 2007).

What is known, however, is that the response to alleged offending remains rather arbitrary. Where people are already living in health or social care provision for people with intellectual disabilities, support workers are reluctant to involve the police (McBrien and Murphy 2006). This reluctance seems to reflect a variety of factors, including:

- fear amongst support workers of criticism or investigation, as a result of reporting illegal behaviour by service users (McBrien and Murphy 2006);
- a lack of relevant guidelines to help support workers identify and deal with alleged offences (Thompson *et al.* 1997; McBrien and Murphy 2006);
- a misguided belief – traditionally shared by the criminal justice system – that the person is already 'taken care of' if they are known to health and/or social care services (Carson 1989);
- assumptions that allegations by victims and other witnesses, especially if they also have intellectual disabilities, will not be taken seriously by the police and the Crown Prosecution Service;
- a belief amongst support workers that individuals with intellectual disabilities need more 'help and understanding' than others who break the law (McBrien and Murphy 2006).

In addition, at a practitioner level, there is some confusion, and considerable room for professional discretion, at the intersection of the criminal justice system and other arrangements that may be relevant, such as Adult Safeguarding procedures.

Nevertheless, people with mild intellectual disabilities who are not already known to adult intellectual disability services are at risk of coming into contact with the criminal justice system – and of being vulnerable within it – if it is alleged that they have committed an offence (Loucks 2007). The majority of people with mild intellectual disabilities merge into the general population after leaving school (Richardson and Koller 1985) because, under ordinary circumstances, they either do not need or do not wish for further support. If their intellectual disability is not identified by the police, the special provision introduced in England and Wales under the *Police and Criminal Evidence Act 1984* to protect 'vulnerable' adult suspects cannot be implemented; this can lead, and has led, to miscarriages of justice (see Gudjonsson 2003). However, even when alleged offenders are identified, it is not unusual for them to proceed through at least some stages of the criminal justice system repeatedly before specialist health and social care services for people with intellectual disabilities accept responsibility for working with other agencies to meet their needs. Clinical experience suggests that this reluctance to respond reflects a number of factors: these men and women do not immediately appear to meet eligibility criteria, which are often rather arbitrary (Commission for Social Care

Inspection 2008); they are seen by commissioners and providers as likely to require expensive placements; and/or they are believed to be 'too difficult' for services with people with intellectual disabilities and therefore 'the responsibility of forensic services'.

Since the 1990s (see, for example, Department of Health/Home Office 1992), there have been a number of initiatives to provide a more consistent approach to alleged or convicted offenders with complex needs such as intellectual disabilities and/or mental health problems. Like previous initiatives, the most recent of these, the Bradley Report (Department of Health 2009a), which is supported by the Government, endorses the involvement of the criminal justice system in dealing with alleged offending, including through prosecution where there is sufficient evidence and this is 'in the public interest' (for example, because there is a risk to the public, there is a pattern of allegedly escalating behaviour, etc). *Nowhere* is it suggested that alleged offending should not be reported to, and investigated by, the police. However, it is very important that the rights of the alleged offender should be protected: this will mean that, as a suspect at a police station, the person needs to have a solicitor with relevant experience, and someone who is independent of the police (the 'Appropriate Adult') present to assist him/her to understand what is happening and the possible consequences of any admissions (for practical guidance, see Hollins *et al.* 1996a and b; see Gudjonsson 2003, for a review of some of the problems relating to Appropriate Adults).

The Bradley Report (Department of Health 2009a) also reaffirms previous Government policy in stating that, as far as possible, contact with the criminal justice system should not lead to imprisonment. Early intervention strategies for men and women with intellectual diabilities who are starting to engage in illegal behaviour should be considered, and where necessary, provided within the framework of the 'community safety' measures introduced under the *Crime and Disorder Act 1998*. Where people with intellectual disabilities and/or mental health needs have been convicted of criminal offences, they should also, as far as possible, be provided with treatment and support:

- on a multi-agency basis. A variety of agencies may be involved, including health (both General Practitioners and specialist health care providers), social care, criminal justice agencies such as the police and probation services, housing, and substance misuse services. Some of these will be statutory, while others will be third sector organisations, and not all will have the same underlying philosophy. As in work with other people with complex needs, a case-management or key-worker role is often needed to ensure a consistent approach;
- in a range of services, providing different levels of supervision and support but, as far as possible, in community rather than in institutional

settings. Where necessary, community services can be provided within a criminal justice framework (e.g. through a Community Rehabilitation Order with conditions, such as of treatment or residence) or through the *Mental Health Act 2007* (for example, a s. 37 Guardianship Order);

- in such a way as to be person-centred, to maximise rehabilitation and social inclusion and promote the possibility of sustaining an independent life,
- as near as possible to the person's home or family;
- involving, as far as possible, the person him/herself, caregivers and others who know him/her well.

Many developments for offenders and alleged offenders with intellectual disabilities described in the literature so far still reflect a traditional forensic model where the prototypical service-user is a person whose difficulties can be addressed within a hospital-based service (Murphy *et al.* 1991; Taylor and Novaco 2005). Increasingly, however, community-based assessment and treatment services are being developed (Willner *et al.* 2002; Lindsay *et al.* 2006; Murphy *et al.* 2007; Lindsay, 2009), and most practitioners agree that the emphasis needs to be on community-based services with access to hospital facilities (locally, as far as possible) when necessary (see Chapter 2).

## WHAT IS KNOWN ABOUT OFFENDERS/ALLEGED OFFENDERS WITH INTELLECTUAL DISABILITIES?

Until recently, it was thought that offenders and alleged offenders with intellectual disabilities were similar to their counterparts without disabilities (Noble and Conley 1992; Thompson 1997): they were said to be mostly male, young, with backgrounds of social deprivation, and, frequently, to have additional substance misuse problems (Lindsay *et al.* 2006). More recent research (McBrien 2003; Wheeler *et al.* 2009), which has included those already known to community services for people with intellectual disabilities, rather than more specialist settings, is starting to develop this picture. It now appears that a significant minority of offenders and alleged offenders are women, and that, whilst alcohol may be problematic, other forms of substance misuse may be less relevant.

Regardless of their gender, there is now considerable evidence that offenders and alleged offenders with intellectual disabilities have histories of chronic adversity. They are likely to have had childhood backgrounds characterised by chronic financial and social disadvantage, including family instability (Barron *et al.* 2004; Hatton and Emerson 2004). In many cases, this has not merely involved loss (such as the absence of a parent), but also placements (often multiple) away from their families of origin and extended families. Since studies show consistently that intellectual competence is a protective factor for children whose lives are very difficult (Rutter, Giller and Hagell 1998), these disruptions of appropriate sustaining relationships with adults in a 'parenting' role and the feelings generated by unwanted separations are likely to have a particular effect on those with intellectual disabilities. Such disruptions may also place young people at increased risk of specific forms of abuse, such as sexual abuse. Emerging evidence suggests that the experience of being sexually abused in childhood increases the likelihood that, in later life, men with intellectual disabilities will themselves engage in illegal sexual behaviour (Lindsay *et al.* 2001; Murphy *et al.* 2010).

The impact of familial adversity is likely to be exacerbated by the limited opportunities for, and difficulties in maintaining, friendships with their peers that affect many people with intellectual disabilities. Such experiences undermine further the possibility of developing resilience (Masten and Coatsworth 2000) and, in turn, increase the risk of developing unusual styles of attachment, restricting the possibilities for supportive relationships in adulthood (Allen 2001; Rholes and Simpson 2004). All these factors may contribute to the enhanced vulnerability to adult mental health difficulties that is found among offenders and alleged offenders (Lindsay *et al.* 2002; O'Brien 2002; Lindsay *et al.* 2004a; Murphy *et al.* 2010). There has been some debate about the relevance of specific conditions, particularly autism spectrum conditions, to offending. While it is clear that people with autism spectrum conditions do sometimes commit offences, the evidence does *not* suggest that the condition is itself is a risk factor (Woodbury-Smith *et al.* 2006; Clare and Woodbury-Smith 2009).

## GENERAL PRINCIPLES OF ASSESSMENT AND TREATMENT OF THE PERSON AND MANAGEMENT OF FURTHER OFFENDING/ALLEGED OFFENDING

### Assessment

The purpose of the assessment is to understand the behaviour and the context in which it occurs in order to implement interventions to minimise the risk of re-occurrence.

*Background to Assessment*

Sometimes the outcome of a conviction by a court has implications for assessment and treatment (for example, following a Community Rehabilitation Order with a condition of treatment in hospital, or a

Hospital Order under s.37 of the *Mental Health Act 2007* is made – see Chapter 5), so that the person is legally obliged to comply with, if not engage with, assessment and /or treatment. At other times, there are no such implications, even when the person has accepted that s/he has committed an offence (e.g. when the police give a formal caution). In any case, on many occasions, the outcome is indefinite (for example, because the families of alleged child victims do not wish them to go to court). In these circumstances, the person may need encouragement to participate in assessment and treatment. Often, offenders and alleged offenders are very reluctant to discuss their behaviour (e.g. Lindsay 2009; Murphy *et al.* 2010). Perkins (1991) suggests that praise, persuasion, and some communication that the therapist is able to detect evasion and side-stepping are likely to be helpful, and they may all be necessary at times. In addition, it may be possible to assist the person to acknowledge that there is some area in which 'help' might be useful, and to work from there towards the behaviour which constitutes the alleged offence. Even where the person is unwilling to accept any assistance, work can still be carried out with him/her and with support workers or caregivers to reduce the risk of re-offending by providing a framework for minimising the possibility of further allegations and ensuring a consistent response if they do occur.

Before carrying out any assessment, there are a number of issues which need to be addressed (see summary in Table 12.1). Some particularly important matters are discussed in more detail below.

### Ethical Issues

*Consent*   The *Mental Capacity Act 2005* (and equivalent legislation in Scotland) makes it clear that the starting-point is that adults (i.e. those aged 16 years or more) are able to make (that is, have the capacity to make) decisions for themselves. Consent for an intervention needs to be sought from the person him or herself, not from others. If s/he is *able* to consent but does not do so, then his/her decision must be respected. This does *not*, however, mean simply accepting a person's reluctance to cooperate. Part of the task of clinicians is to engage those who may initially be hesitant about participating in assessments and/or treatments that may improve the quality of their lives.

There are, of course, situations in which capacity is challengeable. Having followed the guidance in the *Mental Capacity Act* and its accompanying *Code of Practice* (Department for Constitutional Affairs 2007), and having made all practicable efforts to support the person, it sometimes appears, on the balance of probabilities, that someone lacks the capacity to consent to an intervention considered 'necessary' for his or her life, health or well-being. In such cases, a decision about the proposed intervention needs to be made on the person's behalf. The responsibility

**Table 12.1** Preliminary issues to be clarified before the assessment.

*The person and his/her behaviour*

⇒ What are the referral issues in this case (often, the issues are presented as questions: how can the person's offending/alleged offending best be understood?; what interventions are most likely to minimise the probability that the behaviour will occur again?). Which of these referral issues are appropriately carried out by health (rather than with, or by, a criminal justice or social care agency)?

⇒ Is it clear what behaviour is involved in the offending/alleged offending (written, contemporaneous accounts should be sought whenever possible), what action has, is to be, or may be, taken by the police and by other agencies? Has all the available documentation been read, notes requested etc.?

⇒ What arrangements are in place to ensure that issues relating to confidentiality, including its limits, are discussed at an early stage?

⇒ What has the offender/alleged offender been told so far and has his/her consent to the assessment and treatment been sought and given?

⇒ Have arrangements been made to see the person somewhere which is not threatening to him or her but is safe to those involved?

⇒ What will happen if the person engages in offending/alleged offending during the session?

*The service response*

⇒ Who is the named contact person in each agency involved in the case (i.e. the person to whom letters should be written, who attends meetings)?

⇒ Who is the case-manager (i.e. the person coordinating the work)?

⇒ Who is the person's key-worker? Has contact been made to ensure that s/he knows about the involvement of the assessment and treatment service and the purpose of carrying out the assessment and treatment?

⇒ What arrangements have been made to meet with the other people involved to discuss progress? Multi-agency meetings are difficult to set up and need to be organised weeks in advance.

for making the judgement about capacity and for substitute decision-making belong to the individual who will be carrying out the decision, acting in the person's 'best interests' (see Chapter 5, Joyce 2007). To assist in establishing 'best interests', clinicians should follow the 'checklist' set out in the MCA and the Code of Practice, taking into consideration the person's wishes and feelings, if ascertainable, and the views of caregivers and others involved in his/her life. It is also important also to support the person to participate as much as possible in the decision that is made on his/her behalf. The basis for the judgement about the person's capacity to consent, the efforts made to help him/her gain or regain capacity, the consultations with others, and the support provided to facilitate partici-pation in the decision made, and the decision itself, all need to be documented fully.

The only exception to this framework relates to the small number of people who fulfil the criteria for detention, primarily in hospital, for assessment and/or treatment under the MHA. Controversially, this legislation is not capacity-based (see Chapter 5) and therefore allows interventions to be carried out regardless of whether the person can, or does, consent to them. It is good practice, nevertheless, to follow the process by which consent is normally sought (providing relevant information, and so on).

*Confidentiality*  In practice, there is little direct psychological work which can be carried out without the individual's cooperation. Sometimes, though, the person is cooperative but puts the clinician in a difficult situation by divulging information, particularly about recent behaviour which may constitute an offence, which s/he asks not to be shared. Frequently, the person also asks that notes are not taken. Clinicians and clients need to be aware, however, that *confidentiality can-not be restricted to a single person* and that those members of a multi-agency team who are directly involved in assessment, treatment and manage-ment will have access to all necessary information; it is unwise to keep information from other team members who have a 'need to know'. However, any further sharing should be considered within the frame-work of the British Psychological Society's comprehensive guidelines for professional practice in applied psychology (British Psychological Society 2008; Department of Health 2007). The advice of other members of the team involved should also always be sought; occasionally, legal advice may be needed.

Typically, initial interviews should begin with statements that clarify the degree of confidentiality that can be relied on. For example, the clinician can say 'What you tell me here can be private. But if you tell me that you or someone else is at risk of harm or in danger, I will need to tell others. I cannot keep it secret between you and me'. Such statements are complex and hard to simplify. They will need to be repeated and explained for many clients and a written agreement (or videotape, if this is better suited to the person's abilities) should be made with the person so s/he is clear about information sharing. A model is provided by the 'agreement of nonconfidentiality' (Salter 1988, p. 263), which can be adapted. Signed copies (or an equivalent, if another medium has been used) should be held in each agency's notes.

*Areas of Assessment*

Assessment can be divided into three stages, not all of which need be carried out together or by the same person:

(i) The initial investigation of the alleged incident (for the purposes of this chapter, we shall assume this has been completed by the police or by others and that witness statements have been obtained).
(ii) The assessment of the day and residential services (if any) the person currently receives (the principles here are similar to those widely used for people with intellectual disabilities.
(iii) the assessment of the person.

In 'mainstream' forensic work, the dominant psychological approach to assessment is cognitive-behavioural. This includes the person's interpretations of his/her experiences (i.e. thoughts, feelings and beliefs) as part of the 'functional analysis' (Carr *et al.* 1994; Carr and O'Reilly 2007; O'Reilly *et al.* 2007) on which the formulation, and subsequent treatment, is based. In most areas of clinical practice, the research literature would be used as a basis for selecting topics relevant to the person's particular difficulty for use in the assessment. However, the literature relating to people with intellectual disabilities who have, or are alleged to have, committed offences remains rather limited (see below under specific types of offences). This means that assessment needs to be very broad-based in order to produce information on the background of the person, his/her present functioning and social circumstances, and the behaviour (including the person's thoughts and feelings about the behaviour) that constitutes the offence/alleged offence.

The information needed is summarised in Table 12.2.

The material is obtained using the established methods of *self-report*, *reports from others*, *behavioural observations*, and *archival data*. However, there are some differences between work with offenders or alleged offenders and other people with intellectual disabilities and challenging behaviour. First, and not withstanding that their skills are often over-estimated, men and women at risk of offending are much more likely to have relatively good expressive verbal language and comprehension, so self-report measures, such as interviews and questionnaires are very frequently used. It is clear that, when they are interviewed properly (see Chapter 6), even when they are very distressed, people with intellectual disabilities are often well able to provide information about themselves and their experiences, their thoughts, and their feelings (Dagnan *et al.* 2000; Oathamshaw and Haddock 2006), provided that care is taken to avoid

**Table 12.2** Information required for an assessment of alleged offending or offending.

*Background*

⇒ Developmental history – particularly:
  • 'milestones';
  • imaginative play, communication, social interaction
⇒ Social history – particularly:
  • periods away from biological family;
  • physical/sexual/emotional abuse or neglect;
  • bereavements;
  • friendships and social networks
  • attachment and other significant (including intimate) relationships;
⇒ Medical and psychiatric history – particularly:
  • periods in hospital for physical and/or mental health problems;
  • response to treatment in the community
⇒ Forensic history – including allegations *but their status must be made clear;*
  • witness statements wherever possible;
  • transcripts (and, if possible, tapes) of formal police interviews (often obtainable through the person's solicitor);
  • level of violence used
  • degree of planning
  • responses to treatment and/or management

*The person*

⇒ Mental health needs
⇒ Cognitive skills – particularly:
  • global intellectual ability, and profile of intellectual strengths and weaknesses;
  • executive functioning;
⇒ Communication –
  • understanding of single words, sentences and concepts (verbally and through other systems of communication);
  • verbal and other means of expression
⇒ Life skills – daily living skills; particular strengths; interests
⇒ Other challenging behaviours (apart from the offending/alleged offending)
⇒ Coping strategies
⇒ Thoughts, feelings, beliefs about past experiences, the present and the future

*(Continued)*

**Table 12.2** (*cont'd*)

*This offence/alleged offence and any previous ones*

⇒ Antecedents, behaviour, consequences – what happened and the person's thoughts, feelings, and beliefs about each of these. To include:
  - interests (excitement resulting from the behaviour; fantasies; planning and use of subterfuge);
  - knowledge about the behaviour (whether it is against the law, its possible consequences for him/her);
  - setting conditions (arguments with others, substance misuse, life events);
  - how the victim (if any) was selected (to include 'stalking' and 'grooming');
  - attitudes (beliefs about the impact of the behaviour on others; the extent to which victims 'deserved' the behaviour); whether the consequence was desired (for example, in a physical assault which was interrupted by staff, was the person pleased to be stopped, or resentful that s/he did not succeed in injuring the victim);

Also:

⇒ Details of times when the person felt like committing an offence but did not do so.

asking questions in a way that promotes acquiescence, suggestibility, or compliance (see Gudjonsson 2003, for a discussion of the distinctions between these concepts). It is often particularly helpful to give concrete assistance (for example, a choice of pictures of emotions).

Nevertheless, as in all forensic work, great care is needed in interviews. This is partly because the person may be very reluctant to admit to his/her part in what has, or is alleged to have, happened, and partly because, by the time the person is seen for assessment and treatment, s/he has often had to give an account of the same event(s) on many occasions (e.g. to the police, a solicitor, clinical psychologists and psychiatrists preparing reports for the court). Since all interviews are social interactions, almost inevitably, the account becomes 'shaped' (see Antaki *et al.* 2008, for examples of this process in services for people with intellectual disabilities). It is very important to try to counteract, or at least minimise, this process (see Bull 1995, for helpful guidance). Assisting the person to provide his or her account in a different way (such as through explaining drawings or other visual material related to the event) may help. Providing the person consents, it can be useful to audio-tape interviews since this allows the interviewer to concentrate fully on the conversation. Similarly, it can be useful to have two interviewers, particularly where the alleged offence is very serious, so that each has more time to think about what s/he is saying. In addition it is extremely important to cross-check data as far as possible (for example, against the accounts of witnesses), to highlight discrepancies.

In 'mainstream' forensic work, self-report measures relating to specific offences have been developed to supplement interview data. Unfortunately, with few exceptions, these are unsuitable for people with intellectual disabilities because they:

- require sophisticated reading skills. Despite the claims made for 'easier read' materials, they still demand some literacy skills, and there is limited evidence that the additional of symbols is always helpful (Poncelas and Murphy 2007). Reading material out loud, however, makes very high demands on working memory, which, it is increasingly apparent, is impaired in people with intellectual disabilities (Henry and MacLean 2002; Schuchardt *et al*. 2010);
- use long sentences, unusual words, abstract concepts or refer to experiences that are unlikely to be familiar to people with intellectual disabilities,
- use rating scales that are too complex.

In any case, there are rarely norms for people with intellectual disabilities. Nevertheless, these self-report measures can still be used as a source of ideas about areas in which information needs to be obtained.

Secondly, the balance of reports from others and of archival data is different from that usually encountered in work with people with intellectual disabilities and challenging behaviour. Far more use is made of archival data in forensic work. In part, this is so that a detailed history of offending and alleged offending can be obtained. There are a number of reasons why this is useful: (i) the extent of previous offending is a predictor of (poor) outcome; (ii) since much of the behaviour of interest is infrequent, it is often difficult for the person him/herself to recall previous occasions on which it occurred; and (iii) since it is not unusual, particularly in poorly-resourced and developed local services, for someone to experience multiple placement changes, current support workers often have very limited information about his or her previous history. While, in the past, it was often not sufficiently recognised or acknowledged by health care providers, it is now accepted that, where it is possible to contact them, families provide an invaluable long-term perspective on the person and their difficulties.

Finally, in contrast with assessments with people with more severe disabilities, behavioural observations are carried out infrequently with individuals who have, or are alleged to have, committed offences. In part, this is because the behaviours in question are often infrequent. Moreover, there are, of course, practical and ethical problems in setting up situations (such as experimental analogues) which might increase the possibility of offending and any such strategies could only be implemented after careful consideration by the agencies involved. Nevertheless, given the uncertainty which often surrounds challenging behaviour, particularly when it takes place outside the home, such observations are often essential. This does not necessarily require the observer to be present, however. Increasingly, modern technological devices are being developed that can be used by the person when he or she is alone are being developed for use in routine clinical practice. What is important is that the information obtained enables the therapist to develop an understanding of the person's thoughts and feelings during his or her experiences.

## Formulation

As in any area of psychological treatment, formulation, the *provisional* summary, which integrates the available information to provide (i) an understanding of the way in which the person's offending or alleged offending has developed and been maintained, and (ii) the rationale for the interventions, is essential in order to clarify the issues for both the treatment provider and others (including the offender/alleged offender). Flow-charts, rather than written formulations, appear to be particularly helpful because:

- a large amount of information derived from complex assessments by different agencies with different perspectives, can be integrated, with the process of integration itself helping the team to develop a coordinated plan of intervention;
- they provide a clear focus for the intervention, keeping the team 'on track' during what is often a long, and complicated, process;
- the expected impact of specific interventions in assisting the person is clear, allowing evaluation to be planned more easily;
- a visual format is more accessible to people with intellectual disabilities, and support workers and caregivers, encouraging a partnership.

Whilst the precise style of a formulation will depend on the theoretical backgrounds of the people involved, the style is generally likely to have historical information at the top, working downwards chronologically to the offending/alleged offending and its maintaining factors, with arrows implying causal and not just temporal connections. Two examples are provided later in this chapter (see Figures 12.1 and 12.2).

## Treatment of the Individual and Management of Further Offending/Alleged Offending

The nature of the intervention(s) will depend on the formulation. Almost always, successful interventions will involve a range of components: educational, psychological, pharmacological, supportive, and practical. Some of the components will be general, and would be used by all kinds of people for all kinds of difficulties (for example, coping strategies for dealing with feelings of distress), a few will be specific to the particular nature of the person's behaviour. Whatever the particular combination, a successful intervention is likely to involve three main types of components:

(i) Lifestyle changes, based around O'Brien's (1987, cited in Emerson 1992) five accomplishments, and the more recent goals of rights, independence, choice and inclusion set out in *Valuing People* (Department of Health) and recently reiterated (Department of Health 2009b), to improve the person's quality of life and combat feelings of helplessness.

(ii) direct treatment with the person both on his/her own and often also in a group to address the particular difficulties which contribute to the person's behaviour. Some of this treatment will involve methods used in mainstream 'forensic' work but is likely to require adaptations so that it is:

  • simpler and more concrete, for example by providing photographs or drawings or symbols;
  • presented visually rather than in text;
  • repeated, encouraging the person to use his or her own words; and also
  • uses materials which are associated with being valued (for example, a personal stereo for relaxation tapes; a pager rather than a 'cue card' to remind a person to carry out particular tasks);
  • is presented in a way which is associated with valued 'ordinary activities' and adult status.

(iii) Prevention and management of further offending/alleged offending, using the multidisciplinary 'positive risk-management' framework outlined by the Department of Health (2007). Whilst there is not enough space to discuss this component in any detail here, prevention and management require identification of the characteristics of the person and his/her victims, and of the situations in which further difficulties are least, as well as most, likely to occur, leading to the development of strategies to minimise the likelihood of offending/alleged offending.

A framework for these overlapping and inter-linking components is provided by the model for the organisation of proactive and reactive intervention strategies proposed by LaVigna *et al.* (1989) and already widely used in work with people with intellectual disabilities; see Chapter 11.

In work with offenders and alleged offenders, there are two particular issues which need to be addressed.

### Working With Caregivers

It is very frequently the case that paid caregivers, such as support workers, will be resentful about the time and attention which the person receives as a result of his or her behaviour; carers, such as families, often seem to be much more accepting. There is no short-cut to listening to the feelings of caregivers, acknowledging the difficulties which they often face, and involving them as far as can be managed (for example, in clinical judgments of risk) without breaching the person's right to confidentiality. In addition to working with the person offender on his/her own and/or in a group, we encourage three-way sessions to enable him or her to feed back to his or her key-worker. We have also found it helpful to:

- explain repeatedly the rationale for working with the person. It is important to avoid unrealistic expectations ('you've seen the person for twelve weeks and he's no better') by providing information about the work which is being carried out, and its (often) long-term nature;
- ensure that victims and alleged victims (including support workers) receive support and assistance from members of the team who are *not* working with the alleged offender (individually and/or as a group);
- ensure that the formulation is shared with, and understood by, all the caregivers involved with the person. To aid this, it is normally helpful to ensure that the key-worker (and his or her manager) are members of the multi-agency team supporting the interventions. Caregivers also need to understand what has been agreed by all the agencies involved to minimise the possibility that the behaviour will happen again, and to respond if it is suspected or known to have taken place. These agreements should be in the form of written guidelines. Caregivers should be consulted very closely during the drafting of these guidelines and the final version should be accessible to all of them, both physically and in terms of their language, content, and format.

### Impact On Practitioners

Whilst, in recent years, there has been a major increase in the number of health care practitioners wishing to work with offenders and alleged offenders with intellectual disabilities, the possible emotional implications are rarely discussed outside the psychoanalytic literature. Indeed, little attention has even be paid, at least within clinical psychology (though see Nicolson 1992) to the fact that those practitioners are likely mostly to be women, mainly working with men (see, for example, the gender balance of those accepted on training courses for clinical psychology for 2009, which is reported to differ little to that of previous recent years, www.leeds.ac.uk/chpccp/BasicEopps). Health care practitioners of all disciplines (and support workers and carers) may develop strong conflicting feelings towards the person: anger at his or her behaviour (particularly when it victimises a vulnerable person), combined with pity and compassion as the frequently harrowing details of his or her life become known; these can become intense, leading to a loss of the ability to think clearly (see Davies 2007; Cottis and O'Driscoll 2009; Hatcher and Noakes 2010). In addition, the consequences of the 'failure' of interventions can be very difficult, for the person being treated as well as for any victims. Moreover, increasingly, therapeutic work has to be carried out within complex multi-agency settings, and in a context that is often openly hostile to the treatment of convicted or alleged offenders within community settings. Unfortunately, until recently these aspects of the work, and their effects on practitioners and on the organizations in which they are based, have rarely been acknowledged.

In this area of work, it is particularly important to:

- have good clinical supervision with opportunities to think about the personal and professional issues raised by the person and his or her behaviour;
- have opportunities to discuss the case with practitioners who are not directly involved. If this cannot be done anonymously, the person's consent must be sought;
- liaise very closely with other members of the multi-agency team (co-working is very helpful; if this is not possible, ensure that at least a proportion of visits are carried out jointly);
- ensure that documents and records are up-to-date and accessible, not only in the health care records but also in the records of other agencies involved. Normally, we write a letter after every meeting with, or substantive 'phone call to, each person involved with the offender/alleged offender, summarising what has been discussed and agreed. Copies are sent to all other members of the multi-agency team involved, to ensure that everyone is aware, and has opportunities for the same understanding, of what has taken place;
- be realistic about what can be achieved, particularly over a period of months, rather than years.

## WORKING WITH SPECIFIC OFFENCES

While the evidence base has expanded, there are still relatively few published data on assessment and treatment involving this group of persons; controlled or comparison studies are virtually unknown. Similarly, few outcome data are available.

### Sexual Offending

As in the general population, there are people with intellectual disabilities, mainly men (Thompson and Brown 1997), who engage in sexual activities with others who do not, or cannot, consent. Despite assertions, there is also very little evidence that people with intellectual disabilities commit a disproportionate number of sexual offences.

In working with people who have, or are alleged to have, committed sex offences, it is important for treatment providers themselves to understand the legislation relating to sex, including those parts which are most likely to affect people with intellectual disabilities (Fanstone and Andrews 2009). In addition, in carrying out assessment and treatment, clinical experience and the very extensive experience of those who practice in 'mainstream' forensic settings suggests that it is important to consider a wide range of issues (for more detail, see Salter 1988; Morrison et al. 1994; Marshall et al. 2000). It should be noted that virtually all this work derives from men; knowledge and experience about the treatment of women with intellectual disabilities who have, or are alleged to have, committed sexual offences remains extremely limited.

*At least* the following should be investigated whenever possible:

- *Attachment and intimacy*: though no measures specifically for men and women with intellectual disabilities are available, the Significant Other Scale (Power et al. 1988), the Social Intimacy Scale (Miller and Lefcourt 1982), and the Emotional Loneliness Scale (Russell et al. 1980) may all be useful, though they may need adapting for people with more severe disabilities.
- *Understanding of consent and abuse* (Murphy and O'Callaghan 2004): the sex education pictorial materials devised for people with intellectual disabilities by McCarthy and Thompson (2007) are particularly useful.
- *Sexual knowledge* (Murphy and O'Callaghan 2004): while it is rarely the case that men with mild intellectual disabilities engage in illegal sexual behaviour because of a lack of understanding of the technical aspects of sexual knowledge (Talbot and Langdon 2006), the possibility needs to be excluded,
- *Consenting sexual experiences* (McCabe and Cummins 1996; Murphy and O'Callaghan 2004): compared with students, men and women with

mild intellectual disabilities are less likely to report a range of sexual experiences.

- *Sexually abusive experiences*: as noted earlier, men who are sexual offenders or alleged offenders are more likely than others to have experienced childhood sexual abuse (Lindsay *et al*. 2001; Murphy *et al*. 2010).
- *Sexual interests and fantasies*: since many of the accepted scales, such as Wilson's Sexual Fantasy Questionnaire (see Salter 1988) need to be adapted, the Affinity test (Glasgow *et al*. 2003; Glasgow 2009) may be easier to use.
- *Cognitive distortions and attitudes to offending*: the best measure is the Questionnaire on Attitudes Consistent with Sexual Offending (QACSO) developed by Lindsay and his colleagues (see Lindsay 2009), to facilitate the assessment of attitudes towards seven different types of sexual offences, including contact as well as non-contact offences.
- *Victim empathy*: an adaptation of Beckett and Fisher's victim empathy scale (see Beckett *et al*. 1994, pp. 136–40) for people with intellectual disabilities has been used clinically (Murphy *et al*. 2010). It may be useful to explore *other aspects of social cognition* (see Gannon 2009) too.
- *Denial and motivation to change*: the measures devised by Bray and Forshaw (1996) have been used recently (Murphy *et al*. 2010) with men with intellectual disabilities.

There is increasing evidence that cognitive-behavioural group treatment appears to be effective in treating men with intellectual disabilities who have, or are alleged to have, committed sexual offences (Keeling *et al*. 2006, 2008; Williams *et al*. 2007; Murphy *et al*. 2007, in press; Lindsay 2009), just as it seems effective in those without disabilities (for example, Beckett *et al*. 1994; Friendship *et al*. 2003; Aos *et al*. 2006; Brooks-Gordon *et al*. 2006). Of course, the CBT model needs some adaptation and simplification in order for it to be used with men with intellectual disabilities and there are now a number of versions of such treatment available, including that of Lindsay *et al*. (2006, in Scotland; the Adapted Sex Offender Treatment or ASOTP programme in some UK prisons and forensic settings; and the SOTSEC-ID model in some community and forensic settings (see www.kent.ac.uk/tizard/sotsec and Murphy and Sinclair, 2009). Most of these programmes include modules on sex and relationships education, enhancing victim empathy, reducing cognitive distortions and relapse prevention (see Murphy and Sinclair 2009, for a full description of the SOTSEC-ID model). The programmes tend to be long and labour-intensive to run, but some outcome predictors are now emerging (Lindsay *et al*. 2004a; Murphy *et al*. 2010). These suggest that treatment may need to be adapted to meet the needs of different people, and that, following thorough assessments, individual formulations are still essential in guiding treatment, especially for those with particular difficulties, such as autism spectrum conditions (see case example 2 below).

In working with sexual offenders or alleged sexual offenders, practitioners need to be particularly aware of the need to use risk management assessment and management strategies at the same time as providing interventions (see Department of Health 2007; Craig 2010). It should be noted, however, that far more research on risk assessment and management for offenders and alleged offenders with intellectual disabilities is required before we can be sure that we are measuring the important variables (Lindsay and Beail 2004; Harris and Tough 2004; Boer *et al*. 2004).

## Fire-setting

The assertion that people with intellectual disabilities are disproportionately likely to set fires is still sometimes made, but there is limited evidence to support it. Rather, since fire-setters of all kinds are at high risk of being prosecuted if they are arrested, and, if they are identified as people with intellectual disabilities, are more likely to be receive a hospital order under mental health legislation than a prison sentence, they are over-represented in medium- and high-secure hospital facilities.

Traditionally, research on arson has tended to focus on typologies of arsonists, often using psychiatric classifications (see for example, Prins *et al*. 1985) and there have been relatively few studies of psychological motivations for fire-setting (but see Jackson *et al*. 1987; Murphy and Clare 1996) or of the provision of psychological treatment (for exceptions, see Clare *et al*. 1992; Taylor *et al*. 2002a, 2004b). Very few assessment measures have been developed specifically for fire-setting but two that are available are:

- *Fire Assessment Schedule* (FAS, Murphy 1990): this is a preliminary structured interview schedule to examine the person's own view of the antecedents and consequences of his or her fire-setting. It comprises 32 statements: 16 statements about antecedents to the fire-setting, ordered randomly, and rated 'usually', 'sometimes' or 'never', in relation to eight types of events, feelings or cognitions (excitement, anxiety, low social attention, low social approval from peers, presence of auditory hallucinations, depression, anger, and avoidance of demands/aversive events); the remaining 16 statements concern consequences to the fire-setting, ordered randomly, also rated 'usually', sometimes' or 'never', in relation to events, feelings or cognitions that are self-reported as consequences. The schedule has reasonable test-retest reliability, which suggests that it may be useful as part of a fire-setting assessment, at least for those with good verbal skills who are able to label their emotions. It may be that the 'antecedents' part of the schedule would be more useful than the 'consequences' part since people seemed to find it easier to report what happened prior to, rather than following, fire-setting (Murphy and Clare 1996). From initial studies, it appeared that an individual's fire-setting often reflected a number of motivations; it may be simplistic to look for a single reason, the implication being that individual formulation is important in deciding treatments.

- *Fire Interest Rating Scale* (FIRS, Murphy 1990): this comprises 14 descriptions of fire-related situations (e.g. watching a house burn down; watching an ordinary coal fire in a house), which the person is asked to rate (from 'very exciting, lovely, very nice' to 'most upsetting, absolutely horrible'). Interestingly, with the exception of the item about a coal fire in a house (which the fire-setters rated as more exciting), there were no significant differences between the ratings of people with mild intellectual disabilities who had, or had not, engaged in fire-setting (Murphy and Clare 1996). Nevertheless, in one sample of people who had been convicted of arson, there were some individuals who obtained unusually high scores on the FIRS and who also identified the excitement of the fire as one of their motivations in the FAS (see above). This suggests that 'interest in fires' (so-called 'pyromania') may be important for some individuals, although, even for them, it may be only part of the motivation for setting fires.

Despite these advances in assessment, there remain few treatment studies in adult populations (see Taylor *et al.* 2004a, and Palmer *et al.* 2007, for reviews). One example, based on a cognitive-behavioural functional analysis, is described in Clare *et al.* (1992). As might be expected, much of the treatment (e.g. relaxation, coping strategies, assertiveness, social-skills training, day-activities and employment) did not relate *specifically* to the person's fire-setting but addressed psychological difficulties thought to increase his vulnerability to the behaviour. In contrast, other strategies (graded exposure to matches, contact with appropriate fires, covert sensitisation) were aimed specifically at his history of very serious fires. It is now about twenty years since the person ('Mr P.R.') described was discharged from an in-patient service. While he has not had an easy life, he lives in his own flat, has a small social network, and importantly, as far as is known, has not set further fires or made more hoax 'phone calls.

More recently, Taylor *et al.* (2002a; 2004a) have developed a cognitive-behavioural treatment package which includes modules on offence cycle review, psycho-education, skills acquisition (coping skills; interpersonal skills) and relapse prevention. Initial results appeared promising but the effectiveness of the intervention requires further evaluation.

## Aggression

While estimates of prevalence vary widely, according to the setting and the definitions used (for a review, see Taylor and Novaco 2005), physically aggressive behaviour by people with intellectual disabilities has a major impact, not only on victims, caregivers (Jahoda and Wanless 2005) and services, but also on the perpetrator him or herself (McMillan *et al.* 2004). It is a major cause of social exclusion and, very often, leads to the involvement of the criminal justice system.

Assessment of the difficulties associated with aggressive behaviour should include many of the broad-based aspects described above (under Treatment of the Individual and Management of Further Offending/ alleged Offending and Table 12.1). In addition, a number of specific self-report anger-related measures have been developed for people with intellectual disabilities:

- The Anger Inventory (Benson and Ivins 1992), which was specifically designed for this population, and has been Anglicized (Rose *et al.* 2005).
- Novaco's Anger Scale and Provocation Inventory (Novaco 2003), which has been adapted for this group (Taylor and Novaco 2005).
- Spielberger's State-Trait Anger Expression Inventory (STAXI-2, Spielberger, 1999), which again has been adapted for this group (Taylor and Novaco 2005).

Anger outbursts are often quite frequent for any individual (c.f. fire-setting and sexual offending), so most practitioners also ask those with whom they work to complete daily anger diaries (see, for example, Benson 1992; Taylor and Novaco 2005). In addition, carers or support workers are often asked to complete individualised measures such ABC charts or incident charts, or standardized measures with good inter-rater reliability, such as the Modified Overt Aggression Scale (MOAS, Kho *et al.* 1998), in order to assess changes in the frequency and/or severity of aggressive outbursts.

For people with more severe intellectual disabilities, treatment programmes for aggressive behaviour tend to be individual and behavioural (see Taylor 2002, for a detailed review). In contrast, while individual treatment is sometimes used with people with mild intellectual disabilities (e.g. Taylor and Novaco 2005), group interventions predominate, particularly in community settings (see Taylor and Novaco 2005). Regardless of the format, most comprise sessions covering at least four components. In addition, there is normally between-session 'homework', usually in the form of an anger-diary, often completed with support from caregivers, to help the person monitor his or her mood and the frequency of, and triggers for, his or her aggressive behaviour. The sessions normally focus on:

- *The development of emotional understanding* (for example, identifying and understanding feelings, thoughts, and behaviours in the self and others), using photographs, drawings, or excerpts from television programmes.

- *Relaxation training*, using progressive relaxation and calming imagery (Taylor and Novaco 2005), or, more recently, mindfulness (Singh *et al.* 2007).
- *Coping skills training*, largely through role-playing difficult situations that have arisen during the week. Sometimes, this involves no more than promoting 'coping' statements (such as 'I can handle this') while decreasing 'trouble' statements (such as 'I'm really going to hit him in a minute'). Increasingly, however, these skills are presented within the framework of cognitive re-structuring, aimed at modifying the attentional focus and expectations that the person brings to difficult situations and, which, in turn, affects his or her judgment (Taylor and Novaco 2005).
- *Problem-solving skills training*, involving some variation of the four stage model developed by Meichenbaum (1985): What is my problem?; What is my plan?; Am I using my plan?; and How am I doing? There is a suggestion, arising from the literature (Pert *et al.* 1999; Jahoda *et al.* 2001) that it may also be helpful to develop a way for the person to minimize the impact of his or her angry behaviour (for example, by going to 'cool down' outside). Again, this is normally carried out through role-playing difficult situations.

While there is some agreement about the components of group interventions, there is wide variation in other aspects, including the number and nature of the therapists, the emphasis given to different components, the number of sessions each week, and, probably importantly, the duration of treatment, from between 18 hours (Benson *et al.* 1986) to 40 hours (Lindsay *et al.* 2004b).

Most studies of group cognitive-behavioural interventions have identified benefits for those completing treatment. However, with rather few exceptions (such as Rose *et al.* 2000; Taylor *et al.* 2002b, Willner *et al.* 2002), comparison groups have not been used, follow-up has been limited, and scant regard has been given to the impact of individual differences. Where these issues have received some consideration, improvements have been noted in performance on provocation inventories (Rose *et al.* 2005), self-reported anger (Willner *et al.* 2002), and staff accounts of anger-coping skills (Taylor *et al.* 2002b). At present, therefore, group CBT is probably the intervention of choice, providing that treatment providers ensure that the needs of each group member are taken into account. Nevertheless, caution is required, given that there is so little evidence that such interventions lead to long-term reductions in the frequency and/or severity of aggressive outbursts and/or to improvements in the quality of life of people with intellectual disabilities and aggressive behaviour.

Some of the points made in this chapter are illustrated by two case studies.

# Case example 1

Mr A's lack of interest in his peers, resistance to changes in his routine, and unusual interests were reported by his mother while he was still a toddler, but her concerns were not addressed. Mr A found school very difficult, and was aggressive, and ran away repeatedly. As he grew older, he was alleged to steal food from shops, though he was never charged by the police. He also made numerous hoax 999 calls, often from places miles from his home. He would wait at the 'phone box for the police. Since he was easily identifiable as a vulnerable person, the police normally took him home.

When he left school, Mr A's parents tried to provide him with an 'ordinary' life at home. However, whenever he was asked to help with domestic tasks, he became aggressive and would run off, very often making hoax calls to the emergency services. In desperation, his parents locked him in. He was referred to a specialist in-patient service for understanding of his: running away; physical aggression; food stealing; and frequent hoax telephone calls

From detailed assessments, the flow-chart formulation in Figure 12.1 was developed: in addition to a mild intellectual disability, Mr A was a person with an autism spectrum condition. His skills were limited and he found it difficult to cope with any 'demands'. Instead, he would try to leave, if possible by taking a bus, since buses were a

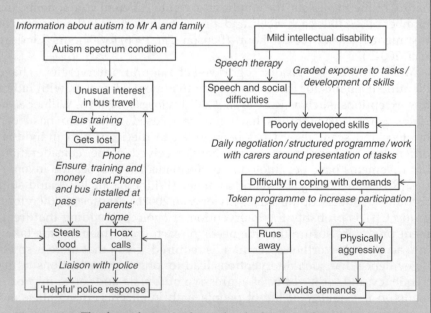

**Figure 12.1** The formulation is shown by the boxes and arrows; the italics show the interventions and their intended effect.

particular interest. If prevented, he would be aggressive. Either way, he avoided tasks, but this meant that his skills remained poor.

Mr A's knowledge of bus routes, time-tables, and so on, suggested a high level of expertise. Behavioural observations indicated that, in practice, his bus skills were very limited: indeed, he often got lost. It was presumed that he stole food because he became hungry while travelling about. Certainly, the hoax calls to the police seemed to be a strategy to enable him to return home.

The italics in Figure 12.1 summarise the interventions carried out by the specialist service with members of his local service. Since Mr A was 'at risk' when he ran away, he was detained in hospital under mental health legislation, but was given leave of absence for increasingly long periods, so that work could be carried out with him in his area of origin. In terms of the framework developed by LaVigna *et al.* (1989), the interventions included:

- ecological manipulations (e.g. graded exposure to tasks; negotiation with him about what were reasonable expectations to help him feel more in control of his life; a structured programme with bus trips scheduled regularly);
- positive programming (e.g. helping him use the telephone to ring his parents and other members of his family; skills training to enable him to help him find his way home);
- direct treatment (such as a token programme, linked to outings to places of particular interest to encourage Mr. A to take part in the skills training); and
- reactive strategies (for his food stealing and hoax calls, such as helping the police in his area recognise that, whilst he was 'vulnerable' suspect (see above), it was not appropriate to ignore his alleged offending).

After leaving the specialist service, Mr A moved to a residential service in his area of origin, attending a local college, and remaining in close contact with his family. For almost two years, things went well. Then, to meet the needs of the service, he was moved to another hostel, and shortly after, was moved again. His increasingly aggressive behaviour resulted in the loss of both his college place and his residential placement. He was moved to an 'out-of-county', independent, service. He reported that he was not happy and his behaviour deteriorated further. Eventually, following a series of hoax calls, the police charged Mr A again. He was convicted and spent a short time in prison. He returned to the same service and his residential placement but his circumstances became more settled. Nevertheless, five years after his discharge from the specialist service, he was still living many miles from his local area and his contact with his family remained more limited than he, or they, would like.

As this example (for more details, see Clare and Mosher 2005) illustrates, even where a good understanding of a person's offending/alleged offending has been developed, and interventions introduced which appear to be effective, long-term success is far from assured. The provision of social care which recognises that offenders/alleged offenders are likely to remain vulnerable and need continuing support, even when they are doing well, is often crucial.

## Case example 2

As a child, Mr J lived with his family and attended mainstream schools, where he had some special support. By his own account, he was socially isolated and was badly bullied. Nevertheless he acquired considerable literacy skills, later attending college and briefly working in paid employment, as a shelf-filler in a supermarket, a charity collector, and as a doorman in a club. He was dismissed from all these jobs, however, because of his difficulties in interacting with others and insistence on routines. He was later diagnosed with an autism spectrum condition.

As an adult, Mr J continued to be extremely socially isolated and to live with his family. He was referred to the local specialist community team for people with intellectual disabilities following illegal sexual behaviour. This included repeated masturbation in public, in front of children in public places (such as parks). He often made attempts to conceal himself, but these were clumsy and he was often seen. He was arrested on four occasions but not charged. Following one of these arrests, the police took him back to his family because of their concerns about his disability. Mr J's behaviour sometimes led to him being abused by the families of his victims and, on at least one occasion, after he was assaulted, he called the police himself. No charges were brought against the alleged perpetrators, exacerbating his view of himself as a victim.

Mr J was offered treatment within services for people with intellectual disabilities because the severity of his social impairments suggested that he met their access criteria. In fact, later, it became clear that his intellectual functioning lay within the borderline range. Further detailed assessment, which included tests of sexual knowledge, victim empathy and cognitive distortions, indicated that, Mr J, who did not deny his offences, was aware that his sexual behaviour was illegal and had relatively good sexual knowledge, but found it difficult to empathise with his victims. Indeed, he blamed the children for his own behaviour.

Mr J's own view was that his problems had originated during his early school years, when he had been isolated and bullied. In the playground, perhaps because he was anxious, he was often incontinent. The staff on duty were very sympathetic, and insisted that he go indoors to find dry clothes. Having discovered that he could both elicit sympathy and escape from the playground, he often wet himself during breaks. Apparently, this behaviour continued into his secondary school years, except that then he would be incontinent near his home, with younger children watching, rather than at school with his peers. At some point, which Mr J was unable to explain, masturbation became incorporated into the 'wetting behaviour'.

When Mr J engaged in such behaviours, he always wore shorts, on the grounds that, despite his unhappy experiences at school, they reminded him of being a child. He looked forward eagerly to the strong positive feelings he gained from masturbation and the sympathy he assumed he would gain from onlookers. He was much more likely to engage in the behavior when he was feeling low, and particularly if he felt he had been bullied. At times, he appeared to use his behaviour as a form of revenge for being bullied, although, or fear of their responses, he did not target the same children as had bullied him; instead, he searched out younger children. He reported that, in the past, he had often felt extremely angry with children,

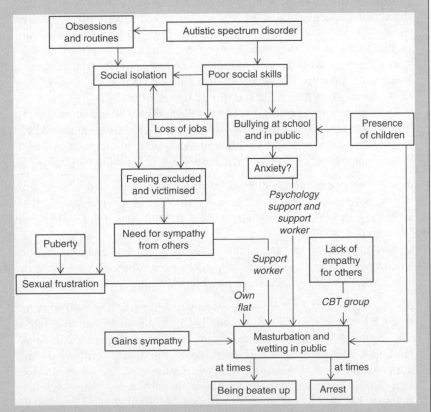

**Figure 12.2** The formulation is shown by the boxes and arrows; the italics show the interventions and their intended effect.

particularly after they had treated him badly, but this had eased over time. Instead, he felt a desperate need for sympathetic and kindly responses both from them, and from others. Figure 2 shows a flowchart formulation of Mr J's difficulties.

Mr J was enrolled in cognitive behaviour therapy treatment for men with mild or borderline intellectual disabilities who were sexual offenders or at risk of sexual offending (see www.kent.ac.uk/tizard/sotsec), attended two consecutive groups. For both, the sessions took place weekly, over about a year, and involved six to eight men (see Murphy and Sinclair 2009). He attended voluntarily and regularly, working hard, and reporting that he found the intervention helpful. The other men in the group found Mr J hard to understand, as, unusually for men with his problems, he was completely frank about his difficulties, and he would always tell the group when he had engaged in masturbation in public during the previous week.

Post-group assessments showed that Mr J had benefited from the groups, in that his sexual knowledge, victim empathy and cognitive distortions had generally improved. From working with him in the groups, it was also clear that he had made great progress in understanding his own behaviour. However, it was also clear that, despite knowing very well the consequences of his sexually inappropriate behaviour, he found it very difficult to stop. It was because of this that he was enrolled in the second programme.

During the same period, Mr J was resettled into an independent flat and he was also receiving individual psychological treatment and help from a support worker, in an attempt to alleviate his social and sexual difficulties. He reported that the following aspects were helpful:

- social support and help in social problem solving (from the cognitive behavioural treatment group and from his own psychologist);
- having a place to masturbate in his own flat so he felt less inclined to go out;
- assistance from the support worker in accessing and engaging in community activities. This support also enable Mr J to share his feelings and alleviated his fear of being bullied when he was out.

Mr J's illegal behaviour only ceased consistently when he was engaged in a CBT group (SOTSEC-ID), was living in his own flat, and had a total of about 16 hours of support each week (from the group, his psychologist, and his support worker). Once the groups ended, and his support hours were reduced, following a decision by social services that funding was no longer available, Mr. J's motivation seriously deteriorated and he began to masturbate in public again. Eventually, he was charged, convicted, and received a probation order. The outcome is unknown as he then moved with his family to a different area.

While Mr J's problems are very different from those of Mr A, this case again illustrates the importance, when a person appears to have made very good progress, of continuing to provide support, including, often crucially, social care support. The barriers to persuading some commissioners and providers of the importance of social care, especially for people with mild intellectual disabilities, should not be under-estimated. While traditional social care will continue to be needed, there may also be other ways in which it could be provided, such as through circles of support or mentoring (see Department of Health 2009b).

## CONCLUSIONS

Over the past decade, the evidence base for the assessment and treatment of people with intellectual disabilities who have, or are alleged to have, committed criminal offences has developed considerably. Increasingly, and particularly where they take into account individualized psychological formulations, it appears that group cognitive-behavioural treatments targeted at specific types of difficulties are useful, at least for men. Nevertheless, so far, the evaluation of such complex interventions remains very limited. This should change over the next few years, as sophisticated methodologies for examining effectiveness continue to be developed (see Craig *et al.* 2008). Meanwhile, and consistent with the recommendations of the Bradley Report (Department of Health 2009a), psychological interventions should be carried out within the framework of strong and committed partnerships between the relevant health, social care, and criminal justice agencies. Such arrangements will maximize the likelihood that any benefits for the offender or alleged offender are supported and developed without increasing the risks to potential victims.

### Further Reading

Cordess, C. and Cox, M. (eds) (1996) *Forensic Psychotherapy. Crime, psychodynamics and the offender patient. Vol. I Mainly Theory. Vol. II Mainly Practice.* Jessica Kingsley: London.
Lindsay, W.R., Taylor, J.L. and Sturmey, P. (eds) (2004) *Offenders with Developmental Disabilities.* Chichester: John Wiley and Sons, Ltd.
Lindsay, W.R. (2009) *The Treatment of Sex Offenders With Developmental Disabilities: a practice workbook.* Chichester: John Wiley and Sons, Ltd.
Taylor, J.L. and Novaco, R.W. (2005) *Anger Treatment for People with Developmental Disabilities: a theory, evidence and manual based approach.* Chichester: John Wiley and Sons, Ltd.

### Acknowledgements

We are grateful to 'Mr A.' and 'Mr J' for giving their consent to the inclusion of the material about their experiences; to the family of 'Mr A' for their support whilst we were seeking his consent; and to colleagues in the clinical teams in which the treatment of 'Mr A' and 'Mr J' was carried out.

# References

Allen, J.G. (2001) *Traumatic Relationships and Serious Mental Disorders*. Chichester: John Wiley and Sons, Ltd.

Antaki, C., Finlay, W.M.L., Walton, C. and Pate, L. (2008) Offering choice to people with an intellectual impairment: an interactional study. *Journal of Intellectual Disability Research*, **52**, 1165–75.

Aos, S., Miller, M. and Drake, E. (2006). *Evidence-based Adult Corrections Programs: what works and what does not*. Olympia, WA: Washington State Institute for Public Policy.

Barron, P., Hassiotis, A. and Banes, J. (2004) Offenders with intellectual disability: A prospective comparative study. *Journal of Intellectual Disability Research*, **48**, 69–76.

Beckett, R., Beech, A., Fisher, D. and Fordham, A.S. (1994) *Community -Based Treatment for Sex Offenders: An Evaluation of Seven Treatment Programmes*.

Benson B.A., Rice C.J. and Miranti S.V. (1986) Effects of anger management training with mentally retarded adults in group treatment. *Journal of Consulting and Clinical Psychology*, **54**, 728–9.

Benson, B.A. (1992) *Teaching Anger Management to Persons with Mental Retardation*. Worthington, OH: International Diagnostics Systems Inc.

Benson, B.A. and Ivins, J. (1992) Anger, depression and self-concept in adults with mental retardation. *Journal of Intellectual Disability Research*, **36**, 169–75.

Boer, D.P., Tough, S. and Haaven, J. (2004) Assessment of risk manageability of developmentally disabled sex offenders. *Journal of Applied Research in Intellectual Disabilities*, **17**, 275–84.

Bray, D. and Forshaw, N. (1996) *Sex Offenders' Self-Appraisal Scale* (Version 1.1). Preston, Lancs: Lancashire Care NHS Trust.

British Psychological Society. (2008) *Generic Professional Practice Guidelines*. Leicester: British Psychological Society.

Brooks-Gordon, B. and Bilby, C. (2006) Psychological interventions for treatment of adult sex offenders. *British Medical Journal*, **333**, 5–6.

Bull, R.H.C. (1995) Interviewing people with communicative disabilities. In R. Bull and D. Carson (eds), *Handbook and Psychology in Legal Contexts* (pp. 247–60). Chichester: John Wiley and Sons, Ltd.

Carr, E.G., Levin, L., McConnachie, G., Carlson, J.I., Kemp, D.C. and Smith, C.E. (1994) *Communication-based Intervention for Problem Behavior: a user's guide for producing positive change*. Baltimore, MD: P.H. Brookes.

Carr, A. and O'Reilly, G. (2007) Diagnosis, classification and epidemiology. In A. Carr, G. O'Reilly, P. Noonan-Walsh and J. McEvoy (eds). *The Handbook of Intellectual Disability and Clinical Psychology Practice* (pp. 3–49). Hove: Routledge.

Carson, D. (1989) Prosecuting people with mental handicaps. *Criminal Law Review*, 87–94.

Carson, D. (1995) Editorial. *Mental Handicap Research*, **8**, 77–80.

Carson, D. and Clare, I.C.H. (1997). Boundaries with the criminal justice and other legal systems. In J. Churchill, H. Brown, A. Craft and C. Horrocks (eds), *There*

*Are No Easy Answers! The provision of continuing care and treatment to adults with learning disabilities who sexually abuse others* (pp. 53–68). Chesterfield: ARC/NAPSAC.

Clare, I.C.H., Murphy, G.H., Cox, D. and Chaplin, E.H. (1992) Assessment and treatment of fire-setting: A single case investigation using a cognitive-behavioural model. *Criminal Behaviour and Mental Health*, **2**, 253–68.

Clare, I.C.H. and Mosher, S. (2005) Working with people with aggressive behaviour. In T. Riding, C. Swann and B. Swann (eds), *The Handbook of Forensic Learning Disabilities* (pp. 73–96). Abingdon: Radcliffe Publishing Ltd.

Clare, I.C.H. and Woodbury-Smith, M.R. (2009) Autism spectrum conditions. In S. Young, M. Kopelman and G. Gudjonsson (eds), *Handbook of Forensic Neuropsychology* (pp. 109–33). Oxford: Oxford University Press.

Commission for Social Care Inspection. (2008) *Cutting the Cake Fairly: CSCI review of eligibility criteria for social care*. London: Commission for Social Care Inspection.

Cottis, T. and O'Driscoll, D. (2009) Outside in: The effect of trauma on organizations. In T. Cottis (ed.), *Intellectual Disability, Trauma and Psychotherapy* (pp.). Hove: Routledge.

Craig, L.A. (2010) Controversies in assessing risk and deviancy in sex offenders with intellectual disabilities, *Psychology, Crime and Law*, **16**, 75–101.

Craig, P., Dieppe, P., Macintyre, S., Michie, S., Nazareth, I. and Petticrew, M. (2008) Developing and evaluating complex interventions: the new Medical Research Council guidance. *British Medical Journal*, **337**, 979–83.

*Crime and Disorder Act 1998*. London: Her Majesty's Stationery Office.

Dagnan, D., Chadwick, P. and Proudlove, J. (2000) Toward an assessment of suitability of people with mental retardation for cognitive therapy. *Cognitive Therapy and Research*, **24**, 627–36.

Davies, R. (2007) The forensic network and the internal world of the offender: Thoughts from consultancy work in the forensic sector. In D. Morgan and S. Ruszczynski (eds), *Lectures on Violence, Perversion and Delinquency* (pp. 221–38). London: Karnac Books.

Department for Constitutional Affairs (2007) *Mental Capacity Act 2005: Code of Practice*. London: The Stationery Office.

Department of Health and Home Office (1992) *Review of Health and Social Services for Mentally Disordered Offenders and Others Requiring Similar Services: Final Summary Report* (Cm 2008.). London: Her Majesty's Stationery Office.

Department of Health (2001) *Valuing People: a new strategy for learning disability for the 21st Century*. London: Department of Health.

Department of Health (2007) *Best Practice in Managing Risk: principles and guidance for best practice in the assessment and management of risk to self and others in mental health services*. London: Department of Health.

Department of Health (2009a) *The Bradley Report: Lord Bradley's review of people with mental health problems or learning disabilities in the criminal justice system*. London: Department of Health.

Department of Health (2009b) *Valuing People Now: from progress to transformation*. London: Department of Health.

Emerson, E. (1992) What is normalisation? In H. Brown and H. Smith (eds), *Normalisation. a reader for the nineties* (pp. 1–18). London: Routledge.

Fanstone, C. and Andrews, S. (2009) *Learning Disabilities, Sex and the Law: a practical guide* (2nd revised edn) London: Family Planning Association.

Fennell, P. (1996) *Treatment Without Consent. Law, psychiatry, and the treatment of mentally disordered people since 1845*. London: Routledge.

Friendship, C., Mann, R.E. and Beech, A.R. (2003) Evaluation of a national prison-based treatment program for sexual offenders in England and Wales. *Journal of Interpersonal Violence*, **18**, 744–59.

Gannon, T.A. (2009) Social cognition in violent and sexual offending: an overview. *Psychology, Crime and Law*, **15**, 97–118.

Glasgow, D.V. (2009) Affinity: The development of a self-report assessment of pae-dophile sexual interest incorporating a viewing time validity measure. In D. Thornton and D.R. Laws (eds), *Cognitive Approaches to the Assessment of Sexual Interest in Sexual Offenders* (pp. 59–83).Chichester: John Wiley and Sons, Ltd.

Glasgow, D.V., Croxen, J. and Osborne, A. (2003) An assessment tool for investigating paedophile sexual interest using viewing time: An application of single case methodology. *British Journal of Learning Disabilities*, **31**, 96–102.

Gudjonsson, G.H. (2003) *The Psychology of Interrogations and Confessions: a handbook*. Chichester: John Wiley and Sons, Ltd.

Harris, A.J.R. and Tough, S. (2004) Should actuarial risk assessments be used with sex offenders who are intellectually disabled? *Journal of Applied Research in Intellectual Disabilities*, **17**, 235–42.

Hatcher, R. and Noakes, S. (2010) Working with sex offenders: the impact on Australian treatment providers. *Psychology, Crime and Law*, **16**, 145–67.

Hatton, C. and Emerson, E. (2004) The relationship between life events and psychopathology amongst children with intellectual disabilities. *Journal of Applied Research in Intellectual Disabilities*, **17**, 109–17.

Henry, L. and MacLean, M. (2002) Working memory performance in children with and without intellectual disabilities. *American Journal on Mental Retardation*, **107**, 421–32.

Holland, T., Clare, I.C.H. and Mukhopadhyay, T. (2002) Prevalence of criminal offending by men and women with intellectual disability and the characteristics of offenders: Implications for research and service development. *Journal of Intellectual Disability Research*, **46**(1), 6–20.

Hollins, S., Clare, I.C.H. and Murphy, G.H. (1996a) *You're Under Arrest*. London: Royal College of Psychiatrists and St George's Hospital Medical School.

Hollins, S., Murphy, G.H. and Clare, I.C.H. (1996b) *You're On Trial*. London: Royal College of Psychiatrists and St George's Hospital Medical School.

*Human Rights Act 1998*. London: Her Majesty's Stationery Office.

Jahoda, A., Trower, P., Pert, C. and Fin, D. (2001) Contingent reinforcement or defending the self? A review of evolving models of aggression in people with mild learning disabilities. *British Journal of Medical Psychology*, **74**, 305–21.

Jahoda, A. and Wanless, L. (2005) Knowing you: The inter-personal perceptions of staff towards aggressive individuals with mild to moderate intellectual disabilities in situations of conflict. *Journal of Intellectual Disability Research*, **49**, 544–51.

Jackson, H.F., Glass, C. and Hope, S. (1987) A functional analysis of recidivistic arson. *British Journal of Clinical Psychology*, **26**, 175–85.

Joyce, T. (2007) *Best Interests: guidance on determining the best interests of adults who lack the capacity to make a decision (or decisions) for themselves [England and Wales]*. Leicester: British Psychological Society Professional Practice Board.

Keeling, J.A., Rose, J.L. and A.R. Beech (2006) An investigation into the effectiveness of a custody-based cognitive-behavioural treatment for special needs sexual offenders. *Journal of Forensic Psychiatry and Psychology*, **17**, 372–92.

Keeling, J.A., Rose, J.L. and A.R. Beech (2008) What do we know about the efficacy of group work for sexual offenders with an intellectual disability? Where to from here? *Journal of Sexual Aggression*, **14**, 135–44.

Kho, K., Sensky, T., Mortimer, A. and Corcos, C. (1998) Prospective study into factors associated with aggressive incidents in psychiatric acute admission wards. *British Journal of Psychiatry*, **172**, 38–43.

LaVigna, G.W., Willis, T.J. and Donnellan, A.M. (1989) The role of positive programming in behavioural treatment. In E. Cipani (ed.), *The Treatment of Severe Behavior Disorders*. (pp. 59–84). Washington, DC: American Association on Mental Deficiency.

Lindsay, W.R. (2009) *The Treatment of Sex Offenders With Developmental Disabilities: a practice workbook*. Chichester: John Wiley and Sons, Ltd.

Lindsay, W.R. and Beail, N. (2004) Risk assessment: Actuarial prediction and clinical judgement of offending incidents and behaviour for intellectual disability services. *Journal of Applied Research in Intellectual Disabilities*, **17**, 229–34.

Lindsay, W.R., Allan, R., Parry, C., MacLeod, F., Cottrell, J., Overend, H. and Smith, A.H.W. (2004b) Anger and aggression in people with intellectual disabilities: Treatment and follow-up of consecutive referrals and a waiting list comparison. *Clinical Psychology and Psychotherapy*, **11**, 255–64.

Lindsay, W.R., Elliot, S.F. and Astell, A. (2004a) Predictors of sexual offence recidivism in offenders with intellectual disabilities. *Journal of Applied Research in Intellectual Disabilities*, **17**, 299–305.

Lindsay, W.R., Law, J., Quinn, K., Smart, N. and Smith, A.H.W. (2001) A comparison of physical and sexual abuse histories: Sexual and non-sexual offenders with intellectual disability. *Child Abuse and Neglect*, **25**, 989–95.

Lindsay, W.R., Smith, A.H.W., Law, J., Quinn, K. anderson, A., Smith, A. and Allan, R. (2002) A treatment service for sex offenders and abusers with intellectual disability: Characteristics of referrals and evaluation. *Journal of Applied Research in Intellectual Disability*, **15**, 166–74.

Lindsay, W.R., Steele, L., Smith, A.H.W., Quinn, K. and Allan, R. (2006) A community forensic intellectual disability service: Twelve year follow up of referrals, analysis of referral patterns and assessment of harm reduction. *Legal and Criminological Psychology*, **11**, 113–30.

Loucks, N. (2007) *No One Knows: offenders with learning difficulties and learning disabilities: review of prevalence and associated needs*. London: Prison Reform Trust.

McBrien, J. (2003) The intellectually disabled offender: Methodological problems and identification. *Journal of Applied Research in Intellectual Disabilities*, **16**, 95–105.

McBrien, J. and Murphy, G. (2006) Police and carers' views on reporting of alleged offences by people with intellectual disabilities. *Psychology, Crime and Law*, **12**, 127–44.

McCabe, M.P. and Cummins, R.A. (1996) The sexual knowledge, experience, feelings and needs of people with mild intellectual disability. *Education and Training in Mental Retardation and Developmental Disabilities*, **31**, 13–21.

McCarthy, M. and Thompson, D. (2007) *Sex and the 3Rs: rights, responsibilities and risks* (3rd edn). Brighton: Pavilion.

McMillan, D., Hastings, R.P. and Coldwell, J. (2004) Clinical and actuarial prediction of physical violence in a forensic intellectual disability hospital: A longitudinal study. *Journal of Applied Research in Intellectual Disabilities*, **17**, 255–65.

Marshall, W.L. anderson, D. and Fernandez, Y. (2000) *Cognitive Behavioural Treatment of Sexual Offenders*. Chichester: John Wiley and Sons, Ltd.

Masten, A.S. and Coatsworth, J.D. (1995) Competence, resilience, and psychopathology. In D. Cicchetti and D.J. Cohen (eds), *Manual of Developmental Psychopathology: Volume 2, risk, disorder and adaptation*, (pp. 715–52). New York: John Wiley and Sons, Ltd.

Meichenbaum, D. (1985) *Stress Inoculation Training*. New York, NY: Pergamon Press.

*Mental Capacity Act (England and Wales) 2005*. London: The Stationery Office.

*Mental Health Act (England and Wales) 2007*. London: The Stationery Office.

Miller, R.S. and Lefcourt, H.M. (1982) The assessment of social intimacy. *Journal of Personality Assessment*, **46**, 514–18.

Morrison, T., Erooga, M. and Beckett, R. (1994) *Sexual Offending Against Children*. London: Routledge.

Murphy, G.H. (1990) *Analysis of Motivation and Fire-related Interests in People With a Mild Learning Disability Who Set Fires*. Paper presented at the International Congress on Treatment of Mental Illness and Behavioural Disorders in Mentally Retarded People, Amersterdam.

Murphy, G.H., Holland, A.J., Fowler, P. and Reep, J. (1991) MIETS: A service option for people with mild mental handicaps and challenging behaviour or psychiatric problems. 1: Philosophy, service, and service users. *Mental Handicap Research*, **4**, 41–66.

Murphy, G.H. and Clare, I.C.H. (1996) Analysis of motivation in people with mild learning disabilities (mental handicap) who set fires. *Psychology, Crime and Law*, **2**, 153–64.

Murphy, G.H. and O'Callaghan, A.C. (2004) Capacity to consent to sexual relationships by adults with intellectual disabilities. *Psychological Medicine*, **34**, 1347–57.

Murphy, G.H. and Mason, J. (2007) People with intellectual disabilities who are at risk of offending. In N. Bouras and G. Holt (eds), *Psychiatric and Behavioural Disorders in Intellectual and Developmental Disabilities* (pp. 173–201). Cambridge: Cambridge University Press.

Murphy, G.H., Powell, S., Guzman, A.M. and Hays, S.J. (2007) Cognitive-behavioural treatment for men with intellectual disabilities and sexually abusive behaviour: A pilot study. *Journal of Intellectual Disability Research*, **51**, 902–12.

Murphy G.H. and Sinclair N. (2009)Treatment for men with intellectual disabilities and sexually abusive behaviour. In A.R. Beech, L.A. Craig and K.D.Browne (eds), *Assessment and Treatment of Sex Offenders: a handbook* (pp. 369–92). Chichester: John Wiley and Sons, Ltd.

Murphy, G.H., Sinclair, N., Hays, S.J. and SOTSEC-ID members (2010) Effectiveness of group cognitive-behavioural treatment for men with intellectual disabilities at risk of sexual offending. *Journal of Applied Research in Intellectual Disabilities*, **23**, 537–51.

Nicolson, P. (1992) Gender issues in clinical psychology. In J.M. Usher and Nicolson, P. (eds), *Gender Issues in Psychology* (pp. 8–38). London: Routledge.

Noble, J.H. and Conley, R.W. (1992) Toward an epidemiology of relevant attributes. In R.W. Conley, R. Luckasson, and G.N. Bouthilet (eds), *The Criminal Justice System and Mental Retardation* (pp. 17–54). Baltimore, MD: P.H. Brookes.

Novaco, R.W. (2003) *The Novaco Anger Scale and Provocation Inventory (NAS-PI)*. Los Angeles, CA: Western Psychological Services.

Oathamshaw, S.C. and Haddock, G. (2006) Do people with intellectual disabilities and psychosis have the cognitive skills required to undertake cognitive behavioural therapy? *Journal of Applied Research in Intellectual Disabilities*, **19**, 35–43.

O'Brien, G. (2002) Dual diagnoses in offenders with intellectual disability: Setting research priorities: A review of research findings concerning psychiatric disorder (excluding personality disorder) among offenders with intellectual disability. *Journal of Intellectual Disability Research*, **46**(1), 21–30.

O'Reilly, M., Sigafoos, J., Lancioni, G.E., Green, V.A., Olive, M. and Cannella, H. (2007). Applied behaviour analysis. In A. Carr, G. O'Reilly, P. Noonan-Walsh and J. McEvoy (eds), *The Handbook of Intellectual Disability and Clinical Psychology Practice* (pp. 253–80). Hove: Routledge.

Palmer, E.J., McGuire, J., Hounsome, J.C., Hatcher, R.M., Bilby, C.A.L. and Hollin, C.R. (2007) Offending behaviour programmes in the community: The effects on reconviction of three programmes with adult male offenders. *Legal and Criminological Psychology*, **12**, 251–64.

Perkins, D. (1991) Clinical work with sex offenders in secure settings. In C.R. Hollin and K. Howells (eds), *Clinical Approaches to Sex Offenders and Their Victims* (pp. 151–77). Chichester: John Wiley and Sons, Ltd.

Pert, C., Jahoda, A. and Squire, J. (1999) Attribution of intent and role-taking: Cognitive factors as mediators of aggression with people who have mental retardation. *American Journal on Mental Retardation*, **104**, 399–409.

*Police and Criminal Evidence Act (England and Wales) 1984*. London: HMSO.

Poncelas, A. and Murphy, G. (2007) Accessible information for people with intellectual disabilities: Do symbols really help? *Journal of Applied Research in Intellectual Disabilities*, **20**, 466–74.

Power, M.J., Champion, L.A. and Aris, S.J. (1988) The development of a measure of social support: The Significant Others (SOS) Scale. *British Journal of Clinical Psychology*, **27**, 349–58.

Prins, H., Tennant, G. and Trick, K. (1985) Motives for arson (fire raising). *Medicine, Science, and the Law*, **25**, 275–8.

Rholes, S.W. and Simpson, J.A. (2004) Ambivalent attachment and depressive symptoms: The role of romantic and parent-child relationships. *Journal of Cognitive Psychotherapy*, **18**, 67–78.

Richardson, S.A. and Koller, H. (1985) Epidemiology. In A.M. Clarke, A.D.B. Clarke and J.M. Berg (eds), *Mental Deficiency: the changing outlook* (4th edn), (pp. 356–400). London: Methuen.

Rose, J., West, C. and Clifford, D. (2000) Group interventions for anger in people with intellectual disabilities. *Research in Developmental Disabilities*, **21**, 171–81.

Rose J., Loftus M., Flint B. and Carey L. (2005) Factors associated with the efficacy of a group intervention for anger in people with intellectual disabilities. *British Journal of Clinical Psychology*, **44**, 305–17.

Russell, D., Peplan, C.A. and Cutrona, C.A. (1980) The revised UCLA Loneliness Scale: Concurrent and discriminant validity evidence. *Journal of Personality and Social Psychology*, **39**, 472–80.

Rutter, M., Giller, H. and Hagell, A. (1998) *Antisocial Behaviour by Young People*. New York: Cambridge University Press.

Salter, A. (1988) *Treating Child Sex Offenders and Victims*. Newbury Park, CA: Sage.

*Safeguarding Vulnerable Groups (England and Wales) Act 2006*. London: The Stationery Office.

Schuchardt, K., Gebhardt, M. and Maehler, C. (2010) Working memory functions in children with different degrees of intellectual disability. *Journal of Intellectual Disability Research*, **54**, 346–53.

Singh, N.N., Lancioni, G.E., Winton, A.S.W., Adkins, A.D., Singh, J. and Singh, A.N. (2007) Mindfulness training assists individuals with moderate mental retardation to maintain their community placements. *Behavior Modification*, **31**, 800–14.

Spielberger, C.D. (1999) *Manual for the State-trait Anger Expression Inventory, STAXI-2*. Odessa, FL: Psychological Assessment Resources.

Talbot, T.J. and Langdon, P.E. (2006) A revised sexual knowledge assessment tool for people with intellectual disabilities: Is sexual knowledge related to sexual offending behaviour? *Journal of Intellectual Disability Research*, **50**, 523–31.

Taylor, J.L. (2002) A review of the assessment and treatment of anger and aggression in offenders with intellectual disability. *Journal of Intellectual Disability Research*, **46**, 57–73.

Taylor, J.L. and Novaco, R.W. (2005) *Anger Treatment for People with Developmental Disabilities: a theory, evidence and manual based approach*. Chichester: John Wiley and Sons, Ltd.

Taylor, J.L., Novaco, R.W., Gillmer, B. and Thorne, I. (2002b) Cognitive-behavioural treatment of anger intensity among offenders with intellectual disabilities. *Journal of Applied Research in Intellectual Disabilities*, **15**, 151–65.

Taylor, J.L., Novaco, R.W., Guinan, C. and Street, N. (2004b) Development of an imaginal provocation test to evaluate treatment for anger problems in people with intellectual disabilities. *Clinical Psychology and Psychotherapy*, **11**, 233–46.

Taylor J.L., Thorne I., Robertson A. and Avery G. (2002a) Evaluation of a psycho-educational group intervention for fire-setters with mild and borderline intellectual disabilities. *Criminal Behaviour and Mental Health*, **12**, 282–93.

Taylor J.L., Thorne I. and Slavkin M. (2004a) Treatment of firesetters. In W.R. Lindsay, J.L. Taylor and P. Sturmey (eds) *Offenders With Developmental Disabilities* (pp. 221–40). Chichester: John Wiley and Sons, Ltd.

Thompson, D. (1997) Profiling the sexually abusive behaviour of men with intellectual disabilities. *Journal of Applied Research in Intellectual Disabilities*, **10**, 125–39.

Thompson, D. and Brown, H. (1997) Men with intellectual disabilities who sexually abuse: A review of the literature. *Journal of Applied Research in Intellectual Disabilities*, **10**, 140–58.

Thompson, D., Clare, I.C.H. and Brown, H. (1997) Not such an 'ordinary' relationship: the role of women support staff in relation to men with learning disabilities who have difficult sexual behaviour. *Disability and Society*, **12**, 573–92.

Trent, J.W. (1994) *Inventing the Feeble Mind. A history of mental retardation in the United States*. Berkley, CA: University of California Press.

Wheeler, J.R., Holland, A.J., Bambrick, M., Lindsay, W.R., Carson, D., Steptoe, L., Johnston, S., Taylor, J.L., Middleton, C., Price, K. and O'Brien, G. (2009) Community services and people with intellectual disabilities who engage in anti-social or offending behaviour: Referral rates, characteristics, and care pathways. *Journal of Forensic Psychiatry and Psychology*, **20**, 717–40.

Williams, F., Wakeling, H. and Webster, S. (2007) A psychometric study of six self report measures for use with sexual offenders with cognitive and social functioning deficits. *Psychology, Crime and Law*, **13**, 505–22.

Willner, P., Jones, J., Tams, R. and Green, G. (2002) A randomized controlled trial of the efficacy of a cognitive-behavioural anger management group for clients with learning disabilities. *Journal of Applied Research in Intellectual Disabilities*, **15**, 224–35.

Woodbury-Smith M.R., Clare I.C. H., Holland A.J. and Kearns, A. (2006) High functioning autistic spectrum disorders, offending and other law-breaking: Findings from a community sample. *Journal of Forensic Psychiatry and Psychology*, **17**, 108–20.

Chapter 13

# SEXUAL EXPLOITATION OF PEOPLE WITH INTELLECTUAL DISABILITIES

Paul Withers and Jennifer Morris

## INTRODUCTION

> 'When I was a little boy, on my way home a man near us asked me into his house for some sweets. He made me have sex with him in the kitchen. He did that every day after that. He said he'd shoot me if I told anyone. He knew I'd believe him, didn't he? Because I've got learning difficulties. He picked on me because of that'

Although this man might be unusual in being able to articulate to the first author the link between his disability and his abuse, the events he describes will be depressingly familiar to most clinical psychologists who work with people with intellectual disabilities. Most of us regularly hear accounts of sexual abuse experienced by our clients, both in childhood and in adulthood, and it often seems that almost all of the people we see, particularly the women, have had sexual encounters in which their feelings and wishes have played no part. In many instances this has been with their 'consent', but nevertheless the impact upon them has clearly been within the realms of what we would consider to be abusive if it happened to us. Where abuse has been intentional their experiences have often been appalling, with their abusers apparently delighting in subjecting them to degrading and humiliating acts.

Despite the apparently overwhelming scale of the problem of the abuse, sexual or otherwise, of people with intellectual disabilities, it is a topic that never appeared in English clinical and theoretical literature until 1979 (Sinason, 2002). Most of our literature on this topic must be considered to be embryonic, and the issues of the assessment and

*Clinical Psychology and People with Intellectual Disabilities*, Second Edition. Edited by
Eric Emerson, Chris Hatton, Kate Dickson, Rupa Gone, Amanda Caine and Jo Bromley.
© 2012 John Wiley & Sons, Ltd. Published 2012 by John Wiley & Sons, Ltd.

treatment of individuals who have experienced abuse but who cannot speak, or who have experienced it before they could speak, have scarcely begun to be considered.

## DEFINITION OF SEXUAL ABUSE

'Sexual assault is a crime of violence, anger, power, and control where sex is used as a used as a weapon against the victim. It includes any unwanted sexual contact or attention achieved by force, threat, bribes, manipulation, pressure, tricks or violence. It may be physical or non-physical and includes rape, attempted rape, incest and child molestation, and sexual harassment. It can also include fondling, exhibitionism, oral sex, exposure to sexual materials (pornography), and the use of inappropriate sexual remarks or language.'

(Davis 2005)

### Prevelance

Despite the fact that determining the prevalence of sexual abuse within the general population has been recognized as a national priority in recent years, little importance has been giving to collecting comprehensive data on the prevalence of sexual abuse of people with intellectual disabilities (Horner-Johnson & Drum, 2006). Whilst the literature on sexual abuse of children and adults with intellectual disabilities has grown quite considerably over the past decade there is still a dearth of reliable data (McCormack *et al.*, 2005).

For the purpose of this chapter, prevalence refers to the proportion of people with intellectual disabilities who at the time of data collection had experienced abuse at some point in their lives (Horner-Johnson and Drum 2006). Comparisons between studies are difficult due to varying methods of data collection, definitions of abuse, sampling strategies and settings (McCormack *et al.*, 2005). Horner-Johnson & Drum, (2006) reviewed 18 studies published between 1995 and 2000 to determine an estimate of the prevalence of sexual abuse among people with intellectual disabilities. They found the prevalence of sexual abuse in children and adolescents with intellectual disabilities (ID) ranged from 11.5% to approximately 28%. The prevalence of sexual abuse in adults with ID was even higher, ranging between 25% and 50%. When comparisons were made to non-disabled groups, people with ID were far more likely to have suffered sexual abuse than people without disabilities, supporting estimates in past research (Sobsey, 1994; Levy & Packman, 2004). Children and adolescents with ID are approximately four times more likely to have been sexually abused than children and adolescents with no disability (Sullivan & Knutson, 2000). One study found sexual abuse was up eight times more prevalent in people with ID (Verdugo *et al.*, 1995).

Therefore, despite limitations, the literature suggests sexual abuse is more prevalent for people with intellectual disabilities, than for people without disabilities.

## Incidence

Incidence studies attempt to ascertain the number of new cases of sexual abuse of people with ID occurring within a specified time period. Research has shown that within the United Kingdom every year there will be almost 1400 new cases of sexual abuse of people with intellectual disabilities ('Behind Closed Doors', Mencap, Respond and Voice UK, 2001). There is a lack of longitudinal large-scale studies of the incidence of sexual abuse of people with intellectual disabilities. However one particularly valuable recent study (McCormack *et al.*, 2005) reviewed all allegations of sexual abuse involving service users as a victim or perpetrator over a 15-year period in a large community based service. Following multidisciplinary investigation approximately half the allegations were confirmed. They found incidence levels of 3.72 new client victims of sex abuse per 1,000 service users per year and 1.76 new client perpetrators per 1,000 per year. In other words approximately one in 200 service users became confirmed victims or perpetrators of sexual abuse each year. However as with all research in this area it must be interpreted with caution as it is highly probable that not all episodes of abuse are disclosed or discovered resulting in figures dramatically underestimating the problem. Furthermore when episodes of abuse are disclosed but are categorised only as 'possible abuse/on going concern' rather than 'confirmed', as was the case in one out of seven cases in McCormack *et al.*'s (2005) study, most are probably not false but rather they lack sufficient evidence to prove they are definitely true (Sobsey, 1994 cited in McCormack *et al.*, 2005). McCormack *et al.* (2005) did note a considerable overall increase in detection rates over the period of the study, which may be due to increased awareness, better legislation, and improved detection.

## Vulnerability Factors

Any type of disability appears to contribute to higher vulnerability to sexual abuse but; *intellectual disabilities, communication disorders, and behavioural disorders appear to contribute to very high levels of risk* (Sullivan and Knutson 2000).

In Sobsey's (1994) comprehensive study of abuse in the lives of adults and children with disabilities, an ecological model of abuse is proposed to explain this level of vulnerability. This structural framework offers a way of understanding the complex roles and interactions of the Macrosystems (cultural and environmental factors) and the Microsystems (victim and offender characteristics and relationship). Hollomotz (2009) has reinforced the need for an ecological approach to understanding the risk of sexual violence against people with intellectual disabilities. She suggests that the concept of vulnerability is an inadequate explanation for this risk, and that risk is better understood by considering the interaction between personal attributes, self-defence skills (including knowledge about sex, awareness of rights, self-esteem, social awareness, vocabulary for reporting abuse and decision-making ability), environments and socio-cultural factors. She highlights the need to address the social processes that create risk.

## Victim Characteristics

Fernandez (1992) suggested that there are several factors that make people with intellectual disabilities vulnerable to sexual abuse: These are detailed below.

### Communication

Communication problems are common among people with intellectual disabilities, and abuse can often remain hidden because of the victim's lack of communication skills. Even for verbally skilled people, describing their experiences of abuse can be very challenging, and for those with limited verbal ability this may be an especially demanding task. People with severe intellectual disabilities may have no way to report or talk about their abusive experiences and they might also have difficulty protesting to offenders and asking others for help, which in turn will put them at greater risk of further episodes of abuse. People with intellectual disabilities may try to use non-verbal behaviours to disclose abuse but this can be ignored or labelled as 'challenging behaviour'. Only in recent years have pictures representing acts of abuse and sexual anatomy been used to help verbally unskilled adults and children to report acts of abuse (Davis, 2004).

### Powerlessness and Compliance

People with disabilities are often not given the power to make decisions for themselves; their caregivers make choices for them and they learn not to question them. This leads to a lack of practical opportunities to develop their own intuition; meaning they may not be able to distinguish between safe and unsafe situations. Individuals may live in over-controlled and authoritarian environments that further intensify their feelings of power-lessness. Abuse by authority figures is unlikely to be reported.

*Dependence*

It is very common for people with intellectual disabilities to rely on others for care and support. Some may be dependent on others for personal and intimate care, which means they often have little control over who touches their bodies. This can cause confusion about boundaries and may leave them open to sexual exploitation.

*Isolation*

Often people with intellectual disabilities are isolated from the rest of the community. This increases both the likelihood that sexual abuse will occur and also that the sexual abuse will go undetected.

*Lack of Sexual Knowledge and Education*

Individuals with ID are rarely adequately educated about sex and sexuality. Their inability to understand and identify abuse and abusive situations increases their vulnerability. People with mild or moderate intellectual disabilities may realise they are being abused but due to lack of education, do not realise it is illegal and that they have the right to say no.

## Perpetrator Characteristics

For people with intellectual disabilities, as for those without disabilities, the victim will often know the perpetrator. In Sobsey and Doe's (1991) study of 166 sexual abuse cases, 96% of victims knew the perpetrator. Perpetrators may actively seek out employment with people with disabili-ties. People with intellectual disabilities are often coerced and manipu-lated by the perpetrator or they feel desperate and perceive no other choice due to threats made to them and others around them. Perpetrators often play a significant role in the lives of their victims; frequently they are fam-ily members, residential care staff, transportation providers and personal care attendants, making disclosure for the person suffering the abuse difficult.

In McCormack *et al.*'s (2005) 15-year longitudinal study, 85% of victims knew the perpetrator. Perpetrators of the 118 confirmed episodes of sexual abuse were predominantly male; 56% were peers with an intel-lectual disability and 24% were relatives, 9% were staff members, only 1% were strangers to the victim. Joyce (2003) noted similar findings;

seven of the 18 alleged sexual abusers were members of staff, three were family members, four were people with intellectual disability in the same residential service as the alleged victim and four were members of the public. This suggests people with intellectual disabilities are particularly vulnerable to those who care for them and those who they live with.

## Environmental and Contextual Factors

Poor retention of direct care staff in learning disability services reduces the chances of building trusting relationships between clients and care staff, meaning clients are less likely to disclose abuse. Current problems of retaining care staff within learning disabilities services mean many establishments are over-stretched causing high service user to staff ratio, which further exacerbates the problem. It is vital to train staff to be aware of the signs of possible abuse and how to respond to it effectively.

Abuse may also remain hidden because victims with intellectual disability make the assumption that they will not be heard or believed. This may in part be true as the legal system in the UK has a number of barriers that still exist in relation to sexual abuse allegations, and are even more profound for those with intellectual disabilities (Joyce, 2003). Each year 1400 new cases of sexual abuse against people with intellectual disability are reported in the UK. Only 6% reach court and conviction occurs in just 1% of cases (Mencap, 2002). Joyce (2003) completed an audit of investigations into allegations of abuse involving adults with intellectual disability. Several main issues were identified; lack of credibility as a witness due to suggestibility and vulnerability to leading and mis-leading questions; lack of communication skills which casts doubt on the ability to accurately report abuse and establishing capacity to consent. These issues make the resolution of allegations made by individuals with intellectual disabilities through the current criminal justice system very challenging. The government has recently recognised the difficulties faced by people with intellectual disabilities who have been sexually abused. Efforts are now being made to ensure that their disability does not prejudice their chances of giving evidence about the abuse they have experienced (Home Office 1999, cited in Joyce, 2003). There is also concern that due to variation of, and in some instances lack of, clear policy and procedures concerning abuse committed against people with intellectual disabilities, individual attitudes and personal values of police officers and other professionals leads to major variations in practise across the UK (Bailey & Barr, 2000). Sobsey (1994) emphasised the importance of developing clearer policies and procedures to ensure that genuine allegations are validated and false or doubtful allegations identified and eliminated, protecting innocent people whilst simultaneously effectively prosecuting those that are guilty.

Attitudes held in service contexts may serve to amplify the impact of abuse. Several authors (Sinason, 2002; Williams, 1993) have noted that acts that would be described as rape or indecent assault in the general population are instead referred to as sexual abuse when the victims have intellectual disabilities. This may reflect discomfort amongst service personnel about accepting what has happened to the people they support. This is perhaps unsurprising when we consider that many staff in services do not feel confident to talk to the people they support about their disabilities (Craig *et al.*, 2002), and are thus unlikely to be able to explore with them the relationship between their disabilities and their abuse. Many of the episodes our clients describe to us cannot be considered to be deserving of anything other than the labels of 'rape' and 'assault'. A woman with intellectual disabilities related the following experiences to the first author of this chapter;

> 'I was out for a drink in the pub talking to three men, and one of them said 'come outside for a cigarette', so I went in the yard behind the pub with him. The others came, and they pushed me over a bin and had sex with me, all of them. They did it in my mouth and up my bum, and some of them were laughing. I think one of them took pictures ... Afterwards the first one bought me a drink.'

Sexual crimes committed against people with intellectual disabilities and indeed in the entire population, also have to be contextualised in terms of gender. McCarthy and Thompson (1997) found in a sample of 65 women and 120 men with intellectual disabilities that 61% of the women and 25% of the men had been sexually abused. Of the 54 non-randomly selected participants in Sequeira *et al.*'s (2003) study who had experienced sexual abuse, 18 were male and 36 were female. By contrast, 89% (48) of the participants had been abused by males, 5.5% (3) by females, and the remaining 5.5% (3) by both males and females. Being male is a risk factor in the aetiology of sexually abusing, whilst being female appears to be a risk factor for being sexually abused. The finding that girls and women are more likely to be sexually abused than boys and men is commonly but not universally repeated (Dube *et al.*, 2005).

Feminist perspectives on the sexual abuse of children have attempted to account for the disparity in gender balances between perpetrators and victims. Mulder (1995) has suggested that the abuse of women with intellectual disabilities is in part motivated by the hatred towards people with disabilities, and is further facilitated by cultural oppression of women. Kelly (1996) has noted the danger and lack of logic in accepting 'cycles of abuse' explanations for sexual assaults upon and rape of children. She points out the fact that most perpetrators are male and most victims are female, significantly undermines these explanations. She also reminds us that in most research, only a minority of perpetrators are in fact, found to have been sexually abused as children; a finding which also holds true for the population of people with intellectual disabilities (e.g. Lindsay *et al.*, 2001). Kelly emphasises the problems inherent in using the term 'paedophile' to describe people who sexually abuse children, noting that it tends to promote the notion that raping and sexually assaulting children is related to a form of sexuality, rather than to the exercise of power and control. Stark and Flitcraft (1988) state that child abuse originates in conflicts over gender identity and male authority. Viewing sexual abuse from a perspective which enables us to see that the exercise of power by men is often at its root, might help us to explain why children with intellectual disabilities may be four times more likely to be sexually abused than children without disabilities. (Sullivan and Knutson, 2000) Prejudice against and oppression of people with intellectual disabilities may also contribute to their vulnerability to sexual abuse and to the impact it has upon them. Olney and Kim (2001) describe the struggles of individuals with 'cognitive' disability to form self-images that positively incorporate their experience of disability, noting the dominance of negative messages about cognitive disability within North American culture. The participants in their study were people with disabilities such as Tourette syndrome, dyslexia or perceptual disability. Pointing out that other oppressed groups have used group identification to counter negative messages, they state:

'People with cognitive disabilities may not have had prior involvement with the disability rights movement or with disability culture to counter the negative messages about disability that are readily available in the majority culture. In this regard the experience of people with cognitive disabilities parallels that of survivors of sexual abuse: both groups experience shame and ambivalence. Neither is likely to encounter or recognise others who share their experiences'

(p.581)

For individuals with intellectual disabilities who have been sexually abused, the probability of accessing meaningful peer support is likely to be very low indeed.

## Sequelae of Sexual Abuse

Sequeira and Hollins (2002) reviewed the literature on the clinical effects of sexual abuse on people with intellectual disabilities. The reviewed studies suggested that psychopathology engendered by such abuse in this population is similar to that in the general population. They noted however, that the methodology of the studies produced up to that time was such that definitive knowledge had to be regarded as limited. Sequeira, Howlin and Hollins (2003) attempted to address this issue by undertaking a case-control study of 54 adults with intellectual disabilities who had been sexually abused, matched 1:1 with 54 adults with intellectual disabilities where there was no evidence of abuse. The abused individuals were more likely than non-abused individuals to demonstrate: irritability, agitation and crying: lethargy and social withdrawal; stereotypical behaviour; hyperactivity; sexualised behaviour; psychiatric symptomatology, including depression, neurosis and symptoms of Post Traumatic Stress Disorder; and self-injurious behaviour. They concluded that the psychological sequelae of the sexual abuse of people with intellectual disabilities were indeed similar to those in the general population. People with intellectual disabilities also shared with their non-disabled peers, the finding that an increased severity of abuse and increased frequency of abuse both correlated with increased severity of disturbance. The authors do note that the methodology they employed does not identify causal relationships between abuse and the psychological and behavioural sequelae they reported, and suggest that longitudinal studies would be needed to demonstrate any such link. Nevertheless, people with intellectual disabilities who have been sexually abused are likely to present to clinical psychologists with a wide range of symptoms of psychological distress.

These are however, not the only sequelae of sexual abuse. Lindsay *et al.* (2001) found that sexual offenders with learning disability were more likely to have been sexually abused than were non-sexual offenders with intellectual disability. Further Lindsay, Elliot and Astell (2004) found that sexual abuse in childhood was a factor predictive of recidivism in a range of offenders with intellectual disabilities.

Sinason (2002) noted that abuse 'involves betrayal, shame, secrecy, stigmatisation and self-blame' (p. 429). She also expressed the opinion that having an intellectual disability is in itself traumatising, and that abusive acts perpetrated against people with intellectual disabilities result in compound trauma. Sexual abuse is, therefore, likely to have the capacity to further damage aspects of psychological functioning which are difficult to measure, such as sense of self and identity, and which have been found to be already corroded in people with intellectual disabilities (Jahoda *et al.*, 1988; Craig *et al.*, 2002).

In the general population, sexual abuse in childhood has been found to be associated particularly with borderline personality disorder (Bradley, Jenei & Westen, 2005), but also with the whole range of conditions referred to as personality disorders (Battle *et al.*, 2004). In non-intellectually disabled women, sexual abuse is associated with images of the self as lacking in romanticism and passion (Meston, Kellini & Heiman, 2006). Hicks (2002) has suggested that for men who have been sexually abused, masculine identity is compromised as the abuse damages the sense of strength via autonomy and potency upon which the masculine self-ideal is founded. It is not known if these findings would be replicated amongst people with intellectual disabilities. It seems clear that the impact of sexual abuse might be regarded as being reflected in the whole of the person, rather than being reducible to a set of conditions or symptoms.

## ASSESSMENT

Each individual's experience of sexual abuse is unique. Whilst there are some common sequelae of abuse, each individual's response to it will have unique components. Assessment needs to cover those factors that impinge upon this response. These might include:

Factors relating to the person who has been abused:

- personality;
- history including history of abuse;
- coping strategies;
- knowledge about sex, sexuality and sexual behaviour;
- communication style and ability to describe what has happened;
- extent of understanding of abuse;
- mood;
- self-image, sexuality and identity, including gender identity;
- likelihood of engaging in one-to-one therapy.

Factors relating to the abuser:

- relationship to the abused;
- gender;
- methods of identifying, accessing and/or grooming the victim;
- likelihood of repeated or continued contact with the victim;
- whether criminal conviction resulted from the abuse.

Factors relating to abuse:

- nature of the abuse;
- frequency and duration;
- use of force coercion or threats;
- physical consequences of the abuse;
- time elapsed since the abuse.

Factors relating to the context:

- the individual's personal and professional support networks;
- how carers/family/friends have responded to abuse;

- previous attempts at therapy;
- opportunities to engage in rewarding leisure or occupational activities;
- opportunities to share experiences of abuse with peers;
- opportunities for privacy.

These lists are not exhaustive, and in many circumstances it may be impossible to acquire much of this information. If the person has no formal means of communication then assessment is likely to be based on observations of their behaviour and may be augmented by the use of alternative methods of communicating, such as via artistic media. Psychodynamic workers (e.g. Sinason, 2002) employ open interpretation of their clients' behaviour as part of their attempts to understand what has happened to them and how it has affected them. This approach is difficult to evaluate objectively, and might be considered to amount to 'guessing' based on a particular theoretical stance. We have to acknowledge, however that there will be many instances in which we are unable to complete assessments without resorting to significant amounts of informed guesswork. This will be particularly true with clients with profound intellectual disabilities, where even when we have employed all our resources of ingenuity and creativity, we may be unable to ascertain what has happened, or how it has affected the client.

Assessing people with intellectual disabilities who have been sexually exploited and who are seeking to prosecute their abusers presents particular challenges. Individuals in these circumstances will not only have to cope with the traumatic memories of their abuse, but also with a police service, which may feel ill-equipped to respond to their needs and a court system within which little meaningful adaptation is made to facilitate the gathering of evidence from witnesses with intellectual disabilities (Kebbell, Hatton & Johnson, 2004). Education and policy development with the judicial system remain crucial to ensuring that it can provide justice to people with intellectual disability (Green 2001).

Gudjonsson et al. (2000) and (Green, 2001) have provided guidance about assessments that might need to be conducted prior to a person with intellectual disabilities giving evidence in court. It is suggested that an intellectual assessment is likely to be required in order to establish whether or not the person has the capacity to enter into a sexual relationship. Green (2001) describes the use of a variety of resources such as the Socio-Sexual Knowledge and Attitudes Test (SSKAT, Wish et al., 1979) to determine the individual's capacity to give and withhold informed consent. It is also likely to be necessary to use a semi-structured interview to explore understanding of the oath, and therefore competence to testify. Reliability of testimony might be established via the use of Gudjonsson suggestibility scales (Gudjonsson, 1997) and in vivo exercises are recommended to test out ability to cope with court procedures. Green (2001) emphasises the importance of the person receiving support form the various agencies involved, such as the police and health and social services professionals. The process of preparing for and appearing in court is emotionally taxing for most people, and is highly likely to be much more so for witnesses with intellectual disabilities.

## INTERVENTION

Intervention might be thought of as existing at three levels: preventative work; therapeutic work with the individual; and therapeutic work via support staff and other agencies.

## Preventative Work

Many people who have been victims of sexual abuse will be unable to relate their experiences, and the often deeply traumatising impact of abuse; therefore, attention needs to be focused on methods of preventing abuse. This means tackling the causes of abusing behaviour, and thus attempting to grapple with issues which are likely to prove contentious, and, which might at first, seem to be outside the remit of clinical psychology. These include addressing the ways in which masculinity is constructed and how those constructions contribute to abusive acts in some men. Understanding this relationship may prove equally important in elucidating the manner in which, for some men, experiences of being abused become factors in going on to abuse. These links may be particularly potent for men with intellectual disabilities, who may often feel that their disabilities compromise their masculinity, making any other experiences which seem to threaten male identity appear even more toxic to them. These are undoubtedly topics which warrant further exploration by research. The available evidence is already sufficiently weighty to suggest that in complying with our duty to promote public awareness of psychological knowledge, clinical psychologists should be clear in stating that current constructs of masculinity are among the factors pertinent to the sexual abuse of vulnerable people (Kelly, 1996).

The professional lives of most clinical psychologists do not encompass activities which have the expressed intent of changing the very broad systems in which their clients live. Instead, the exigencies of the workplace mean that the focus is on activities that relate to specific clients. In this context, preventative work might include:

- Education to improve knowledge about sex and sexual behaviour, with the intention of enabling clients to be better prepared to state what they will or will not accept in their contacts with others.

- Working with groups of people with intellectual disabilities to facilitate the development of healthy identities which incorporate their disabilities and their sexuality (Jahoda *et al.*, 1988; Withers *et al.*, 2001 ).
- Promoting the development of self-advocacy by people with intellectual disabilities in order to begin to foster strong public images, which might nullify perceptions of them as vulnerable potential victims.
- Contributing to staff training which enables staff to recognise and reduce the risk situations for clients and which educates them about potential signs and symptoms of abuse.
- Contributing to the development of policies for responding to abuse of people with intellectual disabilities, including abuse by peers, family members, staff and strangers. Such policies will need to be adopted by all agencies working with people with intellectual disabilities.

## Individual Work

Individual work with people with disabilities who have experienced sexual abuse has been undertaken using all the therapeutic approaches within the arsenal of clinical psychology, although it is noteworthy that much of what has been published in this area has been from authors who have employed psychodynamic techniques. Davis (2005) has suggested that all people with intellectual disabilities who have experienced sexual abuse will need individual therapeutic work, even if they are not able to communicate verbally. Sobsey (1993) has suggested six criteria that should be met in order to achieve effective treatment. These are:

1. Treatment should be individualised by matching it to the client's ability and needs.
2. Treatments should be eclectic, drawing on those elements of the variety of treatment approaches which are relevant to the individual receiving treatment;
3. Treatment should be based on what has been shown to be effective for people who do not have intellectual disabilities, thus emphasising social integration rather than isolation.
4. Treatment needs to be embedded in the individuals' living circumstances, and thus to address the physical and emotional environment.
5. Treatment needs to be conducted in explicit, concrete and simple terms according to the individual's ability.
6. Treatment should follow explicit goals and outcomes should be evaluated against these goals.

These recommendations appear to the authors of this chapter to encapsulate good clinical practice in clinical psychology. However, most of the published work on treatment of people with intellectual disabilities who have experienced abuse has focused on single therapeutic modalities with little or no evaluation of any integrated approaches. Sinason (2002) has suggested that within a psychodynamic framework, the key concepts that are helpful in understanding the clients' response to abuse include:

- Re-enactment, where the individual repeats experiences they have had. The purpose of this may be, for example, to make the experience more bearable, or to hope that the outcome will be different. Re-enactment prevents the tension created by the original experience from being processed and ultimately overcome.
- Splitting, wherein the individual may be unable to tolerate ambivalence in their relationships and instead spilt the important people in their lives into clear categories of 'good' and 'bad'. In their attempts to repair their history they may form delusional attachments to the individual who abused them, describing them as wholly good and loving. Whilst such defences may facilitate coping with the trauma of past abuse, they will also prevent meaningful recovery from its effects.
- Transference, whereby the person relocates past experiences in another individual. In therapy this will often be the therapist. This can help the therapist recognise how their client is feeling, and relating this back to the client can help to free them from painful and unhelpful reliving of abusive experiences.

Sinason (1990, as cited in Sobsey, 1994) noted three principal stages of psychoanalytic treatment of individuals with intellectual disabilities who have experienced sexual abuse. Firstly, the therapist needs to help the client to overcome aspects of their disability which originate from their experiences of abuse, e.g. amplified levels of impairment of communication and cognition. This can be achieved through the formation of a trusting and honest relationship with the therapist. Secondly, the therapist facilitates the client in confronting their feelings about the abuse. Finally, the focus shifts towards practical tasks and decision making, with the therapist helping the client to move towards their optimal level of independent functioning. Such an approach is difficult to evaluate other than via single case descriptions, but it does have the capacity to meet Sobsey's (1993, as cited in Sobsey, 1994) recommendations about how therapy should be conducted.

Few other approaches have been described in such detail. Cooke (2003) proposes a form of solution-focused therapy conducted over six sessions, with a 24-hour availability of emotional support outside the therapy sessions, the first session is used to state explicitly that the abuse and its impact on the person will be discussed, with the aim of moving towards recovery. Goals will be set against which progress can be monitored and in subsequent sessions the therapist adopts a cognitive approach, identifying and challenging with the client negative self-concepts that have been generated by the abuse. Often discussion is around reasons why the individual was selected to be abused, as described in the section on vulnerability factors earlier in this chapter. 'Homework' may be given in various forms including self-expression through art; activities designed to help the person feel positive about their body again, such as massage and dance, and keeping a diary of angry episodes which can be discussed with the therapist. As the end of therapy approaches, the therapist discusses safety with the client, establishing ways in which they would experience a greater sense of safety from abuse in the future, and practising how they might avoid abusive situations or acts. Cooke provides illustrative case histories, but acknowledges that this is another approach which requires formal evaluation.

The lack of empirically evaluated treatments means that clinical psychologists will often have to be creative in work of this type. Moss (1998), listed a range of therapeutic tactics which might be useful in helping people with intellectual disabilities to overcome the impact of abuse. Many of these are familiar from other spheres of clinical psychology. For example, a range of relaxation techniques might be used to assist the client in reducing distressing bodily symptoms and anxiety associated with abuse; distraction techniques may be used in the management of flashbacks and intrusive thoughts; and anger management might assist the person in expressing anger appropriately without denying them the right to feel anger about what has happened to them. A clear focus on the unique experiences of the individual may be the most crucial element in developing successful treatments. This does not mean however, that group work may not also be beneficial (Barber *et al.*, 2000). This may prove to be a powerful forum within which to explore the relationship between the participants' intellectual disabilities and the manner in which they have been exploited. It may also help both men and women to understand the role that their gender may have played in their abuse and, especially for men, any subsequent abusive behaviour that they may engage in. Peckham *et al.* (2007) have described how a 'survivors' group' for women with intellectual disabilities helped the women to be less afraid and depressed.

Whatever therapeutic approach is employed, the evidence base for it will be scant. It is important for clinical psychologists to describe the work they do with people with intellectual disabilities who have been sexually abused in ways that ensure that it can be replicated, and that they evaluate what they have done.

## WORKING WITH SUPPORT STAFF

Many people with intellectual disabilities live in supported accommodation. Staff providing direct care need to identify signs that clients have experienced abuse, be aware of referral procedures for people requiring treatment following abuse, and be able to support clients experiencing distress. They also need to be vigilant about the potential for colleagues to abuse clients. Child protection training is now mandatory in many health service contexts and is likely to improve recognition of the signs of abuse and provide information about referral pathways. Services will also have Vulnerable Adults polices, and it is essential that all staff are familiarised with these. Clinical Psychologists can advise care staff about how to respond to distress, and also ensure that they are aware of clients' potential response to therapy. For example, it is important for them to know that for some people with intellectual disabilities, initial discussions about their abuse may cause increased agitation and distress. Staff need to be confident in monitoring these reactions without necessarily believing that they indicate therapy should be terminated. Consistent staffing, the employment of reassurance, and counselling skills by support staff are likely to optimise benefits from therapy. To achieve this, services will need to train staff in the requisite skills and to adopt policies which ensure that consistent supportive staff teams can be maintained around individuals who have experienced abuse. Where recent abuse is brought to the attention of care staff, there needs to be an awareness of the policy guidance about reporting the abuse in a way that minimises the likelihood of its reoccurrence. This can be a complex issue in intellectual disability services, where abusers will often be other users of the same service and sometimes have no understanding of the abusive nature of their behaviour. In these circumstances multi-disciplinary efforts are likely to be required in order to ensure reasonable outcomes for both parties, although the wishes and needs of the abused party must take precedence.

## SUPERVISION

As a profession, Clinical Psychology has a positive history in terms of recognising the importance of supervision, and there is no area of work in which it is more important than in working with people who have experienced abuse. The functions of supervision will include monitoring and modifying therapeutic approaches employed, and supporting the therapist with their own emotional responses to their clients' experiences. These need to be considered carefully in order to ensure that the client remains the central focus of therapy, and that issues raised within the therapist do not obtrude into the therapeutic process. Supervision will be important for all staff working with people who have been abused, and clinical psychologists may take a role in ensuring that it is available to direct care staff. It is unlikely to be appropriate for a clinical psychologist providing therapy to a client to also provide supervision to their support staff, as this would create a danger of contamination of the therapy with the opinions and feelings of the care staff. However, psychologists may contribute to ensuring that other sources of supervision are available to support staff, and may provide it themselves where they are not the person providing therapy to the client.

A final function of supervision may be to provide support when we feel that our efforts are leading to little benefit for the client. However well we attempt to inform ourselves about therapeutic interventions, the state of our knowledge about what is effective is limited. Moreover, the enormity of the abusive experiences of some of our clients, and the organic limitations on their capacity to understand and overcome these experiences, means that we will be approaching some people with little of substance to offer.

## CONCLUSION

Working with people with intellectual disabilities who have been sexually exploited presents great challenges to clinical psychologists. Factors contributing to the commission of acts of sexual exploitation are deeply embedded in the structure of society. The psychological consequences of sexual abuse can be extensive and profoundly debilitating, whilst the therapeutic tools available to address these consequences are under-researched and often not applicable to all people with intellectual disabilities. Service contexts are often ill-equipped to deal with the sequelae of abuse, and indeed are in some instances are the source of it. Clinical Psychologists will need to be creative in their approaches, committed to evaluation, and supported through reflective supervision in order to respond proficiently to these challenges.

## References

Bailey, A. and Barr, O. (2000) Police policies on the investigation of sexual crimes committed against adults who have a learning disability. *Journal of Learning Disabilities*, 4(2), 129–39.

Barber, M., Jenkins, R. and Jones, C. (2000) A survivors group for women who have a learning disability. *The British Journal of Developmental Disabilities*, 46, 31–41.

Battle, C.L., Shea, M.T., Johnson, D.M., Yen, S., Zlotnick, C., Zanarini, M.C. (2004) Childhood maltreatment associated with adult personality disorders: Findings from the collaborative longitudinal personality disorders study. *Journal of Personality Disorders*, 18, 193–211.

Bradley, R., Heim, A. and Westen, D. (2005) Personality constellations in patients with a history of childhood sexual abuse. *Journal of Traumatic Stress*, 18(6), 769–80.

Brown, H. and Turk, V. (1992) Defining sexual abuse as it affects adults with learning disabilities. *Mental Handicap*, 20, 44–55.

Davis, L.A. (2005) People with Intellectual Disabilities and Sexual Violence. The Arc. Retrieved on August 25th 2006 from http://www.thearc.org/fags/sexuala-buse.doc.

Davis, L.A. (2004) Abuse of Children with Cognitive, Intellectual and Developmental Disabilities. Retrieved on August 25th 2006 from http://www.thearc.org/fags/sexualabuse.doc.

Dube, S.R., Anda, R.F., Whitfield, M.D., Brown, D.W., Felitti, V.J., Dong, M. and Giles, W.H. (2005) Long-Term Consequences of Childhood Sexual Abuse by Gender of Victim. *American Journal of Preventative Medicine*, **28**(5).

Cooke, L.B. (2003) Treating the Sequelae of Abuse in Adults with Learning Disabilities. *The British Journal of Developmental Disabilities*, **49**(1), 23–8.

Craig, J. Craig, F. Withers, P. Hatton, C. and Limb, K. (2002) Identity Conflict in People with Intellectual Disabilities: What Role do Service-providers Play in Mediating Stigma? *Journal of Applied Research in Intellectual Disabilities*, **15**, 61–72.

Fernandez, H. (1992) Issues paper 8: People with an Intellectual Disability and the criminal justice system. 3) Crime and People with Intellectual Disability. Retrieved 29th March 2007 from http://www.lawlink.nsw.gov.au/lrc.nsf/pages/IP8CHP3.

Green, G. (2001) Vulnerability of witnesses with learning disabilites: preparing to give evidence against a perpetrator of sexual abuse. *British Journal of Learning Disabilities*, **29**, 103–9.

Gudjonsson, G.H. (1997) *The Gudjonsson Suggestibility Scales*. Hove, Psychology Press.

Gudjonsson, G.H., Murphy, G.H. and Clare I.C.H. (2000) Assessing the capacity of people with intellectual disabilities to be witnesses in court, *Psychol Med.*, **30**, 307–14.

Hicks, R.B. (2002) Shame and the adult male survivor of sexual abuse. *Dissertation Abstracts International: Section B: the Sciences and Engineering*, **62**(11-B), 5376.

Hollomotz, A. (2009) Beyond 'vulnerability': an ecological model approach to conceptualizing risk of sexual violence against people with learning difficulties. *British Journal of Social Work*, **39**, 99–112.

Horner-Johnson, W. and Drum, C.E. (2006) Prevalence of maltreatment of people with intellectual disabilities: a review of recently published research. *Mental Retardation And Developmental Disabilities Research Review*, **12**, 57–69.

Jahoda, A., Cattermole, M. and Markova, L. (1988) Stigma and the self-concept of people with mental handicap. *Journal of Mental Deficiency Research*, **32**, 103–15.

Joyce, T.A. (2003) An audit of investigations into allegations of abuse involving adults with intellectual disability. *Journal of Intellectual Disability Research*, **47**(8), 606–16.

Kebbell, M.R., Hatton, C. and Johnson, S.D. (2004) Witnesses with intellectual disabilities in court: What questions are asked and what influence do they have? *Legal and Criminological Psychology*, **9**, 23–35.

Kelly, L. (1996) Weasel words: paedophiles and the cycle of abuse. *Trouble and Strife*, **33**.

Levy, H. and Packman, W. (2004) Sexual abuse preventative for individuals with mental retardation: Considerations for genetic counselors. *Journal Genetic Counsel*, **13**, 189–205.

Lindsay, W.R., Elliot, S.F. and Astell, A. (2004) Predictors of sexual offence recidivismin offenders with intellectual disabilities. *Journal of Applied Research in Intellectual Disabilities*, **17**, 299–305.

Lindsay, W.R., Law, J., Quinn, K., Smart, N. and Smith, A.H. (2001) A comparison of physical and sexual abuse: histories of sexual and non-sexual offenders with intellectual disability. *Child Abuse Neglect*, **25**(7), 989–95.

McCarthy, M. and Thompson, D. (1997). A prevalence study of sexual abuse of adults with intellectual disabilities referred for sex education. *Journal of Applied Research in Intellectual Disabilities*, **10**(2), 105–24.

McCormack, B., Kavanagh, D., Caffrey, S. and Power, A. (2005) Investigating sexual abuse: findings of a 15-year longitudinal study. *Journal of Applied Research in Intellectual Disabilities*, **18**, 217–27.

Mencap, (2001) 'Behind Closed Doors', *Respond and Voice*, London UK.

Mencap, (2002) New Bill to Challenge Sex Abuse. Retrieved October 2006, from http://www.mencap.org.uk/download/viewpoint_feb02.pdf.

Meston, C.M., Rellini, A.H. and Heiman, J.R. (2006) Women's history of sexual abuse, their sexuality, and sexual self-schemas. *Journal of Consulting and Clinical Psychology*, **74**(2), 229–36.

Moss, J. (1998). Working with issues of sexual abuse. In E. Emerson, C. Hatton, J. Bromley, & A. Caine (Eds.), *Clinical Psychology and people with intellectual disabilities* (pp. 177–192). Chichester: Wiley.

Mulder, L. (1995) Reclaiming our rights: Access to existing police, legal and support services for women with disabilities or who are deaf or hearing impaired who have been subjected to violence. A report to the Department of Women, NSW.

Olney, M.F. and Kim, A. (2001) Beyond Adjustment: integration of cognitive disability into identity. *Disability and Society*, **16**(4), 563–83.

Peckham, N.G., Corbett, A., Howlett, S., McKee, A. and Pattison, S. (2007) The delivery of a survivors' group for learning disabled women who have been sexually abused. *British Journal of Learning Disabilities*, **35**, 236–44.

Sequeira, H. and Hollins, S. (2002) Clinical effects of sexual abuse on people with learning disability: Critical literature review. *British Journal of Psychiatry*, **182**, 13–19.

Sequeira, H., Howlin, P. and Hollins S. (2003) Psychological disturbance associated with sexual abuse in people with learning disabilities. *British Journal of Psychiatry*, **183**, 451–6.

Sinason, V. (2002) Treating people with learning disabilities after physical or sexual abuse. *Advances in Psychiatric Treatment*, **8**, 424–32.

Sobsey, D. (1994) *Violence and Abuse in the Lives of People with Disabilities: the end of silent acceptance?* Baltimore, MD: Brookes.

Sobsey, D. and Doe, T. (1991) Patterns of sexual abuse and assault. *Sexuality and Disability*, **9**, 243–59.

Stark, E. and Flitcraft A.H. (1988) Women and children at risk: a feminist perspective on child abuse. *International Journal of Health Services*, **18**(1), 97–118.

Sullivan P.M. and Knutson, J.F. (2000) Maltreatment and disabilities: a population based epidemiological study. *Child Abuse Neglect*, **24**, 1257–73.

Turk, V. and Brown, H. (1993) The sexual abuse of adults with learning disabilities: the results of a two year incidence survey. *Mental Handicap Research*, **6**, 193–216.

Verdugo, M.A. Bermejo, B.G. and Fuertes, J. (1995) The maltreatment of intellectually handicapped children and adolescents. *Child Abuse Neglect*, **19**, 205–15.

Williams, C. (1993) Vulnerable Victims? A current awareness of the victimisation of people with learning disabilities. *Disability, Handicap and Society*, **8**, 161–72.

Wish, J., McCombs K.F. and Edmonson, B. (1979) *Manual for Socio-sexual Knowledge and Attitudes Test*. Chicago. IL, Stoelting Corporation.

Withers, P., Ensum, I., Howarth, D., Krall, P., Thomas, D., Weekes, D., Winter, C., Mulholland, A., Dindjer, T. and Hall, J. (2001) A psychoeducational group for men with intellectual disabilities who have sex with men. *Journal of Applied Research in Intellectual Disabilities*, **14**, 327–39.

## Chapter 14

# WORKING WITH PARENTS WHO HAPPEN TO HAVE INTELLECTUAL DISABILITIES

Sue McGaw

## INTRODUCTION

People with intellectual disabilities share the same need as other adults, to form friendships, engage in sexual relationships and to bear children. In fact, there are no legal impediments to prevent them from realising any of these ambitions, should they so wish. Currently, the UK government are developing measures to ensure that 'all disabled people have the same choice, freedom, dignity and control over their lives as non-disabled people' which is the focus of a five year Strategy (Office for Disability Issues 2008). Despite these positive changes in national policy and expressed good intent, currently there are many adults with intellectual disabilities who are still being discouraged from entering sexual relationships. The main anxiety held by many families, carers and supporting professionals is that a sexual relationship might result in an unwanted pregnancy. In themselves, the pregnancy and birth are not usually viewed as problematic, rather it is the couple's inability to manage the complexities of parenthood long term and the child's increased vulnerability to neglect and/or harm which give rise to the major concerns.

To some extent, the research literature does give credence to some of these concerns by reporting that many adults with intellectual disabilities are known to be unprepared and ill-informed on the topic of parenthood. Typically, prospective parents with an intellectual disability have

*Clinical Psychology and People with Intellectual Disabilities*, Second Edition. Edited by
Eric Emerson, Chris Hatton, Kate Dickson, Rupa Gone, Amanda Caine and Jo Bromley.
© 2012 John Wiley & Sons, Ltd. Published 2012 by John Wiley & Sons, Ltd.

limited knowledge, poor understanding and inadequate skills in parent-craft. They tend to be a doubly disadvantaged population and frequently suffer low incomes, sub-standard housing and social isolation, in addition to their intellectual disabilities. Nevertheless, it could be argued that these environmental and social disadvantages are also shared by the non-learning disabled parenting population, many of whom struggle to raise their children despite the hardships of poverty and deprivation. Unfortunately, parents with intellectual disabilities tend to be vulnerable to pejorative attitudes which deem them unfit for parenting and incapable of carrying full 'parental responsibility' solely on the basis of their IQ. Such judgements are, in fact, misplaced. The empirical evidence and proliferation of clinical reports disseminating from parenting programmes around the world indicates that **many** parents 'who happen to have an intellectual disability' **are capable** of providing adequate parenting, providing that they receive the appropriate training and support.

## DEFINITION OF TERMS

### Parents with Intellectual Disabilities

First, it is necessary to define what is meant by the term parents with **intellectual disabilities** as different terms prevail, depending upon the country in which you live. Presently, within the UK, the term **intellectual disability** or **learning disability** is most commonly used (learning difficulty tends to apply to children with special educational needs) when someone's intellectual functioning falls two standard deviations below the mean (IQ of 70 or less) in conjunction with deficits in adaptive behaviour, as assessed during the developmental period (up to age 19 years). Other terms commonly used outside of the UK include **mental retardation, developmental disability, cognitive disability or cognitive limitations.** Regardless of the term adopted by professionals, it is important to remember that parents usually reject such classifications anyhow and view themselves, first and foremost, as a parent rather than someone with an academic label. Whilst a diagnostic approach establishes the level of intellectual functioning of parents, a functional approach to intervention and support is what they really need.

### Parental Responsibilities

The Government's response to the investigation into the death of Victoria Climbie marked a significant change to the way that they viewed the vulnerability of children in the hands of their parents or carers (DfES and DH 2003). Although the notion of 'parental responsibilities' is referred to and defined by the Children Act 1989 (to replace the traditional common law concept of 'parental rights') it fails to specify these responsibilities in clear terms which are understandable to many parents, and especially those who happen to have an intellectual disability. Subsequently, the Children Act 2004 has brought clarification to this situation by encompassing the *Every Child Matters* recommendations in the form of the Outcomes Framework and requiring the statutory, voluntary and community sectors to work together to ensure that:

- *Parents, carers and families promote healthy choices.*
- *Parents, carers and families provide safe homes and stability.*
- *Parents, carers and families support learning.*
- *Parents, carers and families promote positive behaviour.*
- *Parents, carers and families are supported to be economically active.*

Clearly, parents with intellectual disabilities need to aspire to the same standards of child care as that expected of any other parent. However, some parents with intellectual disabilities may be confused and hard pressed to comprehend the term 'parental responsibilities' and 'standards of care' when these criteria were insufficiently met by their own parents during their childhood. Moreover, for many parents with intellectual disabilities they will experience difficulties in accessing the parenting literature (because of deficits in reading skills) and will not be able to learn about alternative parenting styles in a way that non-learning disabled parents might do. As a consequence, parents will rely heavily on support agencies to help them acquire the necessary knowledge and skills so that they can adopt a different parenting style to that experienced as a child. Clinicians need to be sensitive to the vulnerability of parents in this position. Interventions which adhere to 'good-enough' parenting can trigger feelings of anger, guilt and sadness in parents who grieve for the childhood which they might have had, and to which they were entitled. Professionals need insight and specialist skills to help parents with intellectual disabilities deal with these and other sensitive issues. Ideally, this support should include early education of teenagers and prospective parents with intellectual disabilities on the topic of parental responsibilities, prior to them taking on the parenting role. The *Every Child Matters: Change for Children programme* (DfES 2004) has recognised that there is a need for specialist services such as these to work alongside some of the most vulnerable parents in our society.

## EPIDEMEOLOGY

The general parenting population within the United Kingdom is estimated to be 12 million (Smith 1996) and of this number there are 2.1 million parents who have a disability (Stickland 2003). Whilst the actual number of **parents with intellectual disabilities** is unknown it is estimated that as many as 250,000 parents may have an intellectual disability or borderline disability (McGaw 1996). More recently, a survey of 2,898 people with intellectual disabilities (16+ years) living in the UK identified that 1:15 people interviewed had children, and just over half of these parents (52%) currently looked after their children (Emerson, Malam, Davies and Spencer 2005). Overall, the national trend indicates that the numbers of parents with intellectual disabilities involved in support services is increasing rapidly, although this might be an underestimation of the true population size (Tarleton, Ward and Howarth 2006). Eligibility criteria for services can be a contentious issue for adults with borderline intellectual disabilities, many of who are frequently excluded from learning disability services on the grounds that their IQ exceeds 70. Nonetheless, these same parents often have learning deficits and support needs that are insufficiently addressed by many generic parenting services (Mundy and McGaw 2006; Tarleton *et al.* 2006). The Joint Committee on Human Rights (2008) have recently drawn attention to the plight of parents with intellectual disabilities who encounter a lack of support from local authorities, particularly as eligibility criteria tighten.

## RESEARCH

In the past, it was assumed that parents with intellectual disabilities were incapable of providing adequate care for their child and that they could not benefit from teaching programmes. Subsequent studies sought to substantiate or refute possible erroneous assumptions using empirical research. In the main, this research has concentrated on three topics: a) the vulnerability of children born to parents with intellectual disabilities, b) parental competency and c), the efficacy of intervention programmes.

- *Vulnerability of children born to learning disabled parents.* Children born to mothers with intellectual disabilities are at increased risk of a low birth weight and admission to neonatal intensive care or special care nursery (McConnell, Mayes and Llewellyn (2008). Epidemiological studies estimate that the majority of parents (at least 60%) will have offspring who function at a higher intellectual level than themselves although this figure varies (Booth and Booth, 2000; Dowdney and Skuse, 1993). Some of these children will be of normal intelligence or superior intelligence, and will fare well as adolescents and adults providing that their families are given the necessary support that they require (Ciotti 1989). However, for many parents who do not receive this specialist guidance and training, their children may be 'at risk' from abuse, but most probably from unintentional neglect (arising from omission rather than commission). Many of these children will also be vulnerable to a developmental delay, especially in expressive language/cognitive skills and mental/cognitive problems (McGaw, Shaw and Beckley 2007). Across genders it is reported that boys are affected more severely than girls in terms of academic achievements and behaviour problems (Feldman and Walton-Allen 1997).

- *Parental competency*. Conflicting findings have emerged from studies of parenting by people with intellectual disabilities over the past 50 years. On the one hand, parents with intellectual disabilities or borderline intellectual disabilities have been identified as overly-representing parents involved in care proceedings. Between one eighth to one quarter of their children are more likely to be freed for adoption than the children from any other group of families (Booth, Booth and McConnell 2005; Llewellyn, McConnell and Ferronato 2003). Neglect rather than abuse is the most commonly reported concern with sexual, physical and emotional abuse being the other areas of concern cited among professional groups. More recently, children have been identified as especially vulnerable to abuse/neglect and removal from their parents though care proceedings when: a child has special needs, their parent has special needs in addition to their intellectual disabilities, their parent has a history of childhood trauma or a mother with intellectual disabilities has a partner with a higher IQ (McGaw, Scully and Pritchard 2010). Overall, parental competency appears to be affected by a combination of historical, social and environmental factors (Cleaver and Nicholson 2007).

   On the other hand, there are positive reports of good-enough parenting and adequate care which has been the main finding emerging from other studies (Floor, Baxter, Rosen and Zisfein 1975; Feldman 1994a, 1996; McGaw 1994; McGaw, Ball and Clark 2002; Llewellyn, McConnell, Honey, Mayes and Russo 2003). Strong associations are reported across these studies between the availability of intensive intervention programmes, supportive social networks, psychological well-being, positive parenting experiences and child outcomes.

- *Efficacy of intervention programmes*. Reports of parenting training programmes for mothers and fathers who have an intellectual disability tend to focus on describing the curriculum of the parenting programmes with some information of the teaching interventions used. In general, reports assert positive outcomes for families participating in the training. Some programmes claim that before their interventions were provided to families about 80% of parents lost their child through care proceedings and this figure reduced to about 15% following training (Feldman 1994b).

Comparability across these studies is difficult as the definition of 'success' appears to vary across programmes and variance often results from differences in methodologies, changing thresholds for parenting criterion and sample selection. Typically, studies differ in their selected parent population (some concentrate on parents with intellectual disabilities whilst others include parents with borderline intellectual disabilities), the teaching topic (Feldman and Case 1999); age and vulnerability of children studied (Feldman, Sparks and Case 1993) and programme settings which extend to homes, schools, community based settings or a combination of these (Heinz and Grant 2003; McGaw, Ball and Clark 2002, Whitman and Accardo 1989). A review conducted by the New York State Commission (1993) of eight programmes serving 41 families headed by parents with intellectual disabilities in the New York State highlights some of these issues:

'measuring the success of the programmes in meeting the needs of parents with developmental disabilities and their children is difficult ... the programmes differed significantly in the services that they provided and the resources that they had available, confounding evaluative comparisons across programmes. Notwithstanding these significant limitations ... parents themselves gave the programme high marks and generally matched the assessments of Commission staff who were impressed by the dedication of programme staff to the families, as well as their success in making many concrete and measurable positive changes in the lives of the parents and the children they served. However, whilst the parenting programmes received recognition for their short-term gains with families for most of the parents enrolled, parenting programmes helped them to compensate for their cognitive limitations, but they did not change them.'

These findings mirror the present situation within the UK where there exists a paucity of comparative data across programmes. The remainder of this Chapter will offer practical guidance to clinicians regarding assessments and clinical interventions which are known to be helpful in supporting parents with intellectual disabilities and their children.

## ASSESSING PARENTING

### General Intelligence

The research indicates that there is no direct correlation between parenting competency and IQ. However, parents whose IQ falls below 60 tend to experience more difficulties (particularly in their cognitive functioning and social skills) than similarly placed learning disabled parents whose general intelligence is estimated to be in excess of IQ 60. Frequently, it is reported that parents who function below this level become over-whelmed by the multiple demands of parenting. As a consequence, their children are more vulnerable to inadequate parenting and removal from their parent's care. All assessments need to be carried out sensitively and adjusted to the pace of the client.

Typically, support agencies will ask clinical psychologists to provide detailed information regarding a parent's general intelligence, decision-making skills, discriminatory ability, logical sequencing skills, memory span and verbal or visual learning preference to guide them in their work. The *Wechsler Adult Intelligence Scale*[UK] – *Third Edition* is commonly used for the purpose of assessing parent's intellectual functioning, many of whom will present with a mild or borderline intellectual disability classification. This assessment helps to distinguish between those people with normal range abilities from those parents who have a moderate or severe intellectual disability. Similarly, *the British Ability Scales, Non-Reading Tests, SON (Non-Verbal)*, or *Raven's Progressive Matrices* are sometimes used instead of or, in conjunction with the *WAIS*[UK] – *Third Edition* as a means of identifying specific skills or deficits.

### Academic Skills

It is essential to assess a parent's reading, writing and numeracy skills so that support agencies can pitch their teaching accordingly. Often, childcare information is conveyed on the back of packaging, in leaflets, prescriptions and letters which many parents miss because they cannot read or understand the text (the average reading age for this population is about seven years). Frequently, services will request information about a parent's reading age, listening comprehension, receptive and expressive language skills and numerical operations (simple addition, subtraction, multiplication and division). The *WORD, WOLD* and *WOND* are just few of many assessments which can be used for this purpose. Whilst many of these assessments are designed to be used for children aged six to 16 years 11 months nevertheless, they are useful for assessing adults whose academic skills fall within this range of functioning.

## Life Skills

The influence of parent's lifeskills on parental competency (in particular their practical skills and social skills) is outlined in the *Parental Skills Model* (McGaw and Sturmey 1994). Whilst standard assessments of adaptive behaviour such as the *Vineland Scales of Adaptive Behaviour* or the *Comprehensive Test of Adaptive Behaviour* provide useful general information about a person's independent living skills, they are limited in their usefulness. There is a need for instruments to assess a parent's life skills regarding their ability to establish and maintain routines and in areas of hygiene, symptom recognition, safety, emergency responses, etc., all of which are fundamental to childcare. There are a number of checklists which are designed for this purpose but they have a functional rather than a diagnostic role and are not weighted. Most empirically based assessments for use with parents with intellectual disabilities have not been standardised on a UK population of learning disabled parents. The *Parent Assessment Manual Software* has been developed specifically by the Special Parenting Service to capture the strengths and needs of parent's life skills in relation to their parenting capacity (McGaw 2010).

## Family History

Whilst family histories, genograms and eco-maps are usually put together as part of the *Framework for the Assessment of Children in Need and their Families* (DH, 2000) by social workers, clinicians need to ensure that social history reports, along with medical and educational information are supplied by the relevant agencies. Joint and separate interviews need to be conducted with the parents, preferably within their own home. During this process parents often reveal important information about their own nurturing experiences and memories of childhood abuse/neglect which may or may not affect their parenting. In some instances, there will be evidence of parental psychopathology which has a deleterious affect upon the child's health and development. In this instance, clinicians need to provide parents with the opportunity to receive therapy or counselling from specialists in the intellectual disabilities/mental health sectors. Issues may arise as to whether such intervention will benefit the parent within the timeframe of the child's needs.

## Support and Resources

The best predictor of future parental competency for parents with intellectual disabilities is the quality and frequency of social, and practical support, available to them on a daily basis. Such support is usually provided by a partner, family member, friends or neighbour. Social support is helpful when it assists or prompts parents (frequency depends upon parent's needs) in their decision-making and maintenance of child-care routines. Hands-on practical support is needed by some parents to help them access resources such as transport, housing, paid employment, creches, playgrounds, health centres, day-care centres, advocacy service and professional services (especially the parenting and intellectual disabilities services). The *Parent Assessment Manual Software* (McGaw 2010); *Social Support Relationship Matrix* (Tymchuk 1996), *Service Use and Needs Survey* (Feldman 1996) are useful tools that have been designed specifically to capture the needs of parents with intellectual disabilities.

## Childcare and Development

*Childcare* is assessed by trained professionals (social workers, health visitors, paediatricians) on aspects of feeding, hygiene, warmth, safety, continuity of care and independence. Typically, a child's height, growth and weight will be monitored to ensure that they are thriving and growing at a rate appropriate to their birth size and weight. Judgements will be made about the quality of the parenting based on the pattern of growth and gains made by a child during the perinatal period. Nowadays, parents are able to keep their child's health records at home so that they become aware of their child's development and take responsibility for this. Health visitors are well-placed to interpret and simplify these records to parents with intellectual disabilities who may find technical information involving growth centiles rather confusing.

*Child development* is assessed, in particular, by health visitors, psychiatrists, paediatricians, teachers and psychologists. Typically, clinical psychologists will take on the role of assessing a child's development (appropriate to their chronological age) and commenting on the quality of parent/child attachment, bonding, guidance and parental control. Usually, parents with intellectual disabilities have difficulty recognising the indicators of normal child development and have little understanding about their role in facilitating their child's learning. Commonly, parents perceive schools as the place where children learn to read and write and the home is where the child's primary needs (food, shelter, warmth, etc.) are met. Inevitably, problems will arise if parents do not become involved in stimulating their child's development.

## Case Study 1

Tamsin is a twenty-eight year old, single mother who has an IQ of 55 who has been known to the statutory agencies over a number of years. She has had four children removed from her care in the past, and as a consequence, has no experience of raising a child beyond the age of two years. She has poor reading and writing skills and is mostly dependent upon friends, neighbours or professionals to help her read letters and bills. Whilst she enjoys having her fifth child, she recognises that he is a lot brighter and more capable than her in many ways. Nevertheless, she tends to let Terry (who is 6 years old) stay home from school at least three days a week, in part because she enjoys his company and it makes life easier for her. Inevitably, there is a downside. The school, educational welfare officer and social worker are extremely concerned about Terry's education and behaviour which are deteriorating. In their opinion, it is not in Tamsin's interests to ensure that Terry attends school. She will feel less challenged by Terry if he becomes a poor-achiever like herself.

Eventually, the family were referred to the clinical psychologist who spent time building up a rapport with the family before organising a package of intervention and support:

a) Tamsin received practical and financial assistance (including transport) to help her join a local literacy class. Initially, she was filled with anxiety about attending but this lessened over-time and Tamsin's self-esteem increased as she learnt to read and write and she was then well-placed to help Terry in his school-work. Another important outcome was that Tamsin became increasingly independent from other people and more in control of her life as she learnt to read her mail and do things for herself.

b) Also, a training programme was offered to Tamsin on managing Terry's behaviour. However, these sessions only took place when Terry was at school. It was agreed that Tamsin would telephone the therapist beforehand to ensure her that this was the case. During these sessions Tamsin learnt that all children misbehave and it was normal for them to challenge their parent's authority at times. It was a sign they wanted to do things their way and to become independent of their parents. She was taught how to recognise the triggers to Terry's anti-social behaviour and how to avoid, manage and defuse a situation effectively using one approach at a time, and visual resources such as audio-tapes, video-tapes and books.

c) Tamsin was invited into the special parent's group which was about to commence on the theme of 'health and relaxation'. This had been selected by the other parents and the programme (facilitated by the two therapists) included visits to a college where they were shown how to make simple, cheap, healthy meals; a trip to the local health centre when they went into a 'fitness' studio under guidance, and sessions with an aromatherapist and reflexologist. Initially, Tamsin was nervous and would have disengaged from the group if she had not been supported by the other parents. Thereafter, she enjoyed the new experiences resulting from the activities and her shyness diminished as she struck up new friendships within the group.

This case illustrates that professionals cannot make assumptions that all parents will or can teach their child academic skills or that they will play with their child without some guidance, prompting or additional intervention. Usually, parents who do not engage children in this way are not deliberately neglectful, they are simply following the parenting behaviour of their own parents who, for whatever reason, did not teach them basic arithmetic, read stories or enter into play with them each day.

## WORKING WITH PARENTS

### Basic Philosophy

Engaging learning disabled parents in support programmes can be problematic. The research indicates that parents will decline or withdraw from professional services if:

- services do not meet their needs;
- the language and resources used by professionals are inappropriate;
- they become 'over-serviced' by multiple professional input;
- parents suspect or learn that their competency is being questioned covertly;
- professionals are dishonest, disrespectful or negative in their attitude towards them.

Paradoxically, the offer of professional support can trigger anxieties in parents. Many such parents fear that their child will be taken away from them if they reveal that they are not coping. As a consequence, parents may attempt to disguise or hide their parenting difficulties from those who are offering to help them. Sadly, this is sometimes misinterpreted by some professionals as indicating parental resistance and their poor motivation to engage with services. Conclusions are then drawn that such parents would be poor recipients of support programmes and the offer of support is withdrawn. In fact, parents will readily accept the support that is on offer to them if they are given reassurances that support agencies will enter into an honest, open relationship with them and that they will not be prejudged or 'talked about behind their backs', especially when there are concerns about the parenting. Parents benefit most from support which is pragmatic and positive in its delivery. Encouraging parents to self-refer to family/parenting services and to make their preferences known (regarding service input, staff, mode of teaching) is one way of facilitating this process.

## Admission to Programme

In order for services to provide intensive input to those families most in need there will be a requirement for services to formulate admission/ discharge criteria. Typically these might specify that:

- one or both parents have a diagnosed intellectual disability or border-line intellectual disability **in addition** to one or more of the following being present:
  - There is a significant lack of parental knowledge and/or skills in areas of feeding, hygiene, warmth, healthcare, parental responsive-ness, safety and child development.
  - Parents are unable to establish and/or maintain adequate household routines.
  - History or potential risk of neglect and/or abuse for parents/or children.
  - Family is socially isolated.
  - History of psychiatric/substance abuse problems.

## Home-based Programmes

The research literature indicates that a combination of home-based programmes and centre-based programmes work best for families. Home-based programmes involve one-to-one contact with the family which varies according to the specific needs of the parents and child. One family may need guidance from the clinical nurse specialist about weaning whilst another may work with the occupational therapist in developing childcare routines, another may talk with the psychologist about their child's development, while yet another parent may talk with a team member about concerns related to budgeting and benefits. Parents need guidance and teaching across a range of different topics. Most programmes include:

## Feeding

It cannot be assumed that parents with intellectual disabilities know how to provide a balanced diet to their children, or themselves. Frequently, parents require guidance on bottle and breast feeding, weaning, food preparation and cooking skills. Often, parents are unaware of the importance of weaning and the need for infants to chew their food as a prerequisite to language development. Typically, parents may bypass weaning altogether or they may shorten the complicated weaning stage in order to introduce simpler 'adult' foods to their child.

## Hygiene and Warmth

Parents with intellectual disabilities do not always understand the need to keep their offspring clean from germs through regular washing/bathing and the sterilisation of equipment (teats, bottles, spoons). Also, when their children suffer from flea bites, head lice, scabies, ringworm, eczema, asthma and other complaints their parents may struggle to treat the condition, despite advice and medication from their GP, health visitor or community nurse. Typically, such professionals provide parents with complicated verbal or written instructions which they cannot read or understand. Nevertheless, parents can benefit from intensive training on symptom recognition (vomiting, breathing difficulties, constipation, etc.) and first-aid, however this training needs to be generalised within the home setting.

## Safety

Safety presents as a significant risk for many children, especially those under the age of five years (school limits the child's daily exposure to risks within the home). All parents need training a), to recognise potentially dangerous or life-threatening situations, b) to avoid or reduce the risk of such dangers before there is a crisis and c), to learn to deal with emergency situations such as choking, burns, house fires etc., including using the 999 procedure. Whilst parents can benefit from such training it cannot be assumed that such knowledge and skills will automatically generalise to alternative settings or new situations. Generalisation may be facilitated if parents are introduced to new knowledge and skills one at a time. Once parents have mastered these skills to the point of 'over-learning', variations of the skill can be taught across different settings.

## Case Study Two

Megan was referred to the Special Parenting Service by the social worker who was concerned about the safety of two young children within the home. Both girls (aged five years and three years) were being cared for in an erratic fashion by their young mother. They were allowed to wander outside of the home onto a road unsupervised; they were constantly throwing objects around the house (often bouncing off visitors); they tampered with electrical wiring and had suffered minor burns from the coal fire on a number of occasions. Previously, there had been a baby in the home, who had been removed from Megan following an incident when the baby's leg was fractured, a possible non-accidental injury. First a risk assessment was needed in order to a) identify the risks that these children were being exposed to, b) to reduce these risks immediately by offering an intensive teaching/support programme c), to identify the parent's strengths and needs and d), to address maintenance and generalisation of newly learnt skills. This programme was duly offered over a two year period and was simple enough to achieve, except for the maintenance and generalisation of skills which this mother did not seem capable of doing by herself even when a skill had been over-learned. Eventually, it was agreed with Megan that in order to facilitate this process a support net-work would be developed around her, involving her relatives, neighbours, family aides and the Special Parenting Service. Thereafter, Megan was constantly reminded about specific parenting skills and routines (which changed over time) by the support group who called at the home frequently (on an individual basis) and who enquired about the programme and the application of skills. They were aware of the need to be positive in their feedback and to suggest alternative settings in which to apply the skills. Although this approach turned out to be extremely effective, it changed dramatically when Megan found a new partner and he was on the spot to intervene if she forgot to use the skills appropriately or to apply these in naturally occurring, alternative situations. As Megan began to do this for herself, her partner's interventions reduced accordingly.

## Child Development and Stimulation

Parents and their children often benefit from guidance to help them engage in structured and unstructured play with their children as part of a routine or during childcare activities such as dressing, washing or putting their child to bed. Portage is an effective model to use, although it will need adaptations if is to be used with parents with intellectual disabilities (McGaw 1994). Simple, skills based programmes have been developed for teaching parents with intellectual disabilities which focus on different stages of a child's development (DfES, 2006).

*Organisation and Routines*

Children like the predictability of family routines which help them to feel secure. Commonly, parents with intellectual disabilities struggle with organisational tasks which require them to prioritise, sequence and to plan in advance. As a prelude to intervention, it is important to check whether parents are skilled in using diaries, calendars, watches and alarms before tackling the basics of planning, establishing routines and helping them to keep to schedules. Parents can benefit from teaching programmes which uses a range of equipment and visual aides to promote these skills. Useful aides such as *Baby Think it Over* (PSD Import Agency) is an ideal teaching aide which is a realistically weighted, electronic doll which looks, cries and commands attention just like a real baby. It is programmed to present the special needs of a premature or drug-dependent baby as well as the changing demands of healthy babies.

*Supervision and Discipline*

Parents with intellectual disabilities often experience difficulties in establishing ground rules and instilling a sense of discipline within the home. The research indicates that children can be particularly challenging of their parents' decision-making and discipline, especially when they function at a higher intellectual level than their parents (sometimes referred to as the Huck Finn Syndrome, O'Neil 1985). Both parents and children can benefit from guidance from parenting services and/or child guidance clinics which identify and strengthen parent/child boundaries, roles and responsibilities within the family unit.

## Centre-based Programmes

Teaching programmes need to be flexible in their format, chosen settings and delivery in order to suit families various needs. Centre-based programmes offer a useful adjunct to home-based teaching and these can be delivered across various settings such as family centres, churches, community centres and health centres. Groups tend to run for a limited period *during* the year and involve professional staff and small groups of infants (5/6) and their parents. Sessions can adopt a low key, informal style that allows for addressing issues as they arise rather than adherence to a 'curriculum'. Alternatively, structured parenting programmes such as the *Skills for Life. Family life: the growing child* (DfES 2006) or those developed by CHANGE (www.changepeople.co.uk), the Special Parenting Service (Mundy and McGaw 2006) or other agencies, have been developed specifically to meet the needs of parents with intellectual disabilities on topics such as:

- *child care and development;*
- *managing disruptive behaviours;*
- *self-esteem;*
- *diet/health/relaxation;*
- *anger-management;*
- *bereavement;*
- *social skills and relationship;s*
- *independent living skills;*
- *birth control;*
- *behavioural management;*
- *support networks.*

However, simply inviting parents to groups may not guarantee their attendance. Group organisers need to spend sometime educating and preparing parents about group membership and what that entails. Some parents fear entering a social circle because they have difficulty communicating effectively and their natural response is to avoid such situations. In addition, some parents fear having to talk about past painful experiences and/or memories which relate to childhood abuse and/or neglect or about their children when they have been removed from their care. Nevertheless, there are many parents with intellectual disabilities who benefit greatly from group teaching and support, as is the case for the general parenting population at large.

## Support Networks

Even though agency and professional involvement with parents with intellectual disabilities is high across the UK there are various barriers to the provision of the most appropriate support to parents. These barriers include negative, or stereotypical, attitudes about parents with intellectual disabilities on behalf of the professionals whose job it is to help them (Tartleton, *et al*. 2006). Also, intellectually disabled parents often have poor social skills. They rarely approach children's social care for help, much preferring that practitioners seek help on their behalf, which can create a dependency on others. When solutions or suggestions come directly from parents themselves this has been identified as being the most useful vehicle for change (Cleaver *et al*. 2007). CHANGE is a good example of a user-led service comprising a team of people with intellectual disabilities who produce resources in an easy read format for others parents to use. Training is provided by CHANGE to professionals to raise awareness about parenting needs and parenting situations. Such training is vital for intermediaries who are well placed to intervene or bridge between group and community resources and for specialist advocacy services, especially when parents are involved in child care proceedings (Tarleton 2008). A number of surveys have identified how best to help adults with intellectual disabilities in their parenting role and have made useful recommendations as to how practitioners can achieve this (Morris 2003; Tarleton *et al* 2006; Wates 2002). Currently, the Norah Fry Research Centre is working on the dissemination of best practice, networking and policy change, all of which is aimed at strengthening service provision for these vulnerable families, details of which are on their website (www.right-support.org.uk).

## Comprehensive Services

Families benefit most from comprehensive services which acknowledge the multiple determinants affecting the physical and mental health of the child and family which includes unsafe and unhealthy environments, poor housing, lack of transport and poverty. Currently, a number of barriers exist which make it difficult for disabled parents to identify and access services (Tarleton *et al*. 2006; Mundy and McGaw 2006). Services are hindered by the lack of staff training, strategic planning and joint commissioning which would enable them to provide what is needed by parents. Key elements of good practice identified for parents and children with learning/physical disabilities are cited in the *Good Practice Guidance on Working with Parents with a Learning Disability* (DfES, 2007) and the *A Life like any other?* (*Joint Committee on Human Rights* 2008). Essentially, five key features of good practice have been identified which services need to mindful of when working with parents with intellectual disabilities. They should provide:

1. **Accessible information and communication** which will enable parents with intellectual disabilities to engage with services and therefore optimise the care that they provide to their children.
2. **Clear and co-ordinated referral and assessment procedures and processes, eligibility criteria and care pathways**. Together these improved service structures should foster a preventative rather than a reactive approach to family interventions, which are known to result in better child outcomes and less parental stress.
3. **Support designed to meet the needs of parents and** children based on assessment of their needs and strengths. A flexible, range of support that is home-based or centre-based or a combination of the two works

best. Also, children need to be provided with support in their own right as well as their parents. Some of these children are carers who need access to support groups, counselling and practical assistance at various stages of their lives.

4. **Long-term support** where necessary as many families need support at various points of their family's life-cycle. A parent's intellectual disability will remain with them throughout their life whilst their child's physical, emotional and academic needs will transgress different stages of development which parents will need to manage accordingly.

5. **Access to independent advocacy** to enable parents to build confidence and self-esteem. Advocacy and self-advocacy should be made available to enable parents to access and engage with services and especially when parents are involved in child protection conferences/care proceedings or in legal matters.

## CONCLUSION

There are encouraging signs that more and more services across the UK are now becoming involved with parents with intellectual disabilities and that they are developing wide-ranging support programmes to meet the various needs of these families. However, clinicians often report that they feel ill-prepared for this task, despite their training and background across the children's services and intellectual disabilities sector. Clearly, this situation presents as an interesting challenge to professionals who feel obliged to assist such families as best as they can, but in the absence of a national strategy on professional training, policy standards and service guidelines. In response, professionals are turning to the research and models of good practice for guidance, some of which have been referred to in this article. Whatever the issues, it is clear that many **adults who happen to have an intellectual disability** will become parents and professionals will continue to offer these families the support to which they are entitled, despite the difficulties.

## References

Booth, T. and Booth, W. (2000) Against the Odds: Growing up with parents who have learning difficulties, **38**, 1–14.

Booth, T., Booth, W. and McConnell, D. (2005) The prevalence and outcomes of care proceedings involving parents with learning difficulties in the Family Courts. *Journal of Applied Research in Intellectual Disabilities*, **18**, 7–17.

CHANGE. *You and Your Baby 0-1 Year*. www.changepeople.co.uk.

CHANGE. *Planning a Baby*. www.changepeople.co.uk.

Ciotti, P. (1989) Growing up different: when the retarded become parents, perhaps their children know best how it works. *Los Angeles Times*, May 9.

Cleaver, H. and Nicholson, D. (2007) *Parental Learning Disability and Children's Needs*. Jessica Kingsley: London.

DfES (2004). *Every Child Matters: Change for Children*. DfES publications. www. publications.everychildmatters.gov.uk.

DfES (2006) *Skills for Life. Family life: the growing child*. DfES publications. www.dfes.gov.uk/readwriteplus/embeddedlearning.

DfES and DH (2003) *Keeping Children Safe*. The Stationery Office: Norwich.

DH (2003) *Every Child Matters*. The Stationery Office: Norwich.

DH (2000) *Assessing Children in Need and their Families*. The Stationery Office: Norwich.

DH and DfES (2007) *Good Practice Guidance on Working with Parents with a Learning Disability*. Office of National Director: Learning Disabilities: London. www. valuingpeople.org.uk.

Dowdney and Skuse (1993) Parenting provided by adults with mental retardation. *Journal of Child Psychology and Psychiatry*, **34**(1), 25–47.

Emerson, E., Malam, S., Davies, I. and Spencer, K. (2005) *Adults with Learning Difficulties in England 2003/4*. Office for National Statistics.

Feldman, M. (1994a) Parenting education for parents with intellectual disabilities: A Review of Outcome Studies, **15**, 299–332.

Feldman, M. (1994b) Parents with intellectual disabilities. *Network*, **4**, 41–7.

Feldman, M. (1996) *Courses for Parents with Intellectual Disabilities and Their Children*. Parenting with Intellectual Disability Conference: Danish Ministry of Social Affairs.

Feldman, M. and Case, L. (1999) Teaching child-care and safety skills to parents with intellectual disabilities through self-learning. *Journal of Intellectual and Developmental Disability*, **24**, 27–44.

Feldman, M. and Walton-Allen, N. (1997) Effects of maternal mental retardation and poverty on intellectual, academic, and behavioural status of school-age children. *American Journal on Mental Retardation*, **101**, 352–64.

Feldman, M., Sparks, B. and Case, L. (1993) Effectiveness of home-based early intervention on the language development of children of mothers with mental retardation. *Research in Developmental Disabilities*, **14**, 387–408.

Floor, L., Baxter, D., Rosen, M. and Zisfein, L. (1975) A survey of marriages among previously institutionalized retardates. *Mental Retardation*, **13**, 33–7.

Heinz, L.C. and Grant, P. (2003) A process evaluation of a parenting group for parents with intellectual disabilities. *Evaluation and Programme Planning*, **26**, 263–74.

Joint Committee on Human Rights. (2008) *A Life Like Any Other?* House of Commons: London. www.parliament.uk/jchr.

Llewellyn, G., McConnell, D. and Ferronato, L. (2003) Prevalence and outcomes for parents with disabilities and their children in an Australian court sample. *Child Abuse and Neglect*, **27**, 235–51.

Llewellyn, G., McConnell, D., Honey, A., Mayes, R. and Russo, D. (2003) Promoting health and home safety for children of parents with intellectual disability: a randomized controlled trial. *Research in Developmental Disabilities*, **24**, 405–31.

McConnell, D., Mayes, R. and Llewellyn, G. (2008) Women with intellectual disability at risk of adverse pregnancy and birth outcomes. *Journal of Intellectual Disability Research*, **52**, 529–35.

McGaw, S. (1994) Raising the parental competency of parents with intellectual disabilities. *Doctorate: Exeter University*. British Lending Library.

McGaw, S. (1996) Services for parents with intellectual disabilities. *Tizard Intellectual disability Review*, **1**, 1.

McGaw, S. (2010) *Parent Assessment Manual Software*. Pill Creek Publishing: Cornwall. www.pillcreekpublishing.com.

McGaw, S., Scully, T. and Pritchard, C. (2010) Predicting the Unpredictable? Identifying high risk versus low risk parents with intellectual disabilities. *Child Abuse and Neglect*. **34**, 699–710.

McGaw, S., Ball, K. and Clark, A. (2002) The effect of group intervention on the relationships of parents with intellectual disabilities, **15**, 354–66.

McGaw, S., Shaw, T. and Beckley, K. (2007) Prevalence of psychopathology across a service population of parents with intellectual disabilities and their children. *Journal of Policy and Practice in Intellectual Disabilities*, **4**, 11–22.

McGaw, S. and Sturmey, P. (1994) Assessing parents with intellectual disabilities: The Parental Skills Model. *Child Abuse Review*, **3**, 36–51.

Morris, J. (2003) *The Right Support*. Joseph Rowntree Foundation: York.

Mundy, S. and McGaw, S. (2006) *Consultation on Services for Disabled Parents in Cornwall*. Cornwall Partnership Trust. www.cornwall.nhs.uk/specialparenting services.

New York State Commission (1993) *Parenting With Special Needs: parents who are mentally retarded and their children*. New York State Commission on Quality of Care for the Mentally Disabled.

Office for Disability Issues. (2008) *Independent Living*. www.officefordisability.gov.uk/independent/strategy.asp.

O'Neil, A.M. (1985) Normal and bright children of mentally retarded parents: the Huck Finn syndrome. *Child Psychiatry and Human Development*, **15**, 255–68.

PSD Import Agency. *Baby Think it Over*. 1A St. Marks Road, Henley on Thames, Oxon, RG9 1LD.

Stickland H. (2003) *Disabled Parents and Employment*. London, Department of Work and Pensions.

Smith, C. (1996) *Developing Parenting Programmes*. National Children's Bureau.

Tarleton, B., Ward, L. and Howarth, J. (2006) *Finding the Right Support?* The Baring Foundation: London.

Tymchuk, A. (1996) The development, implementation and preliminary evaluation of a cross-agency, multi-site self-healthcare and safety preparatory and prevention education program for parents with intellectual disabilities. In *Parenting with Intellectual Disability*. Danish Ministry of Social Affairs: Denmark.

Wates, M. (2002) *Supporting Disabled Adults In Their Parenting Role*. Joseph Rowntree Foundation: York.

Whitman, B. and Accardo, P. (eds). (1989) *When a Parent Is Mentally Retarded*. Baltimore: Brookes.

Chapter 15

# PEOPLE WITH INTELLECTUAL DISABILITIES AND MENTAL ILL-HEALTH

D. Dagnan and W.R. Lindsay

## INTRODUCTION

In the past 10 years the provision of mental health services for the general population has changed considerably. The NHS plan (Department of Health 2000) identified the need to ensure that evidence-based best-practice was made equally available in all parts of Britain. Part of the process of delivering evidence-based services has been the development of National Service Frameworks (NSFs) which identify the structure of services necessary to meet needs in a broad range of clinical areas. The NSF for Mental Health Services primarily addresses the needs of people with severe mental ill-health and identifies psychosocial structures such as Early Intervention Teams, Assertive Outreach Teams, Crisis Resolution and Home Treatment Teams as necessary to the delivery of these services (Department of Health 2001). The NHS is expected to be able to demonstrate an evidence based approach (Department of Health 2006) and a core part of this is demonstration of compliance with NSF standards and NICE (National Institute for Clinical Excellence; e.g. National Institute for Clinical Excellence 2002) clinical guidelines.

However, the evidence base included in the development of most NSFs and NICE guidance does not include people with intellectual disabilities. This presents challenges to the clinician working with people with intellectual disabilities and therefore the degree to which methods developed in the mainstream literature can be adapted for people with intellectual disabilities needs to be explored. This chapter will consider

*Clinical Psychology and People with Intellectual Disabilities*, Second Edition. Edited by Eric Emerson, Chris Hatton, Kate Dickson, Rupa Gone, Amanda Caine and Jo Bromley.
© 2012 John Wiley & Sons, Ltd. Published 2012 by John Wiley & Sons, Ltd.

the evidence base and clinical issues around identification of mental ill-health in people with intellectual disabilities and the subsequent issues of determining prevalence rates. The chapter will then consider vulnerability issues, assessment within clinical practice, formulation, intervention approaches and service structures through which mental health services are delivered, including the interface of intellectual disability services with mainstream mental health services. Throughout the chapter we will take a psychosocial approach that identifies influences on mental well-being at an individual, immediate and wider social context and attempts to place assessment, formulation and intervention within the same framework. We will present a case study that illustrates some of these themes.

## VULNERABILITY

It is generally assumed that people with intellectual disabilities will be more at risk of mental ill-health. Factors in the lives of people with intellectual disabilities that lead to this assumption include:

1. Some phenotypes that are associated with intellectual disability have particular psychological profiles as part of their presentation. For example, people with Down's Syndrome may be more predisposed to depression and dementia, whilst people with Prader-Willi Syndrome may be more predisposed to psychosis (Cooper 2004).
2. People with intellectual disabilities may have particular deficits in problem solving, emotional control and communication difficulties. These make the person's interaction with their world more demanding and complex. For example, social problem solving skills are an integral aspect of social interaction and associations between lower social skill and self-reported ratings of depressive symptoms have been reported (Payne and Jahoda 2004).
3. People with intellectual disabilities may have particular attachment experiences (Rutgers, Bakermans-Kranenburg, van Ijzendoorn and van Berckelaer-Onnes 2004). The interaction of general developmental factors, such as attachment experiences, with the specific experiences of people with intellectual disabilities in the development of mental ill-health has been explored for some presentations (e.g. Dagnan and Jahoda 2006).
4. People with intellectual disabilities are more frequently exposed to specific social experiences such as abuse, negative expectations, bullying and loss. For example many studies have reported increased rates of sexual and physical abuse in people with intellectual disabilities (e.g. Beail and Warden 1995; Sequeira and Hollins 2003; Lindsay, Steele, Smith, Quinn and Allan 2006).

5. People with intellectual disabilities may be exposed to many of the social factors associated with lower socio-economic status such as social isolation, poor housing, negative life events, unemployment and poverty. These factors have been shown to be associated with mental ill-health in people with intellectual disabilities (e.g. Emerson, Graham and Hatton 2006; Lunsky 2006). Thus people with intellectual disabilities may be at greater risk of mental ill-health because of their generally lower socio-economic status.

These factors suggest a complex interaction between the person and their environment in determining the likelihood of mental ill-health in people with intellectual disabilities.

## PREVALENCE

The actual rate of mental ill-health in people with intellectual disabilities is less clear than might be expected and studies report a wide range of prevalence rates. For example, (Borthwick-Duffy 1994), in a review of eight studies involving adults with intellectual disabilities in both hospital and community settings in the UK, reported rates of mental ill-health of between 10 and 39% depending on the sample selection, definition of psychiatric illness, diagnostic criteria and the diagnostic methods used. There are a number of recent reviews of the prevalence rates of mental ill-health (e.g. Cooper 2004) that suggest that there remains a variation in reported prevalence. This is likely to occur for a number of reasons:

1. Established diagnostic criteria for mental ill-health may need some adaptation in their application to people with intellectual disability (Cooper 2004; Meins 1995; Poindexter 2006). For example, the requirements for diagnosis of some categories of mental ill-health require the person to be able to self-report and, thus, may prevent a complete diagnosis in a person who has communication difficulties.
2. The interpretation of studies on prevalence is complex because of differences in diagnostic methods; studies use a variety of methods from indicative survey measures (Taylor and Hatton 2004) to individual diagnoses based upon clinical interview (Eaton and Menolascino 1982).
3. A further crucial difference between studies is their exclusion and inclusion of specific presentations. For example, some studies have included challenging behaviour in their data (Lund 1990), other have included presentations such as dementia (Lund 1985). Cooper, Smiley, Morrison, Williamson, and Allan (2007) present data that demonstrate the significant variation that can occur when presentations such as challenging behaviour or autism are included in psychiatric diagnostic systems.

4. Finally, studies have used different sampling approaches. Some studies are able to access all people within a known population while others have reviewed specific sub-populations. However, it has been pointed out that the population of people with intellectual disabilities that is known to clinical and social services at any one time might over-represent those with mental ill-health and behavioural problems (Whitaker and Read 2006).

Studies have found it difficult to clearly identify an association between severity of intellectual disabilities and mental ill-health (Cooper 2004). Studies have found epilepsy to be associated with higher levels of mental ill-health, whereas others have not (Deb 1997; O'Dwyer 1997) similarly conflicting results have been reported for ageing (Cooper 1997; Patel, Goldberg and Moss 1993). Finally, it is important to note that the prevalence of mental ill-health in people with intellectual disabilities is unlikely to be a stable figure. The epidemiology of intellectual disability indicates a population that is increasing in size, but is also getting older, with mental health issues of ageing becoming more relevant and with more young people and more severe disabilities and an increased recognition of associated disabilities such as autism.

There are a number of issues that make the clinical assessment of mental ill-health in people with intellectual disability complex (Findlay and Lyons 2001; Rush, Bowman, Eidman, Toole and Mortenson 2004). This chapter will now consider process of assessment and treatment. We place less emphasis on process issues since these will be considered in more detail in Chapter 9.

## ASSESSMENT

Rush *et al.* (2004) describe a comprehensive approach to the assessment of mental ill-health that includes the review of client records, interview with the person themselves and/or carers, direct observation and the use of structured rating scales.

1. *Review of client records.* There will often be useful information in the files and records of people with intellectual disabilities that will help establish a baseline of behaviour or a previous pattern of changes in behaviour which will give a context within which the present instance of behavioural change can be interpreted. However, the diagnostic and theoretical knowledge of mental ill-health has changed considerably over time and information and diagnoses identified in case records should be interpreted with caution.

2. *Direct observation.* The literature on the use of direct observation as a clinical assessment method is considerable (Paclawskyj, Kurtz and

O'Connor 2004). For the psychologist involved in a clinical assessment there is a minimum requirement to observe the client within their own environment (Ball, Bush and Emerson 2004). Within the context of mental ill-health there are examples of the reliable observation of mood in people with more severe disabilities as part of the evaluation of psychological interventions (Toole, Bowman, Thomason, Hagopian and Rush 2003) and there are examples of the comprehensive operationalisation of DSM criteria for direct observation (Sovner and Hurley 1982).

3. *Interviews with the person.* There are a number of complexities when interviewing people with intellectual disabilities about their experience of mental ill-health (Findlay and Lyons 2001). However, where possible the client's perspective on their difficulties should be considered and many people are able to give essential insights into their difficulties. There are an increasing number of structured self-report measures: Dagnan and Lindsay (2004) identify the use of:

   a. Scales that are designed for the general population that are used in the same format as when used with people without intellectual disabilities, such as the Beck and Zung scales (Prout and Schaefer 1985).
   b. Scales that were developed for the general population but which have been adapted for use with people with intellectual disabilities such as the Zung Depression Inventory (Dagnan and Sandhu 1999; Lindsay and Michie 1988; Lindsay, Michie, Baty, Smith and Miller 1994), the Brief Symptom Inventory (Kellett, Beail, Newman and Frankish 2003), and a series of scales for use with people with psychosis (Hatton *et al.* 2005).
   c. Scales specifically developed for use with people with intellectual disabilities. Of particular interest are the Glasgow Anxiety and Depression scales (Cuthill, Espie and Cooper 2003; Mindham and Espie 2003). These scales have particular advantages in that they have been validated against clinical diagnostic judgement and have been developed using people with intellectual disabilities to inform wording of scale items.
   d. Scales to assess underlying concepts associated with mental ill-health such as self-esteem and social comparison (Dagnan and Sandhu 1999), stigma and negative self-evaluation (Dagnan and Waring 2004) and negative automatic thoughts (Nezu, Nezu, Rothenberg, Dellicarpini and Groag 1995).

Interview and assessment of the person themselves may also include consideration of the potential of the person to engage in intervention. For example Dagnan and Chadwick (1997) describe assessments that illustrate core abilities that might make a person more able to take advantage of cognitive therapy. This assessment process includes assessment of language ability, emotional recognition and expression, abilities to relate events to emotions and the ability to understand therapy specific concepts such as the cognitive mediation of emotion and behaviour. The results of such assessment may suggest further input to better enable the use of particular therapy, how therapeutic and supportive interventions may be adapted and offer insights into the formulation of the difficulties experienced by the person.

4. *Interview with carers and/or family members.* Carers and family members may be able to provide information about the developmental history of the presenting problems. It is always important to bear in mind that carers will be presenting their perspective on the presentation and that this will often be affected by their own views of the client and their knowledge of mental ill-health.

There are now a number of structured rating scales that can be used to help identify mental ill-health presentations in people with intellectual disabilities. Rush *et al.* (2004) reviews a number of such scales developed in the United States; within the UK the most commonly used of such scales is the PAS-ADD (Moss *et al.* 1997) which is based upon DSM diagnostic criteria. The PAS-ADD system has 3 levels of assessment; the PAS-ADD checklist is a 25 item rating scale designed to be completed by those with little diagnostic or clinical knowledge such as direct carers or families, the Mini-PAS-ADD Interview is a an interview based scale designed to be used by those with more diagnostic experience. The Mini-PAS-ADD Interview has a carefully constructed reference system to help the interviewer phrase questions and interpret responses. Finally the PAS-ADD 10 is a semi-structured clinical interview designed for use by those with more experience and which can provide clinically reliable diagnoses (Prosser *et al.* 1998; Sturmey, Newton, Cowley, Bouras and Holt 2005).

5. *Assessment of the influence of psychosocial factors.* Given the psychosocial emphasis of this chapter it is important that assessment should also include consideration of the broader psychosocial context of the client (e.g. Allen 1999). The assessment of environmental features associated with mental ill-health problems is underdeveloped. However some examples of assessments that are suitable for this type of assessment exist, for example:

a. Assessments of the beliefs and attitudes of carers about the behaviours shown by their client. A number of assessment approaches developed for carers of people with intellectual disabilities and challenging behaviour may be suitable for assessment of beliefs around those with mental ill-health. For example the Challenging Behaviour Attribution Scale and the associated measure of emotional response to challenging behaviour are useful clinical scales in this context (Hastings 1997a; Mitchell and Hastings 1998) and the measures reported by Dagnan and colleagues within an attribution framework (Dagnan 2004; Dagnan, Trower and Smith 1998).

b. Assessments of the knowledge that carers have of mental ill-health presentations and issues (Munden and Perry 2002; Quigley, Murray, McKenzie and Elliot 2001).

c. Assessments of factors such as expressed emotions which have been found to be important in people without intellectual disabilities is not widely reported in the literature on mental ill-health of people with intellectual disabilities. However there is a beginning literature that suggests that these factors may be equally important for people with intellectual disabilities (Hastings, Daley, Burns and Beck 2006; Weigel, Langdon, Collins and O'Brien 2006).

d. Assessments of aspects of a person's life that may be influenced by or that may influence their mental ill-health. For example the Camberwell Assessment of Need for Adults with Developmental and Intellectual Disabilities (CANDID) (Xenitidis et al. 2000) assesses a broad range of psychosocial needs associated with mental ill-health.

## FORMULATION

A psychological perspective on mental ill-health is essentially formulatory. Psychosocial formulation will examine the interaction of the person and their environment. Given the social vulnerability of people with intellectual disabilities it is particularly important that the social context of the person and their life is taken into account in any formulation. A number of writers have identified a tension between biological and psychological (individual) views of psychological distress and social models of the experience of disability (e.g. Dagnan and Waring 2004). Social models identify social structures or social construction as creating disability (Shakespeare and Watson 1997). A number of writers have begun to develop views of disability that integrate the social and individual approaches (Thomas 2004). There is also a developing model of the influence of social context on self-concept within the clinical literature (Jahoda, Trower, Pert and Finn 2001). Dagnan and Waring (2004) suggest that when stigmatisation and negative social construction is recognised by a person with intellectual disability this will have a profound impact upon a person's psychological well-being. Core cognitive experiences such as negative self-evaluation and negative social-comparison might then be expected as a direct consequence of the long-term experience of discrimination and social isolation. A truly psychosocial intervention may use such a model and encourages the therapist and team to formulate the individual's presentation within their social context and to acknowledge the social processes that shaped their fundamental evaluations, attributions and meanings concerning their world. Thus, based upon an individual formulation, psychosocial interventions may be coordinated to enable support and intervention with family and immediate social contexts, to provide opportunities in work and leisure and to inform therapeutic work with the individual.

## INTERVENTION

At the heart of the NICE and NSF guidance on severe mental ill-health is a psycho-social perspective. Dagnan (2007) identifies psycho-social intervention as bringing together interventions across a number of ecological levels including:

1. *Interventions with the individual.* These include symptom control approaches, problem solving and coping approaches, psycho-educational approaches as well as more typical cognitive and psychotherapeutic approaches.
2. *Interventions in the immediate environment of the client.* These include psycho-educational approaches aimed at families and carers and therapeutic approaches within the family context.
3. *Interventions in the broader environment around the person.* This includes intervention in the areas of activity such as work, leisure and housing as well as education.
4. Finally intervention can be considered as occurring through the structure of the services used to deliver services. The NSF for mental health outlines specific team structures and functions necessary to deliver psychosocial intervention.

This section will consider interventions using the psychosocial structures laid out as above.

### Individual Interventions

*Behavioural Approaches*

There is a considerable evidence base for the importance of behavioural approaches for working with people with mental ill-health. Many of the established interventions for people without intellectual disability for anxiety, depression, and severe mental ill-health have significant behavioural elements (Sturmey 2004). The use of behavioural approaches is usually based upon the theoretical basis upon which the particular difficulty is understood. Thus, for example, the behavioural model of anxiety or anger suggests that part of the presentation is a physiological response to activating events which calls for a physiological management approach such as relaxation (Meichenbaum 1977; Novaco 1977). To illustrate the appropriate use of behavioural approaches we will consider the theoretical assumptions of the behavioural view of anxiety and depression and then identify how these assumptions inform intervention.

Within the behavioural model anxiety is seen as a disorder of fear association and automatic learning rather than operant learning. The literature on the predisposition to learn particular associations significantly informs and develops this model (e.g. Davey 1992). A number of factors are known to affect the potential power of stimuli to become associated with anxiety, for example previous exposure to a conditioned stimulus will weaken its potential to establish a fear response (latent inhibition); thus a person bought up with dogs is unlikely to become phobic of dogs if bitten in adulthood. These insights have treatment implications in encouraging non-aversive exposure to a potential fear provoking stimulus (visiting airports or dentists prior to flights or treatment).

Within a behavioural model depression is seen as the consequence of low levels of reinforcement, possibly resulting from changes in reinforcement availability through loss or bereavement. Lower levels of reinforcement lead to lower levels of behavioural response, which are symptomatic of the observable behaviours of depression such as lack of activity and overt signs of low mood. Functional analytic techniques can be used to identify how such behaviours co-vary with environmental factors (Paclawskyj et al. 2004).

Both of these behavioural approaches are usefully considered in interventions for people with intellectual disabilities and have a number of reported interventions associated with them in the literature.

*Behavioural Treatment Approaches*

Behavioural techniques involving exposure to fear eliciting stimuli have been shown to be effective in most anxiety treatments. Behavioural treatments primarily generally follow a systematic desensitisation structure based upon a counter conditioning logic which follows a three-stage process:

1. Training in relaxation or identification of other counter-conditioning stimulus.
2. Development of a fear producing stimulus hierarchy.
3. The systematic graduated pairing of items in the hierarchy with relaxation. Most studies in people with intellectual disabilities and people without intellectual disabilities would use in vivo methods to achieve this.

A number of alternatives to relaxation training have been used; for example, studies of needle phobia have used anxiolytixc medication (Hagopian, Crockett and Keeney 2001) and although counter-conditioning is the predominant intervention approach, modelling and shaping positive behaviour in response to the feared stimulus have also been used in the treatment of phobia (Jackson 1983).

Depression was one of the first emotional disorders in people with intellectual disabilities to be addressed using psychological therapy. Matson, Dettling and Senatore (1979) reported on the effective treatment of depression in a 32 year old man with borderline to mild intellectual disability who had a 10 year history of depressed mood, feelings of worthlessness, suicidal threats, social withdrawal and sleep difficulties. They reported a behavioural treatment designed to increase positive self-statements, decreased negative self-statements and develop increased sociability through the use of self-monitoring, social reinforcement and encouragement of positive self-statements. Observations showed that negative self-statements decreased and remained low during post treatment and follow-up sessions. A number of subsequent interventions aimed at increasing positive mood have been described (e.g. Green, Reid, Rollyson and Passante 2005) and studies have shown that the behavioural signs of mood can be reliably observed (Toole *et al.* 2003). The use of behavioural approaches to treatment of depression also continues to be developed in people without intellectual disabilities (Hopko, Lejuez, Ruggiero and Eifert 2003).

*Behavioural Approaches: Evidence of Effectiveness*

Jackson (1983) reviewed the use of psychological interventions for phobia, at that time he found 15 studies relating to people with intellectual disabilities and autism. Most interventions used *in-vivo* desensitisation with reinforcement for contact with fear stimulus although some used participant modelling. Since 1983 there have been a continuing series of publications of successful interventions with phobias, these have included phobias of dogs (Newman and Adams 2004), and phobias of blood and needles (Hagopian *et al.* 2001). There are similar behavioural treatments reported for other anxiety presentations such as obsessive compulsive disorder (Matson 1982; McDougle *et al.* 1995) and Post Traumatic Stress Disorder (Lemmon and Mizes 2002).

The evidence base for the use of behavioural approaches to treat with people with intellectual disabilities and depression is less extensive (Matson, Dettling and Senatore 1979; Matson, Senatore, Kazdin and Helsel 1983) although evidence for positive effects of enriched environments in increasing positive affect can also be seen as an example of this type of intervention (Green and Reid 1999; Green *et al.* 2005).

## Cognitive Approaches

There are a number of therapeutic approaches for people without intellectual disabilities that can be considered to be 'cognitive'. Dagnan and Chadwick (1997) suggest that cognitive therapy can be seen as based within 'deficit' or 'distortion' models of the cognitive role in psychological distress. The deficit model suggests that emotional and behavioural difficulties are due to a lack of cognitive skills, including very basic skills such as self-talk through to more complex skills such as problem-solving (Whitman 1990). Interventions constructed within the 'deficit' model include self-regulation, self-monitoring and self-instruction approaches. There is discussion regarding whether approaches such as self-monitoring can be considered truly cognitive; theoretical explanations of change processes have been offered from behavioural and cognitive perspectives (Korotitsch and Nelson-Gray 1999). Whether regarded as predominantly behavioural or cognitive there is a substantial body of research that uses this type of approach with people with intellectual disabilities (Harchik, Sherman and Sheldon 1992).

The second approach to cognitive therapy for people with intellectual disabilities is concerned with 'cognitive distortion', where people are seen as using cognitive mediation to make sense of their world but where their interpretations or the cognitive processes involved are in some way unhelpful. Interventions constructed within this model generally follow those developed by Beck (e.g., Beck, Ward, Shaw and Emery 1979) or Ellis (Ellis 1977). Cognitive therapy of this type aims to help people examine and test the usefulness of the meanings they generate. There is a growing interest in using this approach with people with intellectual disabilities.

### Treatment Approaches

Most of the mental ill-health focused cognitive therapy interventions that are reported include the essential principles and components of treatment as follows: setting an agenda; developing an awareness of the role of underlying beliefs in determining thought; establishing the relationship between thoughts, experiences of emotion and behaviour; monitoring automatic thoughts; determining the content of underlying beliefs and assumptions through themes and automatic thoughts; testing the accuracy of cognitions and challenging maladaptive beliefs; generating alternative cognitions and adaptive automatic thoughts; practising these thoughts during therapy sessions, role-plays and in vivo sessions; reviewing the evidence to contradict maladaptive beliefs and construct new underlying assumptions about the self; and establishing homework assignments to review maladaptive cognitions and test out new underlying assumptions and adaptive automatic thoughts (e.g. Lindsay 1999). A detailed account of the development of therapeutic work within a cognitive framework is given in Chapter 7.

*Cognitive Approaches: Evidence For Effectiveness*

Problems of anxiety in people with intellectual disabilities have received more attention than almost any other area, although, in general, treatments have been more behavioural and physiological in focus than cognitive (Lindsay *et al*. 1999). In both cases anxiety remained stable and low at 18 months follow-up. Lindsay (1999) reports a cohort of 15 individuals with clinically significant levels of anxiety on the Beck Anxiety Inventory or the Zung Anxiety Scale. Treatment (following the principles outlined above) lasted an average of 23 sessions and resulted in a statistically significant reduction in self-report measures of anxiety; improvements were maintained at six-month follow-up.

Lindsay, Howells and Pitcaithly (1993) employed a revised and simplified version of cognitive therapy for depression with two people with intellectual disabilities. They gave examples of each stage of treatment noting the importance of placing a simple, straightforward interpretation on dysfunctional thoughts with a similarly straightforward interpretation of underlying assumptions. Lindsay (1999) reported on a cohort of five individuals with clinically significant levels of depression as measured on the Beck Depression Inventory or Zung Depression Scale. Lindsay, Stenfert-Kroese and Drew (2005) reported on the development of schema-focused cognitive therapy for depression with two cases of a 20 year old man with a measured IQ of 62 and a 28 year old woman with a measured IQ of 69. It is clear that cognitive therapy for depression is a structured treatment which makes it eminently suitable for clients with mild intellectual disabilities. Its very practical structure and the predictable nature of each session allow for clarity and are helpful to clients. Experimental work reviewing depression in relation to stigma, poor self-esteem, experience of repeated failure and negative social comparisons has shown their relationship to depression in this client group (Dagnan and Sandhu 1999; Nezu *et al*. 1995). These findings will not be true for all people with intellectual disabilities but must be considered as vulnerability factors.

A considerable amount of work has been conducted on the emotion of anger and related cognitions. Interventions in this area are almost exclusively based on Novaco's (1977) cognitive analysis of aggression in anger provoking situations. Novaco emphasises the relationship between cognition, emotion, physiological arousal and behavioural consequences. He outlines the way in which activating events are processed leading to emotional arousal. The attribution of this arousal as anger leads to behavioural reactions, such as physical or verbal antagonism, passive aggression or avoidance. Anger management has been adapted for people with intellectual disabilities. For example, Black and Novaco (1993) described a treatment approach that involves three stages; cognitive preparation, skill acquisition and practical applications of the coping skills discussed and rehearsed during treatment. Cognitive restructuring (self-instruction and social problem solving), relaxation (arousal reduction) and skill acquisition are employed as major elements throughout treatment. Others have also reported successful case studies both in individual and group treatment (Benson 1994; T.L. Jackson and Altman 1996; Lindsay *et al.* 2004; Rose 1996; Rose, West and Clifford 2000).

Cognitive therapy has been applied to a range of other areas that are not solely mental health such as social problem solving (Loumidis and Hill 1997) and offending behaviour (Lindsay 2005) and there is a beginning case series literature describing interventions with people with intellectual disability and psychosis using protocols developed for people without disabilities (Haddock, Lobban, Hatton and Carson 2004). However, despite its wide application the current evidence-base for cognitive therapy used with people with intellectual disability is limited (Beail 2003; Sturmey 2004, 2006; Willner 2005). The few randomised control-trial designs of cognitive therapy for people with intellectual disabilities are in the area of group interventions for anger (Taylor, Novaco, Gillmer and Thorne 2002; Benson, Rice and Miranti 1986; Rose *et al.* 2000). In over viewing the outcome literature, it is notable that the reported interventions for people with intellectual disability lack the specificity or sophistication of interventions that exist for people without disabilities. For example, reports a series of distinct models and interventions for a range of distinct anxiety presentations; these have not yet been described or evaluated for people with intellectual disabilities.

## Psychodynamic Psychotherapy

Psychodynamic therapy enables the client to become aware of unconscious distortions in their views of other people to enable them to respond more appropriately to people in the future. The relationship between the therapist and the client is the medium within this work is carried out as it is assumed that the client will begin to enact their experience of the world in their relationhsip with the therapist ands that the therapist will experience the cleint in a way congruent with the client's experience. It is notable that there exists the beginnings of a process oriented approach to studying the effectiveness of this type of work with people with intellectual disbailities (Newman and Beail 2005). Beail and Jahoda (see Chapter 7) give a detailed account of the processes and interventions involved in psychotherapy with people with intellectual disabilities.

*Evidence Base*

There is a stong tradition of psychodynamic therapy and thinking being applied to people with intellectual disbailities. As with cognitive behaviour therapy the main body of evidence is in the form of case studies and case series (Beail and Warden 1996; Beail, Warden, Morsley and Newman 2005; Sinason 1992).

## Interventions in Immediate Social Environment

There is a considerable literature on the effectiveness of intervention within the families of people with mental ill-health who do not have intellectual disabilities (Pharoah, Mari, Rathbone and Wong 2006). Many of these interventions are informed by evidence that that those people with schizophrenia who live in family settings that have high levels of criticism, hostility or over involvement are more likely to experience more frequent relapse. Interventions may be aimed at reducing the level of expressed emotion but also at increasing problem solving skills or maintaining appropriate expectations of the family member. There is no current literature that examines the effect of expressed emotion in family members of people with intellectual disabilities with mental ill-health and thus no literature on intervention using this approach. There is a small literature that shows links between maternal expressed emotion and challenging behaviours (Beck, Daley, Hastings and Stevenson 2004; Weigel *et al*. 2006).

More broadly the impact of carer and family attributions have been explored in carers of people with intellectual disabilities and challenging behaviour (e.g. Dagnan *et al*. 1998; Hastings 1997b) with a small number of studies applying the approach to people with intellectual disability and mental ill-health (e.g. Edelstein and Glenwick 2001). There are few examples of discussion of intervention within these frameworks for families or carers of people with intellectual disabilities (Kushlick, Dagnan and Trower 1998; Kushlick, Trower and Dagnan 1997). There are, however, examples of training and support interventions to support families and carers in the general stresses and challenges of working with people with intellectual disabilities and in particular those with challenging behaviour (Allen 1999). Although there are few examples of evaluated training and support for carers of people with intellectual disability and mental ill-health problems (e.g. Quigley *et al*. 2001; Costello, Bouras and Davis 2007) there are training needs analyses and curricula available for this (Holt, Hardy and Bouras 2005).

## Interventions in the Wider Social Environment

There is a considerable literature on the impact and economic effectiveness of intervention in the areas of supported employment, leisure and housing for people with mental ill-health without intellectual disabilities (e.g. Drake, Becker and Bond 2003). There is also a considerable literature on the impact of housing, leisure and supported employment on the psychological well-being of people with intellectual disabilities (e.g. Braun, Yeargin-Allsopp and Lollar 2006; Holburn and Jacobson 2006; Smith, Webber, Graffam and Wilson 2004) and as a response to the needs of people with intellectual disabilities and other problems such as challenging behaviour (e.g. Lowe, Felce, Perry, Baxter and Jones 1998). However, there is little or no literature in this area specific to the needs of people with intellectual disabilities with mental ill-health.

## Service Systems to Provide Services to People with Learning Disabilities

The structures through which interventions are delivered have often been considered a key part of the psychosocial interventions for people with mental ill-health (e.g. Clark and Samnaliev 2005). A small number of studies have reported the provision of psychosocial interventions for people with intellectual disability and mental ill-health through structured team based approaches (Martin *et al.* 2005; Oliver *et al.* 2005). Martin *et al.* (2005) describe a randomised controlled trial that found no statistically significant differences in the level of unmet needs, carer burden, functioning and quality of life between assertive and standard community treatment for people with intellectual disability. Both service delivery methods decreased levels of unmet needs and carer burden, and increased functioning. However, they point out that the two treatment arms were too similar to show the expected differences, and the study highlights that well functioning community teams might already be offering coherent psychosocial intervention. Well functioning community teams will offer multidisciplinary assessment, specialist psychiatric support, regular contact with community nurses, access to residential, employment, education and day service support, therapeutic input from psychology, nursing and or SALT and expert support in activity and environmental design from OT and physiotherapy. Thus the structures considered important in the delivery of effective mental health care for those without intellectual disability might already be present in well functioning community services for people with intellectual disabilities.

## CONCLUSIONS

Psychosocial intervention is well established within the mental health field but has not been widely developed specifically to people with intellectual disabilities. This may be because the key elements of psychosocial intervention are already core elements of the intervention approach within intellectual disability services. Recent guidelines and self-audit for the delivery of services to people with learning disabilities (Foundation for People with Learning Disabilities 2004) suggest that people with intellectual disabilities and mental ill-health should, where possible, receive services from the same teams and in the same settings as those without intellectual disabilities. However, as the complexity of the presentation of the person increases then the level of involvement from specialist intellectual disability services will increase. This chapter has outlined some of the evidence-base for the provision of psychosocial mental health services and has emphasised that there is considerable potential for cross-fertilisation of evidence from mainstream mental health to mental health delivery for people with intellectual disabilities.

## CASE STUDY

The following case study illustrates a psycho-social team based approach to working with a man with intellectual disabilities and mental ill-health. The reader might want to consider the skills used by the clinical psychologist in the case study and reflect upon the role of the clinical psychologist in such multi-disciplinary interventions.

John was a 28 year old man with intellectual disabilities. He had lived with his mother and older sister since leaving residential school at 21 where he had been living since leaving mainstream school at the age of 18. His mother was a retired teacher, his father an engineer who had died from lung cancer seven years ago, round the time when John returned home from residential school. John was referred on an urgent basis to the Community Intellectual Disability Team by his GP because his mother was reporting aggression towards her and her older sister. John had not previously been referred to the community team as an adult, although he had been referred to the children with disabilities team at the age of 14 when he had become significantly withdrawn and anxious. At that time the presentation was attributed to bullying at school and intervention had been within the school to support its approach to bullying of people with intellectual disabilities and at an individual level where assertiveness training was offered.

Psychometric data was available from educational psychology assessments carried out when John was 12, copies of which John's mother had kept. They suggested that his reading and writing skills placed him at the 4th centile. There had been no other previous psychometric assessment.

The community team had a specialist challenging behaviour team to which John was initially allocated. All pathways within the team used the same core assessments and a PASADD was completed with John's mother. When this was interpreted it showed scores above the threshold for psychosis and anxiety. However during the first visit to her home the challenging behaviour nurses became concerned that there were a number of other significant difficulties. John's sister reported that he had not slept in his bed for five days, sleeping for short periods on the sofa in the living room. It was clear that John believed that people were outside of his house that were a threat to him and was shouting at them to stop taunting him and to leave him alone. When his mother and sister tried to reassure him he became aggressive towards them. The nurses found John difficult to engage but he was able to put names to the people he believed were out-side of the house and his mother believed these were the people who had been bullying him when he had been at school.

The challenging behaviour team asked for an immediate assessment from the learning disability consultant psychiatrist and involved the specialist mental health nurse from the community learning disability team. During the subsequent assessment it became clear that the level of disruption and challenge that John's family were experiencing was con-siderable and that they had to take shifts to stay awake through the night to ensure he was kept safe. The learning disability service offered an admission to the learning disability assessment and treatment unit. An admission to the mainstream mental health acute admission unit was con-sidered but it was decided that John was too vulnerable and too distressed to be admitted to the larger unit. Initially John's family were unwilling for this admission, but when the aims of the admission were discussed and they were given information about the unit they agreed. The consultant psychiatrist tried to engage John in making a decision to come into the unit using accessible information prepared by the unit for people with intellectual disabilities. However, John was unable to make this decision and it was judged that he did not wish to come into the unit voluntarily so he was admitted under the Mental Health Act for assessment.

Once in the unit he settled quickly but remained suspicious of people and unable to sleep. At times at night he became agitated because of the people he believed were calling him names outside of his bedroom win-dow. There was considerable discussion within the multi-disciplinary meetings at the time of John's admission as to whether his behaviour was best understood as extreme anxiety or as schizophrenia. The history given by his family and other features of his current presentation lead to the diagnosis of schizophrenia and he was started on anti-psychotic medica-tion. The Clinical Psychologist associated with the mental health work of the community team met with the family to take a comprehensive history of John's mental ill-heath. It became clear that there had been two earlier periods where John had become distressed and suspicious although the degree of disruption had not been so great. It was also clear that when John returned from his residential college, around the time of his father's death, that the family had noticed that he was more isolated and less happy around other people that he had been before attending residential college. Although there were two clear previous episodes of significant distress the family regarded them as an exaggeration of the John they had become used to rather than distinct episodes. The psychologist was able to discuss with the family why they had not previously asked for help and it was clear they were a close family who believed they should be able to care for John and that John's mother was still very easily upset in talking about John's father's death. There were core beliefs within the family that they might lose John if they asked for help in respect to his behaviours. The psychologist offered regular appointments with John's mother to discuss these issues and John's mother accepted.

After the initial 28 day assessment period John was much more settled and was able to discuss his stay at the unit with the Consultant Psychiatrist and the nurse in charge of the unit. He was now feeling quite comfortable in the unit and was willing to extend his stay on a voluntary basis. The unit began to make plans with John's family for his discharge.

John agreed to a range of intellectual and communicative assessments while at the unit. He was also given the opportunity to talk to a key nurse on a regular basis. The intellectual assessment showed a discrepancy between John's verbal and performance scores, with his verbal IQ in the mid 50s and his performance IQ in the high 60s. This was confirmed in the communication assessments; whilst John had a good structured expressive communication he had some difficulties in receptive and more abstract use of language. Overall the clinical psychologist interpreted this profile as potentially leading to John being communicated with in a way that put him under considerable demand as he initially appeared to be able to express herself well and was very adept at visual spatial tasks. This hypothesis confirmed by the profile of an adaptive behaviour assessment which showed that Carol was highly competent in most community and self-help skill areas. The clinical psychologist also carried out assessments of John's ability to understand and discuss emotions and his ability to understand how his emotions related to his experience of his environment. John showed considerable difficulty in understanding emotional expression in him and others in using emotional language; he seemed to have little insight into how his emotions were related to the things that happened to him. The clinical psychologist considered that the types of therapy that might be offered to people with psychosis to help them reduce the distress they experience in response to their symptoms would be too complex. However, plans were made to build the development of emotional skills into the interactions used within the planned say service.

The clinical psychologist suggested a formulation of the psychosocial context of John's life that identified the early experience at school of bullying as occurring at a key time where many adolescents would be developing greater independence, this was seen as a particular stressor in the development of his subsequent mental ill-health. John's family wished him to gain a high level of independence and so encouraged him to attend mainstream school and to go to college after school. His return home coincided with his father's death and an increased level of anxiety within his family, this was clearly a further stressor. John's receptive language ability had always been overestimated by those around him in way that had added further demand into his life. The detailed history taken with John's family had identified a number of behaviours that seemed to predict an increase in his distress; in particular difficulty in getting to sleep and being awake in the very early hours of the morning had preceded previous more distressed periods.

An intervention plan was developed that included an early signs monitoring process that involved both John's family and John himself in monitoring his sleep pattern. With John's permission the information obtained from assessments was shared with John's family and incorporated into the work carried out with the family as part of helping them understand John's difficulties. The community nurses working with people with learning disabilities and mental ill-health arranged to maintain contact in the initial period after John's discharge and to be the point of contact if the early signs suggested a change in well-being. An outreach day service was commissioned to enable John to participate in other activities away from his family. The staff team employed to work with John received training from the Clinical Psychologist based upon the formulation with particular emphasis on his specific communication difficulties; they jointly developed communication strategies and further strategies and assessments that the team would use to determine how much and what structure of activity to offer to John.

# References

Allen, D. (1999) Mediator analysis: an overview of recent research on carers supporting people with intellectual disability and challenging behaviour. *Journal of Intellectual Disability Research*, **43**, 325–39.

Ball, T., Bush, A. and Emerson, E. (2004) *Psychological Interventions for Severely Challenging Behavious Shown by People with Learning Disabilities*. Leicester: The British Psychological Society.

Beail, N. (2003) What works for people with mental retardation? Critical commentary on cognitive-behavioral and psychodynamic psychotherapy research. *Mental Retardation*, **41**(6), 468–72.

Beail, N. and Warden, S. (1995) Sexual Abuse of Adults with Learning-Disabilities. *Journal of Intellectual Disability Research*, **39**, 382–7.

Beck, A., Daley, D., Hastings, R.P. and Stevenson, J. (2004) Mothers' expressed emotion towards children with and without intellectual disabilities. *Journal of Intellectual Disability Research*, **48**, 628–38.

Beck, A.T., Ward, C.H., Shaw, B.F. and Emery, G. (1979) *Cognitive Therapy of Depression*. New York: John Wiley and Sons, Inc.

Benson, B.A. (1994) Anger management training: a self-controlled programme for persons with mild mental retardation. In N. Bouras (ed.), *Mental Health in Mental*

*Retardation: recent advances and practices* (pp. 224–32). Cambridge: Cambridge University Press.

Benson, B.A., Rice, C.J. and Miranti, S.V. (1986) Effects of Anger Management-Training with Mentally-Retarded Adults in Group Treatment. *Journal of Consulting and Clinical Psychology*, **54**(5), 728–9.

Black, L. and Novaco, R.W. (1993) Treatment of anger with a developmentally handicapped man. In R.A. Wells and V.J. Geinnetti (eds), *Case Book of Brief Psychotherapies* (pp. 33–52). New York: Plenum.

Borthwick-Duffy, S.A. (1994) Epidemiology and prevalence of psychopathology in people with mental retardation. *Journal of Consulting and Clinical Psychology*, **62**, 17–27.

Braun, K.V., Yeargin-Allsopp, M. and Lollar, D. (2006) Factors associated with leisure activity among young adults with developmental disabilities. *Research in Developmental Disabilities*, **27**(5), 567–83.

Clark, R.E. and Samnaliev, M. (2005) Psychosocial treatment in the 21st century. *International Journal of Law and Psychiatry*, **28**(5), 532–44.

Cooper, S.-A. (1997) Psychiatry of elderly compared to younger adults with intellectual disabilities. *Journal of Applied Research in Intellectual Disabilities*, **10**(4), 303–11.

Cooper, S.-A. (2004) Mental Health. In E. Emerson, C. Hatton, T. Thompson and T.R. Parmenter (eds), *The International Handbook of Applied Research in Intellectual Disabilities* (pp. 407–21). Chichester: John Wiley and Sons, Ltd.

Cooper, S.A., Smiley, E., Morrison, J., Williamson, A. and Allan, L. (2007) Mental ill-health in adults with intellectual disabilities: prevalence and associated factors. *British Journal of Psychiatry*, **190**, 27–35.

Costello, H., Bouras, N. and Davis, H. (2007) The role of training in improving community care staff awareness of mental health problems in people with intellectual disabilities. *Journal of Applied Research in Intellectual Disabilities*, **20**, 228–35.

Cuthill, F.M., Espie, C.A. and Cooper, S.A. (2003) Development and psychometric properties of the Glasgow Depression Scale for people with a Learning Disability – Individual and carer supplement versions. *British Journal of Psychiatry*, **182**, 347–53.

Dagnan, D. (2004) Understanding challenging behaviour in older people; The development of the controllability beliefs scale. *Behavioural and Cognitive Psychotherapy*, **32**(4), 501–6.

Dagnan, D. (2007) Psychosocial interventions In N. Bouras and G. Holt (eds), *Psychiatric and Behavioural Disorders in Intellectual and Developmental Disabilities*. Cambridge: Cambridge University Press.

Dagnan, D. and Chadwick, P. (1997) Cognitive behaviour therapy for people with learning disabilities: assessment and intervention. In B.S. Kroese, D. Dagnan and K. Loumides (eds), *Cognitive Behaviour Therapy for People with Learning Disabilities* (pp. 110–23). London: Routledge.

Dagnan, D. and Jahoda, A. (2006) Cognitive-behavioural intervention for people with intellectual disability and anxiety disorders. *Journal of Applied Research in Intellectual Disabilities*, **19**(1), 91–7.

Dagnan, D. and Lindsay, W.R. (2004) Research issues in cognitive therapy. In E. Emerson, C. Hatton, T. Thompson and T.R. Parmenter (eds), *The International*

*Handbook of Applied Research in Intellectual Disabilities* (pp. 517–30). Brighton: John Wiley and Sons, Ltd.

Dagnan, D. and Sandhu, S. (1999) Social comparison, self-esteem and depression in people with intellectual disability. *Journal of Intellectual Disability Research*, **43**, 372–9.

Dagnan, D., Trower, P. and Smith, R. (1998) Care staff responses to people with learning disabilities and challenging behaviour: A cognitive-emotional analysis. *British Journal of Clinical Psychology*, **37**, 59–68.

Dagnan, D. and Waring, M. (2004) Linking stigma to psychological distress: Testing a social-cognitive model of the experience of people with intellectual disabilities. *Clinical Psychology and Psychotherapy*, **11**(4), 247–54.

Davey, G.C.L. (1992). Classical-Conditioning and the Acquisition of Human Fears and Phobias – a Review and Synthesis of the Literature. *Advances in Behaviour Research and Therapy*, **14**(1), 29–66.

Deb, S. (1997) Mental disorder in adults with mental retardation and epilepsy. *Comprehensive Psychiatry*, **38**(3), 179–84.

Department of Health (2000) The NHS Plan: a plan for investment, a plan for reform. In Department of Health (ed) (Vol. Cm 4818-I): Department of Health.

Department of Health (2001) The Mental Health Policy Implementation Guide: Departent of Health.

Department of Health (2006) Standards for Better Health: Department of Health.

Drake, R.E., Becker, D.R. and Bond, G.R. (2003) Recent research on vocational rehabilitation for persons with severe mental illness. *Current Opinion in Psychiatry*, **16**(4), 451–5.

Eaton, L.F. and Menolascino, F.J. (1982) Psychiatric-Disorders in the Mentally-Retarded - Types, Problems, and Challenges. *American Journal of Psychiatry*, **139**(10), 1297–1303.

Edelstein, T.M. and Glenwick, D.S. (2001) Direct-care workers' attributions of psychopathology in adults with mental retardation. *Mental Retardation*, **39**(5), 368–78.

Ellis, A. (1977) The basic clinical theory of rational emotive therapy. In A. Ellis and R. Grieger (eds), *Handbook of Rational-Emotive Therapy* (pp. 10–37). New York: Springer-Verlag.

Emerson, E., Graham, H. and Hatton, C. (2006) The measurement of poverty and socioeconomic position in research involving people with intellectual disability. In *International Review of Research in Mental Retardation, Vol 32* (pp. 77–108).

Findlay, W.M.L. and Lyons, E. (2001) Methodological issues in interviewing and using self-report questionnaires with people with mental retardation. *Psychological Assessment*, **13**, 319–35.

Foundation for People with Learning Disabilities (2004) *Green Light for Mental Health. How good are your mental health services for people with learning disabilities? A service improvement kit*.: Foundation for People with Learning Disabilities.

Green, C.W. and Reid, D.H. (1999) Reducing indices of unhappiness among individuals with profound multiple disabilities during therapeutic exercise routines. *Journal of Applied Behavior Analysis*, **32**(2), 137–47.

Green, C.W., Reid, D.H., Rollyson, J.H. and Passante, S.C. (2005) An enriched teaching program for reducing resistance and indices of unhappiness among individuals with profound multiple disabilities. *Journal of Applied Behavior Analysis*, **38**(2), 221–33.

Haddock, G., Lobban, F., Hatton, C. and Carson, R. (2004) Cognitive-behaviour therapy for people with psychosis and mild intellectual disabilities: A case series. *Clinical Psychology and Psychotherapy*, **11**(4), 282–98.

Hagopian, L.P., Crockett, J.L. and Keeney, K.M. (2001) Multicomponent treatment for blood-injury-injection phobia in a young man with mental retardation. *Research in Developmental Disabilities*, **22**(2), 141–9.

Harchik, A.E., Sherman, J.A. and Sheldon, J.B. (1992) The Use of Self-Management Procedures by People with Developmental-Disabilities – a Brief Review. *Research in Developmental Disabilities*, **13**(3), 211–27.

Hastings, R.P. (1997a) Measuring staff perceptions of challenging behaviour: the Challenging Behaviour Attributions Scale (CHABA). *Journal of Intellectual Disability Research*, **41**, 495–501.

Hastings, R.P. (1997b) Staff beliefs about the challenging behaviors of children and adults with mental retardation. *Clinical Psychology Review*, **17**(7), 775–90.

Hastings, R.P., Daley, D., Burns, C. and Beck, A. (2006) Maternal distress and expressed emotion: Cross-sectional and longitudinal relationships with behavior problems of children with intellectual disabilities. *American Journal on Mental Retardation*, **111**(1), 48–61.

Hatton, C., Haddock, G., Taylor, J.L., Coldwell, J., Crossley, R. and Peckham, N. (2005) The reliability and validity of general psychotic rating scales with people with mild and moderate intellectual disabilities: an empirical investigation. *Journal of Intellectual Disability Research*, **49**, 490–500.

Holburn, S. and Jacobson, J.W. (2006) Residential services research in the developmental disabilities sector. In *International Review of Research in Mental Retardation, Vol 32* (pp. 41–76).

Holt, G., Hardy, S. and Bouras, N. (2005) *Mental Health in learning Disabilities: A Training Resource*. Brighton: Pavilion Publishing.

Hopko, D.R., Lejuez, C.W., Ruggiero, K.J. and Eifert, G.H. (2003) Contemporary behavioral activation treatments for depression: Procedures, principles, and progress. *Clinical Psychology Review*, **23**(5), 699–717.

Jackson, H. (1983) Current trends in the treatment of phobias in autistic and mentally retarded persons. *Australia and New Zealand Journal of Developmental Disabilities*, **9**, 191–208.

Jackson, T.L. and Altman, R. (1996) Self-management of aggression in an adult male with mental retardation and severe behavior disorders. *Education and Training in Mental Retardation and Developmental Disabilities*, **31**(1), 55–65.

Jahoda, A., Trower, P., Pert, C. and Finn, D. (2001) Contingent reinforcement or defending the self? A review of evolving models of aggression in people with mild learning disabilities. *British Journal of Medical Psychology*, **74**, 305–21.

Kellett, S., Beail, N., Newman, D.W. and Frankish, P. (2003) Utility of the brief symptom inventory in the assessment of psychological distress. *Journal of Applied Research in Intellectual Disabilities*, **16**(2), 127–34.

Korotitsch, W.J. and Nelson-Gray, R.O. (1999) An overview of self-monitoring research in assessment and treatment. *Psychological Assessment*, **11**(4), 415–25.

Kushlick, A., Dagnan, D. and Trower, P. (1998) The Birthday Exercise. Introducing cognitive therapy techniques to staff working with people with learning disabilities and challenging behaviour. In K. Cigno and D. Bourne (eds), *Case Studies in Social Work: Cognitive-Behavioural Practice*. Aldershot: Ashgate Publishing Ltd.

Kushlick, A., Trower, P. and Dagnan, D. (1997) Applying cognitive behavioural approaches to the carers of people with learning disabilities. In B.S. Kroese, D. Dagnan and K. Loumides (eds), *Cognitive Therapy for People with Learning Disabilities*. London: Routledge.

Lemmon, V.A. and Mizes, J.S. (2002) Effectiveness of exposure therapy: A case study of post-traumatic stress disorder and mental retardation. *Cognitive and Behavioral Practice*, **9**, 317–23.

Lindsay, W.R. (1999) Cognitive therapy. *Psychologist*, **12**(5), 238–41.

Lindsay, W.R. (2005) Model underpinning treatment for sex offenders with mild intellectual disability: Current theories of sex offending. *Mental Retardation*, **43**(6), 428–41.

Lindsay, W.R., Allan, R., Parry, C., Macleod, F., Cottrell, J., Overend, H., *et al*. (2004) Anger and aggression in people with intellectual disabilities: Treatment and follow-up of consecutive referrals and a waiting list comparison. *Clinical Psychology and Psychotherapy*, **11**(4), 255–64.

Lindsay, W.R., Howells, L. and Pitcaithly, D. (1993) Cognitive Therapy for Depression with Individuals with Intellectual Disabilities. *British Journal of Medical Psychology*, **66**, 135–41.

Lindsay, W.R. and Michie, A.M. (1988) Adaptation of the Zung Self-Rating Anxiety Scale for People with a Mental Handicap. *Journal of Mental Deficiency Research*, **32**, 485–90.

Lindsay, W.R., Michie, A.M., Baty, F.J., Smith, A.H.W. and Miller, S. (1994) The Consistency of Reports About Feelings and Emotions from People with Intellectual Disability. *Journal of Intellectual Disability Research*, **38**, 61–6.

Lindsay, W.R., Olley, S., Baillie, N. and Smith, A.H.W. (1999) Treatment of adolescent sex offenders with intellectual disabilities. *Mental Retardation*, **37**, 201–11.

Lindsay, W.R., Steele, L., Smith, A.H.W., Quinn, K. and Allan, R. (2006) A community forensic intellectual disability service: Twelve year follow up of referrals, analysis of referral patterns and assessment of harm reduction. *Legal and Criminological Psychology*, **11**, 113–30.

Lindsay, W.R., Stenfert-Kroese, B. and Drew, P. (2005) Cognitive-behavioral approaches to depression in people with learning disabilities. In P. Sturmey (ed), *Mood Disorders and People with Mental Retardation*. New York: NADD Press.

Loumidis, K.S. and Hill, A. (1997) Training social problem-solving skill to reduce maladaptive behaviours in intellectual disability groups: The influence of individual difference factors. *Journal of Applied Research in Intellectual Disabilities*, **10**(3), 217–37.

Lowe, K., Felce, D., Perry, J., Baxter, H. and Jones, E. (1998) The characteristics and residential situations of people with severe intellectual disability and the most severe challenging behaviour in Wales. *Journal of Intellectual Disability Research*, **42**, 375–89.

Lund, J. (1985) The Prevalence of Psychiatric Morbidity in Mentally-Retarded Adults. *Acta Psychiatrica Scandinavica*, **72**(6), 563–70.

Lund, J. (1990) Mentally-Retarded Criminal Offenders in Denmark. *British Journal of Psychiatry*, **156**, 726–31.

Lunsky, Y. (2006) Individual differences in interpersonal relationships for persons with mental retardation. In *Mental Retardation, Personality, and Motivational Systems* (Vol. 31, pp. 117–61).

Martin, G., Costello, H., Leese, M., Slade, M., Bouras, N., Higgins, S., *et al.* (2005) An exploratory study of assertive community treatment for people with intellectual disability and psychiatric disorders: conceptual, clinical, and service issues. *Journal of Intellectual Disability Research*, **49**, 516–24.

Matson, J.L. (1982) Treating Obsessive-Compulsive Behavior in Mentally-Retarded Adults. *Behavior Modification*, **6**(4), 551–67.

Matson, J.L., Dettling, J. and Senatore, V. (1979) Treating depression of a mentally retarded adult. *British Journal of Mental Subnormality*, **26**, 86–9.

Matson, J.L., Senatore, V., Kazdin, A.E. and Helsel, W.T. (1983) Verbal Behaviors in Depressed and Nondepressed Mentally-Retarded Persons. *Applied Research in Mental Retardation*, **4**(1), 79–83.

McDougle, C.J., Kresch, L.E., Goodman, W.K., Naylor, S.T., Volkmar, F.R., Cohen, D.J., *et al.* (1995) A Case-Controlled Study of Repetitive Thoughts and Behavior in Adults with Autistic Disorder and Obsessive-Compulsive Disorder. *American Journal of Psychiatry*, **152**(5), 772–7.

Meichenbaum, D. (1977) *Cognitive Behavior Modification: An Integrative Approach.* New York: Plenum.

Meins, W. (1995) Symptoms of Major Depression in Mentally-Retarded Adults. *Journal of Intellectual Disability Research*, **39**, 41–5.

Mindham, J. and Espie, C.A. (2003) Glasgow Anxiety Scale for people with an Intellectual Disability (GAS-ID): development and psychometric properties of a new measure for use with people with mild intellectual disability. *Journal of Intellectual Disability Research*, **47**, 22–30.

Mitchell, G. and Hastings, R.P. (1998) Learning disability care staffs emotional reactions to aggressive challenging behaviours: Development of a measurement tool. *British Journal of Clinical Psychology*, **37**, 441–9.

Moss, S., Ibbotson, B., Prosser, H., Goldberg, D., Patel, P. and Simpson, N. (1997) Validity of the PAS-ADD for detecting psychiatric symptoms in adults with learning disability (mental retardation). *Social Psychiatry and Psychiatric Epidemiology*, **32**(6), 344–54.

Munden, A.C. and Perry, D.W. (2002) *Symptoms of Depression in People with Learning Disabilities: Knowledge of Various Members of the Multidisciplinary Team Involved in the Care and Assessment of Challenging Behaviour* (Vol. 6, pp. 13–22).

National Institute for Clinical Excellence (2002) *Schizophrenia: core interventions in the treatment and management of schizophrenia in primary and secondary care. Clinical Guideline 1.* London: NICE.

Newman, C. and Adams, K. (2004) Dog done good: managing dog phobia in a teenage boy with a learning disability. *British Journal of Learning Disabilities*, **32**, 35–48.

Newman, D.W. and Beail, N. (2005) An analysis of assimilation during psychotherapy with people who have mental retardation. *American Journal on Mental Retardation*, **110**, 359–65.

Nezu, C.M., Nezu, A.M., Rothenberg, J.L., Dellicarpini, L. and Groag, I. (1995) Depression in Adults with Mild Mental-Retardation – Are Cognitive Variables Involved. *Cognitive Therapy and Research*, **19**(2), 227–39.

Novaco, R.W. (1977) *Anger Control: the development and evaluation of an experimental treatment.* Lexicon: Heath.

O'Dwyer, J.M. (1997) Schizophrenia in people wiht learning disability: the role of pregnancy and birth complications *Journal of Intellectual Disability Research*, **41**, 238–51.

Oliver, P.C., Piachaud, J., Tyrer, P., Regan, A., Dack, M., Alexander, R., *et al.* (2005) Randomized controlled trial of assertive community treatment in intellectual disability: the TACTILD study. *Journal of Intellectual Disability Research*, **49**, 507–15.

Paclawskyj, T.R., Kurtz, P.F. and O'Connor, J.T. (2004) Functional assessment of problem behaviors in adults with mental retardation. *Behavior Modification*, **28**(5), 649–67.

Patel, P., Goldberg, D. and Moss, S. (1993) Psychiatric Morbidity in Older-People with Moderate and Severe Learning-Disability .2. the Prevalence Study. *British Journal of Psychiatry*, **163**, 481–91.

Payne, R. and Jahoda, A. (2004) The Glasgow social self-efficacy scale - A new scale for measuring social self-efficacy in people with intellectual disability. *Clinical Psychology and Psychotherapy*, **11**(4), 265–74.

Pharoah, F., Mari, J., Rathbone, J. and Wong, W. (2006) Family intervention for schizophrenia, *Cochrane Database of Systematic Reviews*.

Poindexter, A.R. (2006) Diagnosis of depression in people with developmental disabilities: Progress and problems. In *International Review of Research in Mental Retardation, Vol 32* (pp. 261–81).

Prosser, H., Moss, S.C., Costello, H., Simpson, N., Patel, P. and Rowe, S. (1998) Reliability and validity of the mini PAS-ADD for assessing psychiatric disorders in adults with intellectual disability. *Journal of Intellectual Disability Research*, **42**, 264–72.

Prout, H.T. and Schaefer, B.M. (1985) Self-Reports of Depression by Community-Based Mildly Mentally-Retarded Adults. *American Journal of Mental Deficiency*, **90**(2), 220–2.

Quigley, A., Murray, G.C., McKenzie, K. and Elliot, G. (2001) *Staff Knowledge about Symptoms of Mental Health Problems in People with Learning Disabilities* (Vol. 5, pp. 235–44).

Rose, J. (1996) Anger management: A group treatment program for people with mental retardation. *Journal of Developmental and Physical Disabilities*, **8**(2), 133–49.

Rose, J., West, C. and Clifford, D. (2000) Group interventions for anger in people with intellectual disabilities. *Research in Developmental Disabilities*, **21**(3), 171–81.

Rush, K.S., Bowman, L.G., Eidman, S.L., Toole, L.M. and Mortenson, B.P. (2004) Assessing psychopathology in individuals with developmental disabilities. *Behavior Modification*, **28**(5), 621–37.

Rutgers, A.H., Bakermans-Kranenburg, M.J., van Ijzendoorn, M.H. and van Berckelaer-Onnes, I.A. (2004) Autism and attachment: a meta-analytic review. *Journal of Child Psychology and Psychiatry*, **45**(6), 1123–34.

Sequeira, H. and Hollins, S. (2003) Clinical effects of sexual abuse on people with learning disability – Critical literature review. *British Journal of Psychiatry*, **182**, 13–19.

Shakespeare, T. and Watson, N. (1997) Defending the social model. *Disability and Society*, **12**(2), 293–300.

Sinason, V. (1992) *Mental Handicap and the Human Condition*. London: Free Association Books.

Smith, K., Webber, L., Graffam, J. and Wilson, C. (2004) Employment and intellectual disability: Achieving successful employment outcomes. In *International Review of Research in Mental Retardation, Vol. 29* (pp. 261–89).

Sovner, R. and Hurley, A.D. (1982) Diagnosing depression in the mentally retarded. *Psychiatric Aspects of Mental Retardation Newsletter*, **1**, 1–4.

Sturmey, P. (2004) Cognitive therapy with people with intellectual disabilities: A selective review and critique. *Clinical Psychology and Psychotherapy*, **11**(4), 222–32.

Sturmey, P. (2006) On some recent claims for the efficacy of cognitive therapy for people with intellectual disabilities. *Journal of Applied Research in Intellectual Disabilities*, **19**(1), 109–17.

Sturmey, P., Newton, J.T., Cowley, A., Bouras, N. and Holt, G. (2005) The PAS-ADD Checklist: independent replication of its psychometric properties in a community sample. *British Journal of Psychiatry*, **186**, 319–23.

Taylor, J.L. and Hatton, C. (2004) Measurement of psychiatric symptoms and challenging behaviour in a whole district population of adults with intellectual disabilities (ID) in England. *Journal of Intellectual Disability Research*, **48**, 302.

Taylor, J.L., Novaco, R.W., Gillmer, B. and Thorne, I. (2002) Cognitive-behavioural treatment of anger intensity among offenders with intellectual disabilities. *Journal of Applied Research in Intellectual Disabilities*, **15**(2), 151–65.

Thomas, C. (2004) How is disability understood? An examination of sociological approaches. *Disability and Society*, **19**(6), 569–83.

Toole, L.M., Bowman, L.G., Thomason, J.L., Hagopian, L.P. and Rush, K.S. (2003) Observed increases in positive affect during behavioral treatment. *Behavioral Interventions*, **18**(1), 35–42.

Weigel, L., Langdon, P. E., Collins, S. and O'Brien, Y. (2006) Challenging behaviour and learning disabilities: The relationship between expressed emotion and staff attributions. *British Journal of Clinical Psychology*, **45**, 205–16.

Whitaker, S. and Read, S. (2006) The prevalence of psychiatric disorders among people with intellectual disabilities: An analysis of the literature. *Journal of Applied Research in Intellectual Disabilities*, **19**(4), 330–45.

Whitman, T.L. (1990) Self-regulation and mental-retardation. *American Journal on Mental Retardation*, **94**(4), 347–62.

Willner, P. (2005) The effectiveness of psychotherapeutic interventions for people with learning disabilities: a critical overview. *Journal of Intellectual Disability Research*, **49**, 73–85.

Xenitidis, K., Thornicroft, G., Leese, M., Slade, M., Fotiadou, M., Philp, H., *et al.* (2000) Reliability and validity of the CANDID - a needs assessment instrument for adults with learning disabilities and mental health problems. *British Journal of Psychiatry*, **176**, 473–8.

# Chapter 16

# WORKING WITH PEOPLE WITH AUTISM

Jo Bromley, Elizabeth Crabtree, Christine Mellor and Mary Delaney

## INTRODUCTION

The reported prevalence rates of Autistic Spectrum Disorders (ASD) have risen dramatically over the last few decades. The reason for this increase is not fully clear but is likely to be due in part to increased recognition by parents and professionals, improvements in diagnostic services and a greater understanding of the range of symptoms that would be included within diagnostic assessments. Current prevalence rates suggest 1 in 100 people will have a broad range of presentations across the Autistic Spectrum (Baird *et al.* 2006).

Initial research indicated that 70% of children with ASD had associated Learning Difficulties (Rutter and Schopler 1987) although it is now believed that 75% of people with ASD have IQ within the normal range (MRC 2001). However the co-morbidity of learning disability and ASD is high (Emerson and Hatton 2007) and as such, whilst working with children and young people with learning disabilities, you will find yourself working with someone who has a diagnosis of autism.

## DEFINITIONS

Childhood Autism was originally described by Leo Kanner in America in the 1940s although other, less systematic accounts can be seen throughout the literature before this time.

*Clinical Psychology and People with Intellectual Disabilities*, Second Edition. Edited by Eric Emerson, Chris Hatton, Kate Dickson, Rupa Gone, Amanda Caine and Jo Bromley.
© 2012 John Wiley & Sons, Ltd. Published 2012 by John Wiley & Sons, Ltd.

Kanner identified a group of children who had difficulties with social interaction and communication and who had a need to maintain sameness in their environment and interactions (Kanner 1943). He also identified that these children had difficulties with the development of their play skills and he reported that their emerging skills lacked the level of creativity and imagination seen in typically developing children. Kanner used the term 'Early Infantile Autism' to describe these children.

At around the same time, Hans Asperger also described a group of children who had similar difficulties in the areas of social communication, obsessional interests and a need for routine and sameness (Asperger 1944). He reported that these children were also clumsy but that they did not have any obvious cognitive or language difficulties, being of average, or above average, intelligence. Asperger identified these children as having 'autistic psychopathology'.

The terms Childhood Autism and Asperger's Syndrome have subsequently been used to identify children (and adults) with a range of difficulties in the areas of social interaction, social communication and imagination/flexible thinking. This cluster of difficulties has been referred to as the 'triad of impairment' (Wing and Gould 1979). In addition to this triad of difficulties, children and adults may display repetitive behaviours, have a need for routine/sameness and have difficulties in processing sensory information.

Individuals will vary greatly in how they are affected by autism and each person will have particular strengths as well as difficulties that are caused by their autistic thinking styles and behavioural patterns. However, all individuals who are diagnosed with an Autistic Spectrum Disorder will have core difficulties within the triad and these will impact on their ability to link into the world around them.

Formal diagnostic descriptions of Autistic Spectrum Disorders are listed in DSM IV (American Psychiatric Association 1994) and ICD 10 (World Health Organisation 1993). The range of diagnoses considered includes: Autism, Asperger's Syndrome and Pervasive Developmental Disorder. There is debate regarding whether the diagnoses defined within these manuals are discrete disorders and it is more widely viewed that the range of difficulties presented fall within a spectrum of difficulties. Wing and Gould (1979) introduced the term 'Autistic Spectrum Disorders' (ASD) in order to encapsulate the wide variety of behavioural presentation that occurs across the triad of impairment. The view of a spectrum can help with understanding the range of difficulties experienced by people with ASD but can lead to a view that some forms of autism (e.g. classical autism) are more severe than others (such as Asperger's Syndrome). It is important to recognise that the impact of having ASD can vary significantly and underlying impairments may result in major difficulties for individuals that cannot be wholly mediated by greater cognitive ability. Debates over name continue as some people with autism, would also much rather the term 'Autistic Spectrum Condition' was used as they feel that 'disorder' has unnecessarily negative connotations. Understandably and more accurately; they would prefer the autistic thinking style to be acknowledged as simply being 'different' and celebrated for that difference.

## CAUSES OF AUTISM

At present, a single, specific cause for Autism has not been identified. More recently, it has been proposed that there is not a single cause of autism but that ASD is a complex disorder with a range of core difficulties that may have distinct, and differing, causes (Happé and Ronald 2008).

Early theories of Autism focussed on the parent-child relationship. Kanner (1949) proposed that children developed Autism as a result of lack of parental warmth and this was further developed by Bettleheim (1963) who suggested that the mothers of children with Autism were cold, distant and rejecting. These theories of 'refrigerator mothers' lead to parents of children with Autism feeling guilty and blamed but such theories have now been soundly discredited.

Research has suggested that pre-birth complications may increase the likelihood of children developing ASD (Deykin and MacMahon 1980; Glasson et al. 2004). The causal nature of this relationship is not clear however and other research suggests that, while pregnancy complications are common in women whose children are later diagnosed with ASD, this may result from the foetus already having genetic difficulties rather than the complications causing problems for the foetus. (Zwaigenbaum 2002).

More extensive research indicates that individuals with ASD show some differences in brain structure and development which may account for the range of difficulties that they experience (Courchesne et al. 2001; Sparkes et al. 2002; Acosta and Pearl 2004). There is no single primary structure or pathway identified in the literature but a number of different sites within the brain have been implicated (e.g. amygdala, orbito-frontal cortex, medial frontal cortex) and research is ongoing.

Running parallel to the research on brain function is research into genetic factors. Again, no single gene has been identified as responsible for Autism but a number of genes appear to be implicated in children and adults with ASD (Muhle et al. 2004). This is strengthened by clinical observation which highlights that many families appear to have family histories of ASD or other associated difficulties (e.g. speech and language impairment, dyspraxia). It is known that a number of individuals with other genetic syndromes also have an increased likelihood of having an Autistic Spectrum Disorder (e.g. Tuberous Sclerosis, Fragile X, Congenital Rubella Syndrome and untreated Phenylketonuria).

Wakefield (1998) suggested a link between Autism and MMR immunisations. This research led to much public debate but the article was fully retracted by The Lancet in February 2010. A population study of over 30,000 children in Japan (Honda *et al*. 2005) looked at the incidence of Autism following the withdrawal of MMR as a consequence of concerns of a link to meningitis. The incidence of ASD continued to rise in line with countries where MMR was still routinely given to children suggesting that MMR vaccination was not a causal factor in increased rates of ASD.

## PSYCHOLOGICAL THEORIES OF AUTISM

There are three main cognitive theories of Autism that dominate the literature: Theory of Mind Deficit, Executive Dysfunction and Weak Central Coherence (Rajendran and Mitchell 2007).

### Theory of Mind

'Theory of mind' is the ability to reflect on one's own, and other's mental states minds and allows an individual to read the intentions of others. It was proposed that people with Autism lack this ability and as such struggle to understand the thoughts and intentions of others. Various tests of theory of mind have been invented; the most well known of which is probably the 'Sally Anne' test. The interviewer animates two dolls; 'Sally' and 'Anne'. Anne has a marble that she puts in her basket. She then leaves the room and Sally moves the marble and puts it in a box. The interviewer asks the interviewee where Anne will look for her marble. To answer correctly, the interviewee has to be able to acknowledge that they have seen Sally move the marble but 'Anne' did not. Therefore Anne will look for the marble in the basket because that is where she left it. If the interviewee cannot put themselves in Anne's shoes they will say that she will look in the box because that is where they know it to be.

'Neuro-typical' children (children without ASD) have the ability to track what others are thinking by the age of four years (Wellman, Cross and Watson 2001), (Wimmer, and Perner 1983). When using a test of Theory of Mind, based on that developed by Wimmer and Perner, with a group of children with ASD, Baron Cohen *et al*. (1985) found that 80% of these children were unable to succeed at the task leading him to conclude that people with ASD had a deficit in this area. However, 20% of the group were able to complete the task and as such, Baron-Cohen later adapted his theory to suggest that this was an area of delay rather than deficit in people with ASD (Baron-Cohen 1989). Further research has focussed on using more difficult theory of mind tests but again results have not always been conclusive with some researchers showing larger numbers of people with ASD being able to infer the states of minds of others (Bowler 1992).

As a result of differing findings from the Wimmer and Perner tests, further tasks have been developed to assess the ability to infer states of mind from contextual information focussing on language and face processing in ASD, e.g. The Strange Stories test (Happe 1994), The Eyes Task (Baron-Cohen *et al*. 1997) which again identify that people with ASD may have difficulties identifying the thoughts and emotions of others.

## Executive Dysfunction

The Executive Dysfunction theory of Autism stemmed from research into Specific Brain Injury that hypothesised similar symptom presentation between people with Autism and those experiencing Dysexecutive Syndrome as a result of an Acquired Brain Injury (Ozonoff *et al*. 1991). 'Executive function' refers to the process underlying control of actions, namely attentional control, initiation, planning, inhibition of unwanted responses, flexibility of thought and action and decision making; all known to be areas of difficulty for people with autism.

Research findings have provided mixed support to the Executive Dysfunction theory of ASD; ranging from 96% of people with ASD showing deficits in Executive Function (Ozonoff *et al*. 1991) to only 50% (Pellicano *et al*. 2006). Research authors have also questioned the uniqueness of Executive Dysfunction to ASD, finding similar difficulties in groups of individuals with other psychiatric disorder including ADHD, OCD, Tourette Syndrome and Schizophrenia (Ozonoff and Jensen 1999).

## Weak Central Coherence Theory

Central coherence explains the ability to integrate information into context and extract overall meaning from experiences and situations. For example, the person may find it difficult to integrate someone saying 'I'm sorry'; with a facial expression that indicates otherwise; in the context of the person complaining about something they find unacceptable. The theory of weak central coherence addresses the trait of attention to detail that is found in people with ASD and hypothesises that people with ASD process information by focussing on component parts as opposed to the whole picture (Frith 1989). Tests used to identify central coherence include the 'Children's Embedded Figures Test' (Witkin *et al*. 1971) where researchers have found that people with ASD perform better than matched controls suggesting that they were able to focus on component parts of the test without being distracted by the global whole (Shah and Frith 1993). Again, researchers have found conflicting results when reviewing theories of central coherence and it is not considered to explain all difficulties experienced by people with ASD (Happe and Frith 2006).

In summary, the three main cognitive theories of Autism account for a number of the difficulties experienced by people with ASD but no single theory is able to account for the range of problems experienced. It is likely that no one theory will ever explain such a complex disorder (Ozonoff *et al*. 1991) but that a multiple-deficit account, drawing on a number of different theories will help understand the experiences of people on the Autistic Spectrum.

In addition to the peer reviewed literature, there are numerous first-hand accounts of ASD, which provide a valuable insight into the experiences of those with a diagnosis of ASD and propose alternative views on the underlying strengths and deficits experienced by people with ASD (Lawson 2000; Williams 1996; Grandin 2006). This literature tends to better convey the more positive aspects of the autistic experience and the strengths of the autistic thinking style (http://www.wrongplanet.net/postt40354.html; http://autism.about.com/od/postiveaspectsofautism/Postive_Aspects_of_Autism.htm).

## ASSESSMENT AND DIAGNOSIS

The assessment process is often quite complex and sometimes families and individuals with autism are less interested in the eventual diagnosis at the end of assessment than in the process itself. Some people find the end diagnosis reassuring; having always felt 'different'. Unfortunately, some find that only a formal diagnosis will help them gain access to appropriate services and support. However, others take the view that the main aim of an assessment should be to give a better understanding of an individual's profile; their strengths and difficulties and the type of support they might need and that this, rather than a diagnosis per se, that needs to drive the assessment.

The development of good practice guidelines and tools to aid diagnosis has tended to focus on children and adolescents but much of the good practice can be extrapolated to adult settings. The National Autism Plan for Children (NAP-C; NIASA 2003), highlights a code of good practice for assessment in children. It suggests that assessment should be multi-disciplinary and should involve assessment by Child Psychiatrists/Community Paediatrician, Clinical Psychologists, Speech and Language

Therapists and Educational Psychologists. It sets targets for the length of an assessment process and gives families a guideline as to what an assessment should look like. It notes, for example, that as part of the process there should be:

- a medical overview – screenings as necessary;
- a developmental history;
- observations of the child across settings;
- use of semi structured interviews (such as the Autism Diagnostic Interview or the Autism Diagnostic Observation Schedule – see below);
- an assessment of communication.

and in some cases; a cognitive assessment.

The developmental history is essential to an assessment of Autism as it should highlight that problems with social communication and inflexibility have existed from the child being an infant or from the adult being a child. By its nature; autism takes a developmental path; therefore even with very young children; there may be areas of development that can be identified as being unusual. Filipek *et al.* (1999) identified a number of Red Flags for Autism and these can be used as a basis for questioning parents of young children who are being seen for assessment (see Table 16.1).

Questions also need to ascertain that the difficulties are pervasive across settings. For example; as children get older; information about social skills can be gained by asking about their relationships at nursery and at school. Is it just parents or do teachers and support workers show concern about the child and what exactly have they noticed that they feel is different?

Taking a developmental history will constitute at least two sessions as you will need to be absolutely sure that you have exact details about an individual's:

- social development;
- communication style;
- special interests;
- repetitive behaviours;
- ability to be flexible (in actions and thought);
- sensory issues;
- additional difficulties with learning;
- additional difficulties with coordination;
- strengths and motivators.

How does the individual fill their time? What happens when routines are changed? When there is a different route home from school or if they have to go and see the dentist rather than returning home as usual? What motivates the individual? What is the parent/carers experience of having a

**Table16.1** Filipek's red flags for autism.

*Key issues in early infant development*

- No big smiles or other warm, joyful expressions by six months or thereafter.
- No back-and-forth sharing of sounds, smiles, or other facial expressions by nine months or thereafter.
- No babbling by 12 months.
- No back-and-forth gestures, such as pointing, showing, reaching, or waving by 12 months.
- No words by 16 months.
- No two-word meaningful phrases (without imitating or repeating) by 24 months.
- Any loss of speech or babbling or social skills at any age.

*Other indicators that may cause concern*

- The child does not respond to his/her name.
- The child cannot explain what he/she wants.
- The child's language skills are slow to develop or speech is delayed.
- The child doesn't follow directions.
- At times, the child seems to be deaf.
- The child seems to hear sometimes, but not other times.
- The child doesn't point or wave 'bye-bye.'
- The child used to say a few words or babble, but now he/she doesn't.
- The child throws intense or violent tantrums.
- The child has odd movement patterns.
- The child is overly active, uncooperative, or resistant.
- The child doesn't know how to play with toys.
- The child doesn't smile when smiled at.
- The child has poor eye contact.
- The child gets 'stuck' doing the same things over and over and can't move on to other things.
- The child seems to prefer to play alone.
- The child gets things for him/herself only.
- The child is very independent for his/her age.
- The child does things 'early' compared to other children.
- The child seems to be in his/her 'own world.'
- The child seems to tune people out.
- The child is not interested in other children.
- The child walks on his/her toes.
- The child shows unusual attachments to toys, objects, or schedules (i.e., always holding a string or having to put socks on before pants).
- Child spends a lot of time lining things up or putting things in a certain order.

conversation with their child? Even for children without formal language; parents can often give evidence of conversational 'babble'; of turn taking in making noise. For individuals who can speak; ask parents/carers how it feels to have a conversation with them. Does it feel comfortable? Is there the normal to and fro quality of speech and is the person able to integrate gesture into conversation? Many people with autism find this kind of verbal/non verbal integration difficult. Some individuals can speak eloquently about topics they enjoy but do not converse about other things; others will talk in monologues leaving their conversational partner little room to join them. Carers may speak about conversations being 'one sided' and rather rigid and note that their individuals fails to pick up on their normal social cues that they need to end the conversation or that they want to inject a comment into it. How does the person express their emotions? What do they do well?

As with any assessment you will need to consider contextual factors such as the environment in which the child is living; their school experiences; any trauma or past history of neglect or abuse; factors which may provide alternative explanations to behaviours that may be puzzling or unusual. One must always consider differential diagnoses such as Specific Language Impairments, Attachment Difficulties or Developmental Co-ordination Difficulties and consider why these might be ruled out and why ASD is a better fit.

A good developmental history is often easier to obtain for children as they are usually still living with their parents who can give a fairly good account of the child's early years. However, it can be more complicated when assessing an adult as they may no longer have relatives who can remember their early years. In this instance; it is important to try and get hold of medical records to look for that developmental trajectory of difficulties. It is also helpful to talk to friends and carers who know the individual now to get a sense of current functioning. With adults, one can ask more questions about how social relationships have evolved; how the person has managed relationships with prospective partners; how they individual functions at work. Rather than discuss play, one can think about current leisure activities and interests and how the person pursues those. As we get older we have more choice over how and what we do and this can in itself be revealing as a person who finds social contact stressful may avoid that contact more easily and pursue gaming activities on the internet or more solitary leisure pursuits.

It is undoubtedly useful to be aware of semi structured interviews such as the Diagnostic Interview for Social Communication DisOrders (DISCO; Wing *et al.* 1999, 2002) or the Autism Diagnostic Interview (ADI-R); (Rutter *et al.* 2003) both of which can be used to guide good history taking. Both these tools require further training in administration and can be lengthy to administer but both ensure that detailed, relevant information about current and past functioning is gathered from carers who know the individual well.

Whilst vital, of course; the developmental history is not the whole picture and it is also important to undertake observation of the individual under assessment in a variety of settings. Most people can be seen in clinic and whenever appropriate it is helpful to interview the individual directly who is being assessed to gain first hand feedback about their social communication skills as well as gather information about interests, etc. However, it is also helpful to observe individuals at home and with children and young adults; to see them at nursery, school or college. This provides additional information regarding the individual's social communication skills in a much more naturalistic way. Observations should include the individual's responses to those around them; how much do they initiate contact and how responsive are they when others make social overtures? It is important to note whether people respond to their name, whether they understand whole group instructions as being relevant to themselves and how they act in both structured and unstructured times within their everyday settings. Observers may want to watch for the individual showing sensory sensitivities, obsessions and rituals and consider how easily they follows social cues in the environment (e.g. in a school; if everyone lines up to go outside do they understand they need to line up too?). If possible, it can be helpful to have a sense of others' experiences of the individual and their views of any difficulties being experienced. For a child in school, for example, on might ask a teacher to complete a questionnaire (e.g. the Australian Scale for Asperger's Syndrome; Attwood and Garnett 1995; Attwood 2002).

The ADOS (Autism Diagnostic Observation Schedule Lord *et al.* 1999, 2000) is a semi structured interactive measure that can be used with children or adults which is designed to draw out the kinds of difficulties in social communication that one sees in ASD. It again requires further training but can be a useful guide to observation and assessment. For adults; it takes the form of a semi structured interview but for children it is more like a play session. It looks, for example, at how children develop their own play themes as well as how they interact to other's themes and ideas in their play (e.g. Will they let the therapist join the play for example, or do they have set repetitive ideas which the therapist has to join in with? Is the play a verbatim copy of a favourite TV show or is it self generated?).

## INTERVIEWING PEOPLE WITH ASD

Whether during assessment or intervention, you will need to interview the person with social communication difficulties. The principles that apply to interviewing people with intellectual disabilities also apply to interviewing people with autism, however there are some additional factors that relate to Autism which you might want to consider. For example, it is important to check how 'Autism friendly' your environment is (http://www.nas.org.uk/nas/jsp/polopoly.jsp?d=2004). Pay attention to sensory issues and try to have an environment that is as distraction free as possible to ensure that the individual has the best chance of understanding the session.

Make sure that you have the person's attention before asking questions. They may have difficulty filtering out stimuli from their environment and may not hear what you are saying. Be consistent with the words you use and ensure that body language is clear. Hold a facial expression that is congruent with your verbal communication and try and avoid ambiguity, sarcasm or irony. It may take longer for the individual with ASD to process verbal information so adjust the assessment/intervention to their speed. It may be that the individual has difficulties with physical proximity or eye contact that need to be taken into account when planning sessions.

The social interaction inherent in Clinical Psychology work may be stressful and anxiety provoking for people with ASD. It may be necessary to provide sessions with breaks or to have sessions that are much shorter in length and it is helpful to use a visual timetable to let clients know what the session will be about.

## INTERVENTIONS AND ASD – GENERAL PRINCIPLES

People with ASD have a range of difficulties within the 'triad of impairment' and the strengths and challenges that individual experiences will vary widely. Moreover, while individuals vary widely between each other, the presentation of each individual also changes over time so it is necessary to be flexible with approaches to assessment and intervention. No single intervention works for all people with ASD and no single intervention will work consistently with one individual over time. There are, however, a number of general principles which are important to consider in intervention:

- View difficulties through an 'autism lens'; identify the individual, autism specific reasons for behaviour/difficulties. Autism specific or sensitive interventions are much more likely to be successful than those that remain unadapted.
- Encompass the individual's strengths and skills, utilising routines and special interests/obsessions where appropriate.
- Take account of possible communication difficulties and include the use of visual support whenever necessary.
- Question the social norms. Why does something have to happen in a certain way? Is there scope to change an environment or an experience so it fits better with the person with autism? It doesn't have to be down to the person with ASD to make all the change.
- Take your time; make small changes that are less likely to phase the person with ASD and give them time to accommodate to these changes

**Table 16.2** SPELL – the NAS framework for intervention.

**Structure** – Make the world more predictable and accessible.

**Positive** – Assessment and interventions should account for the strengths, interests and abilities of people with ASD in order to help develop potential whilst providing an appropriate level of support based on an accurate assessment of need.

**Empathy** – It is necessary to explore the issues from the perspective of the individual with ASD.

**Low Arousal** – Environments should be managed to provide calm and ordered experiences for individuals that reduces anxiety and encourages attention.

**Links** – links need to be made across aspects of an individual's life to ensure communication between support networks and increase consistency and communication.

e.g. with eating difficulites; if someone has a very restricted diet; try and introduce very similar foods first; just change the type of pasta someone eats for example; rather than try and introduce a whole new range of food (Legge 2002).

- Utilise the skills, knowledge and expertise of the individual themselves, their parents, carers and other professionals who know that person well. Evidence suggests that working in a multiagency way, in partnership with the person with autism and their carers, produces more accurate diagnoses and more successful interventions (National Autism Plan for Children 2003).
- Promote generalisation; a significant issue for children and adults with ASD is difficulty generalising skills across a range of settings. Ensure that strategies are in place to help the individual to transfer skills across environments.
- Provide information regarding ASD and support organisations for individuals and their families, e.g. information about the National Autistic Society (NAS); Contact a Family, etc.
- Ensure all staff and carers supporting people with ASD have appropriate training on autism so they too can better understand the individual.
- Consider the NAS framework (SPELL) when organising clinical work (see Table 16.2).

## BEHAVIOURAL INTERVENTIONS

As for people with intellectual disabilities who do not have autism; behaviour theory is key to providing evidence based interventions for those people who do have Autism (Howlin and Rutter 1987). The most common reason for referral to a clinical psychologist is likely to be related to a person exhibiting some kind of challenging or problematic behaviour. Whether it be feeding, sleeping or self injury; the key principles remain the same (see Chapter 11 on behavioural interventions). In essence, one needs to think about the STAR approach Settings, Triggers, Action and Response (STAR; Zarkowska and Clements 1994 – see Clements and Zarkowska 2000). What are the environmental or wider contextual factors in which this behaviour is occurring (Setting)? What exactly seems to trigger the behaviour (Trigger)? What does the person do (Action)? What is the response to the behaviour (Response)? This format helps the clinician to think through the possible function of the challenging behaviour and in doing so, find solutions for change. Rather than a linear ABC model; it can be drawn out as a STAR shape to help parents or carers understand that behaviours do not happen out of the blue but are part of a larger system of interactions.

Often, with people with autism; the setting events and context to the behaviour is key. With carers and parents, we often talk about putting on autism glasses and imagining for a moment how the world felt just before a difficult-to manage behaviour occurred. Bearing in mind that between 45% and 95% of people with ASD are thought to have some sensory sensitivities (see Ben-Sasson *et al.* 2009 for overview); the person's reaction to their sensory environment is a good example of how setting might influence behaviour (see also Williams 1996; Holliday-Willey 1999).

Sensory sensitivities can take different forms:

- **Visual sensitivity** – individuals may become very interested and engaged in visual information, patterns and shapes, e.g. the light coming through the trees, the pattern of the carpet. They may also have a dislike of certain visual information, e.g. fluorescent lights, bright lights
- **Auditory sensitivity** – Individuals can either be over-sensitive to certain sounds or under sensitive to noise. For example, it may be that the sound of the vacuum cleaner or the traffic outside is unbearable and individuals with ASD are frequently observed to place their hands over their ears to block out the noise. Equally, they may be fascinated by certain sounds and want these played repeatedly.
- **Pain** – for some individuals with ASD they appear to have a high pain threshold and there are reports of people with extremely painful injuries of which they seem unaware. These reports are complicated however, in that it may be difficult for the individual to demonstrate the social behaviour that usually accompanies pain. Contrastingly, some individuals seem to have heightened pain experiences and may find it painful to have their hair cut/brushed.
- **Taste** – Individuals report both heightened and lowered senses of taste and this may well relate to some of the difficulties with feeding detailed above.

- **Smell** – Again, sense of smell can be affected and individuals with ASD indicate that many smells may become overpowering – this can have an impact on areas such as toilet training and feeding.

By recognising, for example, that someone has sensory sensitivities; one might think about a supermarket differently. How many senses might be assaulted by the strong smells, bright overhead lights, background 'muzak' and smells of fresh bread? Thinking about the wider context, one can see how the person with autism might feel quickly overwhelmed in a supermarket and how a seemingly innocuous event (e.g. being pushed by someone else's trolley) might lead to a behavioural outburst. Thinking about the situation in these terms can help parents, carers and individuals themselves to come up with ideas for managing the original anxiety and sensory overload – does it help to wear glasses? Your own MP3 player with your own music on? Does it help to know that the shop will be brief; does it help to have a visual reminder of what you need; a list that you can tick things off and so see that the end of the shop is coming?

Aside from sensory sensitivities; one might also want to consider if the person is experiencing any communication difficulties and if; as part of a broader set of interventions; they might need support to express themselves better or to understand the demands of those around them. Working alongside colleagues in speech and language therapy; it can be helpful to consider alternative communications strategies such as Picture Exchange Communication System (PECS) (Bondy and Frost 2001) to aide expression and understanding.

Once you have thought about settings, it is important to consider key triggers to behavioural change. Whilst the setting event may be that a person does not like change; the trigger could be that something unexpected has happened e.g. if a person likes to take a familiar route to a favourite place and that route is diverted due to roadworks. It is often useful to think about how much visual information the person is given at these times to help them understand what is happening and what is likely to happen next. Ensuring that people with Autism have the right information in the right format can help to reduce anxiety levels at such times and may avert behavioural challenge.

Finally, one needs to think about the response and how this impacts on the person. If, for example, the STAR reveals that a bout of self injury usually results in the individual being removed from a stressful environment into a calmer one; then one might want to consider if the individual is engaging in self injury in order to get to that calm space. Perhaps it would be better to try and reinforce an alternative way of them asking for a break e.g. 'I need a break' cards. When trying to alternative behaviours, you may have to be inventive as standard reward strategies are often socially based and may not be that effective. The challenge is to be creative and to use whatever the individual finds rewarding. For instance, you may grant the individual five minutes to flap their hands if that's what they enjoy, or time to look at a web page or book that is related to their special interest whatever that may be.

## COGNITIVE-BEHAVIOUR THERAPY

People with ASD are at increased risk of developing mental health difficulties (Melville *et al.* 2008) with particular evidence to suggest that the incidence of anxiety and depression in this population may be higher than in the general population (Gilliot *et al.* 2001; Kim *et al.* 2000). In some cases, as noted above, changing the environment may help to reduce stress and anxiety. However where direct work with the individual is indicated, Cognitive Behaviour Therapy (CBT) is the most appropriate intervention to offer. CBT is based on the underlying principle that our interpretations and understanding of events are mediated by our beliefs about ourselves, others and the world (Beck 1976). Faulty or negatively biased beliefs lead to misinterpretations, in turn leading to negative emotional or behavioural responses. Intervention aims to challenge and change faulty beliefs and biased thinking, leading to more adaptive responses. CBT is the psychological treatment of choice for managing both anxiety and depression in adults (NICE 2004) and children (Cartwright-Hatton *et al.* 2004; NICE 2005). In recent years there has been a growing acceptance that people with intellectual disabilities can engage in CBT and there is an increasing body of research suggesting its effectiveness for people with ASD (Hare and Paine 1997; Sofronoff *et al.* 2005; Lang *et al.* 2010; Wood *et al.* 2009). CBT has certain characteristics that play to the strengths and preferences of people with ASD, such as using logical argument to challenge faulty cognitions, that make it particularly applicable and acceptable (Hare and Paine 1997).

## SPECIFIC INTERVENTIONS WITH AUTISM

When searching the internet for references relating to 'autism' and 'interventions', thousands of potential sites are available, many claiming to have found a cure for ASD. Many of these sites have no research evidence for their claims and have not been subject to systematic analysis. These sites are understandably seductive to parents, carers and families of people with ASD and part of the clinician's role is to help carers of people with ASD and individuals themselves to negotiate this minefield. It is important to help people to understand the available research and to assess the claims that support different interventions.

Helpful information is available from the NAS website on how to understand research articles and there are also summary sheets on various common approaches or interventions such as TEACCH (Mesibov *et al.* 1997, 2005), Social Stories (Gray 2002, 2010; Lorimer *et al.* 2002; Smith 2001) which are used to support people with ASD.

## CONCLUSION

In conclusion, no single chapter is going to tell you all you need to know about autism nor can it encapsulate the exciting and challenging clinical work that ensues from getting to know those with autism. However, we hope that we have conveyed the main skills that you need; to keep an open mind; wear your autism glasses and celebrate the strengths of the autistic experience and the fortitude and creativity that people with autism show whilst managing that experience within a neuro-typical world.

## References

Acosta, M.T. and Pearl, P.L. (2004) Imagery data in autism: from structure to malfunction. *Seminars in Pediatric Neurology*, **11**(3), 205–13.

American Psychiatric Association (1994) *Diagnostic and Statistical Manual of Mental Disorders* (4th edn). Washington, DC: APA.

Asperger, H. (1991/1944) "Autistic Psychopathology" in Childhood. Translated and annotated by Frith, U. In Frith, U. (ed.) *Autism and Asperger syndrome*. New York: Cambridge University Press.

Attwood, T. (2002) *Asperger's Syndrome: a guide for parents and professionals*. London: Jessica Kingsley Publishers.

Attwood, T. and Garnett, M. (1995) *The Australian Scale for Asperger Syndrome*. Paper presented at the 1995 Australian National Autism Conference. Brisbane, Australia.

Baird, G., Simonoff, E., Pickles, A., Chandler, S., Loucas, T., Meldrum, D. and Charman, T. (2006) Prevalence of disorders of the autistic spectrum in a population cohort of children in South Thames: The Special Needs and Autism Project (SNAP). *The Lancet*, **15**, 210–16.

Baron-Cohen, S. (1989) The autistic child's theory of mind – a case of specific developmental delay. *Journal of Child Psychology and Psychiatry and Allied Disciplines*. **30**(2), 285–97.

Baron-Cohen, S., Joliffe, T., Mortimore, C. and Robertson, M. (1997) Another advanced test of theory of mind: evidence from very high functioning adults with autism or Asperger Syndrome. *Journal of Child Psychology and Psychiatry and Allied Disciplines*, **38**(7), 813–22.

Baron-Cohen, S., Leslie, A. and Frith, U. (1985) Does the autistic-child have a theory of mind? *Cognition*, **21**(1), 37–46.

Beck, A. (1976) *Cognitive Therapy and the Emotional Disorders*. International Universities Press.

Ben-Sasson, A., Hen, L., Fluss, R., Cermack, S., Engel-Yeger, B. and Gal, E. (2009) A meta-analysis of sensory modulation symptoms in individuals with autism spectrum disorders. *Journal of Autism and Developmental Disabilities*, **39**(1), 1–11.

Bettelheim, B. (1963) *The Empty Fortress*. Chicago: Free Press.

Bondy, A. and Frost, L. (2001) The picture exchange communication system. *Behavior Modification*, **25**, 725–44.

Bowler, D. (1992) Theory of mind in Asperger's Syndrome. *Journal of Child Psychology and Psychiatry and Allied Disciplines*, **33**(5), 877–93.

Cartwright-Hatton, S., Roberts, C., Chitsabesan, P., Fothergill, C. and Harrington, R. (2004) Systematic review of the efficacy of cognitive behaviour therapies for childhood and adolescent anxiety disorders. *British Journal of Clinical Psychology*, **43**(4), 421–36.

Clements, J. and Zarkowska, E. (2000) *Behavioural Concerns and Autistic Spectrum Disorders: Explanations and Strategies for Change*. Jessica Kingsley Publishers.

Courchesne, E., Karns, L.M., Davis, H.R., Ziccardi, B.S., Carper, R.A., Tigue, Z.D., Chisum, H.J., Moses, P., Pierce, K., Lord, C., Lincoln, A.J., Pizzo, S., Schreibman, L., Haas, R.H., Askhoomoff, N.A. and Courchesne, R.Y. (2001) Unusual brain growth patterns in early life of patients with autistic disorder. *Neurology*, **57**(2), 245–54.

Deykin, E. and MacMahon, B. (1980) Pregnancy, delivery, and neonatal complications among autistic children. *American Journal of Diseases of Children*, **134**(9), 860–4.

Emerson, E. and Hatton, C. (2007) Mental health of children and adolescents with intellectual disabilities in Britain. *The British Journal of Psychiatry*, **191**, 493–9.

Filipek, P., Accardo, P., Baranek, G., Cook, E., Dawson, G., Gordon, B., Gravel, J., Johnson, C., Kallen, R., Levy, S., Minshew, N., Prizant, B., Rapin, I., Stone, S., Teplin, S., Tuchman, R. and Volkmar, F. (1999) The screening and diagnosis of autistic spectrum disorders. *Journal of Autism and Developmental Disorders*, **29**(6), 439–84.

Fitzpatrick, M. (2004) *MMR and Autism: What Parents Need to Know*. London: Routledge.Taylor and Francis.

Frith, U. (1989) *Autism: Explaining the Enigma*. Oxford: Blackwell.

Frost, L. and Bondy, A. (1994) *The Picture Exchange Communication System Training Manual*. Cherry Hill, NJ: PECs.

Gilliot, A., Furniss, F. and Walter, A. (2001) Anxiety in high-functioning children with autism. *Autism*, **5**(3), 277–86.

Glasson, E., Bower, C., Petterson, B., De Klerk, N., Chaney, G. and Hallmayer, J. (2004) Perinatal factors and the development of autism. A population study. *Archives of General Psychiatry*, **61**, 618–27.

Grandin, T. (2006) *Thinking in Pictures*. Bloomsbury Publishing.

Gray, C. and Leigh-White, A. (2002) *My Social Stories Book*. London: Jessica Kingsley Publishers.

Gray, C. (2010) *The New Social Story Book*. Arlington, TX: Future Horizons Inc.

Happé, F. (1994) An advanced test of theory of mind – understanding of story character's thoughts and feelings by able autistic, mentally-handicapped and normal children and adults. *Journal of Autism, and Developmental Disorders*, **24**(2), 129–54.

Happé, F. and Frith, U. (2006) The weak coherence account: detail-focused cognitive style in autism spectrum disorders. *Journal of Autism and Developmental Disorders*, **36**(1), 5–25.

Happé, F. and Ronald, A. (2008) The 'fractionable autism triad': a review of evidence from behavioural, genetic, cognitive and neural research. *Neuropsychological Review*, **18**(4), 287–304.

Hare, D. and Paine, C. (1997). The use of cognitive-behavioural therapy with people with Asperger Syndrome: a case study. *Autism*, **1**(2), 215–25.

Holliday-Willey, L. (1999) *Pretending to be Normal: Living with Asperger's Syndrome*. Jessica Kingsley Publishers.

Honda, H., Shimizu, Y. and Rutter, M. (2005) No effect of MMR withdrawal on the incidence of autism: a total population study. *Journal of Child Psychology and Psychiatry*, **46**, 572.

Howlin, P. and Rutter, M. (1987) *Treatment of Autistic Children*. Chichester: John Wiley and Sons, Ltd.

in treatment of sleep Disorders in children with autism. *Journal of Autism and Developmental Disorders*, **36**, 741–52.

Kanner, L. (1943) Autistic disturbances of affective contact. *Nervous Child*, **2**, 217–50.

Kanner, L. (1949) Problems of nosology and psychodynamics in early childhood autism. *American Journal of Orthopsychiatry*, **19**(3), 416–26.

Kim, J., Szatmari, P., Byrson, S., Streiner, D. and Wilson, F. (2000) The prevalence of anxiety and mood disorders among children with autism and Asperger Syndrome. *Autism*, **4**(2), 117–32.

Lang, R., Regester, A., Lauderdale, S., Ashbaugh, K. and Haring, A. (2010) Treatment of anxiety in autism spectrum disorders using cognitive behaviour therapy: a systematic review. *Developmental Neurorehabilitation*, **13**(1), 53–63.

Lawson, W. (2000) *Life behind Glass: a personal account of autism spectrum disorder*. Jessica Kingsley Publishers.

Legge, B. (2002) *Can'tEeat, Won't Eat: dietary difficulties and autistic spectrum disorders*. Jessica Kingsley Publishers.

Lord, C., Risi, S., Lambrecht, L., Cook, E., Leventhal, B., DiLavore, P., Pickles, A. and Rutter, M. (2000) The autism diagnostic schedule-generic: a standard measure of social and communication deficits associated with the spectrum of autism. *Journal of Autism and Developmental Disorders*, **30**, 205–24.

Lord, C., Rutter, M., DiLavore, P. and Risi, S. (1999) Autism diagnostic observation schedule – generic. Los Angeles, CA: Western Psychological Services.

Lorimer, P.A., Simpson, R.L., Myles, B.S. and Ganz, J.B. (2002) The use of social stories as a preventative behavioural intervention in a home setting with a child with autism. *Journal of Positive Behavior Interventions*, **4**(1), 53–60.

Melville, C., Cooper, S., Morrison, J., Smiley, E., Allan, L., Jackson, A., Finlayson, J. and Mantry, D. (2008) The prevalence and incidence of mental ill-health in adults with autism and intellectual disabilities. *Journal of Autism and Developmental Disabilities*, **38**, 1676–88.

Mesibov, G.B. (1997) Formal and Informal Measures on the Effectiveness of the TEACCH Programme. *Autism*, **1**(1), 25–35.

Mesibov, G.B., Shea, V. and Schopler, E. (2005) *The TEACCH Approach to Autism Spectrum Disorder: Issues in Clinical Child Psychology*. Kluwer Academic/Plenum Publishers.

MRC (2001) *Review of Autism Research: Epidemiology and Causes*.

Muhle, R., Trentacoste, S.V. and Rapin, I. (2004) The genetics of autism. *Pediatrics*, **113**, 472–86.

*National Autism Plan for Children* (2003) *Review of Autism Research: Epidemiology and Causes*. NIASA.

National Institute for Clinical Excellence (NICE) (2005) *Depression in Children and Young People: Identification and Management in Primary, Community and Secondary Care*. London: National Institute for Clinical Excellence.

National Institute for Clinical Excellence (NICE) (2004) *Depression: Management of Depression in Primary and Secondary Care*. London: National Institute for Clinical Excellence.

Ozonoff, S. and Jensen, J. (1999) Brief report: specific executive function profiles in three neurodevelopmental disorders. *Journal of Autism and Developmental Disorders*, 29(2), 171–7.

Ozonoff, S., Pennington, B. and Rogers, S. (1991) Executive function deficits in high functioning autistic individuals – relationship to theory of mind. *Journal of Child Psychology and Psychiatry and Allied Disciplines*, 32(7), 1081–1105.

Pellicano, E., Mayberry, M., Durkin, K. and Maley, A. (2006) Multiple cognitive capabilities/deficits in children with an autism spectrum disorder: 'weak' central coherence and its relationship to theory of mind and executive control. *Development and Psychopathology*, 18(1), 77–98.

Rajendran, G. and Mitchell, P. (2007) Cognitive theories of autism. *Developmental Review*, 27, 224–60.

Rutter, M. and Schopler, E. (1987) Autism and pervasive developmental disorders: concepts and diagnostic issues. *Journal of Autism and Developmental Disorders*, 17, 159–86.

Rutter, M., LeCouteur, A. and Lord, C. (2003) Autism Diagnostic Interview – Revised (ADI-R). Los Angeles, CA: Western Psychological Services.

Shah, A. and Frith, U. (1993) Why do autistic individuals show superior performance on the block design task. *Journal of Child Psychology and Psychiatry and Allied Disciplines*, 34(8), 1351–64.

Smith, C. (2001) Using Social stories to enhance behaviour in children with autistic Spectrum Difficulties. *Educational Psychology in Practice*, 17(4), 337–45.

Soffronoff, K., Attwood, T. and Hinton, S. (2005) A randomised controlled trial of a CBT intervention for anxiety in children with Asperger Syndrome. *Journal of Child Psychology and Psychiatry*, 46, 1152–60.

Sparks, B.F., Freidman, S.D., Shaw, D.W., Aylward, E.H., Echelard, D., Artry, A.A., Maravilla, K.R., Giedd, J.N., Munsen, J., Dawson, G. and Dager, S.R. (2002) Brain structural abnormalities in young children with autistic spectrum disorder. *Neurology*, 59(2), 184–92.

Wakefield, A.J., Murch, S.H. and Anthony, A. (1998) Ileal-lymphoid-nodular hyperplasia, non-specific colitis, and pervasive developmental disorder in children. *Lancet*, 351, 637–41.

Wellman, H., Cross, D. and Watson, J. (2001) Meta-analysis of theory of mind development; the truth about false belief. *Child Development*, 72(3), 655–84.

Williams, D. (1996) *An Inside-out Approach*. London: Jessica Kingsley Publishers

Williams, D. (1998) *Nobody Nowhere: the remarkable autobiography of an autistic girl*. Jessica Kingsley Publishers.

Wimmer, H. and Perner, J. (1983) Beliefs about beliefs – representation and constraining function of wrong beliefs in young children's understanding of deception. *Cognition*, 13(1), 103–28.

Wing, L. and Gould, J. (1979) Severe impairments of social interaction and associated abnormalities in children: epidemiology and classification. *Journal of Autism and Developmental Disorders*, 9(1), 11–29.

Wing, L. (1999) *Diagnostic Interview for Social and Communication Disorders, DISCO*. Bromley, Kent: The National Autistic Society.

Wing, L., Leekam, S.R., Libby, S.J., Gould, J. and Larcombe, M. (2002) The DISCO: background, inter-rater reliability and clinical use. *Journal of Child Psychology and Psychiatry*, **43**(3), 307–25.

Witkin, H. *et al.* (1971) *A Manual for the Embedded Figures Test*. California: Consulting Psychologists Press.

Wood, J., Drahota, A., Sze, K., Har, K., Chiu, A. and Langer, D. (2009) Cognitive behavioral therapy for anxiety in children with autism spectrum disorders: a randomized, controlled trial. *Journal of Child Psychology and Psychiatry*, **50**(3), 224–34.

World Health Organisation (1993) *The ICD-10 Classification of Mental and Behavioural Disorders. Diagnostic Criteria for Research*. Geneva: World Health Organization.

Zwaigenbaum, L., Szatmari, P., Jones, M.B., Bryson, S.E., MacLean, J.E., Mahoney, W.J., Bartolucci, G. and Tuff, L. (2002) Pregnancy and birth complications in autism and liability to the broader autism phenotype. *Journal of the American Academy of Child and Adolescent Psychiatry*, **41**(5), 572–9.

Chapter 17

# OLDER ADULTS WITH INTELLECTUAL DISABILITIES: ISSUES IN AGEING AND DEMENTIA

Sunny Kalsy-Lillico, Dawn Adams
and Chris Oliver

## INTRODUCTION

The biological, psychological and social factors of ageing in people with intellectual disabilities are similar to those seen in the general population. Physical health difficulties and the psychological and social consequences of these increase with age. A decline in an individual's cognitive and behavioural functioning is increasingly evident and socially, there is a diminishing of networks and opportunities as individuals age. Service responses to these issues, including those by psychology, may not differ in principle to those service responses to ageing needs of the general population. However, given the significant variability in the characteristics of individuals who use intellectual disability services, there is a range of demographic, service and social factors that warrant consideration particularly as these factors interact with the ageing process of individuals with intellectual disabilities.

The average life expectancy of people with intellectual disabilities has, as in the general population, risen significantly with the life expectancy for those with mild intellectual disabilities being almost equal to that of the general population (Bittles *et al.* 2002; Janicki *et al.* 1999). There are a number of immediate consequences to this increased longevity and services for people with intellectual disabilities must respond to the needs of this new, older population.

*Clinical Psychology and People with Intellectual Disabilities*, Second Edition. Edited by
Eric Emerson, Chris Hatton, Kate Dickson, Rupa Gone, Amanda Caine and Jo Bromley.
© 2012 John Wiley & Sons, Ltd. Published 2012 by John Wiley & Sons, Ltd.

## THE SOCIAL AND HEALTH CARE CONTEXTS
## PERTINENT TO AGEING

The social context in which people with intellectual disabilities live is core to their experience of ageing. Poorer health is generally associated with the accumulation of risk across the lifespan (Emerson 2004). Those risks that are specifically attributed to poor health in people with intellectual disabilities include disadvantaged lifestyles, the late recognition of illness and underlying genetic disorder (Cooper 1999). In addition to socioeconomic deprivation, unemployment is the norm, even for people with mild intellectual disabilities. Access to services for older adults with intellectual disabilities is also compromised; levels of preventative care are lower than for the general population (Ouellette-Kuntz 2005) as is frequency of contact with general practitioners (Cooper 1998) and recognition and diagnosis of health problems (Beange, McElduff and Baker 1995).

Previous work has demonstrated that there are barriers in accessing appropriate health care for people with intellectual disabilities (Wilson and Haire 1990; MENCAP 1998, 2007). These problems have been found to be more pronounced for older as compared with younger adults with intellectual disabilities (Cooper 1997a) as older adults have greater health needs, poor health promotion uptake, inadequate care for serious morbidity, unrecognised health need and poor access to health care. Consequently, there is a great disparity between the health of people with intellectual disabilities and that of the general population (Kerr 2004; MENCAP 2007). Furthermore, older people with intellectual disabilities tend to receive residential and day services from a range of providers, some intended for use by adults with intellectual disabilities and others designed primarily for use by the older general population (Cooper 1997a; Thompson and Wright 2001). In both these settings, older people with intellectual disabilities are in the minority. There is the potential for inexperienced intellectual disabilities care staff to attribute the health needs of older people as being part of 'normal' old age and therefore not refer the person for health care. Similarly, inexperienced care staff in facilities designed for use by older people may inadvertently attribute health needs of the person with intellectual disabilities such as physical pain as a 'typical' characteristic of the pre-existing intellectual disability and thus not refer the person for health care (Singleton and Kalsy 2008). Healthcare staff may also not be aware of the raised prevalence of some health conditions in people with intellectual disabilities, some of which are age related (MENCAP 2007). People with intellectual disabilities therefore fit poorly into a health care system where no care is received unless requested (Cooper 1998) creating a real threat to healthy ageing.

## INTELLECTUAL DISABILITY AND AGEING

The differences in previous life experiences, degree and cause of intellectual disabilities are significant influences on the ageing process and the person's experience of ageing. Some older people with intellectual disabilities will have experienced early separation from their family, socially and materially lacking living environments, including long-stay hospital placements and limited educational opportunities prior to community living placements.

The degree of intellectual disability also creates variability in the ageing process and impacts on predictions of longevity. People with profound intellectual disabilities may expect to live into their late thirties, people with severe intellectual disabilities may expect to live into their 50s and those with moderate/mild intellectual disabilities into their sixties (Strauss and Eyman 1996). Thus, it may be assumed that services and families may be supporting people with severe intellectual disabilities and significant care needs into their 50s and 60s whilst parents approach their 80s. Currently, the carers of older people with intellectual disabilities are challenged by their extended duration of caring, their own additional age-related health concerns as well as those of their relative and the psychological stress that can be brought on by anxiety over future care after the carer's death (Hatzidimitriadou and Milne 2005; McCallion and McCarron 2004; Morgan and Magrill 2005). Furthermore, there is an obvious implication for older parents of people with severe intellectual disabilities given the need for basic care on a daily basis. A final degree of intellectual disability by ageing process interaction is emerging in the study of dementia in Down syndrome with some evidence suggesting that people with Down syndrome may evidence decline at an earlier stage if they have a more substantial degree of intellectual disability (Oliver et al. 1998).

With the shift to social models of disability, clinical psychology has paid less attention to cause of intellectual disabilities, despite substantial evidence that genetic and other causes can be related to physical disorder and difference alongside cognitive, behavioural and emotional presentation (O'Brien and Yule 1995). These differences inevitably interact with ageing. As previously noted, the most obvious example is the reduced longevity in individuals with Down syndrome compared to the general population of people with intellectual disabilities, combined with a higher prevalence of age related disorders such as cataracts, hearing loss, alopecia and Alzheimer related dementia (Oliver and Holland 1986).

## AGEING AND PHYSICAL HEALTH IN PEOPLE WITH INTELLECTUAL DISABILITIES

People with intellectual disabilities experience high rates of physical health problems with increasing age (Cooper 1998; Janicki, Davidson, Henderson *et al.* 2002). This highlights the need for vigilance amongst caregivers (Janicki *et al.* 2002) although eliciting reliable self-reports of health problems from people with intellectual disabilities is becoming increasingly possible (Ruddick and Oliver 2005). Common age related physical changes that are experienced by both the general population and those with intellectual disabilities include mobility problems, incontinence, hypertension, sensory impairments and obesity (Cooper 1998; Evenhuis 1995a, b; Janicki *et al.* 2002; Nieuwenhuis-Mark 2009).

Adults with intellectual disabilities may also present with disability-related conditions that are not found to the same extent in the general population (Janicki *et al.* 2002). Epilepsy (Branford and Collacott 1994), acquired cataracts (Zigman *et al.* 2004) and otitis media (middle ear infections) (Hagerman, Altshul-Stark and McBogg 1987) are all reported to affect at least 20% of adults with intellectual disabilities. Alongside these physical health concerns is that of undiagnosed and untreated pain which is compounded by pre-existing cognitive and other impairments including restricted communication ability resulting in caregivers often misattributing pain/discomfort as a challenging behaviour (British Psychological Society 2009; Singleton and Kalsy 2008; Wilkinson *et al.* 2004; Zwakhalen *et al.* 2004).

With regards to specific syndromes of intellectual disability, Down syndrome is associated with a number of health concerns related to ageing including a greater prevalence of obesity (Braunschweig, Gomez, Sheean *et al.* 2004), hypothyroidism (Rubello *et al.* 1995), atlantoaxial instability (an instability between the first and second cervical vertebrae) (Pueschel and Scola, 1987), obstructive sleep apnoea (Stebbens *et al.* 1991) and dementia (discussed below). Premature menopause i.e. mid-forties, is also experienced by women with Down syndrome (Cosgrave, Tyrrell, McCarron *et al.* 1999; Seltzer, Schupf and Wu 2001).

## AGEING AND MENTAL HEALTH NEEDS IN PEOPLE WITH INTELLECTUAL DISABILITIES

As with physical health difficulties, older adults with intellectual disabilities may exhibit the same types of mental health difficulties as the general population (Foelker and Luke 1989) including depression (Harper and Wadsworth 1990) and anxiety (Cooper 1999). Prevalence estimates of mental health problems are consistently higher for individuals with intellectual disabilities than for the general population although the methodological limitations of such data have been raised (Campbell and Malone 1991; Hatton 2002). Transitions such as loss and bereavements also have significant impacts upon people with intellectual disabilities. The death of a caregiver can lead to additional associated losses for the individual, such as leaving their home, residing in emergency accommodation, followed by multiple residential moves and the disruption of relationships, activities and sense of emotional well-being. Thus a significant proportion of older people with intellectual disabilities may be experiencing mental health concerns due to age-related physical illness and associated end-of-life/palliative care issues and bereavement associated with loss of a carer, compounded by limited access to and support from mental health services (Dodd, Dowling and Hollins 2005; Hatzidimitriadou and Milne 2005; Tuffrey-Wijne 2003).

The recognition and diagnosis of a mental health difficulty in people with intellectual disabilities is further compromised by language limitations, diagnostic overshadowing or misinterpretation of syndrome-specific behaviours (Moss et al. 2000). Furthermore, age-associated psychiatric disorders have also been noted; dementia is reportedly common among adults with intellectual disabilities and adults with Down Syndrome (British Psychological Society 2009; Cooper 1997b; Zigman et al. 2004).

# DEMENTIA IN ADULTS WITH INTELLECTUAL DISABILITIES AND DOWN SYNDROME

Down syndrome is the most common genetically caused intellectual disability, accounting for 15–20% of the intellectual disability population (Busciglio and Yankner 1995; Down Syndrome Association 2007). The life expectancy of people with Down syndrome has, like that of the general population, increased significantly from under 10 years old in the 1920s, to over 60 at present (Watchman 2003). The possible reasons for this are associated with advances in medical and social care (Holland 2004; Wilkinson et al. 2004).

Functional deterioration in adults with Down Syndrome was first noted in the nineteenth century when in 1876, Fraser and Mitchell reported that individuals with Down Syndrome had a form of 'precipitated senility'. Although the understanding of this relationship was for a long time a largely neuropathological one, many studies have now confirmed that age-related cognitive decline and dementia affecting individuals with Down syndrome occur some 30 years earlier in life than in the general population (Holland 2004; Zigman et al. 2004).

Dementia (a term used to describe a collection of symptoms including a decline in cognitive ability and functional skills caused by structural changes in the brain) affects one person in 20 over the age of 65 and one person in five over the age of 80 (Alzheimer's Disease International, 1999). The numbers of people with dementia in the UK are forecast to increase by 38% over the next 15 years and 154% over the next 45 years (Alzheimer's Society 2007). Alzheimer's disease is the most common form of dementia, making up 55% of all cases of dementia. Alzheimer's disease leads to a progressive loss of brain tissue. This is generally reflected in a number of symptoms such as a loss of daily living skills, short-term memory loss, disorientation, confusion and difficulties in concentration and speech production. Table 17.1 describes estimated population prevalence rates.

Virtually all adults with Down syndrome over the age of 40 show the neuropathological signs of Alzheimer's disease at autopsy (Wisniewski, Wisniewski and Wen 1985). However, a clinical diagnosis is only given in 0–2% of 30–39 year olds, 5.7–13.8% of 40–49 year olds, 25–36.1% of 50–59 year olds and 33.3–54.5% of 60–69 year olds (Prasher 1995; Holland, Hon, Huppert, Stevens, and Watson 1998; Tyrrell *et al.* 2001). This inconsistency between neuropathological and clinical prevalence rates may be due to survivor effects (Carr 2000), diagnostic criteria used (see Holland *et al.* 1998) or variable presentation (see Oliver and Holland 1986).

Furthermore, people with intellectual disabilities from ethnic minority groups face a wider set of barriers to accessing statutory services. Research indicates that older people from ethnic minority groups who develop dementia find that some services are inappropriate and hard to access (Bowes and Wilkinson 2003; Patel *et al.* 1998). Indeed, research has also highlighted that the presence of higher levels of dementia amongst non-English speaking community groups and a higher prevalence of dementia related behaviours in ethnic minorities in comparison to their Caucasian peers (McCracken, Boneham, Copeland, Williams, Wilson *et al.* 1997; Sink, Covinsky, Newcomer and Yaffe 2004) Thus, understanding and appreciating the impact of social, cultural and environmental factors are important in recognising signs of dementia and in meeting needs.

## ASSESSMENT AND DIAGNOSIS OF DEMENTIA IN PEOPLE WITH INTELLECTUAL DISABILITIES

There is no single diagnostic test for Alzheimer's disease and the diagnosis of dementia in people with intellectual disabilities presents a significant clinical challenge that increases with the degree of pre-existing

**Table 17.1** Estimated population prevalence rates.

| Age group | 30–39 years | 40–49 years | 50–59 years | 60–69 years | 70–79 years | 80–89 years | 90–99 years |
|---|---|---|---|---|---|---|---|
| General population (Alzheimer's Society 2007) | 0.008–0.009% | 0.01–0.03 % | 0.06–0.14 % | 0.16–1.3 % | 2.9–5.9 % | 12.2–20.3 % | 28.6–32.5 % |
| People with intellectual disabilities excluding Down Syndrome (Cooper 1997b) | | | | 15.6% (65–74 year olds) | 23.5% (75–84 year olds) | 70.0% (85–94 year olds) | |
| People with Down Syndrome (Zigman et al. 2004) | 0–10 % | 10–30 % | 20–55 % | 30–75 % | | | |

intellectual disability. There are a number of strategies that may be adopted with regard to the assessment of dementia in people with intellectual disabilities (Oliver 1999). The 'retrospective' strategy involves waiting for referral (commonly triggered by observation of inexplicable change) and then undertaking assessments and comparing results compared to past assessments (which are rarely available or applicable). Difficulties with this approach include inaccuracy in estimating and appraising the rate of decline, especially for individuals with low baseline scores (see Oliver and Kalsy 2005). The alternative 'prospective' strategy ensures that adults with intellectual disabilities who are at high risk (typically those with Down syndrome) for developing dementia have a baseline assessment as they approach high risk age. This too is associated with problems including high cost, persistent floor effects and differential diagnosis at an early stage (Oliver 1999).

With reference to the clinical (diagnostic) assessment for people with intellectual disabilities this should include medical, psychiatric, physical, cognitive, adaptive, behavioural and psychosocial functioning in addition to gathering detailed background information (see McQuillan *et al.* 2003 for description). Assessments should be both comprehensive, by combining both informant based and neuropsychological measures, and specific, by using assessment methods and measures developed for the detection of dementia in adults with intellectual disabilities that are more sensitive to change (e.g. Kalsy and Oliver 2005; Crayton *et al.* 1998). Those that have been used and evaluated in the current literature include global carer screening questionnaires (Dementia Questionnaire for Persons with Mental Retardation, Evenhuis 1992, 1996; Dementia Scale for Down syndrome, Gedye 1995; and the CAMDEX-DS. Holland *et al.* 2005), questionnaires specifically concerned with behavioural change relating to dementia (Assessment for Adults with Developmental Disabilities, Kalsy, McQuillan, Oliver and Hall 2001) and neuropsychological tests of cognitive functioning (e.g. Neuropsychological Assessment of Dementia in Adults with Intellectual Disabilities (formerly Crayton and Oliver), Oliver *et al.* 1998; Rivermead Behavioural Memory Test for Children, Aldrich and Wilson 1991; The Dalton-McMurray Visual Memory Test: Delayed Matching to Sample Cognitive Test, Dalton 1995). Extensive reviews and recommendations of methods and measures are provided in Oliver (1999), Aylward, Burt, Thorpe, Lai and Dalton (1997), Burt and Aylward (2000), Nieuwenhuis-Mark (2009), British Psychological Society (2009) and Kalsy and Oliver (2005).

If dementia is suspected, a thorough evaluation procedure or 'differential diagnosis' is strongly recommended to exclude any other conditions or disorders and should include an assessment of the individual's cognitive and behavioural functioning as well as reports from key informants:

- Sensory, particularly visual and hearing impairments, such as cataracts and impacted earwax.
- Hormonal and endrocine disorders e.g. hypo/hyperthyroidism, menopause, diabetes, etc.
- Depression (and other psychiatric disorders such as anxiety or the exacerbation of an existing psychotic condition).
- Physical health conditions, e.g. anaemia, uncontrolled epilepsy, undiagnosed pain, musculoskeletal problems, stroke, atlanto-axial instability, urinary tract infections, cardiac disorders, nutritional deficiencies, etc.
- Medication effects, e.g. side-effects of anticonvulsant therapy and medication for Parkinson's disease, polypharmac.
- Impact of life events, bereavements, transitions, situational crises and environmental changes.

The main principle for a diagnostic assessment is to establish a progressive loss of skills in more than one area of functioning, that has continued for at least six months and the observed changes are not due to any of the conditions described above. Once information from the neuropsychological and informant based measures have been collated, it should be compared to diagnostic criteria for dementia. The preference is currently for ICD-10 diagnostic criteria as these consider both 'cognitive' and 'non cognitive' aspects of dementia such as apathy or irritability (Aylward *et al.* 1997).

It should be noted that there are several benefits of early diagnosis. The functional decline as a result of the dementia and its consequences can be better managed if identified and intervened with early. Prompt identification can help the individual and their carers understand changes in behaviour that are often early signs, as well as positively supporting any interventions for managing cognitive symptoms. Associated conditions such as depression, anxiety and aggression are more likely to respond to intervention if identified early. Furthermore, an early diagnosis enables individuals and their carers more time for long-range planning (including financial and end-of-life considerations) to manage the impact of the dementia.

## BEHAVIOURAL PRESENTATION OF DEMENTIA IN PEOPLE WITH INTELLECTUAL DISABILITIES

The perception of decline and clinical presentation of dementia in people with intellectual disabilities will depend on the individual's premorbid level of functioning and demands presented in everyday life (Aylward *et al.* 1997). Contemporary research (e.g. Holland, Hon, Huppert and Stevens 2000; Nelson *et al.* 1995) suggests that behavioural and personality changes, similar to those seen in frontal type dementia, are the earliest changes observed by carers. There is increasing evidence for frontal type presentation in Down syndrome. This may be due to the pre-existing neurological difference in Down syndrome interacting with Alzheimer like pathology in a way that confirms and extends the reserve capacity hypothesis, which states that both the magnitude of brain atrophy and premorbid brain size determine the volume of the brain affected by Alzheimer's disease (Holland *et al.* 1998, 2000).

Adults with Down syndrome have a much higher probability of developing Alzheimer's disease at a younger age, on average 20 years earlier than would be expected in the general population. From a clinical perspective, change of any magnitude in adults over the age of 30 with Down syndrome (and, arguably, any person with intellectual disabilities over the age of 50) should be investigated for two reasons. Firstly, to facilitate prompt and accurate assessment and diagnosis and intervention (including the use of the anti-dementia drug treatment of symptoms of mild-moderate Alzheimer's disease in adults with Down syndrome and thus, early diagnosis is imperative (NICE 2006a, 2006b; Prasher 2004) Secondly for quality of life issues; to allow for future life-planning, health and social care interventions and for carers, who report changes relating to cognitive decline as problematic, to receive support (Oliver *et al.* 2000).

Generally the expression of Alzheimer's disease in adults with Down syndrome is comparable to the decline observed in the general population. The early presentation of Alzheimer's Disease in people with Down syndrome is characterised by prominent personality and behaviour changes associated with executive dysfunction (Ball *et al.* 2006). Other research has highlighted that severe cognitive deterioration such as acquired apraxia is increasingly prevalent in ageing adults with Down syndrome and that deterioration in memory, learning and orientation, preceded the acquisition of aphasia, agnosia and apraxia (Oliver *et al.* 1998). Changes in cognitive, behavioural, psychiatric and adaptive functioning have been documented in people with intellectual disabilities and literature relating to the presence of behavioural and psychiatric features in dementia has suggested that people with intellectual disabilities may present with a higher incidence of low mood, restlessness or over-activity, disturbed sleep, uncooperativeness and aggression (Cooper and Prasher 1998). A three-stage model is often used to describe the clinical progress of the disease and these stages occur over different time periods in different people (Dalton and Janicki 1999). Table 17.2 describes the typical

**Table 17.2** Symptom progression.

| Stage of Alzheimer's Disease | Presentation |
|---|---|
| 1. Onset/Early | • The initial symptoms often appear very gradually and can easily go unnoticed.<br>• Subtle changes in behaviour and mood e.g. loss of interest in others, slowing of physical movements and changes in bodily functioning such as bladder control.<br>• There is a decline in social, community and daily living skills, e.g. not initiating conversations with others, not wishing to take part in previously enjoyed activities, struggling with personal care tasks.<br>• Language and word finding difficulties e.g. tip of the tongue type behaviours.<br>• There are some problems with memory e.g. disoriented in time, difficulty remembering some names or recent events.<br>• There are some difficulties learning new information and making decisions, e.g. choosing what to wear. |
| 2. Progressive/ Middle | • Disturbances in personality, mood and behaviour increase e.g. increased episodes of tearfulness or anxiety, wandering, sleep disturbances, increased agitation.<br>• Language problems are more evident, e.g. speaking and responding less, understanding requests or naming familiar objects.<br>• Difficulties with perceptions may be noted, e.g. struggle to carry out personal care tasks or recognising common objects.<br>• As the disease progresses, memory losses are more pronounced, e.g. difficulty remembering names of close friends/family, repeating questions, statements and actions, becoming more disorientated.<br>• Physical problems also become more apparent, e.g. increased risk of seizures and weight loss and movements becoming slower and jerky such as stop-start when walking. |

*(Continued)*

**Table 17.2**  (*cont'd*)

| Stage of Alzheimer's Disease | Presentation |
| --- | --- |
| 3.  Severe/End | • Further confusion and deterioration is all areas including an inability to recognise close family or friends, difficulty with swallowing and continence, loss of language and some agitation.<br>• Once the disease has progressed, balance and ability to walk may be lost and the individual may be confined to bed.<br>• Person is totally dependant on others for all needs.<br>• The risk of developing infections, particularly pneumonia, dehydration and nutritional deficiencies, increases. |

symptom progression of Alzheimer's disease in people with Down syndrome.

As compared to the general population, the rate of progression of Alzheimer's disease in people with intellectual disabilities is considerably more rapid, with some people with Down syndrome moving quickly through the disease stages. The average age of onset of Alzheimer's disease in people with Down syndrome has been estimated to be 52 years with the average duration of the illness being less than five years (Prasher and Krishnan 1993). However, anecdotally, clinicians have reported people with Down syndrome progressing through the disease at a rate of up to 12 months from the point of diagnosis to death (Dodd 2003). This significantly impacts on the individual, those around them including other service users, their caregivers and indeed on service planning and provision.

Despite this uniquely high prevalence rate of dementia and more rapid rate of decline amongst those with Down syndrome, the exact course and determinants of decline are as yet unknown. Described below are four people with Down syndrome who demonstrate the wide variation in both the presence and presentation of dementia as highlighted by their performance on the Neuropsychological Assessment of Intellectual Disabilities (NAID) battery for assessment of dementia (Crayton *et al.* 1998).

# Case Studies

## Case 'Laura' – Long-term Decline

Upon baseline assessment, Laura, a 55 year old woman with Down syndrome, showed high level of both adaptive behaviour and receptive language. Her performance on the NAID and informant based interviews did not indicate any signs of cognitive deterioration. Laura was very independent, travelling on public transport to her day placement and managing her own money. After three years of stable neuropsychological assessments, Laura began to show decline. Despite these changes being identified, it was not until her final assessment that Laura's carers reported behavioural and cognitive changes that were of a significant magnitude to warrant a diagnosis of early stage Alzheimer's disease on the CAMDEX-DS (Holland *et al.* 2005). Laura was 49 years old when her baseline assessment was made and 54 years when the early signs of Alzheimer's disease became apparent. Her case highlights the importance of longitudinal, prospective screening assessments in individuals with Down Syndrome.

## Case 'Ralph' – Older But No Decline

Ralph was 51 years old when his baseline neuropsychological assessment was made. These assessments were considered within the expected limits for an individual with intellectual disabilities of his age. Although he showed significant physical signs of ageing such as reduced gait speed and rapid alopecia, Ralph's carers did not report any behavioural or cognitive changes. Almost five years after his initial baseline assessment, Ralph, now aged 55 years old, remains stable on both his neuropsychological and informant based measures of dementia.

## Case 'Kara' – Reversible Signs

Kara is a 39 year old woman with Down syndrome, who enjoyed an independent life both in and outside of her family home. Over the past three years, she has shown changes of concern. The initial changes identified by neuropsychological assessments and carer interviews prompted a referral to a specialist psychology service for older adults with intellectual disabilities (see Kalsy *et al.* 2005). The referral was accompanied by a recommendation of a full physical assessment and as a result, Kara received a diagnosis of hypothyroidism and depression, for which she was prescribed a low dosage of antidepressants. At her last neuropsychological assessment, Kara showed scores that did not differ from those obtained at her initial baseline assessment. This case highlights the importance of differential diagnosis of hypothyroidism and depression when diagnosing dementia in individuals with Down syndrome.

## Case 'Mac' – Early Stages

Mac, a 47 year old man with Down syndrome had his initial baseline assessment when he was 44 years old. Residing in semi-supported living, he had minimal contact with staff outside of mealtimes. His carers did not report any behavioural or cognitive concerns. Over the last three years, changes that were reported by carers were always explained by the arrival of a new member of staff or changes in Mac's day placements. However, his performance on some sub-tests of the NAID were at a lowered level that could not be accounted for by his age or degree of intellectual disabilities and cautious statistical procedures for identifying decline on the NAID indicated that Mac was presenting with more than mild cognitive impairment. This case highlights the importance of seeking possible alternative explanations for behavioural change especially in individuals such as Mac who are in the relatively high risk age range for developing dementia.

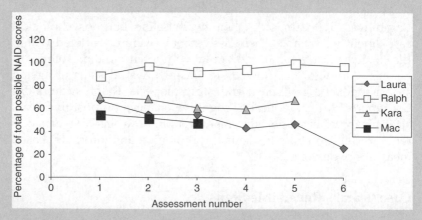

**Graph A:** Percentage of total possible NAID scores for each case study.

Case 'Laura' a 55-year old woman with Down syndrome showing long-term decline.

Case 'Ralph' a 55-year old man with Down syndrome showing no decline.

Case 'Kara' a 36-year old woman with Down syndrome showing reversible signs.

Case 'Mac' a 47-year old man with Down syndrome showing early signs.

**Case studies NAID scores**

# THE SERVICE AND POLICY CONTEXTS FOR OLDER ADULTS WITH INTELLECTUAL DISABILITIES

With regards to service responses to the issues raised thus far, local services need to develop strategies to detect and reduce the physical and mental health problems in older adults with intellectual disabilities that often go unaddressed by healthcare systems (Janicki, Heller, Seltzer and Hogg 1996). With an increasing number of surviving ageing adults with intellectual disabilities, practitioners are increasingly being asked to provide appropriate services, including dementia diagnostic ones (Turk, Dodd and Christmas 2001). In England, these services are developing within overall service policy and strategic frameworks such as 'Valuing People' and the 'National Service Framework for Older People' (Department of Health 2001a, b). The former highlights a number of issues for people with intellectual disabilities, including the need for co-ordinated services, support for family carers, and choice for the individual. It recognises the healthcare needs of older people with intellectual disabilities, identifying person-centred planning as key to ensuring that age-related changes in physical and mental health are monitored and attended to (Department of Health 2001a). The National Service Framework for Older People reflects a generic policy that also emphasises the need for person-centred care by promoting health and independence and the tailoring of local services to meet age-related changes in service user and carer needs (Department of Health 2001b, 2006). There is an emphasis on early detection and diagnosis of dementia to allow access to treatment and planning of future care relating to prognosis (Department of Health and CSIP 2005; National Audit Office 2007). This has been further developed into the 'National Dementia Strategy' (Department of Health 2009) which details a five-year cross-service strategy to achieve seventeen objectives that focus on improving knowledge, early diagnosis, support and treatment and the need to develop services to meet changing needs of people with dementia in England, including people with intellectual disabilities. These strategic drivers emphasise that mainstream guidelines must include the needs of people with intellectual disabilities. This is reflected in the National Institute for Clinical Excellence (NICE) publications on dementia (NICE 2006a, b), which although limited in their understanding of the assessment process for dementia in people with intellectual disabilities, do highlight the needs of ageing adults with intellectual disabilities in a broadly non-discriminatory way.

Recent reports have indicated that few statutory services have comprehensive plans to meet the needs of older adults with intellectual disabilities (DoH 2004). This patchy picture of services is compounded by an unspoken expectation that once a person with intellectual disabilities reaches old age (however arbitrarily defined) that they leave intellectual disabilities services and access generic older adult services

(Hatzidimitriadou and Milne 2005). The transfer of individuals on the basis of chronological age to a different service provider has significant implications in terms of quality of care received and issues of normalisation, empowerment and independence. This is highlighted by the growing number of older adults with intellectual disabilities being placed in generic care homes for older people, supported by staff who are ill-equipped to meet their specific changing needs (Thompson and Wright 2001). Service providers and families must confront problems associated with in-home and community-based support and a lack of investment in specialist services further compounds this situation as does deficits in meeting the physical, social and emotional care needs of people with intellectual disabilities who have dementia (British Psychological Society 2009; Dodd 2003; Wilkinson and Janicki 2002).

## MODELS OF SERVICE DELIVERY AND PROVISION

There is some variation around where and how services should be directed in order to best meet the needs of ageing adults with intellectual disabilities and dementia (NICE 2006a). Research has suggested a range of critical issues for service planners and providers such as the appropriateness of accommodation, care management, diagnosis and carer/staff training, knowing the local population and their changing ageing needs as well as carefully planned budgets and financial flexibility (Watchman 2003; Turk *et al.* 2001). Furthermore, planning should ensure that older people with intellectual disabilities at risk of developing dementia have the same access to appropriate services and supports as those without an intellectual disability (British Psychological Society 2009; Department of Health and CSIP 2005). This is a challenge for adults with Down syndrome who typically develop the symptoms of dementia at an age that is too young to access generic dementia services and the paucity of working-age dementia services is also highlighted as is the potentially exclusionary description of this latter service for people with intellectual disabilities.

It is thus important for services to develop care pathways that emphasise effective support for practitioners and carers in the recognition and assessment of ageing needs. This would encourage a multidisciplinary response across the different levels of statutory health, social care and third sector (community/voluntary) services. This is also linked with the need for a comprehensive awareness packages for staff and the need to influence strategic planners. Indeed, in response to international policy influences, it is recommended that services adopt the seven *'Edinburgh Principles'* for people with intellectual disabilities and dementia, (Wilkinson and Janicki 2002). These include the promotion of quality of life and person centred approaches, the involvement of the individual and caregivers in assessment, planning and provision, access to appropriate services and support for ageing people with intellectual disabilities and dementia. A framework for service care provision has also been described, highlighting service strategies such as 'ageing in place', 'in place progression' and 'referral out' (see Janicki and Dalton 1999). This framework has been expanded to include outreach models of community service provision to support individuals in their home (Wilkinson *et al.* 2004).

## PSYCHOLOGICAL SERVICE RESPONSES

With specific reference to the response of psychological services, descriptions are available of factors involved in the instigation of clinical referrals for diagnostic assessments, proactive psychological assessments and intervention models that have the primary goal of enhancing quality of life for the person with intellectual disabilities as they age, with appropriate supports to compensate for losses or changes in ability and circumstances, whilst maintaining personal dignity and respect (Adams, Oliver, Kalsy, Peters, Broquard *et al.* 2008; Auty and Scior 2008; British Psychological Society 2009; Dodd 2003; Kalsy *et al.* 2005; Jervis and Prinsloo 2007). Furthermore, the continuity of service delivery described with interdisciplinary and cross-agency working emphasises a long-term service commitment to older adults with intellectual disabilities and their ageing family carers.

With regards to clinical practices, in addition to the clinical roles of assessment and diagnosis of age-related conditions such as dementia and delivery of training, psychologists are called on to develop and implement interventions to facilitate the understanding and management of behaviour concern and emotional distress expressed by people with intellectual disabilities as they age. However, the literature is sparse on models of psychological formulation and intervention other than at the level of broad practice guidelines (British Psychological Society 2009; Janicki *et al.*1996; Kalsy *et al.* 2005).

Psychological interventions described in the general older adults' literature could be adapted for use with people with intellectual disabilities (Opie, Rosewarne and O'Connor 1999) as a similar three-stage model is used to describe the clinical progress of the disease in both populations (Dalton and Janicki 1999). Interventions must consider multiple systemic influences on behaviour in order to support the individual and carers to understand, cope with and manage behaviour concerns and emotional distress. This consideration of behavioural and systemic contexts alongside a biomedical appreciation (of any associated medical conditions and/ or the stages of dementia) enables greater intervention choice. This more person-centred approach is consistent with social models of dementia that emphasise personhood, adjustment and coping, considering contextual influences such as environment and caregiver relationships as influences on behaviour (Kerr 1997; Kitwood 1997) and firmly placing the responsibility for change on those around the person with dementia. Practically this means that the onus is on others to appropriately communicate with the person with dementia, for the environment to enhance the individual's capability rather than compound their disabilities and a recognition that an individual is a valued person who has remaining skills that need to be supported. Table 17.3 presents a framework for organising psychological interventions and practices into four broad groups.

**Table 17.3** A framework for psychological interventions.

| | |
|---|---|
| **Behaviour-oriented** | A full functional analysis of the behaviour in question will enable a systemic understanding of the behaviour as a form of communication. The best practice principles that should be considered when supporting ageing adults with intellectual disabilities and dementia include simplifying multistep activities/skills, matching the level of demand on the individual with that of their current capacities, employing a range of prompts to facilitate communication and to modify the environment insofar as possible to compensate for deficits and capitalise on the individual's strengths. For carers, recommended practice also encourages the adoption of a proactive approach to identity potential stressors (or triggers) that can lead to distressed behaviours and moderate change as necessary. |
| **Emotion-oriented** | The underlying principles for such interventions are to reduce distress, validate a sense of self, enhance emotional wellbeing and support coping strategies. Psychodynamic approaches appear helpful for understanding intrapsychic concerns, cognitive/behavioural techniques assist individuals in the early stage to build coping strategies and reduce distress, reminiscence and life review approaches provide individuals in the mild to moderate stage of dementia with interpersonal connections, (Kasl-Godley and Gatz 2000). |
| **Cognition-oriented** | The aim of these techniques is to compensate cognitive deficits, by utilising behavioural approaches to focus on specific cognitive and behavioural impairments and help to optimise remaining abilities These techniques include reality orientation and skills training. |

*(Continued)*

**Table 17.3**  (*cont'd*)

| | |
|---|---|
| **Stimulation-oriented** | These treatments include recreational activities (e.g., crafts, games, pets) and art therapies (e.g., music, dance, art) to provide stimulation and enrichment that will engage the individual's available cognitive and emotional resources. Approaches such as life work that include life stories, valuables and memorable pictures/ photographs/objects are powerful ways of relating to the individual with dementia in a person-centred way (McKeown *et al.* 2006). Reminiscence work is also important as a process of recalling experiences and events memorable for the individual by using different mediums such as verbal, visual, musical, tactile and smell. Anecdotally, in using reminiscence with groups of ageing adults with intellectual disabilities, the first author has found that its associative process i.e. one memory leads to another so that one person's shared recollection usually sparks off associated recollections or 'memories' in others, has had positive effects on engagement and communication as reminiscence makes connections between a person's past, present and future. |

To reiterate, the core aims of psychological interventions with older adults with intellectual disabilities and dementia are to enable the retention/maintenance of skills, optimise a sense of personhood and emotional well-being and compensate for changes in an individual's functional abilities. These psychological interventions are postulated upon a number of systemic influences, some specific to the person concerned (and their circumstances) and others more broadly related to general conceptual understanding about dementia, e.g. Buijssen's two laws of dementia (2005) – law of disturbed inculcation (the individual is no longer able to successfully encode information from their short-term working memory and store it in their long-term memory) and law of roll back memory, (the individual is unable to form any new long-term memories and overtime the individual may be able to recall childhood events but struggles with more recent events, i.e. their memory is rolling back), both of which have significant cognitive and behavioural consequences for the person with dementia that change as their condition progresses through the different stages. Kalsy *et al.* (2005) provide a comprehensive three-stage of dementia model of psychological interventions (Table 17.4).

**Table 17.4** Kalsy *et al.* (2005) dementia stage-defined psychological practices (reproduced with permission).

| Early Stage | Middle Stage | Late Stage |
|---|---|---|
| • Maintaining skills and independence by increasing supervision and prompting. | • Preserving abilities, using life story work, reminiscence, favoured activities, low-level behavioural interventions, reality orientation, etc. | • Contributing to multidisciplinary, family and other care providers planning of palliative/end of life care |
| • Minimising changes in the environment and daily routine. | • Monitoring behavioural changes (typically excesses) e.g. verbal agitation, wandering, stereotyped actions or disturbed sleep, etc. | • Supporting and working with families, other care providers and peers with intellectual disabilities around issues of loss and bereavement |
| • Structuring and simplifying routines to help orientation. | • Supporting behaviours that challenge such as anxiety and agitation, with reassurance, patience, redirection, avoiding confrontation. | • Working with families, other care providers and peers with intellectual disabilities around reminiscence and remembering |
| • Using multimodal memory aids e.g. picture calendars to support understanding. | • Offering alternative means of communication incorporating visual images, pictures and objects, touch, sounds and smells. | • Contributing to multidisciplinary, family and other care providers ethical decision making around further physical health interventions such as percutaneous endoscopic gastronomy (PEG) feeds |
| • Keeping communication simple and clear, using additional prompts when necessary. | • Offering appropriately stimulating and failure-free activities that promote cognition, physical health, social roles, emotional wellbeing and self-care. | |
| • Using a prompting system of 'tell' (verbal), 'show' (model), 'guide' (physical). | | |
| • At times of expressed confusion, offer sensitive reminders of where the person is, what they are doing, etc. | | |

- Reducing demands by breaking tasks down, easing choice, clutter and noise.
- Behavioural strategies and validation to manage affective and anxiety symptoms.
- Encouraging engagement with activity by the individual setting their own pace, e.g. observing or participating.
- Psychotherapeutic techniques promoting dignity, self-esteem, emotional well-being.
- Monitoring and documenting change closely.

- Offering activities that balance sensory stimulation with sensory calming / relaxing
- Maintaining environments that are safe, calm, predictable, familiar, suitably stimulating and make sense for the individual.
- Working with caregivers and peers with intellectual disabilities on understanding the individual's condition.
- Monitoring and documenting change closely.

With reference to supportive interventions for the carers of ageing adults with intellectual disabilities and dementia, various practical principles of care practices that aim to facilitate more enabling care experiences are currently available, e.g. British Psychological Society 2009; Dodd, Kerr and Fern 2006; Kerr and Wilkinson 2005. The common key principles that are highlighted include:

- *Embracing positive philosophies of care*: key factors include being person-centred, flexible and adaptable care system, individualised care, regular and consistent staff, provision of stress- and failure-free activities, creative use of compensatory strategies to support changes in communication, memory, etc, future planning considerations.
- *Taking a life-story perspective*: by understanding a person's past and knowing their likes and dislikes, carers can endeavour to support people with their emotions. This background knowledge can also help in the form of reassurances offered to the person with dementia should they become distressed. The main focus is to preserve as much quality of their previous lifestyle as is possible. This not only retains the person's dignity but also helps to maintain their orientation and sense of reality. Table 17.5 highlights particular dementia stage-specific activities (this is not an exhaustive list) to help the person with dementia maintain their skills, facilitate interactions with others and sustain engagement with their environment (activities can be interchanged, depending on needs, abilities and interests of the person).
- *Consideration of carer characteristics*: the key characteristics include the carers' ability to understand and properly know the person they are caring for, to understand issues in ageing and dementia and crucially to proactively work to support the individual to cope with the challenges that dementia causes, for example by predicting potential stressors that may challenge the individual and lead to distressing behaviours. There is also a role for clinicians in relation to the information and training provided for carers, for whilst carers may be better resourced to cope with changes in cognitive ability, many report difficulties in understanding and managing behavioural changes in relation to acquired conditions such as dementia (Kalsy, Heath, Adams and Oliver 2007; Lloyd, Kalsy and Gatherer 2008).
- *Providing 'enabling' environments*: the main constituents of these environments are that they are calm, predictable, familiar, suitably stimulating and safe. The impact of an environment upon a person's well-being particularly for those people who may have dementia has also been acknowledged. There is increasing evidence that 'dementia unfriendly' environments further disable people whereas 'dementia friendly' environments help people to maintain levels of independence as well as remain in their own homes (Hutchings *et al.* 2000; Kalsy *et al.* 2005; Kerr 1997; Marshall 2001; Wilkinson *et al.* 2004).

**Table 17.5** Dementia stage-specific activities to help the person with dementia maintain their skills, facilitate interactions with others and sustain engagement with their environment (activities can be interchanged, depending on needs, abilities and interests of the person).

| Early Stage | Early – Middle Stage | Middle Stage | End Stage |
|---|---|---|---|
| • Board Games – card games such snap are good as are large-sized dominoes. | • Music – play something that resonates and has a good bass and beat. | • Movement and exercise – can be done standing or sitting. | • Smiling and laughing – don't underestimate this as an activity. |
| • Ball Games – throwing soft balls to each other, standing or sitting. | • Dance – chair dancing is good, swaying and rocking in time to music. | • Multi-sensory environments – use lights, sounds, smells, touch, Snoezlen. | • Singing – humming along to popular tunes, radio jingles or TV adverts. |
| • Discussions – about people, places and things. | • Art and 'pottery' – working with dough, clay, plasticine or sand. | • Massage – hand and feet spa treatments. | • Stroking – positive touch of people and objects that have different textures. |
| • Relaxation – progressive relaxation, massage or aromatherapy activities. | • Movement – guided walks, progressive relaxation. | • One-step cooking tasks – such as mixing items, peeling food. | • Gentle rocking – can relax and establish physical contact. |
| • Arts and Crafts – painting, colouring in, making bean bags, posters, etc. | • Drama. | • One-step gardening tasks – such as watering plants, digging pots. | • Holding – as above. |
| • End-product Activities – anything where there is an immediate end result such as flower arranging, drawing, cooking, baking, etc. | • Reminiscence – using familiar items, mementoes touch, taste, smells, sounds, pictures or photos that remind people of times gone by. | • One-step daily living tasks – such as plumping up cushions. | • Cuddling – as above. |
| • Use visual planner and cues to structure activities/day. | • Story-telling – talking about old friends, stories about special times, memories or what's on TV. | • Walking – along routes that are circular with focus points. | |
| | • Spiritual or religious activity. | • Stacking and folding – clothes, papers, magazines, etc. | |
| | | • Soft toys – touch can help anxious feelings. | |
| | | • Balls, bubbles, balloons – remind people of fun. | |

- *Engaging in proactive service planning*: the key factor is a consideration of the person's current needs alongside their future changing needs, particularly given the relatively faster rate of decline experienced by people with Down syndrome and dementia. Considerations such as taking a wider quality of life perspective and discussions of end-of-life and palliative care issues must be carefully thought about. Furthermore, services need to plan ahead for their sustainability and capacity to meet future demand over the coming years (British Psychological Society 2009; Department of Health 2009).

## EMERGING ISSUES

There are a number of emerging issues experienced by practitioners and caregivers working alongside older adults with intellectual disabilities and dementia, which are highlighted below:

- *Informed consent*: it is vitally important to use existing consent to treatment guidance (coherent with contemporaneous statutory and professional requirements) whilst also clarifying the reasons for seeking consent and recognising that at times best interest needs to be considered. The current Mental Capacity Act code of practice (DCA 2007) must be sourced for support. Furthermore, the Alzhiemer's Society has produced a resource aimed at everyone working with and supporting people with dementia using the Mental Capacity Act (Alzheimer's Society 2009).
- *Sharing information*: consideration as to how to explain the rationales for assessments, particularly baseline longitudinal assessment and disclosure of diagnosis needs to well thought out (see Table 17.6 for general guidance on sharing diagnosis and prognosis). The onus is to balance the need for detailed information with that of causing undue distress/anxiety whilst also ensuring that adequate support networks are available and accessible for both the individual and their caregivers (Fearnley *et al.* 1997; Watchman 2003).
- *Anti-dementia medication*: further work is needed on cognitive enhancers with older adults with intellectual disabilities, particularly Down syndrome although preliminary work has been promising (Mohan, Carpenter and Bennett 2009a, 2009b, 2009c; Prasher 2004). There is inequity at present, in that access to these drugs is not uniformly available. Partly this may be because the assessment tool advised by NICE guidelines is unsuitable for the majority of people with intellectual disabilities due to floor effects which has led to a cautious approach to the use of this medication.
- *Insight of service users and other people with intellectual disabilities*: issues of interdependency between older adults with intellectual disabilities and dementia, their co-residents and family caregivers do impact on the

**Table 17.6** General guidance on discussing a diagnosis of dementia and prognosis.

- *Use the individual's preferred form of communication* – The individual with dementia should dictate the pace, form (verbal and non-verbal means) and level of information during the discussion. The focus is on what the individual wants to know, what he or she is ready to know and is able to understand: they are at the centre of all discussions, which must be respectful and supportive.
- *Identify potential benefits of knowing (and not knowing) the diagnosis* – Explore how much the individual knows already and how much they want to know. The challenge is having a discussion based on probability rather than certainty. Determine who other than the individual with dementia is to be told: consider the principle of confidentiality against the standard of best interests
- *Tailor the approach for each individual* – The diagnosis should be given by someone who has positive contact with the individual, carers/family as part of an ongoing therapeutic relationship. Furthermore, the information given must be considered in the context of stage of dementia: an individual presenting with early signs, may be able to manage a greater level of information than someone in the late stages of the condition.
- *Use a multi-disciplinary approach to answer questions and make recommendations* – Give an explanation as to why these changes are happening. Sensitively discuss how the individual's current behaviours, health difficulties etc may progress in the light of the probable diagnosis and means of sustaining their strengths and abilities for as long as possible. Endeavour to address fears and thoughts about the future, in a realistic and supportive way.
- *Repetition* – Individuals and their carers may need to have more than one discussion around both diagnosis and prognosis. This is a dynamic process that requires time to talk and facilitation to ask questions, so additional discussions may be necessary.
- *Access resources* – Its important to provide written/pictorial information to support the discussion. There are resources available from the Down Syndrome Association (UK), Down Syndrome Scotland and British Institute for Learning Disabilities (BILD) for people with intellectual disabilities, their peers and carers. It is also helpful if information on local community supports is made available
- *Arrange for further support if required* – In addition to any further support for the person with dementia (individual counselling etc), the health of the carer needs to be considered, particularly in relation to their own ageing needs, levels of stress and ability to cope.
- *Agree a care plan* – This should focus on both current and future needs and highlight intervention strategies and reviews, with supportive information. It is helpful to consider future social care support needs, especially in the light of changes in residential, day program or short-breaks placements that may be being considered.

understanding of changes taking place. (Lloyd, Kalsy and Gatherer 2007; Lynggaard and Alexander 2004).

- *Life after assessment*: the main thrust of published literature has been on recognising signs, assessment and diagnosis of dementia in people with intellectual disabilities. There is limited information available on what happened after diagnosis, including issues such as the process of diagnostic counselling, continuing care, the needs of ageing care givers, accessing day, residential and respite services, residential supports and future life planning to determine needs and wishes (Kalsy *et al.* 2005; Thompson and Wright 2001; Watchman 2003). However, the wider detrimental effects include the probable moving of a person with Alzheimer's disease to alternative (but often inappropriate) accommodation (Thompson and Wright 2001, Wilkinson *et al.* 2004).
- *End of life issues*: these encompass old age, palliative care needs, terminal illness, dying, grief, mourning and bereavement faced by the ageing individual with intellectual disabilities and their ageing family caregivers. Strategies such as end of life education, grief counselling, bereavement services, support groups, crisis teams, and end of life committees are options for providing more responsive end of life care (Botsford and King 2005; Tuffrey-Wijne 2003; Watchman 2005).
- *Workforce concerns*: broadly speaking, there is international consensus on the need of caregivers to be both intellectual disability and dementia aware in order to meet the changing needs of older adults with intellectual disabilities. This does have significant workforce implications in relation to high resource implications of prospective screening and early diagnosis, skills and knowledge development, staff and family caregiver training, support, communication and sharing of skills (Hussien and Manthorpe 2005; Tuffrey-Wijne *et al.* 2005; Turk *et al.* 2001).

## CONCLUSIONS AND RECOMMENDED READING

The increased life expectancy for individuals with intellectual disabilities has given rise to an older population about whom knowledge is limited and only recently has there been a consideration of the cause and level of intellectual disabilities when estimating life expectancies (Strauss and Eyman 1996) and reporting physical and mental health problems (Janicki *et al.* 2002). This has created a field of growing but inconsistent literature on the ageing process.

Age-related physical and mental health problems, such as depression, arthritis and cataracts are being increasingly reported in the ageing intellectual disability population alongside syndrome-specific disability linked conditions. Of note is the elevated prevalence of dementia in adults with intellectual disabilities and, in particular, adults with Down syndrome. The exact course and presentation of dementia in intellectual disabilities and Down syndrome remains unclear despite the extensive availability of assessment tests and batteries. For this reason, it is recommended that for diagnostic and quality of life purposes, behavioural or cognitive changes in adults with Down syndrome over the age of 30 (and intellectual disabilities over the age of 50) should be investigated.

As the older population of people with intellectual disabilities has risen dramatically over recent years, the need for coherent, planned and effective services has also grown (Janicki *et al.* 1999; Thorpe *et al.* 2001). Furthermore, the closure of the long-stay hospitals has moved people with intellectual disabilities into changing community-based systems with uncoordinated and variable primary care practices. Currently, there are reactive service responses to the emerging needs of older adults with intellectual disabilities rather than proactive responsive needs-led service provision that has the capacity to take into account current and future age-related needs (Adams *et al.* 2008; Hatzidimitriadou and Milne 2005, Kalsy *et al.* 2005). There is a need to work in partnership alongside older people with intellectual disabilities and their carers to bring about positive futures for those concerned, so that people have personal control over their own lives, make everyday choices, are in good physical and mental health until death and have reciprocal and respectful relationships with others (Lloyd *et al.* 2007). Services should be educated and equipped to recognise and manage both physical and mental health changes associated with the ageing process. Frameworks and guidelines that emphasis multidisciplinary and multiagency working have been produced, highlighting the key issues for the individuals, carers and service providers. However, there is comparatively less literature regarding specific interventions for ageing adults with intellectual disabilities which must consider a complex interaction of genetics, socioeconomic and ethnic background and context alongside environmental and caregiver relationships. This focus is necessary to ensure that the increased life expectancy of older adults with intellectual disabilities can be matched by increased quality of life.

## RECOMMENDED READING

Fray, M. (2000) *Caring for Kathleen: A Sister's Story*. Kidderminster: British Institute for Learning Disabilities.

Hogg, J. and Langa, A. (2005) *Assessing Adults with Intellectual Disabilities*. Oxford: Blackwell Publishing.

Janicki, M.P. and Dalton, A.J. (1999) *Dementia, Aging and Intellectual Disabilities: A Handbook*. Philadelphia: Bruner/Mazel.

## References

Adams, D., Oliver, C., Kalsy, S., Peters, S., Broquard, M., Basra, T., Konstantinidi, E. and McQuillan, S. (2008) Behavioural characteristics associated with dementia assessment referrals in adults with Down syndrome. *Journal of Intellectual Disability Research*, **54**(4), 358–368.

Aldrich F. and Wilson B. (1991) Rivermead Behavioural Memory Test for Children (RBMT-C): a preliminary evaluation. *British Journal of Clinical Psychology*, **30**, 161– 68.

Alzheimer's Society (2007) *Dementia UK: A report into the prevalence and cost of dementia*. London: Alzheimer's Society.

Alzheimer's Society (2009) *Supporting People With Dementia Using the Mental Capacity Act*. London: Alzheimer's Society.

Alzheimer's Disease International (1999) *The Prevalence of Dementia: a factsheet*. London: Alzheimer's Disease International.

Auty, E. and Scior, K. (2008) Psychologists' clinical practices in assessing dementia in individuals with Down syndrome. *Journal of Policy and Practice in Intellectual Disabilities*, **5**(4), 259–68.

Aylward, E., Burt, D., Thorpe, L., Lai, F. and Dalton, A. (1997) Diagnosis of dementia in individuals with intellectual disability. *J. Intellect. Disabil. Res.*, **41**, 152–64.

Ball, S., Holland, A.J., Hon, J., Huppert, F., Treppner, P. and Watson, P. (2006) Personality and behaviour changes mark the early stages of Alzheimer's disease on adults with Down syndrome: Findings from a prospective population-based study. *International Journal of Geriatric Psychiatry*, **21**(7), 661–73.

Beange, H., McElduff, A. and Baker, W. (1995) Medical disorders of adults with mental retardation: a population study. *Am. J. Ment. Retard.*, **99**, 595–604.

Bittles A., Petterson B., Sullivan S., Hussain R., Glasson E. and Montgomery P. (2002) The influence of intellectual disability on life expectancy. *Journal of Gerontology Series A – Biological Sciences and Medical Sciences*, **57**, M470–M472.

Botsford, A.L. and King, A. (2005) End-of-life care policies for people with an intellectual disability. *Journal of Disability Policy Studies*, **16**, 22–30.

Bowes A. and Wilkinson, H. (2003) 'We didn't know it would get that bad': South Asian experience of dementia and the service response. *Health and Social Care in the Community*, **11**(5), 387–96.

Branford, D. and Collacott, R. (1994) Comparison of community and institutional prescription of antiepileptic drugs for individuals with learning disabilities. *J. Intellect. Disabil. Res.*, **38**, 561–6.

Braunschweig, C., Gomez, S., Sheean, P., Tomey, K., Rimmer, J. and Heller, T. (2004) Nutritional status and risk factors for chronic disease in urban-dwelling adults with Down syndrome. *Am. J. Ment. Retard.*, **109**, 186–93.

British Psychological Society (2009) *Dementia and People with Learning Disabilities: Guidance on the assessment, diagnosis, treatment and support*. Leicester: British Psychological Society.

Buijssen, H. (2005) *The Simplicity of Dementia*. London: Jessica Kingsley Publishers.

Burt, D. and Aylward, E. (2000). Test battery for the diagnosis of dementia in individuals with Intellectual Disability. *J. Intellect. Disabil. Res.*, **44**, 175–80.

Busciglio, J. and Yankner, B. (1995) Apoptosis and increased generation of reactive oxygen species in Down's syndrome neurons in vitro. *Nature*, **378**, 776–9.

Campbell, M. and Malone, R.P. (1991) Mental retardation and psychiatric disorders. *Hosp. Community Psychiatry*, **42**, 374–9.

Carr, J. (2000). Intellectual and daily living skills of 30-year-olds with Down's syndrome: Continuation of a longitudinal study. *J. App. Res. Intellect. Disabil.*, **13**, 1–16.

Cooper, S-A (1997a) Deficient health and social services for elderly persons with learning disabilities. *J. Intellect. Disabil. Res.*, 41, 331–8.

Cooper, S.A. (1997b) High prevalence of dementia among people with learning disabilities not attributable to Down's syndrome. *Psychol. Med.*, 27, 609–16.

Cooper, S.A. (1998) Clinical study of the effects of age on the physical health of adults with mental retardation. *Am. J. Ment. Retard.*, 102, 582–9.

Cooper, S.A. (1999) The relationship between psychiatric and physical health in elderly people with intellectual disability. *J. Intellect. Disabil. Res.*, 43, 54–60.

Cooper, S. A., Prasher, (1998). Maladaptive behaviours and symptoms of dementia in adults with Down's syndrome compared with adults with intellectual disability of other aetiologies. *Journal of Intellectual Disability Research*, 4, (4).

Cosgrave, M.P., Tyrrell, J., McCarron, M., Gill, M. and Lawlor, B.A. (1999) Age at onset of dementia and age of menopause in women with Down's syndrome. *J. Intellect. Disabil. Res.*, 43, 461–5.

Crayton, L., Oliver, C., Holland, A. and Hall, S. (1998) The neuropsychological assessment of age-related cognitive deficits in adults with Down syndrome. *J. App. Res. Intellect. Disabil.*, 11, 255–72.

Dalton, A.J. (1995) *Dalton/McMurray Visual Memory Test*: Delayed matching to sample cognitive test. Canada: Byte Craft Ltd.

Dalton, A.J. and Janicki, M.P. (1999) Ageing and dementia. In M.P. Janicki and A.J. Dalton (eds) *Dementia, Aging and Intellectual Disabilities: A Handbook* (pp. 5–31). Philadelphia: Bruner/Mazel.

Department of Constitutional Affairs (2007) *The Mental Capacity Act: Code of Practice*. London: The Stationery Office.

Department of Health (2001a) *Valuing People: a new strategy for learning disability for the 21st century*. London: The Stationery Office.

Department of Health (2001b) *National Service Framework for Older People*. London: The Stationery Office.

Department of Health (2004) *New Provision for Older People with Learning Disabilities*. London: The Stationery Office.

Department of Health (2006) *New Ambition for Old Age: next steps in implementing the NSF for older people*. London: The Stationery Office.

Department of Health (2009) *Living Well With Dementia: a national dementia strategy*. London: The Stationery Office.

Department of Health and CSIP (2005) *Everybody's Business: integrated mental health services for older adults – a service development guide*. London: The Stationery Office.

Dodd, K. (2003) Supporting people with Down syndrome and dementia. *Tizard Intellectual Disability Review*, 8, 14–18.

Dodd, K., Kerr, D. and Fern, S. (2006) *Down's Syndrome and Dementia Workbook for Carers*. Teddington: Down Syndrome Association.

Dodd, P., Dowling, S. and Hollins, S. (2005) A review of the emotional, psychiatric and behavioural responses to bereavement in people with intellectual disabilities. *J. Intellect. Disab. Res.*, 49, 537–43.

DSA (2007) Down Syndrome. DSA: Teddington, Essex.

Emerson, E. (2004) Poverty and children with intellectual disabilities in the world's richer countries. *Journal of Intellectual and Developmental Disability*, 29, 319–38.

Evenhuis, H.M. (1995a) Medical aspects of ageing in a population with intellectual disability: II. Hearing impairment. *J. Intellect. Disabil. Res.*, 39, 27–33.

Evenhuis, H.M. (1995b) Medical aspects of ageing in a population with intellectual disability: I. Visual impairment. *J. Intellect. Disabil. Res.*, **39**, 19–25.

Evenhuis, H.M. (1992) Evaluation of a screening instrument for dementia in ageing mentally retarded persons. *J. Intellect. Disabil. Res.*, **36**(4), 337–47.

Evenhuis, H.M. (1996) Further evaluation of the Dementia Questionnaire for Persons with Mental Retardation (DMR). *J. Intellect. Disabil. Res.*, **40**(4), 369–73.

Fearnley, K., McLennan, J. and Weaks, D. (1997) *The Right to Know? Sharing the Diagnosis of Dementia*. Edinburgh: Alzheimer's Scotland, Action on Dementia.

Foelker, G.A. and Luke, E.A. (1989) Mental Health Issues for the aging mentally retarded population. *The Journal of Applied Gerontology*, **8**, 242–50.

Fraser, J. and Mitchell, A. (1876) Kalmuc idiocy: report of a case with autopsy, with notes on sixty-two cases. *J. Ment. Sci.*, **22**, 161–79.

Gedye, A. (1995) *Development of the Scale. Dementia Scale for Down Syndrome Manual*. Vancouver: Gedye Research and Consulting.

Hagerman, R.J., Altshul-Stark, D. and McBogg, P. (1987) Recurrent otitis media in the fragile X syndrome. *Am. J. Dis. Child*, **141**, 184–7.

Harper, D.C. and Wadsworth, J.S. (1992) Improving health care communication for persons with mental retardation. *Public Health Rep.*, **107**, 297–302.

Hatton, C. (2002) Psychosocial interventions for adults with intellectual disabilities and mental health problems: a review. *Journal of Mental Health*, **11**, 357–74.

Hatzidimitriadou, E. and Milne, A. (2005) Planning Ahead: Meeting the needs of older people with intellectual disabilities in the United Kingdom. *Dementia*, **4**, 341–59.

Holland A.J. (2004) Down's syndrome and Alzheimer's Disease. Down Syndrome Association: Teddington, Essex.

Holland, A., Huppert, F., Ball, S., Teppner, P. and Dodd, K. (2005) *CAMDEX-DS: Dementia Test for People with Down's Syndrome*. Cambridge: Cambridge University Press.

Holland, A.J., Hon, J., Huppert, F.A., Stevens, F. and Watson, P. (1998) Population-based study of the prevalence and presentation of dementia in adults with Down's syndrome. *Br. J. Psychiatry*, **172**, 493–8.

Holland, A.J., Hon, J., Huppert, F.A. and Stevens, F. (2000) Incidence and course of dementia in people with Down's syndrome: findings from a population-based study. *J. Intellect. Disabil. Res.*, **44**, 138–46.

Holland AJ (2004) Down's syndrome and Alzheimer's Disease. Down Syndrome Association: Teddington, Essex.

Hussein, S. and Manthorpe, J. (2005) Older people with learning disabilities: work-force issues. *Journal of Integrated Care*, **13**, 17–23.

Hutchings, B.L., Olsen, R.V. and Ehrenkrantz, E.D. (2000) Modifying Home Environments. In M.P. Janicki and E.F. Ansello (eds) *Community Supports for Aging Adults with Lifelong Disabilities*. Baltimore: Paul H. Brookes.

Janicki, M.P., Dalton, A.J., Henderson, M. and Davidson, P.W. (1999) Mortality and morbidity among older adults with intellectual disabilities: Health services considerations. *Disability and Rehabilitation*, **21**, 284–94.

Janicki, M.P., Davidson, P.W., Henderson, C.M., McCallion, P., Taets, J.D., *et al.* (2002) Health characteristics and health services utilization in older adults with intellectual disability living in community residences. *J. Intellect. Disabil. Res.*, **46**, 287–98.

Janicki, M.P., Heller, T., Seltzer, G.B. and Hogg, J. (1996) Practice guidelines for the clinical assessment and care management of Alzheimer's disease and other dementias among adults with intellectual disability. *J. Intellect. Disabil. Res.*, **40**, 373–82.

Janicki, M.P. and Dalton, A.J. (1999) *Dementia, Aging and Intellectual Disabilities: a handbook*. Philadelphia: Bruner/Mazel.

Jervis, N. and Prinsloo L. (2007) How we developed a multidisciplinary screening project for people with Down syndrome given the increased prevalence of early onset dementia. *British Journal of Learning Disabilities*, **36**, 13–21.

Kahn, R.L. (2002) Successful aging and well-being. *Gerontology*, **42**, 725–6.

Kalsy, S., Heath, R., Adams, D. and Oliver, C. (2007) Effects of training on controllability attributions of behavioural excesses and deficits shown by adults with Down syndrome and dementia. *Journal of Applied Research in Intellectual Disabilities*, **20**, 64–8

Kalsy, S., McQuillan, S., Adams, D., Lloyd, V., Basra, T., *et al.* (2005) A proactive psychological screening strategy for dementia in adults with Down syndrome: Preliminary description of service use and evaluation. *Journal of Policy and Practice in Intellectual Disabilities*, **2**, 116–25.

Kalsy, S., McQuillan, S., Oliver, C. and Hall, S. (2002) *Assessment for Adults with Developmental Disabilities (A.A.D.S.)*. Birmingham: The University of Birmingham and South Birmingham Primary Care NHS Trust.

Kasl-Godley, J. and Gatz, M. (2000) Psychosocial interventions for individuals with dementia: an integration of theory, therapy, and a clinical understanding of dementia. *Clinical Psychology Review*, **20**, 755–82.

Kerr, D. (1997) *Down's Syndrome and Dementia: a practitioner's guide*. London: Venture Press.

Kerr, M. (2004) Improving the general health of people with learning disabilities. *Advances in Psychiatric Treatment*, **10**, 200–6.

Kerr, D. and Wilkinson, H. (2005) *In the know, implementing good practice. Information and tools for anyone supporting people with a learning disability and dementia*. Brighton: Pavilion Publishing Ltd.

Kitwood, T. (1997) *Dementia Reconsidered: the person comes first*. Buckingham: Open University Press.

Lynggaard, H. and Alexander, N. (2004) Why are my friends changing? Explaining dementia to people with learning disabilities. *British Journal of Learning Disabilities*, **32**, 30–9.

Lloyd, V., Kalsy, S. and Gatherer, A. (2007) The subjective experience of individuals with Down syndrome living with dementia. *Dementia: The International Journal of Social Research and Practice*, **6**, 63–88.

Lloyd, V., Kalsy, S. and Gatherer, A. (2008) The impact of dementia upon residential carers for individuals with Down syndrome. *Journal of Policy and Practice in Intellectual Disabilities*, **5**(1), 33–38.

McCallion, P. and McCarron, M. (2004) Ageing and intellectual disabilities: a review of recent literature. *Current Opinion in Psychiatry*, **17**, 1–4.

McCracken, C., Boneham, M., Copeland, J., Williams, K., Wilson, K., Scott, A., McKibbin, P. and Cleave, N. (1997) Prevalence of dementia and depression among elderly people from black and ethnic minorities. *British Journal of Psychiatry*, **171**, 269–73.

McKeown, J., Clarke, A. and Repper, J. (2006) Life story work in health and social care. *Journal of Advanced Nursing*, **55**, 237–24.

Marshall, M. (2001) Care settings and the care environment. In *A Handbook of Dementia Care* (ed. C. Cantley). Buckingham: Open University Press.

Mencap (1998). *The NHS – Health for all?* People with learning disabilities and health care. London: Mencap Publications.

Mencap (2007) *Death By Indifference*. London: Mencap Publications.

Mohan, M., Carpenter, P.K. and Bennett, C. (2009a) *Donepzil for Dementia in People with Down Syndrome: a review*. The Cochrane Collaboration, John Wiley Press.

Mohan, M., Carpenter, P.K. and Bennett, C. (2009b) *Galantamine for Dementia in People with Down Syndrome: a review*. The Cochrane Collaboration, John Wiley Press.

Mohan, M., Carpenter, P.K. and Bennett, C. (2009c) *Memantine for Dementia in People with Down Syndrome: a review*. The Cochrane Collaboration, John Wiley Press.

Morgan, H. and Magrill, D. (2005) *Supporting Older Families of People with Learning Disabilities*. London: The Mental Health Foundation.

Moss, S., Bouras, N. and Holt, G. (2000) Mental health services for people with intellectual disability: a conceptual framework. *J. Intellect. Disabil. Res.*, 44, 97–107.

National Audit Office (2007) *Improving Services and Support for People with Dementia*. London: Stationery Office.

Nelson, L., Lott, I., Touchette, P., Satz, P. and D'Elia, L. (1995) Detection of Alzheimer disease in individuals with Down syndrome. *Am. J. Ment. Retard.*, 99, 616–22.

National Institute for Health and Clinical Excellence (NICE) (2006a) *Dementia: supporting people with dementia and their carers*. NICE guideline number 42. London: NICE.

National Institute for Health and Clinical Excellence (NICE) (2006b) *Donepezil, Galantamine, Rivastigmine (Review) and Memantine for the Treatment of Alzheimer's Disease. NICE technology appraisal guidance 111*. London: NICE.

Nieuwenhuis-Mark R.E. (2009) Diagnosing Alzheimer's dementia in Down syndrome: Problems and possible solutions. *Research in Developmental Disabilities*, 30, 828–38.

O'Brien, G. and Yule, W. (1995) *Behavioural Phenotypes*. London: MacKeith Press.

Oliver, C. (1999) Perspectives on Assessment and Evaluation. In M.P. Janicki and A.J. Dalton (eds) *Dementia, Aging, and Intellectual Disabilities: a handbook*. Philadelphia PA: Taylor and Francis/Bruner/Mazel, pp. 123–40.

Oliver, C., Crayton, L., Holland, A.J. and Hall, S. (2000) Acquired cognitive impairments in adults with Down syndrome: Effects on the individual, carers and services. *Am. J. Ment. Retard.*, 105, 455–65.

Oliver, C., Crayton, L., Holland, A., Hall, S. and Bradbury, J. (1998) A four year prospective study of age-related cognitive change in adults with Down's syndrome. *Psychol. Med.*, 28, 1365–77.

Oliver, C. and Holland, A. (1986) Down's syndrome and Alzheimer's disease: a review. *Psychol. Med.*, 16, 307–22.

Oliver, C. and Kalsy, S. (2005) The Assessment of Dementia in People with Intellectual Disabilities: Context Strategy and Methods. In J. Hogg and A. Langa (eds), *Assessing Adults with Intellectual Disabilities*. Blackwell Publishing: Oxford.

Opie, J., Rosewarne, R. and O'Connor, D.W. (1999) The efficacy of psychological approaches to behaviour disorders in dementia: a systematic literature review. *Australia and New Zealand Journal of Psychiatry*, 33, 789–99.

Ouellette-Kuntz, H. (2005) Understanding health disparities and inequities faced by individuals with intellectual disabilities. *J. Applied. Res. Intellect. Disabil.*, 18, 113–21.

Patel, N., Mirza, N., Lindbla, P., Amstrup, K. and Samaoli, O. (1998) *Dementia and Minority Ethnic Older People: managing care in the UK, Denmark and France*. London: Russell House.

Prasher, V.P. (1995) Age specific prevalence, thyroid dysfunction and depressive symptomatology in adults with Down's syndrome and dementia. *Int. J. Geriatric Psychiatry*, **10**, 25–31.

Prasher, V.P. (2004) Review of donepezil, rivastigmine, galantamine and memantine for the treatment of dementia in Alzheimer's disease in adults with Down's syndrome: implications for the learning disability population. *Int. J. Geriatric Psychiatry*, **19**, 509–15.

Prasher, V.P. and Krishnan, V.H.R. (1993) Age of onset and duration of dementia in people with Down syndrome. *Int. J. Geriatr. Psychiatry*, **8**, 915–22.

Pueschel, S.M. and Scola, F.H. (1987) Atlantoaxial instability in individuals with Down syndrome: epidemiologic, radiographic, and clinical studies. *Pediatrics*, **80**, 555–60.

Rubello, D., Pozzan, G.B., Casara, D., Girelli, M.E., Boccato, S., Rigon, F., *et al.* (1995) Natural course of subclinical hypothyroidism in Down's syndrome: prospective study results and therapeutic considerations. *J. Endocrinol. Invest.*, **18**, 35–40.

Ruddick, L. and Oliver, C. (2005) The Development of a Health Status Measure for Self-report by People with Intellectual Disabilities. *J. Applied. Res. Intellect. Disabil.*, **18**, 143–50.

Seltzer, G.B., Schupf, N. and Wu, H.S. (2001) A prospective study of menopause in women with Down's syndrome. *J. Intellect. Disabil. Res.*, **45**, 1–7.

Singleton, J. and Kalsy, S. (2008) It Hurts! Pain and older adults with learning disabilities and dementia. *Clinical Psychology and Learning Disabilities*. Leicester: British Psychological Society.

Sink, K., Covinsky, K., Newcomer, R. and Yaffe, K. (2004) Ethnic differences in the prevalence and patterns of dementia realted behaviours. *Journal of the American Geriatric Society*, **52**, 1272–83.

Stebbens, V.A., Dennis, J., Samuels, M.P., Croft, C.B. and Southall, P. (1991) Sleep related upper airway obstruction in a cohort with Down's syndrome. *Arch. Dis. Child.*, **66**, 1333–8.

Strauss, D. and Eyman, R. (1996) Mortality of people with mental retardation in California with and without Down syndrome. *Am. J. Ment. Retard.*, **100**, 643–53.

Thompson, D. and Wright, S. (2001) *Misplaced and Forgotten? People with learning disabilities in residential services for older people*. London: Mental Health Foundation.

Thorpe, L., Davidson, P. and Janicki, M. (2001) Healthy ageing – adults with intellectual disabilities: bio-behavioural issues. *J. Appl. Res. Intellect. Disabil.*, **13**, 218–28.

Tuffrey-Wijne, I. (2003) The palliative care needs of people with intellectual disabilities: a literature review. *Palliative Care*, **17**, 55–62.

Tuffrey-Wijne, I., Hollins, S. and Curfs, L. (2005) Supporting patients who have intellectual disabilities. *International Journal of Palliative Care*, **11**, 182–8.

Turk, V., Dodd, K. and Christmas, M. (2001) *Down's Syndrome and Dementia: a Briefing for Commissioners*. London: The Foundation for People with Learning Disabilities.

Tyrrell, J., Cosgrave, M., McCarron, M., McPherson, J., Calvert, J., *et al.* (2001) Dementia in people with Down syndrome. *Int. J. Geriatr. Psychiatry*, **16**, 1168–74.

Watchman, K. (2003) Critical issues for service planners and providers of care for people with Down's syndrome and dementia. *British Journal of Learning Disabilities*, **31**, 81–4.

Watchman, K. (2005). Practitioner raised issues and end of life care for adults with Down's syndrome and dementia. *J. Pol. Pract. Intellect. Disabil.*, **2**, 156–62.

Wilkinson, H. and Janicki, M.P. (2002) The Edinburgh Principles. *J. Intellect. Disabil. Res.*, **46**, 279–84.

Wilkinson, H., Kerr, D., Cunningham, C. and Rae, C. (2004). *Home for Good? Preparing to support people with learning difficulties in residential settings when they develop dementia.* Brighton: Pavilion Publishing/Joseph Rowntree Foundation.

Wilson, D.N. and Haire, A. (1990) Health screening for people with mental handicap living in the community. *British Medical Journal*, **301**, 1379–81.

Wisniewski, K.E., Wisniewski, H.M. and Wen, G.Y. (1985) Occurrence of neuropathological changes and dementia of Alzheimer's disease in Down's syndrome. *Ann. Neurol.*, **17**, 278–82.

Zwakhalen S.M.G., Van Dongen K.A.J., Hamers J.P.H. and Huda Huijer A.S. (2004) Pain assessment in intellectually disabled people: non-verbal indicators. *Journal of Advanced Nursing*, **45**, 236–45.

Zigman, W.B., Schupf, N., Devenny, D.A., Miezejeski, C., Ryan, R., Urv, T. K., et al. (2004) Incidence and prevalence of dementia in elderly adults with mental retardation without down syndrome. *Am. J. Ment. Retard.*, **109**, 126–41.

# INDEX

*A Vision for Adult Social Care: Capable Communities and Active Citizens* (2010) 38

A–B–C analysis 214–15

AAIDD *see* American Association on Intellectual and Developmental Disabilities

ABA *see* Applied Behavioural Analysis

abstract questions 114

abuse
  autism spectrum disorders 347
  legislative context 83, 85, 89–90, 99–101
  mental health disorders 314
  offending behaviour 240, 252–3
  social context 54, 55–6
  *see also* sexual abuse

academic skills 299–300

acquiescence 108, 113, 185, 246

active verbs 114

adaptation 4, 5–6, 142, 144

ADHD *see* Attention Deficit Hyperactivity Disorder

ADOS *see* Autism Diagnostic Observation Schedule

Adult Safeguarding procedures 237

adult social care
  ageing 360, 374
  organisations 162, 171, 176–7
  service provision 36–7

*Adults with Incapacity (Scotland) Act* (2000) 91, 102

Advancing Practice Conference 196

advice to courts 97

advising organisations 164–77

advocacy 43–4, 310

aetiology *see* causes of intellectual disabilities

ageing 359–92
  assessment and diagnosis 364–7, 383–4
  behavioural presentation of dementia 367–70, 378
  case studies 371–2
  context 359
  dementia 361, 363–85
  direct interventions 375–82
  Down syndrome 361–6, 368–74, 382, 384–5
  emerging issues 382–4
  epidemiology of intellectual disabilities 9–11
  intellectual disability impacts 361
  mental health disorders 316, 328, 362–3, 384–5
  physical health 362, 384–5
  policy contexts 373–4
  prevalence of dementia 364–5
  psychological service responses 375–82
  service provision 359, 373–5
  sharing prognostic information 382–3
  social and health care contexts 360
  socio-economic position 51–2
  stage-specific activities 381–2
  symptom progression of dementia 369–70

*Clinical Psychology and People with Intellectual Disabilities*, Second Edition. Edited by Eric Emerson, Chris Hatton, Kate Dickson, Rupa Gone, Amanda Caine and Jo Bromley.
© 2012 John Wiley & Sons, Ltd. Published 2012 by John Wiley & Sons, Ltd.

aggressive behaviour 255–63
  ageing 367, 368
  mental health disorders 324–5, 328–9
alleged offending 235–9
Alzheimer's disease 361, 363–85
  assessment and diagnosis 364–7
  behavioural presentation 367–70, 378
  case studies 371–2
  direct interventions 375–82
  emerging issues 382–4
  prevalence 364–5
  service provision 372–5
  stage-specific activities 381–2
American Association on Intellectual and Developmental Disabilities (AAIDD) 4–6
anchor events 115
Angelman syndrome 16
anger management 130, 133, 324–5
anger-related measures 256–7
Antecedent Behaviour Consequence (ABC) analysis 214–15
anti-dementia medications 382
anxiety
  ageing 362, 367
  autism spectrum disorders 352
  direct interventions 128–9, 131, 133–4
  mental health disorders 321–2, 324, 329–31
  parents with intellectual disabilities 303–4
anxiolytic medications 322
Applied Behavioural Analysis (ABA) 207, 210, 220, 227
appropriate vocabulary 114–15
arson 85–6, 254–5
art therapies 377, 381
ASD see Autistic Spectrum Disorder
Asperger's syndrome 85, 340
assessment
  academic skills 299–300
  ageing 364–7, 384
  autism spectrum disorders 344–8
  challenging behaviour 211–28
  childcare and development 301
  epidemiology of intellectual disabilities 8

family history 300
general intelligence 299
life skills 300
mental health disorders 316–19, 328–31
National Health Service 186–7, 195–6
offending behaviour 240–8
parents with intellectual disabilities 299–303, 309
sexual abuse 282–4
social support 301
Assimilation Model 136
attachment theory
  mental health disorders 314
  offending behaviour 252
  parents with intellectual disabilities 301
attention 76–7
Attention Deficit Hyperactivity Disorder (ADHD) 70
auditory sensitivity 351
augmented communication 109, 117
authority figures 136, 161
Autism Diagnostic Observation Schedule (ADOS) 348
autism spectrum disorders (ASD) 339–58
  assessment and diagnosis 344–8
  behavioural therapy 350–3
  causes 341–2
  cognitive assessment 70
  cognitive behavioural therapy 353
  context 339
  definitions 339–41
  direct interventions 349–54
  executive dysfunction 343
  family members 142, 144, 155
  interviews 347–9
  mental health disorders 315
  offending behaviour 240, 258–63
  organisations 172
  psychological theories of autism 342–4
  sensory sensitivities 351–2
  specific interventions 353–4
  theory of mind 342–3
  weak central coherence theory 343–4

autonomy
    direct interventions 133
    legislative context 83, 90–3, 97–9, 100

BADS *see* Behavioural Assessment of
    Dysexecutive Functioning
Beck Depression Inventory 317, 324
Behaviour Problems Inventory 134
Behavioural Assessment of
    Dysexecutive Functioning
    (BADS) 77
behavioural observations 244, 247–8
behavioural phenotype 13
behavioural presentation of demen-
    tia 367–70, 378
behavioural sequence questions 151–3
behavioural therapy
    ageing 375–6, 378
    autism spectrum disorders 350–3
    challenging behaviour 207–8
    family members 154–6
    mental health disorders 320–2
    National Health Service 183, 185,
    187
*Behind Closed Doors* (2001) 275
*Better Services for the Mentally
    Handicapped* (1971) 27, 88
Big Society 44
biomedical factors 14, 18
block design sub-test 73–4
borderline personality disorder
    (BPD) 281
boundary issues in work 194–5
BPD *see* borderline personality
    disorder
BPS *see* British Psychological Society
BPVS-2 *see* British Picture Vocabulary
    Scale
Bradley Report (2009) 238–9, 263
Brief Symptom Inventory 134, 317
British Picture Vocabulary Scale
    (BPVS-2) 75–6
British Psychological Society (BPS)
    cognitive assessment 65, 71
    legislative context 98
    National Health Service 181–2, 196
    offending behaviour 243
Buijssen's two laws of dementia 377
bullying 260–1, 328

capacity to consent 65, 241–3, 278, 283
care homes 39, 99–100, 374
    *see also* residential care
care management 34
care plans 162, 383
Care Programme Approach (CPA) 33,
    163–4
Care Quality Commission 176
carers
    ageing 361, 363, 378–80, 382–5
    autism spectrum disorders 345, 347,
    350
    challenging behaviour 220–7
    direct interventions 122–3, 128
    interviews 118
    mental health disorders 318, 326,
    328–9
    offending behaviour 250
    organisations 165–7, 172
    parents with intellectual
    disabilities 310
    sexual abuse 277–8, 287–8
*Caring for People* (1989) 36
causes of intellectual disabilities 12–19
    biomedical factors 14, 18
    environmental factors 15, 18–19
    genetic factors 12–17
    perinatal causes 15–18
    postnatal causes 18–19
    prenatal causes 14–15
CBT *see* cognitive behavioural therapy
central coherence 343–4
centre-based programmes 304, 307–8
cerebral palsy 12
challenging behaviour 205–33
    ageing 362
    altering behaviour
    consequences 223–4
    assessment and formulation 211–28
    behavioural models 207–8
    cognitive assessment 64
    communication-based models
    206–7
    definition and context 205–6
    direct interventions 134, 212, 220–7
    effectiveness of interventions 212,
    227
    environmental/contextual
    factors 208–9, 212, 213–14

challenging behaviour   (*Continued*)
  epidemiology of intellectual
    disabilities 12
  establishing operations 217, 220–1
  family members 148, 154
  formulating hypotheses 212, 219
  functional assessment 212, 217–19
  functional relationships 208
  hypothesis testing 212, 219–20
  increasing alternative
    behaviours 221–3
  individualised risk management
    plans 224–7
  informant-based functional
    assessment 218–19
  information about the person 212,
    213–14
  intervention design, training and
    support 212, 220–7
  legislative context 85–6
  maintaining positive strategies 212,
    227
  mental health disorders 315, 327,
    328–9
  National Health Service 187
  neurological models 206
  offending and alleged offend-
    ing 235–6, 245–6
  organisations 170, 172–3, 175
  Positive Behavioural Support 210,
    228
  problem identification and target
    behaviour 211–13, 217
  psychiatric models 207
  reducing challenging
    behaviour 220–1
  sexual abuse 276
  understandings and models 206–10
CHANGE 307–8
childcare and development 301, 306–7
children
  interviews 110
  organisations 163
  sexual abuse 273, 274–5, 279–80, 288
*Children Act* (1989/2004) 34, 176–7, 295
chromosomal disorders 14–17
chronic adversity 239–40
circular questions 151–3
citizen advocacy 43–4

classification of intellectual
    disabilities 4–7
  AAIDD 2010 definition 5–6
  cultural and linguistic diversity 6–7
  epidemiology 8
  levels of intellectual disability 6
  operational definitions 5–6
  present functioning 7
  service settings 7
classification questions 151–3
Clinical Governance 197
closed questions 112–13
cognition-oriented interventions 323–
    5, 376
cognitive assessment 63–81
  attention 77
  communication 75–6
  definition of cognition 66–7
  definition of learning disability 65–6
  developmental theory 60, 66
  errorless learning 73–4
  executive functioning 77
  global assessments of intelli-
    gence 67–8, 69–70, 72–5
  historical context 63–4
  intelligence quotient 65–70, 71–2
  memory 76, 77–8
  neuropsychological assessment 74,
    75–9
  Person Centred Planning 63, 64–5
  potential pitfalls 71–2
  psychometric assessment 64–6,
    68–70, 71–3
cognitive behavioural therapy
    (CBT) 121, 123–6, 130–6
  autism spectrum disorders 353
  family members 147–8, 154–6
  National Health Service 185
  offending behaviour 253, 255, 257,
    262
cognitive restructuring 325
colloquialisms 115
Commission for Social Care
    Inspection 34
commissioning health and social
    care 34–6, 37–8, 163
communication
  ageing 362, 383
  challenging behaviour 206–7

cognitive assessment 75–6
ethnicity 56
mental health disorders 331
organisations 168
parents with intellectual
    disabilities 309
sexual abuse 276
Community Care 23–4, 26–7, 33–4, 36
community psychology practice 188,
    196–7
Community Rehabilitation
    Orders 239, 240–1
community safety 238
community services 327
community support teams 43
Community Teams for people with
    Learning Disabilities
    (CTLD) 188–90
Community Treatment Orders
    (CTO) 97
compliance
    interviews 107
    offending behaviour 246
    organisations 165–6, 176–7
    sexual abuse 276–7
compulsory hospitalisation 101–2
conduct disorders 155
confidentiality 110, 177, 195, 243–4
consent
    ageing 382
    direct interventions 122
    interviews 109
    National Health Service 194–5
    offending behaviour 241–3, 252–3
    sexual abuse 273, 278, 283
constraint minimisation 175
Continuing NHS Care (1995) 32
continuing professional development
    (CPD) 182–3, 186, 191–4, 196–7
coping mechanisms 145–8
coping skills 257, 325
Coughlan Review (1999) 32–3
counter-conditioning 322
counter-transference 128
Court of Protection 98–100
CPA see Care Programme Approach
CPD see continuing professional
    development
Cri-du-chat syndrome 16

Crime and Disorder Act (1998) 238
criminal justice system 94–5, 237–9
Criminal Procedure (Insanity) Act
    (1964/1991) 96
CTLD see Community Teams for
    people with Learning Disabilities
CTO see Community Treatment
    Orders
cultural factors 6–7, 56
cycles of abuse 279–80

day services 41–2
Death by Indifference (2007) 90–1
decision-making capacity 83, 90–3,
    97–9, 100
defense mechanisms 128–9
deficit model 130, 323
delayed recall 77–8
dementia 315, 361, 363–85
    assessment and diagnosis 364–7
    behavioural presentation 367–70,
        378
    case studies 371–2
    direct interventions 375–82
    emerging issues 382–4
    prevalence 364–5
    service provision 372–5
    stage-specific activities 381–2
    symptom progression 369–70
denial 253
dependence 277
depression
    ageing 362, 367
    direct interventions 130
    family members 155
    gender effects 54
    mental health disorders 317, 322,
        324
Deprivation of Liberty safeguards
    (DoLS) 92, 93–4
developmental history 245, 345, 347–8
developmental theory
    autism spectrum disorders 341, 345,
        347–8
    cognitive assessment 60, 66
    life cycle theory 143–5, 146
    parents with intellectual
        disabilities 301
diachronic questions 151–3

Diagnostic and Statistical Manual
    of Mental Disorders
    (DSM-IV-TR) 65, 198, 340
diet and nutrition 305
differential reinforcement 222–3
direct interventions 121–39
    accessing psychotherapy and
        assessment 121–7
    ageing 375–82
    autism spectrum disorders
        349–54
    challenging behaviour 212, 220–7
    cognitive behavioural therapy 121,
        123–6, 130–6
    contraindications 124–5, 135
    ending therapy 156
    family members 147–8, 154–6
    mental health disorders 320–31
    National Health Service 185–6
    offending behaviour 249, 253, 255,
        257
    parents with intellectual
        disabilities 297–8
    physical space 126–7
    psychodynamic psychotherapy 121,
        123–6, 127–9, 134–6
    routine evaluation of outcomes 134
    sexual abuse 283, 284–7
    suitability for psychotherapy and
        assessment 123–4
    therapeutic relationship 123, 125–6,
        129, 130–1, 135–6
    treatment length 133–4
direct observation 316–17, 348
direct payments 42
Disability Discrimination Act
    (1995/2005) 29–31, 87
disablism 57–8
discipline 307
discrimination
    challenging behaviour 208–9
    disablism 57–8
    ethnicity 55–6
disengagement 153
distortion model 253, 262, 323
disturbed inculcation 377
DoLS see Deprivation of Liberty
    safeguards
domestic violence 54

Down syndrome
    ageing 361–6, 368–74, 382, 384–5
    causes of intellectual disabili-
        ties 14–15, 16
    mental health disorders 314
    organisations 169
DSM-IV-TR see Diagnostic and Statistical
    Manual of Mental Disorders
Duchenne's muscular dystrophy 17
dyspraxia 70

eating disorders 84–5
ecological manipulations 259
ecological models 276
Education Act (1944) 26
educational approaches in CBT 130–1
Edward's syndrome 16
effectiveness of interventions 212, 227
ego 128–9
either/or questions 113
emotional functioning
    autism spectrum disorders 343, 346
    direct interventions 130, 135
    family members 142–3, 144, 149
    interviews 107
    mental health disorders 322, 330
    offending behaviour 251, 256
emotional-oriented interventions 376
empathy 350
employment see labour markets
enabling environments 380
end-of-life care 363, 384
ending therapy 156
environmental factors
    causes of intellectual disabilities 15,
        18–19
    challenging behaviour 208–9, 212,
        213–14
    mental health disorders 326–7
    offending behaviour 239–40
    sexual abuse 278–80
EO see establishing operations
epidemiology of intellectual disabili-
    ties 3, 7–12
    disorders and associated
        conditions 12
    incidence 8, 10
    mild intellectual disabilities 9
    prevalence 8–11

service needs 10–11
severe intellectual disabilities 9–10
epilepsy 12
equity 52–3
*Equity and Excellence: Liberating the
NHS* (2010) 31–2, 37–8
errorless learning 73–4
establishing operations (EO) 209, 217,
220–1
ethical issues
National Health Service 194–5
offending behaviour 241–4
organisations 172–3
*see also* confidentiality; consent
ethnicity
ageing 364
epidemiology of intellectual
disabilities 11
service provision 43
social context 55–7
eugenics 25
*European Declaration on the Health of
Children and Young People with
Intellectual Disabilities and their
Families* (2010) 28
*Every Child Matters* (2004) 295
executive functioning 77, 343
exploitation 83, 99–101
*see also* sexual abuse
external locus of control 132, 135
extinction approach 222, 223

face processing tests 343
FAI *see* Functional Analysis Interview
*Fair Access to Care Services* (2003) 34
*Fair Society; Healthy Lives* (2010) 38
family adversity 239–40
family history 300
family members 141–60
ageing 361, 363, 378–80, 382–5
autism spectrum disorders 345, 347,
350
context 141
describing the problem 150–1
direct interventions 122–3, 128–9,
147–8, 154–6
ending therapy 156
inclusion of person with intellectual
disabilities 150

individual work 155–6
interviews 118, 149–53
joining other professionals 150
life cycle theory 143–5, 146
mental health disorders 318, 326,
328–9
offending behaviour 250
parenting groups 154–5
sexual abuse 277–8
sharing the diagnosis 141–3, 144
siblings 146, 148–9
stress and coping mechanisms
145–8, 155
systemic interview
techniques 151–3
who to invite to interview 149
family routines 307
family support services 42–3
fantasies 253
FAS *see* Fire Assessment Schedule
FCT *see* functional communication
training
fear association 321
feeding 305
feminist theory 279–80
Filipek's Red Flags for Autism 345–6
Fire Assessment Schedule (FAS)
254–5
Fire Interest Rating Scale (FIRS) 255
fire-setting 85–6, 254–5
FIRS *see* Fire Interest Rating Scale
fitness to plead 96
forensics 244–7, 252
formulation
challenging behaviour 211–28
mental health disorders 319–20
offending behaviour 248
fragile-X syndrome 17
free association 127
Frontal Systems Behaviour Scale
(FrSBe) 77
functional analyses
challenging behaviour 210, 217–18,
219–20
family members 141, 155
mental health disorders 321
National Health Service 183
offending behaviour 244, 255
organisations 170

Functional Analysis Interview
    (FAI) 218
functional assessment 212, 217–19
functional communication training
    (FCT) 222
functional displacement 221–2
functional relationships 208
funding 32–3, 42
further education 42
future questions 151–3

gender effects
    epidemiology of intellectual
        disabilities 9–10
    offending behaviour 239, 251
    sexual abuse 273, 279–80, 281–2
    social context 53–4
generalisation of skills 305–6, 350
genetic factors
    autism spectrum disorders 341
    causes of intellectual
        disabilities 12–17
    challenging behaviour 209
    mental health disorders 314
Getting It Right (2010) 31
Glasgow Anxiety and Depression
    scales 134, 317
global assessments of intelli-
    gence 67–8, 69–70, 72–5
group homes 40
group referral 171
Guardianship Orders 97, 100, 239

head teachers 172
Health Act (1999) 35
health issues
    ageing 360
    parents with intellectual
        disabilities 305
    socio-economic position 52
Health and Social Care Bill (2011) 38
Healthy Lives, Healthy People: Our
    strategy for public health in England
    (2010) 38
hidden agendas 171
hoax calls 258–9
home-based programmes 304–5
Hospital Orders 96–7, 241
hospitalisation 101–2

hostels 40
housing service provision 39–41
human rights
    legislative context 83, 87, 91
    parents with intellectual
        disabilities 296
    service provision 28, 29–31
hygiene 305
hypothesis testing 74–5, 212, 219–20
hypothetical questions 151–3

ICD see International Classification of
    Diseases
ICF see International Classification of
    Functioning, Disability and Health
idiocy 23–5
IMCA see Independent Mental
    Capacity Advocate
immediate recall 77–8
incidence of intellectual disabilities 8,
    10
independent living 36–7, 40
Independent Mental Capacity
    Advocate (IMCA) 93, 100
index scores 67–8
individual support services 42–3
individual work
    family members 155–6
    mental health disorders 320–2
    sexual abuse 285–7
individualised risk management
    plans 224–7
informant-based functional
    assessment 218–19
information seeking responses 128
informed consent see consent
inherent vulnerability 90
institutions 24, 26–7
intellectual functioning 5
intelligence quotient (IQ)
    classification of intellectual
        disabilities 5–6
    cognitive assessment 65–70, 71–2
    epidemiology of intellectual
        disabilities 8–10
    mental health disorders 330
    parents with intellectual
        disabilities 299
    service provision 25

International Classification of Diseases
(ICD) 6, 65, 340, 367
International Classification of
Functioning, Disability and Health
(ICF) 4
international legislation 28, 86–7
interventions *see* direct interventions
interviews 107–20
acquiescence 108, 113
anchor events 115
appropriate vocabulary 114–15
autism spectrum disorders 347–9
carers and family members 118
challenging behaviour 213, 218
circular questions 151–3
closed questions 112–13
considerations peculiar to
intellectual disabilities 107–8
content of the interview 110–18
creative approaches 117–18
family members 149–53
mental health disorders 317–18
offending behaviour 244–6
open questions 111–12
opening the interview 109–10
procedural and setting
considerations 109
profound intellectual disabilities
117
questions to avoid 113–14
self-report measures 116–17
suggestibility 110, 113
summarising responses 115
systemic interview
techniques 151–3
video 115–16
intimate relationships
offending behaviour 252
parents with intellectual
disabilities 293
social context 54
Inventory of Interpersonal
Problems 134
IQ *see* intelligence quotient

jargon 115, 165
Joint Commissioning 35

Klinefelter syndrome 16

labour markets
ageing 360
gender effects 53
National Health Service 181–2
socio-economic position 52
language 6–7
autism spectrum disorders 343, 346–7
interviews 109, 114–15
Lasting Power Attorney (LPA) 99
LDPB *see* Learning Disability
Partnership Boards
leadership 191–3, 196–7
leading questions 113
Learning Disability Partnership Boards
(LDPB) 35
legislative context 83–103
abuse, exploitation and neglect 83,
85, 89–90, 99–101
autonomy and decision-making 83,
90–3, 97–9, 100
background 86–97
case scenarios 84–6
clinical practice 97–102
international conventions and
declarations 86–7
mental capacity 90–3
national legislation, policy and
practice 87–8
offending behaviour 84, 94–6, 101–2,
236–9
organisations 163, 176–7
recent developments in policy and
practice 89–97
safeguarding of vulnerable
adults 89–90, 100
service provision 27–38
Leiter–International Performance Scale
Revised (LIPS-R) 68–9, 76
Lesch-Nyhan syndrome 17
life chances 51–3
life cycle theory 143–5, 146
life expectancy 11, 359
life skills 300
life-stories 377, 380
lifestyle changes 249
likert scales 116
linking responses 128
LIPS-R *see* Leiter–International
Performance Scale Revised

Local Authorities 162–3, 171,
    176–7, 199
local authority-funded direct
    payments 42
logical memory 77
long-stay mental handicap
    hospitals 41
long-term care funding 32–3
LPA see Lasting Power Attorney
lunacy 23

Makaton 109
Malan's triangles of conflict 129
management style 170
masturbation in public 260–2
MCA see Mental Capacity Act
MDT see multidisciplinary teams
measles–mumps–rubella (MMR)
    vaccinations 342
medical history 245, 316
medical model 4
memory
    ageing 366, 368, 377–8
    cognitive assessment 76, 77–8
Mencap 30–1
mental capacity
    legislative context 90–4, 97–9, 100
    offending behaviour 241–3
Mental Capacity Act (2005) 91–4,
    98–100, 102, 241–3
Mental Deficiency Act (1913) 25,
    87–8
Mental Health Act (1959) 88, 91
Mental Health Act (1983) 65, 96–7,
    99–100
Mental Health Act (2007) 239, 241–3
mental health disorders 313–38
    ageing 316, 328, 362–3, 384–5
    assessment 316–19, 328–31
    case study 328–31
    cognitive approaches 323–5
    context 313–14
    direct interventions 320–31
    epidemiology of intellectual
        disabilities 12
    formulation 319–20
    gender effects 54
    immediate social environment 326
    individual work 320–2

    prevalence 315–16
    service provision 327
    vulnerability 314–15
    wider social environment 326–7
MHA see Mental Health Act
Mini-PAS-ADD checklist 318
minority ethnic communities see
    ethnicity
MMR see measles–mumps–rubella
Model District Service (1983) 191–2
modes of working 187–8
Modified Novaco Anger Scale 134
moral imbecility 25
motivation
    challenging behaviour 208–9, 218
    to change 253
Motivational Assessment Scale
    (MAS) 218
motor impairments 12
MSA see Motivational Assessment
    Scale
multidisciplinary teams (MDT)
    ageing 385
    clinical psychology within
        teams 189–90
    National Health Service
        188–90
    offending behaviour 251
    organisational features 189
    organisations 177
    practice and overlapping
        roles 190
    service provision 43
multiple choice questions 112

NAID see Neuropsychological
    Assessment of Intellectual
    Disabilities
National Autism Plan for Children
    (NAP-C) 344, 350
National Autistic Society (NAS) 350
National Dementia Strategy 373
National Health Service
    (NHS) 181–201
    addressing complexity in
        evaluation 187
    assessment 186–7, 195–6
    boundary issues in work 194–5
    clinical activity 183–4

context for Clinical
Psychologists 181–2
continuing professional
development 182–3, 186, 191–4,
196–7
current challenges 196–8
direct clinical work 184–8
establishing effective work
venues 184–5, 195
ethical issues 194–5
mental health disorders 313
modes of working 187–8
multidisciplinary teams 188–90
organisational features 189, 197
organisations 163
practice and overlapping roles 190
psychological models 185–6
research issues 191
service development and leadership 191–3, 196–8
service provision 26–7, 31–4
staff training 182, 184, 192–3
supervision 193–4
*National Health Service and Community
Care Act* (1990) 33–4, 89
*National Health Service Plan* (2010) 31
National Institute for Health and
Clinical Excellence (NICE) 32,
313, 373
national policy and legislation 28–31,
35, 87–8
National Service Frameworks
(NSF) 313, 373
negative reinforcement 208
negative transference 129
neglect 83, 99–101
neurological models 206
Neuropsychological Assessment of
Intellectual Disabilities
(NAID) 74, 75–9, 186, 370–2
NHS *see* National Health Service
NICE *see* National Institute for Health
and Clinical Excellence
*No Secrets* (2000) 90, 100
non-verbal communication 71–3, 127
normalisation 27, 63
now/then questions 151–3
NSF *see* National Service
Frameworks

offending behaviour 235–71
aggressive behaviour 255–63
assessment of person 240–8
case examples 258–63
challenging behaviour, offending
and alleged offending 235–6,
245–6
context 235
environmental/contextual
factors 239–40
ethical issues 241–4
fire-setting 254–5
formulations 248
impact on practitioners 250–1
legislative context 84, 94–6, 101–2
management of further
offending 249–51
service responses 236–9, 242
sexual abuse 281
sexual offending 252–4, 260–2
specific offences 252–63
treatment of person 249–51
working with caregivers 250
older adults *see* ageing
open questions 111–12
opening an interview 109–10
operant behaviour 207–8
organisations 161–80
attitudes, beliefs and theories 170
broader policies 163–4
clarifying the plan 165
commissioning provision 163
constraint minimisation 175
context 161–2
difficulties between providers 171–2
ethical problems 172–3
follow through 166
giving advice 164–77
good housekeeping 166–7
group referral 171
hidden agendas 171
lack of experience/knowledge 169
lack of staff 168
management style 170
poor communication 168
presenting formulations and
plans 164–5
problems in the psychologist 167–8
range of provision 162

organisations   (*Continued*)
  staff assessments  173–4
  staff stress  168
  staff training  175–6
  weak links  169
  whistleblowing  176–7
  working environment  162–4
  working with recipients of
    advice  168–77
  *see also* National Health Service
orientation  142–3, 144
*Our Health, Our Nation, Our Care, Our
  Say* (2006)  35–6, 37, 163
*Our Strategy for Public Health in
  England* (2010)  44

PACE *see Police and Criminal Evidence Act*
paedophilia  280
pain  351
palliative care  363, 384
parent-child relationship  341
parental competency  297, 304, 306
parental dissatisfaction  142
parental relationships  128–9
parental responsibilities  294–5
parenting groups  154–5
parents with intellectual
    disabilities  293–312
  academic skills  299–300
  admission to programme  304
  assessment  299–303, 309
  case studies  302–3, 306
  centre-based programmes  304,
    307–8
  childcare and development  301,
    306–7
  comprehensive services  309–10
  context  293–4
  definition of terms  294–5
  direct interventions  297–8
  epidemiology  296
  family history  300
  general intelligence  299
  home-based programmes  304–5
  life skills  300
  parental competency  297, 304, 306
  parental responsibilities  294–5
  research  296–8
  support networks  308–9

  support and resources  301
  vulnerability of children  296–7
  working with parents  303–10
PAS-ADD *see* Psychiatric Assessment
    Schedule for Adults with
    Developmental Disability
passive verbs  114
Patau's syndrome  16
PBC *see* Practice Based Commissioning
PBS *see* Positive Behavioural Support
PD *see* personality disorders
PDD *see* pervasive developmental
    disorder
PECS *see* Picture Exchange
    Communication System
perinatal causes of intellectual
    disabilities  15–18
person centred planning
  ageing  374–6
  challenging behaviour  213
  legislative context  89
  National Health Service  184
  service provision  42, 63, 64–5
Personalisation Agenda  36–7
personality disorders (PD)  281
pervasive developmental disorder
    (PDD)  340
phenylalanine  13
phenylketonuria  13
phobias  322
physical abuse  54, 314
physical health  362, 384–5
pica  144
pictorial questions  113
Picture Exchange Communication
    System (PECS)  109, 352
*Police and Criminal Evidence Act*
    (1984)  95, 237
policy context
  ageing  373–4
  legislative context  83, 87–97
  National Health Service  199
  organisations  163–4
  service provision  27–38
Poor Laws  23–4
Positive Behavioural Support
    (PBS)  210, 228
positive programming  259
positive reinforcement  208

positive risk management 224–6, 249
positive transference 129
postnatal causes of intellectual
    disabilities 18–19
POVA see Protection of Vulnerable
    Adults
poverty 51–2
powerlessness 276–7
Practice Based Commissioning
    (PBC) 36
Prader Willi Syndrome (PWS) 16,
    84–5, 99, 314
pregnancy 293
pre-hand knowledge 113
prenatal causes of intellectual
    disabilities 14–15
present functioning 7
presenting formulations and
    plans 164–5
prevalence of intellectual
    disabilities 8–11
preventative work 284–5
Primary Care Trusts 163
private hospitals 39
problem identification 211–13
problem-solving skills training 257
Protection of Vulnerable Adults
    (POVA) 90
Psychiatric Assessment Schedule for
    Adults with Developmental
    Disability (PAS-ADD) 111, 318
psychiatric history 245, 316
psychiatric models 207
psychodynamic psychotherapy 121,
    123–6, 127–9, 134–6
  ageing 376
  mental health disorders 325–6
  sexual abuse 283, 285–6
psychometric assessment 64–6, 68–70,
    71–3
  mental health disorders 328
  National Health Service 186–7, 196
psychosis 125, 325
psychosocial factors 318–20, 327–31
psychotherapy see direct interventions
public health 38
public masturbation 260–2
punishment approach 223–4
pyromania 255

quality of life (QoL) 187, 198, 221,
    374–5
Questionnaire on Attitudes Consistent
    with Sexual Offending
    (QACSO) 253
questionnaires
  ageing 366
  challenging behaviour 218–19
  family members 147–8
  interviews 111, 115
Questions About Behavioural Function
    (QABF) 219

racism 55–7
range of provision 162
ranking questions 151–3
rapport 109
Ravens Coloured Matrices 71–2
RBMT see Rivermead Behavioural
    Memory Test
reactive strategies 259
reasonable adjustments 29–31, 57–8
Red Flags for Autism 345–6
re-enactment 286
referrals 187–8
reinforcement 208, 221, 321–2
relationship differences 151–3
relaxation training 257, 287, 321
religious factors 56
reminiscence work 377, 380–1
reports from others 244, 247
research issues 191
residential care
  organisations 177
  service provision 39–41
  sexual abuse 278–9, 287–8
respite services 42–3
response bias 113
review of client records 316
risk assessments 213
risk management plans 224–6, 249
Rivermead Behavioural Memory Test
    (RBMT) 76
role-plays 132, 165
roll back memory 377
routines 307, 345–6, 349
Royal Commission on the Care
    and Control of the Feeble-
    Minded 25

safeguarding of vulnerable adults
(SOVA) 89–90, 100
safety issues 305–6
Sally Anne test 342
sampling strategies 8
scaled scores 67–8
scatter plots 215–17
schizophrenia 329
scientist practitioner model 134
self-advocacy 310
self-instructional approaches in
CBT 130–1
self-referrals 187–8
self-reporting 244, 247
semi-structured interviews 111
sensory impairments 12
sensory sensitivities 351–2
SEP *see* socio-economic position
sequential analysis 215
service development 191–3, 196–8
service provision 23–49
advocacy schemes 43–4
ageing 359, 373–5
classification of intellectual
disabilities 7
commissioning health and social
care 34–6, 37–8
current picture 39–44
day services 41–2
*Disability Discrimination Act* and
reasonable adjustments 29–31
epidemiology of intellectual
disabilities 10–11
ethnicity 56–7
family and individual support
services 42–3
funding for long-term care 32–3
historical context 23–7
housing and residential
services 39–41
institutions as social reform 24
international legislation 28
mental health disorders 327
national policy and legislation 28–31, 35
NHS and Community Care 26–7,
33–4
NHS reforms 31–2
offending behaviour 236–9, 242

parents with intellectual disabilities 296, 309–10
Personalisation Agenda 36–7
policy and legislative context 27–38
Poor Laws and Community
Care 23–4
public health 38
social threats 24–5
sexual abuse 273–92
assessment 282–4
context 273–4
definition 274
direct interventions 283, 284–7
environmental/contextual
factors 278–80
incidence 275
individual work 285–7
legislative context 85
mental health disorders 314
offending behaviour 240, 253
perpetrator characteristics 277–8
prevalence 273–4
preventative work 284–5
sequelae 280–2
social context 54
supervision 288–9
victim characteristics 276–7
vulnerability factors 275–6
working with support staff 287–8
sexual disorders 25
sexual knowledge 252, 260, 262, 277,
283–4
sexual offending 252–4, 260–2
sharing prognostic information 382–3
shock 142, 144
siblings 146, 148–9
single gene disorders 15, 17
smell sensitivity 351
social anxiety 131, 133
social approval 108
social care *see* adult social care
Social Education Centres 27
social exclusion 52, 56
offending behaviour 256, 260–1
sexual abuse 277
social gradients 51
social history 245
social reform 24
social role valorisation (SRV) 63, 184

social skills 314
social support 301
socio-economic position (SEP) 51–3
    ageing 360
    epidemiology of intellectual
        disabilities 9–10
    mental health disorders 315
    offending behaviour 239–40
Socratic questioning 131–2
solution-focused therapy 286–7
SOVA *see* safeguarding of vulnerable
    adults
Special Parenting Service 306, 308
specialisation 191
specialist residential services 40–1
SPELL framework 350
splitting 286
SRV *see* social role valorisation
staff assessments 173–4
staff stress 168
staff training 175–6, 182, 184, 192–3
staffed houses 40
stage-specific activities 381–2
Standard Progressive Matrices 71–2
STAR framework 351
stereotypes 56
Sternberg's triarchic model of
    intelligence 66–7
stimulation for children 306–7
stimulation-oriented interventions 377
stress 145–8, 155, 168
structural analyses 219
substance abuse 124–5
suggestibility
    cognitive assessment 72–3
    interviews 110, 113
    offending behaviour 246
    sexual abuse 278, 283
suicidality 101
summarising responses 115
supervision
    National Health Service 193–4
    parents with intellectual
        disabilities 307
    sexual abuse 288–9
support networks 308–9
supported living 40, 89
systemic interview techniques 151–3
systemic practice 185

target behaviour 211–13, 214–17
taste sensitivity 351
Test of Everyday Attention (TEA) 77
Test of Reception of Grammar
    (TROG-2) 75–6
theory of mind 342–3
therapeutic relationship 123, 125–6,
    129, 130–1, 135–6
training
    National Health Service 182, 184,
        192–3
    organisations 175–6
    parents with intellectual disabili-
        ties 297–8, 309
transference 128–9, 195, 286
*Transparency in outcomes: a framework
    for adult social care* (2010) 36, 44
triangles of conflict 129
triarchic model of intelligence 66–7
TROG-2 *see* Test of Reception of
    Grammar
trust 109, 278

ULO *see* user-led organisations
UN *see* United Nations
unfit to plead 96
unified intelligence 25
United Nations (UN) Conventions and
    Declarations 28, 86–7
Universal Declaration of Human
    Rights 87
unwanted pregnancy 293
user-led organisations (ULO) 43–4

*Valuing People: A New Strategy for
    Learning Disability for the 21st
    Century* (2001)
    ageing 373
    cognitive assessment 63
    National Health Service 190, 192,
        199
    service provision 28–9, 35, 39,
        41, 44
*Valuing People Now* (2009) 29, 35
VAS *see* visual analogue scale
victim empathy 253, 262
Victorian reforms 24
video interviews 115–16
violence 54, 55–6

*Vision for Adult Social Care Capable Communities and Active Citizens* (2010)  36, 44
visual analogue scale (VAS) 116–17, 156
visual rating scales  153
visual sensitivity  351
vocabulary  114–15

WAIS-III *see* Wechsler Adult Intelligence Scale
warmth  305
WASI *see* Wechsler Abbreviated Scale of Intelligence
Ways of Coping Questionnaire  147–8
weak central coherence theory  343–4
weak links  169
Wechsler Abbreviated Scale of Intelligence (WASI)  69, 71
Wechsler Adult Intelligence Scale (WAIS-III)  67–70, 72–4

Wechsler Intelligence Scale for Children (WISC-IV)  68–9
Wechsler Memory Scale (WMS-III) 76, 77
wetting behaviour  260–1
whistleblowing  176–7
Williams syndrome  16
WISC-IV *see* Wechsler Intelligence Scale for Children
withdrawal  144, 146
witness advice to courts  97
witness credibility  278
WMS-III *see* Wechsler Intelligence Scale for Children
working environment  162–4

yes/no questions  112
*Youth Justice and Criminal Evidence Act* (1999)  101

Zung Depression Inventory  317, 324